Neoliberalism

Critics of globalization often portray neoliberalism as an extremist laissez-faire political–economic philosophy that rejects any sort of government intervention in the domestic economy. Like most over-used terms, it is more complicated than this introductory sentence suggests. This volume seeks to move beyond these caricature depictions and definitions as well as the emotional rhetoric that has unfortunately dominated both the scholastic and political debate on neoliberalism and global market-oriented reform. This book emphasizes that there are in fact a variety of *neoliberalisms* that share a common emphasis on market-oriented approaches. Beyond this however, its usages and applications appear much more varied according to the cultural, economic, political, and social context in which it is used.

A host of eminent contributors, including Douglass C. North, Arthur T. Denzau, Thomas D. Willett, Mark Blyth, Colin Hay, Craig Parsons and others provide a rigorous assessment of the significance of neoliberal ideas on economic policy. Through their detailed international case studies, the contributors to this book show how varied its impact has in fact been and the result is a book that will stimulate further debate in this most controversial of subject matters.

Ravi K. Roy is a Research Scholar at the Claremont Institute for Economic Policy Studies. **Arthur T. Denzau** is Professor of Economics at Claremont Graduate University. He is also a Research Associate at the Center for American Business at Washington University (St. Louis). **Thomas D. Willett** is Horton Professor of Economics at Claremont Graduate University. He is also Director of the Claremont Institute for Economic Policy Studies.

Routledge frontiers of political economy

1 **Equilibrium Versus Understanding**
Towards the rehumanization of economics within social theory
Mark Addleson

2 **Evolution, Order and Complexity**
Edited by Elias L. Khalil and Kenneth E. Boulding

3 **Interactions in Political Economy**
Malvern after ten years
Edited by Steven Pressman

4 **The End of Economics**
Michael Perelman

5 **Probability in Economics**
Omar F. Hamouda and Robin Rowley

6 **Capital Controversy, Post Keynesian Economics and the History of Economics**
Essays in honour of Geoff Harcourt, volume 1
Edited by Philip Arestis, Gabriel Palma and Malcolm Sawyer

7 **Markets, Unemployment and Economic Policy**
Essays in honour of Geoff Harcourt, volume 2
Edited by Philip Arestis, Gabriel Palma and Malcolm Sawyer

8 **Social Economy**
The logic of capitalist development
Clark Everling

9 **New Keynesian Economics/Post Keynesian Alternatives**
Edited by Roy J. Rotheim

10 **The Representative Agent in Macroeconomics**
James E. Hartley

11 **Borderlands of Economics**
Essays in honour of Daniel R. Fusfeld
Edited by Nahid Aslanbeigui and Young Back Choi

12 **Value, Distribution and Capital**
Essays in honour of Pierangelo Garegnani
Edited by Gary Mongiovi and Fabio Petri

13 **The Economics of Science**
Methodology and epistemology as if economics really mattered
James R. Wible

14 **Competitiveness, Localised Learning and Regional Development**
Specialisation and prosperity in small open economies
Peter Maskell, Heikki Eskelinen, Ingjaldur Hannibalsson, Anders Malmberg and Eirik Vatne

15 **Labour Market Theory**
A constructive reassessment
Ben J. Fine

16 **Women and European Employment**
Jill Rubery, Mark Smith, Colette Fagan and Damian Grimshaw

17 **Explorations in Economic Methodology**
From Lakatos to empirical philosophy of science
Roger Backhouse

18 **Subjectivity in Political Economy**
Essays on wanting and choosing
David P. Levine

19 **The Political Economy of Middle East Peace**
The impact of competing trade agendas
Edited by J.W. Wright, Jnr

20 **The Active Consumer**
Novelty and surprise in consumer choice
Edited by Marina Bianchi

21 **Subjectivism and Economic Analysis**
Essays in memory of Ludwig Lachmann
Edited by Roger Koppl and Gary Mongiovi

22 **Themes in Post-Keynesian Economics**
Essays in honour of Geoff Harcourt, volume three
Edited by Claudio Sardoni and Peter Kriesler

23 **The Dynamics of Technological Knowledge**
Cristiano Antonelli

24 **The Political Economy of Diet, Health and Food Policy**
Ben J. Fine

25 **The End of Finance**
Capital market inflation, financial derivatives and pension fund capitalism
Jan Toporowski

26 **Political Economy and the New Capitalism**
Edited by Jan Toporowski

27 **Growth Theory**
A philosophical perspective
Patricia Northover

28 **The Political Economy of the Small Firm**
Edited by Charlie Dannreuther

29 **Hahn and Economic Methodology**
Edited by Thomas Boylan and Paschal F. O'Gorman

30 **Gender, Growth and Trade**
The miracle economies of the postwar Years
David Kucera

31 **Normative Political Economy**
Subjective freedom, the market and the state
David Levine

32 **Economist with a Public Purpose**
Essays in honour of John Kenneth Galbraith
Edited by Michael Keaney

33 **Involuntary Unemployment**
The elusive quest for a theory
Michel De Vroey

34 **The Fundamental Institutions of Capitalism**
Ernesto Screpanti

35 **Transcending Transaction**
The search for self-generating markets
Alan Shipman

36 **Power in Business and the State**
An historical analysis of its concentration
Frank Bealey

37 **Editing Economics**
Essays in honour of Mark Perlman
Hank Lim, Ungsuh K. Park and Geoff Harcourt

38 **Money, Macroeconomics and Keynes**
Essays in honour of Victoria Chick, volume 1
Philip Arestis, Meghnad Desai and Sheila Dow

39 **Methodology, Microeconomics and Keynes**
Essays in honour of Victoria Chick, volume 2
Philip Arestis, Meghnad Desai and Sheila Dow

40 **Market Drive and Governance**
Reexamining the rules for economic and commercial contest
Ralf Boscheck

41 **The Value of Marx**
Political economy for contemporary capitalism
Alfredo Saad-Filho

42 **Issues in Positive Political Economy**
S. Mansoob Murshed

43 **The Enigma of Globalisation**
A journey to a new stage of capitalism
Robert Went

44 **The Market**
Equilibrium, stability, mythology
S.N. Afriat

45 **The Political Economy of Rule Evasion and Policy Reform**
Jim Leitzel

46 **Unpaid Work and the Economy**
Edited by Antonella Picchio

47 **Distributional Justice**
Theory and measurement
Hilde Bojer

48 **Cognitive Developments in Economics**
Edited by Salvatore Rizzello

49 **Social Foundations of Markets, Money and Credit**
Costas Lapavitsas

50 **Rethinking Capitalist Development**
Essays on the economics of Josef Steindl
Edited by Tracy Mott and Nina Shapiro

51 **An Evolutionary Approach to Social Welfare**
Christian Sartorius

52 **Kalecki's Economics Today**
Edited by Zdzislaw L. Sadowski and Adam Szeworski

53 **Fiscal Policy from Reagan to Blair**
The Left veers Right
Ravi K. Roy and Arthur T. Denzau

54 **The Cognitive Mechanics of Economic Development and Institutional Change**
Bertin Martens

55 **Individualism and the Social Order**
The social element in liberal thought
Charles R. McCann Jnr

56 **Affirmative Action in the United States and India**
A comparative perspective
Thomas E. Weisskopf

57 **Global Political Economy and the Wealth of Nations**
Performance, institutions, problems and policies
Edited by Phillip Anthony O'Hara

58 **Structural Economics**
Thijs ten Raa

59 **Macroeconomic Theory and Economic Policy**
Essays in honour of Jean-Paul Fitoussi
Edited by K. Vela Velupillai

60 **The Struggle Over Work**
The "end of work" and employment alternatives in post-industrial societies
Shaun Wilson

61 **The Political Economy of Global Sporting Organisations**
John Forster and Nigel Pope

62 **The Flawed Foundations of General Equilibrium Theory**
Critical essays on economic theory
Frank Ackerman and Alejandro Nadal

63 **Uncertainty in Economic Theory**
Essays in honor of David Schmeidler's 65th birthday
Edited by Itzhak Gilboa

64 **The New Institutional Economics of Corruption**
Edited by Johann Graf Lambsdorff, Markus Taube and Matthias Schramm

65 The Price Index and its Extension
A chapter in economic measurement
S.N. Afriat

66 Reduction, Rationality and Game Theory in Marxian Economics
Bruce Philp

67 Culture and Politics in Economic Development
Volker Bornschier

68 Modern Applications of Austrian Thought
Edited by Jürgen G. Backhaus

69 Ordinary Choices
Individuals, incommensurability, and democracy
Robert Urquhart

70 Labour Theory of Value
Peter C. Dooley

71 Capitalism
Victor D. Lippit

72 Macroeconomic Foundations of Macroeconomics
Alvaro Cencini

73 Marx for the 21st Century
Edited by Hiroshi Uchida

74 Growth and Development in the Global Political Economy
Social structures of accumulation and modes of regulation
Phillip Anthony O'Hara

75 The New Economy and Macroeconomic Stability
A neo-modern perspective drawing on the complexity approach and Keynesian economics
Teodoro Dario Togati

76 The Future of Social Security Policy
Women, work and a citizen's basic income
Ailsa McKay

77 Clinton and Blair
The political economy of the Third Way
Flavio Romano

78 Marxian Reproduction Schema
Money and aggregate demand in a capitalist economy
A.B. Trigg

79 The Core Theory in Economics
Problems and solutions
Lester G. Telser

80 Economics, Ethics and the Market
Introduction and applications
Johan J. Graafland

81 Social Costs and Public Action in Modern Capitalism
Essays inspired by Karl William Kapp's Theory of Social Costs
Edited by Wolfram Elsner, Pietro Frigato and Paolo Ramazzotti

82 Globalization and the Myths of Free Trade
History, theory and empirical evidence
Edited by Anwar Shaikh

83 **Equilibrium in Economics: Scope and Limits**
Edited by Valeria Mosini

84 **Globalization**
State of the art and perspectives
Edited by Stefan A. Schirm

85 **Neoliberalism**
National and regional experiments with global ideas
Edited by Ravi K. Roy, Arthur T. Denzau and Thomas D. Willett

Neoliberalism

National and regional experiments with global ideas

Edited by Ravi K. Roy, Arthur T. Denzau and Thomas D. Willett

Preface by Eric Helleiner

Routledge
Taylor & Francis Group
LONDON AND NEW YORK

First published 2007
by Routledge
2 Park Square, Milton Park, Abingdon, Oxon, OX14 4RN

Simultaneously published in the USA and Canada
by Routledge
270 Madison Ave, New York NY 10016

Routledge is an imprint of the Taylor & Francis Group, an informa business

Transferred to Digital Printing 2007

Typeset in Baskerville by Wearset Ltd, Boldon, Tyne and Wear

British Library Cataloguing in Publication Data
A catalogue record for this book is available from the British Library

Library of Congress Cataloging in Publication Data
A catalog record for this book has been requested

ISBN10: 0-415-70090-6 (hbk)
ISBN10: 0-415-45866-8 (pbk)
ISBN10: 0-203-02066-9 (ebk)

ISBN13: 978-0-415-70090-0 (hbk)
ISBN13: 978-0-415-45866-5 (pbk)
ISBN13: 978-0-203-02066-1 (ebk)

For Joan and Nicole. May the Lord Shine His Light upon You.

Contents

Figures

Tables

Preface

Eric Helleiner

This important book provides one of the most convincing statements yet about the significance of ideas within economic policymaking. Over the past decade, political scientists have shown new interest in the explanatory role of ideas. They have often been responding to the growing use of "rationalist" formal models that analyze policy-making by assuming actors are guided by materialist, interest-maximizing behavior. According to their critics, these models – largely imported from economics – oversimplify by neglecting the fact that interests themselves are "ideationally-bound." As one of the contributors to this volume has put it, "agents cannot have interests without reference to their ideas about their interests."[1]

It may come as a surprise to political scientists working in this emerging "constructivist" school to learn that a growing number of economists agree with them. This book marks one of the first serious attempts to develop a dialogue between these economists and political scientists, both of whom share the goal of trying to understand how ideas shape economic policy. The result is "political economy" in the truest sense of the word. The volume demonstrates convincingly that the concept of "shared mental models" provides an excellent basis for this dialogue.

Alongside this theoretical contribution, this book also advances our understanding of the role of neoliberalism in economic policymaking in major ways. Certainly, this is not the first book to call attention to the growing influence of neoliberal thought in economic policy since the early 1980s. But many past works have been both too imprecise in their description of neoliberalism as well as too general in their assessment of its impact. This volume corrects both mistakes.

It highlights how there are in fact many "neoliberalisms". At its core, neoliberal thought is best understood as the revival of some of the basic nineteenth-century classical economic liberal ideas underscoring the importance of the market. That case rested on the argument that markets would promote both greater economic efficiency and individual freedom. But beyond this core belief, there are many disagreements among neoliberals, just as there were among nineteenth-century economic liberals.

From monetarists to supply-siders to the supporters of the "Washington consensus," neoliberals are a less coherent intellectual movement than is often suggested.

The influence of neoliberal mental models has also been highly uneven across the world. Critics of neoliberalism sometimes talk of an emerging global hegemony of neoliberal ideas. The authors in this volume provide a much more nuanced – and in my view, more accurate – picture of the significance of neoliberal ideas on economic policy. To be sure, neoliberal ideas have been in the ascendancy since the early 1980s. But through their detailed case studies of so many regions of the world, the contributors to this book show how varied its impact has in fact been.

Some of this variation can be explained by the interaction between neoliberal ideas and the differing material interests of societal and state actors in the various contexts. But perhaps the most interesting finding is that the influence of neoliberalism often depended heavily on its compatibility with other kinds of shared mental models. In the European Union, neoliberal values had sway largely because they dovetailed with a broader Europeanist ideal. In many ex-Communist bloc countries and East Asian countries, nationalist sentiments were often the most important source of support for the neoliberal cause.[2] In other contexts, neoliberalism's fate has often been determined by its perceived compatibility with local cultural, religious and even "civilizational" values.

These findings remind us that neoliberalism does not stand alone in the universe of mental models. It exists within a broader ideational environment and its political success is contingent on its relationship with other ideals, identities and values. Interestingly, classical liberals in the nineteenth century learned the same lesson. They found that their ideas often had their greatest influence when they were seen to reinforce or reflect both national identities and even certain religious and civilizational values.[3]

The turn to more market-oriented policies since the 1980s, in other words, has been influenced by an ideational environment that is wider than neoliberalism. This insight only reinforces the volume's central thesis that we need to learn more about the explanatory role of ideas in economic policymaking. More specifically, it suggests that the relationship between neoliberalism and other mental models deserves much more scholarly attention than it has received to date. In this way, this volume does more than just convince readers of the importance of ideas. It also sets out an important research agenda for future scholarship in this area.

Notes

1 Quotes from Mark Blyth, *The Great Transformation* (Cambridge: Cambridge University Press, 2002: 34, 270).

2 This has been true in many other contexts too; see Eric Helleiner and Andreas

Pickel, eds., *Economic Nationalism in a Globalizing World* (Ithaca: Cornell University Press, 2005).

3 Eric Helleiner, "Economic Nationalism as a Challenge to Neoliberalism? Lessons from the 19th Century" *International Studies Quarterly* 46(3) (2002): 307–329; C. Rojas de Ferro, *Civilization and Violence* (Minneapolis: University of Minnesota Press, 2002); Frank Trentmann, "Political Culture and Political Economy: Interest, Ideology and Free Trade" *Review of International Political Economy* 5(2) (1998): 217–251.

Acknowledgments

I would like to express sincere and deep gratitude to my co-editors and dear friends, Tom Willett and Art Denzau for their tireless work on this project as well as their intellectual and financial support. I would also like to extend a heartfelt word of appreciation to the contributing authors whose excellent work appears in this volume including: Nicholas Amponsah, Nancy Neiman Auerbach, Graham Bird, Mark Blyth, Nigel Boyle, Colin Hay, Anil Hira, Shale Horowitz, Stephen Marks, Doug North, Craig Parsons, Sunil Rongala, and Lew Snider. Much gratitude is also expressed to Eric Helleiner who has provided a lucid and captivating preface to introduce our volume. I would also like to mention Tom Borcherding, Yi Feng and Peter Katzenstein who offered insightful comments and suggestions that are deeply appreciated.

On a personal note, I would like to acknowledge my loving wife Joan and our new baby girl, Nicole, to whom I have dedicated this volume. I would like to acknowledge my father Professor Ram M. Roy who is retiring as this book goes to print after 50 dedicated years of service to the field of Political Science. I would also like to extend a personal word to Art and Connie Denzau for all they have done. Also, I would like to mention my dear friends Kevin and Norma Gerrity as well as my sister Lia and her husband, Mike Nanda.

Ravi K. Roy

Part I

Conceptual analysis

Shared mental models and neoliberalism

1 Introduction

Neoliberalism as a shared mental model

Ravi K. Roy, Arthur T. Denzau, and Thomas D. Willett

Introduction

This book is about events and ideas and their interrelationships. Its focus is on the dramatic shifts in economic policy across the globe brought about by the greater recognition by governments of economic realities as seen through the lens of mainstream economic analysis. The most visible of the "victories" for mainstream economics and the market-oriented policies that it recommends are the fall of the command-and-control system of the former Soviet Union and the rapid shift toward greater use of the market in China. But the shifts are more widespread than this. Many governments of the left on many continents have adopted more market-oriented approaches and given greater weight to longer-run macroeconomic stability in their policies. Tony Blair in the UK, Bill Clinton in the United States, and Lula in Brazil are prominent examples.

Two points emphasized by many of our contributors, however, are that the same events can be interpreted quite differently by different people and that market-oriented policies – or neoliberalism, as they are often called – can have quite different meanings to different observers and in different national contexts. Experience has clearly shown that the total victory of the market predicted by some after the fall of the former Soviet Union was greatly overstated. This view not only overlooked the likelihood of continuing opposition from many quarters but also failed to understand the conditions necessary for markets to work well. To economists who specialize in political economy and the new institutional economics, it was not surprising that in countries without a tradition of effective property rights and democratic accountability, privatization sometimes looked more like thievery than like the well-functioning competitive markets of economists' blackboards. Without social and political stability and many other aspects of social and institutional infrastructure, no economic system will work well. As John Kay (2004) has stressed in his recent book on *Culture and Prosperity*, there are many varieties within the general class of market-oriented economic systems, and there is no solid evidence that one particular version always works best in terms of either economic performance or social equity.

Discussions of different economic systems often quickly turn into discussions of ideology, sometimes in the form of how one's opponents' blindly-held ideologies keep them from seeing the obvious truth of one's own point of view. In the writings on the economic reforms that have swept the globe over the past three decades we find many examples of such assertions combined with a tendency to equate all of the opposition with their most extreme members. Just as some market triumphalists saw almost any government intervention as a return to a command-and-control system, the advocates of middle-of-the-road market-oriented policies that critics associated with the Washington Consensus as being part and parcel with the most extreme forms of laissez-faire ideology.

A reading of the outpouring of literature makes clear that there are those who have such strong commitments to particular views that it is virtually impossible for arguments or events to influence their views. And somewhere there may be someone who is completely open-minded. Between the extremes lie most of us. Values and biases can slip in almost anywhere, and even with tremendous soul-searching, few if any of us are likely to be aware of all of our biases. But being aware of this problem is still a big help even if we cannot hope to attain perfection. Generally others are much better at perceiving our biases than we are ourselves. Thus we wanted to make sure that this volume contained contributions from leading scholars with a wide range of theoretical orientations and political leanings as well as giving us coverage across a broad range of countries and regions.

Studying neoliberalism as a shared mental model

This volume has several purposes. One is to emphasize that differences in theories, paradigms, and mental models are key variables in explaining disagreements about what economic policies should be pursued and which should be ignored. This volume therefore, aims to provide a refinement of interest-based and rational choice approaches. Given how much effort economists put into debating the "correctness" of different economic theories, it is surprising how little attention is paid by the economics profession to the role that differences in positive views can have on policy debates. In policy discussions, debates about right versus wrong views are still much more prevalent than attention to the role of uncertainty about what is the correct model.

A second purpose is to explore how Arthur T. Denzau and Douglass C. North's Shared Mental Models framework (1994) can help us better understand distinct neoliberal experiments across regions and nations. This volume examines the relevance of neoliberalism as a shared mental model and its various related strands (examined as a subset of mental models) in shaping the political economies of various states and regions in an era of globalization. Neoliberalism as a shared mental model refers to the spread of market-oriented ideas across the globe that has been occurring over the past three decades. The contributors to this volume collectively demonstrate that while these ideas have had an important effect in shaping global economic reform, this importance has varied greatly across countries and regions. Additionally, in cases where neoliberal ideas have been influential, they have not always been successful. We should emphasize that our arguments regarding the potency of ideas in this volume lie in their influence in shaping choices and not necessarily in their leading to successful outcomes. There is a variety of market-oriented systems that fall under the general category of neoliberalism. There are thus a number of distinct, but related *neoliberalisms.* Unfortunately, most writings on the topic have often ignored these distinctions, often painting all neoliberals monochromatically. This volume seeks to address the complexity of the neoliberal debate.

A third purpose is to serve as a catalyst for a continuing dialogue among economists, political scientists and other social scientists who study the role of ideas in shaping state policy. It is an interesting phenomenon that mainstream economists seldom use the term liberalism, neoliberalism or globalization. (They prefer terms such as classical and neoclassical.) It is largely non-economists, especially political scientists, who use these terms. And while writers on international relations such as Gilpin (1987) would most likely treat the term in a neutral sense, it is most commonly used in policy debate, especially in the United Kingdom and Latin America, to portray economic reforms in those countries in a negative light. Many advocates both for and against neoliberalism have been guilty of characterizing their opponents' views in the most extreme terms and associating them with the most extreme positions. Such uncharitable characterizations obstruct a genuine and productive dialog about this critical topic. This volume seeks to move beyond the emotional rhetoric that has unfortunately dominated both the scholastic and political debate on neoliberalism and global market-oriented reform.

Shared mental models and rational choice

A key aspect of Denzau-North's Shared Mental Models framework concerns refinements of rational choice theory. The work on ideas and political economy is a highly fertile area of academic and policy research that will reveal many truths about human behavior that purely rational choice studies have been unable to uncover. This stems mainly from the fact that "rationalist" views are sometimes greatly oversimplified. They frequently assume that everyone knows the true model of the economy and that there is broad agreement on how the world works. Goldstein and Keohane (1993) argue that "utility" itself is ultimately realized through a set of ideas and beliefs of what furthers one's interest and what does not. This is not to suggest, of course, that interests are irrelevant; indeed interests are vital to understanding behavior. Rather, our argument is simply that ideas are an integral component in determining how individuals and groups come to understand what their interests are in the first place, and how best to further them (Denzau and North, 1994: 1). Denzau and North argue that rational behavior is itself determined by the information and knowledge one possesses when making decisions. In some cases a person's or group's self-interest is so obvious that it may seem pedantic to argue that these interests are perceived through ideas or mental models. Often, however, one's interests are not so clearly apparent and differing mental models would lead to quite different perceptions of interests (such as patent protection, or different perceptions about military deterrence).

Denzau and North (1994) argue that mental models are systematic sets of ideas, and related principles that individuals use to interpret the world around them. They involve internal mental constructions, as well as the interpretations and meanings of terms, data, and other forms of information governing a particular subject matter. Even policymakers who disparage theoretical analysis typically rely on implicit mental models to help them make causal connections or draw causal inferences about how the economy works. Mental models help them make predictions about what policy strategies and tools might work under certain sets of circumstances as well as provide policymakers with an interpretative lens of the policy environment in which they operate. In *A Brief Tour of the Human Consciousness*, V.S. Ramachandran (2004) provides a relevant quote:

> Our brains are essentially model-making machines. We need to construct useful, virtual reality simulations of the world that we can act on. Within the simulation, we need also to construct models of other people's minds, because we primates are intensely social creatures ... we need to do this so that we can predict their behavior.
>
> (p. 105)

Mental models thus help actors discern what their interests are as well as which strategies are desirable and which are not. Shared mental models involve shared meanings and understandings of a subject matter. These shared interpretations and meanings are conveyed through shared language, rhetoric, terms, symbols, analogies, and material referents. They involve intersubjectively-accepted mental constructions that individuals may use to develop shared interpretations of the world around them and the developments that occur in it.

Neoliberalism as both a set of distinct but related mental models and a shared mental model

The chapters in this volume apply Denzau and North's Shared Mental Models framework (1994) to help us examine distinct neoliberal experiments across regions and nations. The concept of shared mental models is quite wide, and encompasses other more specific notions of ideas. For example, Kuhn's (1970) notion of a paradigm represents a consensus among a group of scientists on a set of examplar questions and basic approaches to answering them. Paradigms are a class of shared mental models. Although Kuhn used "paradigm" in several different ways, all are intended to be mental models that are shared among a group of people. Similarly, Sowell's (2002) notion of a preanalytic vision is also a class of shared mental model. Sowell classifies visions into two categories, the constrained and the unconstrained visions. The constrained vision sees the human state as having a specific limited content, such that various utopias requiring certain types of humans to make them work are impossible. Constrained humans create institutions to further their interaction and reduce the cognitive and behavioral requirements that an unconstrained vision might require. Mainstream economic analysis adopts this constrained vision in its models of human behavior. In the unconstrained vision, humans are malleable and perfectable, leaving the notion of a human as an empty shell. These visions are clearly shared mental models, although not all shared mental models are necessarily visions or paradigms.

The neoliberal shared mental model has been expressed in the various experiments with market-oriented ideas including the adaptations and innovations that often occur in their application in real political contexts. How market or neoliberal ideas are interpreted as well as applied are informed by these contexts. Distinct market-oriented experiments have been informed (to varying degrees) by a common set of ideas that can be collectively defined as a neoliberal shared mental model. These ideas are consistent with Sowell's constrained vision, and have often been explicitly tied to an economic paradigm of market-generated growth. Precise understandings of what Neoliberalism is and how it should be applied tend to vary according to the context in which the word is used. Context shapes meanings and understandings of ideas and words used to describe them. Distinct experiments with market reforms represent different manifestations of neoliberalism.

The various experiments and manifestations may be regarded as distinct, though related, mental models or strands of a broad neoliberal shared mental model. Some strands emphasize certain liberal principles and policy priorities over others. These individual strands help explain the divergence in policy trajectories of the nations and regions under study in this volume. Some strands are rooted in, or at least sympathetic with, more ardent laissez-faire approaches that are associated with Hayek and the Austrian School, or the Chicago School. The leaderships of Thatcher, Reagan, and Pinochet are well-known examples. Other strands however, such as the Washington Consensus, first termed by John Williamson in 1990, shares some agreement with these approaches while disagreeing (in some cases fundamentally) with others. For example, the Washington Consensus would share broad agreement on issues such as fiscal discipline, tax reform (to lower marginal tax rates and broaden the tax base), privatization, deregulation, and securing property rights (Global Trade Negotiations Home Page, 2006: 1). Williamson however, never intended the Washington Consensus to imply policies such as capital account liberalization, monetarism, supply-side economics, or reducing the state in areas such as welfare provision or income redistribution. The Washington Consensus advocates "redirecting public expenditure priorities toward fields offering both high economic returns and the potential to improve income distribution, such as primary health care, primary education, and infrastructure" (ibid: 1). Nancy Neiman Auerbach discusses these distinctions in much greater depth in Chapter 3. And while these distinct mental models or strands may differ over the appropriate degree to which governments should intervene in markets as well as over policy priorities, and prescriptions, most share broadly similar philosophical positions regarding the superiority of the market mechanism over state intervention in sustaining growth and tend to emphasize the principles of individual and entrepreneurial economic freedom ahead of more collectivist approaches.

Contending shared mental models in political economy: liberalism and neoliberalism versus mercantalism and dirigisme

Robert Gilpin (1987) classifies political–economic systems into three broad political economy world views or what we call contending shared mental models. They are the nationalist (also called realist or modern mercantilist), Marxist, and liberal political–economic world views or shared mental models. We briefly examine them in relation to our discussion of neoliberalism.

When Adam Smith (1776) wrote his classic advocacy of the market system, *The Wealth of Nations*, in the eighteenth century, the dominant economic doctrine of the time in western Europe was mercantilism, which saw the state as the regulator of most economic activity with the goal of maximizing national power. Indeed, the major purpose of Smith's writing was to challenge this mercantilist doctrine with its emphasis on national power and belief that international trade was a zero-sum game, i.e. that one party could gain only at the expense of another. As conceived by Smith, laissez faire was not meant to imply that there were no legitimate roles for government in the economy, but rather that at that time government intervention was far too intrusive and that many markets would work far better if the government would keep its hands off and "let them be." Economic liberalism does not assume that are no conflicts of interest in a competitive market economy and that there is never a case for government intervention. What economic liberalism does argue is that unlike the Marxist and mercantilist view of economic activity as a zero-sum game (such that anyone's gain comes only at the expense of someone else's loss), economic activity is usually a positive-sum game. Over the years, the market economy ideas that Smith pulled together and expounded upon have had a tremendous influence on the evolution of the world economy. They are generally credited with having had a large impact on Britain's move from protectionism toward freer trade in the nineteenth century and formed a key (albeit not total) underpinning of the rise of the United States as a global economic power.

If we fast forward to the middle of the twentieth century, we see the world economy dominated by a bitter contest between two contrasting economic doctrines or contending shared mental models, the Marxist-oriented central planning approach of the Soviet Union and its satellites versus the market-oriented economics of the western industrial nations, with the third (developing) world being pulled, bullied, and cajoled back and forth between these two poles. As Mandelbaum (2002) usefully discusses, in the contest between capitalism and Soviet-style central planning, the outcome was in an ambiguous zone in the middle part of the twentieth century. In the 1950s and 1960s, more than a few western economists thought that heavy central planning was superior.

Neoliberalism is a "new" variation on nineteenth century classical liberalism. Classical liberalism was long the core of western capitalist ideology. Since the late 1990s, activists have used the word "neoliberalism" for global market-liberalism ("capitalism") and for free-trade policies. In this sense it is now widely used in South America. Some people use the word interchangeably with "globalization." The point must be emphasized that there are a variety of neoliberal mental models. The neoliberal shared mental model, however, comprises the distinct applications of various classical liberal ideas in distinct political contexts across the globe. There are substantial differences between, say, the US economy and that of France or many of the newly industrializing economies of Asia. While much more market-oriented than the typical African or Latin American economy of the 1950s and 1960s, the Asian NICs (Newly Industrialized Countries) practiced considerable government intervention. Compared with France, there is no question that the US economy is much closer to "free market capitalism." But even the United States has more government intervention and corporate welfare than a classical liberal such as Milton Friedman would favor. While many Europeans contrast their social market approach with American "cowboy capitalism," political scientists in the United States have cogently depicted its evolving political economy as one of "embedded liberalism" (Ruggie, 1982), that is, the heavy use of markets embedded in a framework of social protection.

Introducing the chapters in this volume

In order to have a fruitful and constructive debate about the evolution of the global economy, the ideas that underpin them must be fleshed out and genuinely discussed by demonstrating fidelity for their complexities. When seeking to augment deregulation and privatizations programs in the United States and Britain for example, Reagan and Thatcher, well known neoliberals belonging to the partisan right, actually expanded public expenditure for many social policies and imposed new taxes on businesses and corporations. And on the left, Clinton and Blair proposed neoliberal reforms in welfare policies by presenting them within a context of social justice that included substantial increases in public funding for job retraining for the unemployed as well as proposing historic increases in the minimum wage for the working poor in their respective nations. Unfortunately, many discussions and writings on the subject of neoliberalism often ignore these complexities and many critics of neoliberalism paint its supporters as apologists for what they regard to be the ruthless and exploitive activities of multinational corporations. Such uncharitable and inaccurate characterizations cannot lead to a genuine dialog on the subject of neoliberalism that it both requires and deserves.

The work on ideas has become increasingly influential in the field of international political economy over the last decade and a half. And the influence of market-oriented ideas on the evolution of the global economy is an area that warrants greater study and genuine in-depth analysis. The collective work of the authors in this volume represents a solid step in this direction.

Arthur T. Denzau, Douglass C. North, and Ravi K. Roy include a chapter, *Shared mental models: a postscript.* When "Shared Mental Models" (Denzau and North, 1994) was being written over ten years ago, Denzau and North sought to make changes in the economic model of choice that preserved the valuable contributions of that model, but avoided some of the obvious flaws. This postscript illuminates some of the uses of the Shared Mental Model framework in the field of political economy over the past 12 years and suggests its usefulness in exploring the influence of neoliberalism across the globe.

Nancy Neiman Auerbach presents a chapter on *The meanings of neoliberalism.* Neoliberalism has always been more of a political label than an economic label. The exploration of neoliberalism in this book seeks to understand neoliberalism in a more constructivist sense by asking how its uses have shaped its meaning rather than seeking agreement over the one true meaning of the term.

Colin Hay provides a chapter on *The genealogy of neoliberalism.* Hay argues that the cultural political economy has been characterized in recent years by the rise and consolidation of neoliberal economic assumptions. This is reflective of a broader shift from a normative to a normalized neoliberalism. Whilst the former normative phase of neoliberalism was largely restricted to an anglophone enclave (centered on the US and the UK), the latter normalized phase has proved far more contagious.

Mark Blyth shares a chapter that discusses macroeconomic regime change from "embedded liberalism" to "neoliberalism" entitled *When liberalisms change: comparing the politics of inflations and deflations.* Blyth argues that this regime change is rooted in a shift of shared mental models.

Graham Bird offers a chapter entitled *Evolution in macroeconomics: principles, policy and performances* in which he traces out the interaction between mainstream macroeconomic principles, policy and performance over a protracted period of time. He asserts that on occasion, advances in economic theory lead to changes in policy that then affect performance, while at other times, changes in performance lead to a reassessment of both underlying principles and policy design. Rather than concentrating on any particular country, this chapter tries to identify a global pattern to evolution in macroeconomics.

Ravi K. Roy and Arthur T. Denzau include a chapter entitled *The neoliberal shift in US fiscal policy from the 1980s to the 1990s: a shared mental model approach to understanding coalition-driven policy shifts.* In this chapter, they explore the influence of neoliberal ideas in shaping US fiscal policy focusing on deficit reduction, from the 1980s to the 1990s. They argue that distinct fiscal strategies pursued by the Reagan and Clinton administrations were informed by the distinct strands of the neoliberal shared mental model that each adopted. They further explore the influence of these mental models in providing the *coalitional glue* that brings like-minded actors together in support of common policy agendas and strategies.

Nigel Boyle submits a chapter entitled *Shared mental models and active labor market policy in Britain and Ireland: ideational coalitions and divergent policy trajectories.* In examining this issue, he examines the institutional setting in which policy was formed, the shared understandings of policy that were forged in key episodes as well as considering the uncertainty that confronted policymakers in these episodes and settings.

Craig Parsons presents a chapter entitled *Neoliberalism isn't enough: on the interaction of neoliberal and Europeanist shared mental models in the European Union.* In particular he seeks to understand the role of neoliberal ideas in driving the process of change since the 1980s. He argues however, that neoliberal ideas intersected with "Europeanist" ideas that represented a distinct agenda about the appropriate institutional locus of authority in postwar Europe. Only for this reason he argues, did the European Union become the locus of a strong neoliberal program.

Shale Horowitz provides a chapter entitled *Neoliberal reform in the post-communist world: mental models in the transition from plan to market.* He argues that in adopting and sustaining neoliberal economic reforms, the post-communist countries stand out from the rest of the developing world in two ways. First, there is greater diversity in economic policy outcomes than in other regions. Second, a large proportion of post-communist countries adopted and sustained ambitious neoliberal reforms under democracy rather than authoritarianism.

Lewis Snider offers a chapter entitled *The clash of mental models in the*

Middle East: neoliberal versus Islamic ideas. Although the preservation of Islam and the war against non-believers (jihad) are the commonly cited reasons for launching a campaign of global terror against the West (and the US in particular) in fact what is being resisted is the extension of neoliberal values into the Middle East through the extension of capitalism. This conflict can be thought of as a clash of mental models. One based on neoliberal values and capitalist economics, the other based on Islamic ideals and clientalist economies.

Sunil Rongala provides a chapter entitled *Experiments with neoliberalism in India: shattering of a mental model.* He shows how the old mental model of India came about and how some minor attempts were made to change it. It also explains how this mental model is being shattered and the tasks ahead in order for India to complete its transition from its old mold. He then highlights recent efforts by India to move in a more neoliberal direction.

Arthur T. Denzau and Ravi K. Roy present a chapter entitled *East Asia and neoliberal mental models.* They assert that most of the successful growth of the East Asian economies coincided with market-friendly policies at the macro-level and micro-policies that usually allowed considerable scope for private businesses to choose how and where to invest – in a word, neoliberal. However, in all cases other than Hong Kong, a nationalist element often accompanied the purely economic approach, with governments attempting to build up specific industries, often attempting to pick economic winners. These approaches were all distinguished from the Latin American inward-oriented ideas by their explicit export orientation. Noteworthy, however, is that when such attempts ran into major troubles, governments usually returned to policies prescribed by neoliberal mental models.

Stephen V. Marks offers a chapter entitled *Mental models of the economy and economic policy in Indonesia.* He examines how neoliberal imperatives have run into resistance from more traditional cultural orientations. Indonesian mental models on the economy tend to include suspicion toward free markets and private ownership of natural resources, and toward foreign and ethnic Chinese ownership in general. Marks asserts that differences between neoliberalism and the prevalent Indonesian mental models are not only about the details of the operation of the economy or the impact of economic policy, but also about how the world is interpreted at a deep level. He focuses on three major influences on shared mental models: indigenous patron-client traditions, the colonial period under the Dutch, and Islam as a world view and a normative guide, and the influence of foreign education of various elites.

Anil Hira includes a chapter entitled *The usefulness of the shared mental model framework for understanding Latin American economic history: from dependencia to neoliberalism.* Hira seeks to address whether Denzau and North's Shared Mental Models framework can successfully explain different periods in Latin American economic history. In this chapter he demonstrates the usefulness of the Shared Mental Models framework to explain simultaneous learning, stickiness, and punctuated equilibria in the fit between ideas and interests, as well as its limitations, principally the neglect of political variables, including discount rates. He concludes however, that the Shared Mental Model framework can be modified to accommodate these limitations.

Nicholas Amponsah presents a chapter entitled *The absence of social capital and the failure of the Ghanian neoliberal mental model.* They argue that neoliberal-based structural adjustment programs (SAPs) prescribed by the IMF and the World Bank place greater emphasis in developing social capital among affected economic and political actors. They argue that this is crucial to the success of SAPs that are aimed at promoting entrepreneurial development and investment-led growth.

References

Boskin, M.J. (1989) *Reagan and the Economy: The Successes, Failures and Unfinished Agenda.* San Francisco: ICS Press.

Denzau, A.T. and North, D.C. (1994) "Shared mental models: ideologies and institutions," *Kyklos* 47.

Gamble, A. (1996) *Hayek: The Iron Cage of Liberty.* Boulder, CO: Westview Press.

Gilpin, R. and Gilpin, J.M. (1987) *The Political Economy of International Relations.* Princeton: Princeton University Press.

Global Trade Negotiations Home Page; www.cid.harvard.edu/cidtrade/issues/washington.html accessed 2006.

Goldstein, J. and Keohane, R.O. (1993) *Ideas and foreign policy: beliefs, institutions, and political change.* Ithaca: Cornell University Press.

Kay, John (2004) *Culture and Prosperity: The Truth About Markets: why some nations are rich but most remain poor.* HarperCollins Publishers.

Kuhn, T.S. (1970) *The Structure of Scientific Revolutions.* Chicago: University of Chicago Press.

Ramachandran, V.S. (2004) *A Brief Tour of the Human Consciousness.* New York: Pi Press.

Ruggie, J.G. (1996) *Winning the Peace: America and world order in the New Era.* Columbia University Press.

Smith, A. (1776) *Wealth of Nations* [electronic resource]. Hoboken, NJ: BiblioBytes; Boulder, CO: NetLibrary.

2 Shared mental models

A postscript

Arthur T. Denzau, Douglass C. North, and Ravi K. Roy

From the perspective of ten years, how do we view our ideas about shared mental models now? We are gratified that so many people have noted our work and attempted to make use of its ideas. So far, almost 100 publications have cited our *Kyklos* paper.

One of the key issues we raised in that paper that has not been adequately addressed in subsequent research, so far as we can tell, is the interaction of learning with the pre-existing shared mental models in a person's head, and in the heads of the people of a society. This is closely related to the question of how shared mental models evolve, and thus how institutions and ideologies might evolve.

Introduction

"For most of the interesting issues in political and economic markets, uncertainty, not risk, characterizes choice-making" (Denzau and North, 1994: 2). When "Shared Mental Models" was being written over ten years ago, our intention was to make changes in the economic model of constrained choice that preserved the valuable contributions of that model, but avoided some of the obvious flaws. The value of the model in some situations of choice was clear to us, and worth preserving. It seemed nonsensical to believe that people did anything other than maximize their expected utility (recognizing that concerns for others can be included in that utility). However, the model assumed not only maximizing, but that people were substantively rational; i.e. they make the best feasible choice at all times.

This involves not just the simple behavioral assumption that, as Ronald Coase has said, given the choice, people prefer more money to less. It also heroically assumes that people have correct models of the world in their heads when they make choices. Such models are assumed to accurately predict the set of possible outcomes and a probability distribution over those outcomes. In this approach, the only role of learning is truly Bayesian, that of improving the parameters of the probability distribution estimates relating actions to outcomes. It leaves no room for people to have the wrong model of the world.

Wrong models may not have been that important as long as one only applied the choice model to everyday market choices. Such regular choices provide frequent feedback of information that helps make the choices good and the chooser behaves as if substantively rational. But the economic model has been taken into many areas that do not involve choices that are that "simple," and this means that there is little reason to believe the chooser has accurate models of the world for the choices being made.

Denzau and North attempted to lay out some of the implications of the idea that people have models in their heads, mental models, that may typically start out wrong. When man first confronted living in the world, he was not provided with an owner's manual stating the relevant action–outcome relations for all possible choices that he could make. With the entrance of Her, the problem multiplied in complexity.

If the mental models people have are not always accurate, then we need to explain the similarity of the models that people seem to have as well as why they remain different, failing to converge. We noted that people live in families and societies, and socialization in those settings trains people to have similar models, hence *shared* mental models. Such things as language and culture involve sets of mental models that make communication and cooperation possible, and seem essential to understanding how humans deal with the economic problem.

Our rudimentary gathering of ideas from psychology and anthropology seemed to us the obvious way to extend the economic model of choice to allow for people to have disparate and often wrong models of the things they were choosing. A fundamental theme of our paper was that one never sees things as they are, but rather only through the lens of the mental models in our heads.

Shared mental models and its reception in various literatures

Quite unexpected to us was the wide variety of literatures in which our paper has had some sort of impact. Our audience was economists, both neoclassical and those already working within the New Institutional Economics (NIE) approach (see Eggertsson, 1990). There have been almost 100 citations to the original paper. Over half were reasonably classifiable as NIE topics, but the next most frequent field for citations was in Public Administration/Public Policy. Also consistent with our expectations were a similar number of citations in Public Choice/Political Economy. But over one-third of the hits were outside our expected audience, with several citations in the following areas: World Politics, Technology Assessment/Management, International Relations and Comparative Politics. Even beyond this variation in fields, there was also a wider set of fields whose journals published these papers citing ours: Development, Business and Law journals, Regional Studies, General Social Science, and a single citation each in Evolutionary Economics, Ergonomics and Ecology.

What are some of the ideas that have been taken from the paper? Thinking in terms of mental models helps one understand certain ideas that are meaningless in terms of the usual rational choice approach. The importance of framing in how we interpret external reality becomes clearer, as does the difficulties with game theory as ordinarily taught. In the next section, we take up the issue of framing. Following that, we consider the problem of learning models of the world, as opposed to parameter learning within a given model. In the final section of this chapter, we apply the Shared Mental Models framework to help us explain neoliberalism in various conceptual dimensions.

Mental models and framing

The importance of the mental model being used to interpret the world can be seen in the notion of framing. Framing involves a set of concepts used to interpret the world (one aspect of mental models), highlighting certain features and ignoring others. In looking at market transactions, a neoclassical economist's focus is on the transaction price and quantity, not on the class, wealth or accents of the exchange partners. A Marxist or sociologist might be drawn to those latter features instead.

In William Riker's (1986) *The Art of Political Manipulation*, framing involves the use of language, symbols, and rhetoric for strategic purposes to build political support for policy agendas.[1] For example, framing some public expenditure as necessary to national defense has always seemed to make it easier to gain political acceptance for that spending. Thus, the US Interstate Highway System was actually authorized as the National Interstate and Defense Highways Act of 1956 (PL627) with the stated aim of making it easier to move military troops and materiel around the nation.

Another example illustrates the powerful cognitive implications of framing. The Wason experiment (1966) involves presenting a set of cards to a person and a rule as to how the symbols on the front and back of the cards are related. The subject is to determine which cards should be turned over to determine if they violate the rule. Presented as such an abstract problem of logic, some 25 percent of subjects make the correct choice. However, the exact same logical problem can be framed as one involving cheating in a social situation. Presented in this form, some 70 percent to 80 percent of subjects get the problem right (see Barkow, Cosmides and Tooby, 1992: 181–185). Framing seems to cue different modules of our mental capabilities to operate on the problem unconsciously, so that it becomes a simple question of detecting cheaters in situations of exchange – this ability is well developed in a social species such as man. Abstract logic does not cue the same cognitive skills in most people.

The relevance of mental models and framing to learning can also be seen in the ways we teach. With students with a strong mathematical background, one might begin teaching economics from solely a mathematical viewpoint, eschewing verbal and graphical presentation. We would consider that a mistake, from several viewpoints. Learning purely in a symbolic manner, such as mathematically, may not provide one with the mental models needed for intuitive discovery or metaphorical leaps. These may come from combining elements from several areas of knowledge that may be linked by related metaphors or concepts. Further, the two types of thinking, conceptual and logical, seem to be processed in different halves of our brains. The right brain usually focuses on conceptual, holistic thinking, while the more linear and logical approaches of mathematics are usually done in the left brain. These different types of processors can act as parallel, partially independent discovery engines, and the standard jury theorem argument suggests that even two independent processors trying to learn the same thing can learn it faster than can one.

How does all this affect social science reasoning? The strong assumptions about rationality embodied in standard game theory can be weakened to create a new version that is more consistent with the above view of human neurocognition. The result is one in which standard game theory is a particular subset.

Mental models and game theory: three notions of equilibrium

How can the notion of mental models affect our interpretation of game theory? Game theory utilizes the notion of common knowledge of the game to avoid the communication issues focused on in our paper. We can consider this an *objective* interpretation of a game – the stated game is common knowledge to all participants, and is objectively true.

If we see the world through mental models, as argued in Denzau–North, and not as it is, then this objective interpretation of game theory is problematic. The people interacting in a game may see the world through different mental models, not a common objective one (see Appendix A). And even if they do agree on the same mental model for their interaction, that mental model may not be objectively true. We acknowledge that even science is about tentative truths, using a method we believe may lead us *toward* the truth. To assume at the outset that agents know that truth seems a curious contradiction.

To avoid assuming the participants know the objective truth, we can consider a game that is common knowledge among the participants, but which is not necessarily a true statement of objective circumstances. This incorporates the basic Popperian notion of science as a tentative set of statements about reality, always viewed as hypotheses and as potentially wrong. We thus need to replace the Nash Equilibrium (NE) solution concept, which involves each player doing the best for themselves as they can, given what all the other players are doing. Our approach to game theory would be an intersubjective interpretation, with a corresponding ISNE (InterSubjective Nash Equilibrium) solution. In this case, the game could be viewed as a shared mental model among the players. This leaves traditional objective game theory as a subset of the intersubjective, and the Objective ONE (Nash Equilibrium) an element (if unique) of the possible ISNE that might exist.

Finally, if the game is not even common knowledge among the players, then we have a purely subjective interpretation, with corresponding Subjective Nash Equilibrium (SNE). The players may have quite different notions about the game they are playing, but achieve a Nash nonetheless. Whether or not players might learn the same game, or the objectively true game, is a question that can be pursued, but it seems likely that this would often not be the case. This would especially be true to the extent that out-of-equilibrium play is essential to sustain an equilibrium, as these plays may never actually occur in the usual view of finding a Nash. This approach to game theory is further developed in Denzau and Roy (2005) (see also Cardenas and Ostrom, 2001).

Of course, if the players consciously realize this problem, then their play would probably not correspond to the prescriptions of Nash. If players are not sure about their model of the game, they may purposely explore the possibilities in order to learn more about it. With both players doing the same, it may be very difficult for each player to learn much – the complexity of the situation could be substantial.

In the theoretical world, the assumptions of ONE and ISNE can be easily made. But the real world is much more problematic. First of all, human understanding of what is rational and what is not rational are often based on imperfect, imprecise, and asymmetric information about the world in which we live. According to Denzau and North (1994), "people act in part upon the basis of myths, dogmas, ideologies and 'half-baked' theories." As a result their preferences are often shaped by limited and imprecise information about their environment. Under these conditions, players' knowledge about their options is often unclear, making objective rational decision-making extremely difficult. As a result their preferences and strategies they pursue relative to others may often result in solutions that are objectively sub-optimal, even if the outcomes are subjectively Nash equilibria.

As noted above, if the players realize the tentative veracity of their mental models, then their play might not correspond to the prescriptions of Nash. When unsure about the game, each player may explore the possibilities in order to learn more about it, thus greatly increasing the complexity of the learning problem. This type of exploration was done by just a few of the participants in the Coursey and Mason (1987) study in which participants were asked to maximize an unknown function. Just as different mental models can induce different behavior in the same objective circumstances, different players may react to their lack of certainty in different ways.

The usual economist's model of learning, that of Bayes, ill fits with our view of mental models. The basic problem is that a Bayesian learner may be very slow to update, in the light of new data, and more importantly, cannot learn things that were not previously viewed as conceivable (see Blume and Easley, 1982). This latter limitation can be very problematic, as is argued in Denzau and Roy (2005), when it is necessary to learn entirely new models of the world.

Mental models and learning: learning models versus learning parameters

Even in such a setting involving learning, traditional game theory would still be descriptive and prescriptive if people could learn sufficiently so they could be substantively rational. As noted in Denzau and North (1994), the choice situation must be relatively simple (with low dimensionality of the model to be learned); information must be good and be based on sufficient feedback from choices; and the learner must be sufficiently motivated to incur the costs of learning. Under those circumstances, a learner may be able to learn the correct mental model through which to see the world, and choice models based on such an assumption are more likely to be accurate.

Without those assumptions, we must consider an alternative situation in which our mental models are not accurate, and may differ substantially across individuals. Mental models help shape the way human beings structure their environment and how they operate in it. According to Denzau and North (1994) an understanding of how "mental models evolve and the relationship between them is the single most important step that research in the social sciences can make to replace the black box of the 'rationality' assumption used in economics and rational choice models."

The gradual learning by economic writers about the causes of international trade is instructive about this learning process. The oldest views about trade are usually termed as the "vent for trade" argument – nations export their excess production of some products. This was joined by a model of absolute advantage – nations export those products that they can produce at the cheapest cost. Both arguments involve the use of prices that are viewed as given, either output or input prices, and do not provide a way to predict from prior considerations the pattern of trade. Ricardo, in 1817, presented the comparative advantage argument for trade – nations export those products which they have a relative, or comparative, advantage in producing. This advanced the model, but left open the more ultimate causes of the assumed productivity differences. It was only with the Heckscher–Ohlin model that relative endowments of resources (capital and labor, or land and human capital, etc.) enabled one to predict a priori the resulting pattern of trade. At each step, the current best model was believed by many and used to draw policy recommendations, even though none of these models is necessarily objectively true.

Based on the model one believes, one can attempt to learn the parameters of that model. For example, a Marxist might believe in the labor theory of value; i.e. that the labor content of a product determines its exchange value. The parameters to measure are thus the labor content and the exchange prices. As Stigler (1958) notes, this gives a relatively good predictive model for many goods. But it is precisely the cases it fails to predict accurately that provide the most information as to what to bring into a better model. Much, if not most, of the value of a piece of electronic gadgetry is in the semiconductor devices (the chips) used in the gadget. However, the labor content in these devices is very small, and remains small even if one adds in the labor content equivalent of the capital used in their production (this labor is termed stored labor in some analyses). These measurements of labor content fail to predict the market prices by a substantial margin. One needs a much more substantial theory of capital to build a better understanding of the production cost of such products and a model of market power to better understand the pricing of such goods. Instead of just learning the labor content parameter, one needs to find a better model that deals with more variables than the simple labor theory of value.

If learning has to do with gaining greater understanding about how the world functions and operates, then our ability to do so to rests upon our ability to distill and organize facts. But what facts we focus on and which we ignore are largely determined by the mental models or beliefs we hold about a subject. In such settings, it has been argued that we think not as sequential logic engines, but rather by pattern recognition and neural nets (see Bechtel and Abrahamsen, 1991) or by the use of metaphors (Lakoff and Johnson, 1980).

In both of those approaches, learning is often contextual. We learn in relationship to what else we know, what we believe, our prejudices and our fears. We assimilate new knowledge by building upon our existing structure of beliefs. And in contexts where existing knowledge of a subject matter is scarce or incomplete, uncertainty looms. In such contexts mental models become critical in shaping how individuals process, construe, and regard new and unfamiliar facts and evidence. Under conditions where there is no preexisting knowledge of a subject matter or where new or unfamiliar facts present themselves in the face of existing knowledge, mental models becomes pivotal in shaping our understanding of what is rational and what is not. It is in such situations when our existing models fail that Bayesian learning gets us nowhere, and new approaches are required.

Neoliberalism as a shared mental model

One application of the study of the influence of shared mental models is in the field of Political Economy and the study of the various experiments with market ideas around the world. The collapse of the Soviet Union in the early 1990s caused many policymakers to rethink Marx-based dependencia and statist political–economic ideas in various countries around the world. Neoliberalism is a term often used in political economy very broadly and vaguely to refer to market-oriented policy ideas and strategies in the second half of the twentieth century. Unfortunately, the conceptual analysis on this subject has been rather scant. We can apply the Shared Mental Models framework to explain how neoliberalism can be understood as both a reference to the distinct but related experiments applying market-oriented ideas in various political, social, and economic contexts. The term is also used as a broader reference to certain core ideas that are shared among them.

The Shared Mental Models framework can be used to help develop an improved conceptual understanding of neoliberalism and the variations and innovations that occurred in its application across regional and national contexts. When applying the Shared Mental Models framework, we begin with the premise that individual countries develop and adopt internal understandings and constructions of the world that are shaped by their unique social, political, economic, and institutional contexts. This affects how policymakers in individual countries and regions construe the meanings of ideas such as what markets are, how they work and what they accomplish. This in turn has shaped distinct neoliberal experiments within individual countries and regions and explains divergences in their respective neoliberal paths. What unites them is that they all converge to varying degrees, emphasizing the primacy of the market and the importance of fostering economic environments that encourage entrepreneurial-led growth. We may analyze neoliberalism as a set of distinct but related mental models that are informed by a similar set of shared ideas, which we refer to as a *shared* mental model.

APPENDIX 2A: SUBJECTIVE GAME THEORY

An Objective Nash Equilibrium example

Consider an asymmetric coordination game of the form shown in Table 2.1. Row has a strategy of playing {Up} if she believes her opponent would

Table 2.1 ONE form of a game

	Left	*Right*
Up	3, 1	−1, 2
Down	−1, −1	0, 0

play {Left}, and {Down} if {Right}, while Column's play is similarly contingent. It has two Nash equilibria at {Up, Left} and {Down, Right}.

The example with mental models for both players

As the game is not common knowledge among the players, then we have a subjective interpretation, with corresponding Subjective NE (SNE). Here, Table 2.2 shows the initial beliefs of the players about the game. Player Row misperceives the game. She has the right general mental model, but has details of the game wrong – note the off-diagonals. Column also misperceives the game, but as a Prisoner's Dilemma, perhaps due to unfamiliarity or the use of signals that trigger the wrong mental model of the situation. Given their subjective notions of the game, the only ones they have to determine best responses, Row chooses {Up} as a dominant strategy, and Column chooses {Right} also as a dominant strategy. This yields the payoff of (−1, 2) for the players from the objective version of the game.

Note that at this point, Column, the player with the completely wrong view of the game, finds her beliefs confirmed by the result. Row, on the other hand, has the right general model, but finds the payoff to not be what she expected, −1 instead of 2.

From this failure, it is not clear what Row would learn, but Column has no reason to change his view of the game. Not only is the payoff what he expected, but Row's play in his view is her dominant strategy. For illustrative purposes, we can simply have Row learn through discussion with Column, who might be quite persuasive, that the game is as Column sees it, a PD.

Table 2.2 SNE forms of the same game

	Player Row	
	Left	*Right*
Up	3, 3	2, 0
Down	0, 1	0, 0
	Player Column	
	Left	*Right*
Up	1, 1	−1, 2
Down	2, −1	0, 0

The example with the same mental models for both players

Table 2.3 illustrates that this would lead to the players playing a PD they now both believe themselves to be playing, and choosing {Down, Right}, leading to a payoff of (0, 0).

Table 2.3 ISNE form of the same game

	Left	*Right*
Up	1, 1	−1, 2
Down	2, −1	0, 0

We can interpret this as a game that is common knowledge among the participants, but which is not necessarily a true view of objective circumstances. This incorporates the basic Popperian view of science and results in an ISNE solution. They have intersubjective agreement on the same model of reality, and play to a Nash equilibrium given those beliefs (mental models). In this case, the game could be viewed as a SMM among the players. Mental models are the internal representations that individual cognitive systems create to interpret the environment. Shared mental models by players are shared inter-subjectively, but do not necessarily relate as a true one-to-one with reality. Different individuals with convergent models will likely entail shared interpretations about problems, solutions, and preferences. This leaves traditional objective game theory as a subset of the intersubjective.

Note

1 According to Benford and Snow (2000), the conceptual applications of framing have been significant in the social sciences. They argue that framing has gained currency in the field of cognitive psychology such as Bateson's (1972) *Steps to an Ecology of the Mind* and Tversky and Kahneman's (1981) "The framing of decisions and psychology of choice." In the field of linguistics and discourse analysis, important applications of framing have been developed in Tannen's (1993) *Framing in Discourse* and Van Dijk's (1977) *Text and Context Exploration in the Semantic and Pragmatics of Discourse.* Similarly, framing has been applied in the field of communication and media studies in Pan and Kosicki's (1993) "Framing analysis: an approach to news discourse," and Scheufele's (1999) "Framing as a theory of media effects" in important ways. In the field of Political Science and policy studies, Benford and Snow cite the seminal work of Schon and Rein's (1994) *Frame Reflection: Toward the Resolution of Intractable Policy Controversies* and Triandafyllidou and Fotiou's (1998) "Sustainability and modernity in the European Union: A Frame Theory Approach to Policymaking." And, Joshua William Busby (2003) cites Sidney Tarrow, Mayer Zald, and David Snow as important contributors to the application of framing to the literature on social movements (p. 8).

Zald (1996) defines frames as "the specific metaphors, symbolic representations, and cognitive cues used to render or cast behavior and events in an evaluative mode and to suggest alternative modes of action" (p. 262). Busby (2003) asserts that frames provide a method "by which policymakers can sort information and provide a number of concomitant functions" (p. 8).

References

Barkow, J.H., Cosmides, L. and Tooby, J. (1992) *The Adapted Mind: Evolutionary Psychology and the Generation of Culture.* New York: Oxford University Press.

Bateson, G. (1972) *Steps to an Ecology of the Mind.* New York: Ballantine.

Bechtel, W. and Abrahamsen, A. (1991) *Connectionism and the Mind: An Introduction to Parallel Processing in Networks.* Cambridge: Blackwell.

Benford, R.D. and Snow, D.A. (2000) "Framing processes and social movements: an overview and assessment," *Annual Review of Sociology* 26: 611–639.

Blume, Larry and Easley, David (1982) "Learning to be rational," *Journal of Economic Theory* 26: 340–351.

Busby, J.W. (2003) "Framing truths for power: the strategic character of persuasion," Georgetown University, paper prepared for the International Studies Association conference, Portland, OR, February 25–March 1.

Busby, J.W. "Bono made Jesse Helms Cry: Jubilee 2000; debt relief: and Moral Action in International Politics." Center for Globalization and Government, Woodrow Wilson School. Princeton University: Working Paper.

Cardenas, J.-C. and Ostrom, E. (2001) "What do people bring into the game? How norms help overcome the tragedy of the commons," unpubl. manuscript, W01-5, presented at Washington University (St. Louis) Conference on Social Norms and the Law, 9 March.

Coursey, D.L. and Mason, C.F. (1987) "Investigations concerning the dynamics of consumer behavior in uncertain environments," *Economic Inquiry* 25(4) (October), 549–564.

Denzau, A.T. and North, D.C. (1994) "Shared mental models: ideologies and institutions," *Kyklos* 47.

Denzau, A.T. and Roy, R.K. (2005) "Mental models and game theory: cognitive constructions of multiple Nash equilibria," Presented at Public Choice Society, March.

Eggertsson, T. (1990) *Economic Behavior and Institutions.* Cambridge: Cambridge University Press.

Kahneman, D. and Tversky, A. (1984) "Choices, values and frames," *American Psychologist* 39: 341–350. (Reprinted as Chapter 1 in Kahneman, D. and Tversky, A. (eds) *Choices, Values and Frames.* New York: Cambridge University Press and the Russell Sage Foundation, 2000.)

Lakoff, George and Johnson, Mark (1980) *Metaphors We Live By.* Chicago: University of Chicago Press.

McClure, Harold J. and Willett, Thomas D. (1983) "Understanding the Supply-Siders," in Stubblebine, C. and Willett, T.D. (eds) *Reaganomics: A Midterm Report.* San Francisco: ICS Press.

Pan, Z. and Kosicki, G.M. (1993) "Framing analysis: an approach to news discourse," *Political Communication* 10: 55–75.

Riker, William (1986) *The Art of Political Manipulation.* New Haven: Yale University Press.

Scheufele, D.A. (1999) "Framing as a theory of media effect," *Journal of Communication* 49: 103–122.

Schon, Donald A. and Rein, Martin (1994) *Frame Reflection: Toward the Resolution of Intractable Policy Controversies.* New York: Basic Books.

Snow, David A. and Benford, Robert D. (1988) "Ideology, frame resonance, and participant mobilization," in *From Structure to Action: Comparing Social Movement Research Across Cultures.* Klandermans, B., Kriesi, H. and Tarrow, S.G. (eds) pp. 197–218. Greenwich: JAI Press.

Stigler, George (1958) "Ricardo and the 93% labor theory of value," *American Economic Review* 48(3) (June), 357–367.

Tannen, D. (ed.) (1993) *Framing in Discourse.* New York: Oxford University Press.

Tarrow, S. (1998) *Power in Movement.* New York: Cambridge University Press, 2nd edn.

Triandafyllidou, A. and Fotiou, A. (1998) "Sustainability and modernity in the European Union: A frame theory approach to policymaking," *Sociological Research Online* 3 (1): www.socresonline.org.uk/socresonline/3/1/2.html.

Tversky, A. and Kahneman, D. (1981) "The framing of decisions and psychology of choice," *Science* 211: 453–458.

Van Dijk, T.A. (1977) *Text and Context Exploration in the Semantic and Pragmatics of Discourse.* London: Longman.

Wason, P. (1966) "Reasoning," in Foss, B.M. (ed.) *New Horizons in Psychology.* Harmondsworth: Penguin.

Zald, Mayer N. (1996) *Culture, Ideology, & Strategic Framing,* in McAdam, D., McCarthy, J. and Zail, M.N. (eds) *Comparative Perspectives on Social Movements.* Cambridge: Cambridge University Press, 261–274.

3 The meanings of neoliberalism[1]

Nancy Neiman Auerbach

Introduction

Before we can analyze neoliberalism as a shared mental model (Denzau and North, 1994), we must define it. But the task of defining neoliberalism is not an easy one. There is certainly widespread disagreement as to the effects of neoliberalism, but there is also significant disagreement over the nature of neoliberalism. For example, many anti-globalization activists have used the word "neoliberalism" as a synonym for globalization or global market-liberalism (otherwise known as capitalism). From this perspective, neoliberalism is just another dirty word, capable of representing any number of injustices in the world loosely attributed to globalization. But interestingly, many traditional and neo-conservatives have also conceived of neoliberalism in broad ideological terms, equating its meaning with "freedom and liberty" in the broadest sense of the word. This often entails the spreading of a liberal society and the conflation of expansionist political goals with an economic agenda. For example, the Bush administration has justified war on the basis of the spreading of liberal ideas both political and economic. Bush's nomination of Wolfowitz to head the World Bank is a perfect example of the seamless enmeshing of politics and what is, at least rhetorically, referred to as free market economics.

But as it turns out, the use of the term neoliberalism reveals complexities even beyond this clear political divide that cannot necessarily be measured along a single axis. One of the reasons that no satisfying definition of neoliberalism really exists is that its uses can only be measured multidimensionally. Here it may be helpful to broadly characterize who uses it and who does not, when the term is used to describe a specific set of policies, when the term is used to reference a historically-grounded time period characterized by the dominance of particular ideas concerning economic policymaking, and when the term is used broadly to describe a process of globalization perpetuated by a capitalist, ideological orientation.

First, who does not use the term, and why? Neoliberalism has always been more of a political label than an economic label. Mainstream economists have never been comfortable using this term "neoliberalism" in part because it is historically associated with the Reagan and Thatcher revolutions. Therefore, if an economist uses neoliberalism to refer to a concrete set of policies, these policies might include Laffer curve supply-side economics policies and monetarism: policies which were never accepted by mainstream economists. But the hesitancy of economists to use the term neoliberalism can be traced back even further to include an avoidance of paradigmatic labels at all. For the purposes of this book, one way to think about neoliberalism is as a revived form of economic liberalism, as both concepts share critical common core market-oriented ideas and directives and thus represent a shared mental model in the broadest sense (Denzau and North, 1994). Here, the key point is that economists never in any significant way used the term economic liberalism, let alone neoliberalism. The main reason for this is that mainstream economists fall so squarely within the paradigm of economic liberalism that there is no need to ever think or talk about it as a shared mental model. Rather, it is political scientists who have more commonly used the term economic liberalism and later neoliberalism as a paradigmatic model set up against realism in the international relations context, or perhaps Marxism in the political economy context. Robert Gilpin's in-depth comparison of the dominant paradigms (or "shared mental models", as used here) of Marxism, liberalism, and mercantilism and their contrasting tenets exemplifies this use (Gilpin, 1987). Other political scientists, especially comparativists, have used the term "neoliberalism" to describe a historical trend or period, often modifying the word "era", as in neoliberal era. Here the term was used as often during the 1980s and 1990s to describe the period as it was unfolding as it has been used since 2000 to refer to the end of the neoliberal era. The latter use is particularly common among Latin Americanists and journalists attempting to describe or explain the increasing popularity of leftist leaders in that region since 2000. Left-oriented academics and anti-globalization protestors have increasingly used the term to refer to a broad range of market-oriented policy trends as well as the actual process of globalization. As this latter use of the term gained popularity in the 1990s, market-oriented reformers who thought of themselves as non-ideological seemed to distance themselves from the term neoliberal, while at the same time concretizing their approach to market reform by enumerating a set of policies that would become known as the Washington Consensus (Williamson, 1990). Increasingly, this has left the term neoliberal almost exclusively in the anti-globalization camp. The most common usage at present among the anti-capitalist, anti-globalization left is as a modifier to globalization as in "neoliberal globalization." This is actually an important development worth commenting on because of what it says about the particular critique being made. The anti-globalization movement, which gained international attention in 2000 after the WTO protest in Seattle, came under attack from market reformers for being naive about the reality of markets. According to economic liberals, market forces and, particularly, the process of globalization underscore a kind of inevitability. They might ask: "how can you protest the globalization of markets?": Globalization just is, whether you like it or not. Anti-globalization protestors have countered by arguing that the form that globalization takes is not inevitable, and that the rules of the game are being set within a neoliberal–ideological framework and enforced though institutions like the WTO. Hence, neoliberal globalization is not merely a tautology, but rather a description of the belief system and values that underlie the particular processes of market integration that are underway.

Obviously, the meaning of neoliberalism depends in part on who is using it, which renders the idea of a concrete and unchanging definition near impossible. The exploration of neoliberalism in this book seeks to understand neoliberalism in a more constructivist sense by asking how its uses have shaped its meaning rather than seeking agreement over the "one true meaning" of the term.

So we "know", that the Reagan and Thatcher revolutions helped to set in motion an entire era of global market reform known to many as "neoliberalism." We also know that neo-conservative and radical voices have been comfortable either wearing, or disparaging, the neoliberal label and that economists have avoided the term altogether. Furthermore, policy reformers, those responsible for implementing market-oriented reform, have for years tried to rehabilitate the term by redefining it as a concrete set of policies that represent the lowest common denominator of policies agreed upon in mainstream policymaking circles. More specifically, pro-market reformers have turned to the "Washington Consensus" as a grounded, and rational approach both to defining neoliberalism and to conducting economic policy. From this perspective, the Washington Consensus constitutes a less ideological middle-ground between the "true believers" on both sides of the debate who tend to wear ideological blinders when it comes to analyzing policy outcomes.

But just as the use of the term neoliberalism and the process of globalization that it attempts to describe have changed over time, so too have the range of critiques. Some opponents of neoliberalism draw inspiration from the three ideologies which presented the most prominent critiques of nineteenth-century classical economic liberalism: economic nationalism, Marxism, and embedded liberalism. Robert Gilpin's 1975 version of this "grand narrative" sets economic liberalism (akin to neoliberalism) against Marxism and Mercantilism (ideologically akin to economic nationalism or neo-realism). Gilpin's mental model equated economic liberalism, and, by extension, neoliberalism, with mainstream economics. But "newer" critiques of economic liberalism, most notably those inspired by feminist thought and environmental concerns are building powerful coalitions based on a shared mental model that directly challenges the neutral, or non-ideological, claims of neoliberal practitioners by employing the language of efficiency themselves.

Ultimately, this paper comes to a constructivist conclusion that the "rational" and positivist middle, economists and policymakers, as well as the "true believers," are biased by the limits of their respective mental models when considering the definition, the value and the dynamics of neoliberalism. That is, ideological blinders are worn not just by many globalization protestors on the left and hyper-capitalists on the right, but also by mainstream practitioners of the Washington Consensus and mainstream economists. One might assume that economists are mostly immune from such biases because economics as a discipline draws such clear distinctions between positive analysis, a statement of fact, and normative analysis, a value judgment. Moreover, economics as a discipline places much greater value on positive economics than it does on normative economics. Under these conditions, it makes sense to assume that economists face much greater incentives than other observers to be unbiased. But it could also be that economists face a greater incentive to believe that their models are unbiased, even when they diverge significantly from reality. Normative values can tend to bias positive analysis in unconscious ways. Thomas Kuhn suggested that even in the hard sciences, working within a particular paradigm can literally affect a scientist's initial observations, which calls into question the whole idea that positive analysis contains no value judgments. Often this presumption about market efficiency leads economists to model deregulation in a way that automatically assumes pareto-improvement. However, if multiple market failures exist, there is no economic law that guarantees that deregulation in one area will necessarily be pareto-improving. This phenomenon is sometimes referred to as the theory of Second Best. While the theory of Second Best is perfectly consistent with positive economic analysis, it often gets forgotten in analyses of economic reform. Especially in development economics, the notion of efficiency in the form of growth maximization tends to overshadow distributive issues precisely because equity falls under the purview of normative analysis. For example, one of the most important assumptions of economic reform models is that growth can be pursued first, and redistribution or equity issues can be implemented at relatively low cost later. But because political variables often work to maintain inequality, the assumption of low-cost redistribution is often unrealistic. That is, because the positive analysis points to the fastest growth path, while analyzing the outcome of inequality requires normative value judgments, the quality of underlying assumptions often receives little attention. This paper asserts that equity should be considered an a-priori condition for efficient economic growth. It addresses the problem of equity in economic analyses directly by proposing that an "infrastructure of justice," similar to the physical and legal infrastructures that have more typically been considered prerequisites to development, be pursued as well. With such an infrastructure in place, the promise of market reform in terms of welfare benefits could truly be realized.

In order to even address the confusion over the meaning and nature of neoliberalism, this paper begins with an historical analysis of the deceptively simple question: "What is neoliberalism?" The next section of this paper defines neoliberalism as an era in a specific historical context bounded by dramatic events and policy changes. As such, the neoliberal era constitutes a period when neoliberalism enjoyed hegemonic status both as a shared mental model, and as a set of policies instituted by market-oriented governments across the globe. The trajectory of the world economy due to a global wave of policy reform, both domestic and system-wide, ushered in a period of rapid globalization which consequently has come to be seen by some as synonymous with neoliberalism. However, while the reign of neoliberal hegemony in terms of accepted ideas for economic reform and supportive governments has arguably declined since its heyday of the 1980s and 1990s, the same cannot necessarily be said about globalization. This suggests that an exploration of the meaning of neoliberalism cannot be based solely on historical context. Rather, a deeper understanding of neoliberalism must explore both the concrete nature of neoliberalism as a policy agenda as well as the multiple ideologically-informed meanings of neoliberalism.

Using the Washington Consensus as a jumping-off point to define neoliberalism, the next part will explore the multiple, and at times contradictory understandings of neoliberalism. This section will attempt to answer the question: "If neoliberalism does in fact refer to a coherent shared mental model and related set of policies, and if evidence is widely available as to the welfare effects of these policies, how can proponents and opponents continue to differ so radically in their opinions as to the nature of neoliberalism?" As Kuhn suggests, are both sides so embedded in their paradigms (or shared mental models) that they are missing crucial evidence? Is there a fundamental misunderstanding on either side as to what neoliberalism actually is?

The last part focuses on fundamental differences over the implementation of neoliberal policies that remain once it is established that both sides are in fact talking about the same policies. In this section, neoliberalism in the form of rational policy-making based on economic analysis is stripped of its neutral non-ideological status. Only at this point will it be possible to engage in meaningful dialogue across the divide: a dialogue hopefully capable of producing policies that indeed can fulfill the promise that proponents of neoliberalism have claimed market-oriented reforms would bring but have up until now largely failed on their own terms.

A neoliberal era? Defining neoliberalism in historical context

As a set of policies or shared mental models, it is difficult to distinguish in any meaningful way between neoliberalism and more classical forms of economic liberalism except by placing neoliberalism in an historical context. This is in part because the content of neoliberalism mirrors its intellectual antecedent, economic liberalism, and in fact, argues for a return to economic liberalism in an age of big governments and widespread interventionism. The "neo-" can really be thought of as meaning "a return to" liberal market economic ideals, with some compromises away from classical ideals, due to political constraints (Denzau and North, 1994). The only question is: "When did this return really begin?" The exact timing, as it turns out, depends on which set of world events one focuses on, though a strong case can be made that neoliberalism began to take form with all of these events. One could mark the beginning of the neoliberal era as early as 1971, with the end of the Bretton Woods and the abandoning of capital controls in the United States, or with the election of Margaret Thatcher, in 1979, and Ronald Reagan in 1980, or with the beginning of the Latin American Debt Crisis in 1982, or perhaps with the fall of the Berlin Wall in 1989. But regardless of the "start date" or particular world events that symbolize it, neoliberal economic policy reform became widespread in the 1980s, and continued to spread dramatically throughout the last two decades of the twentieth century. The historical analysis presented here attempts to search out and underscore the deepest roots of neoliberal dominance by focusing on the most recent event first and analyzing its roots in the form of earlier events. The analysis thus proceeds in reverse chronological order.

The fall of Communism

For many pro-market reformers, the fall of the Berlin Wall was the ultimate symbol that market liberalism and democracy had won the final battle with Communism and socialist ideology. Francis Fukayama, for example, proclaimed not only the victory of market economics, but the end of history (Fukuyama, 1992). Denzau and North see the failure of the Soviet Union as a crack in a "pure" ideology due to internal contradictions that are likely to lead to crisis and rapid change (Denzau and North, 1994). These interpretations are, of course, based on a series of dramatic events like the mass protests that took place in Eastern Europe in 1989. Nor was this simply the perspective of outside observers. Free markets were also exalted in writing by Russians, Poles, Hungarians, Romanians, Czechs, East Germans, and Bulgarians (McKenzie and Lee, 1991: 7). Many neoliberals argue that it was in fact market forces in the form of rapid capital movements that ultimately defeated the Soviet Union and the dominance of socialist ideology that supported it:

> the growing transnational mobility of capital forced world governments to become competitors for the globe's expanding capital base – by cutting tax rates, curbing unnecessary and wasteful expenditures, eliminating inefficient regulations, and renouncing all the trappings of state central planning.
>
> (McKenzie and Lee, 1991: 9)

But regardless of cause and effect, the end result of the collapse of the Soviet Union was the reintegration into the global market economy of the entire Eastern Bloc and, ultimately, all previously-socialist planned economies, with the exception of North Korea and Cuba. This phenomenon by itself constitutes a significant process of market liberalization which helped to define an era of neoliberalism. Yet, regardless of how symbolic the opening-up of the Communist Bloc to market reform was to the era of neoliberalism, it would be difficult to argue that the process began there.

Latin American Debt Crisis[2]

Alternatively, the beginning of the neoliberal era could be placed seven years earlier, in 1982, with Mexico's announcement that it could no longer meet interest payments on its debt. This marked the official beginning of the "Latin American Debt Crisis." As Mexico made the announcement, private banks that had lent billions of dollars to developing countries over the past decade suddenly stopped lending. The IMF was called in to clean up the "mess." Together with the US government, the IMF put together the Baker Plan to help bailout Mexico. The IMF also went about offering its seal of approval to other heavily-indebted developing countries so that private-bank lending might resume. Throughout the 1980s, Latin American countries gave up import-substitution policies and adopted trade-liberalization policies. They also privatized banks and other industries, lifted interest rate ceilings, and cut back considerably on deficit spending. Whether this wave of neoliberal policies came as a result of Latin American governments having "learned from the error of their ways" or because they needed the IMF's seal of approval, it can safely be said that the Debt Crisis triggered the beginning of the neoliberal wave in Latin America. Actually, this policy shift toward neoliberal policy reforms took place throughout the developing world and also in the developed world in the form of widespread deregulation.

Reagan and Thatcher

Reaganism and Thatcherism can certainly be thought of as distinct but related strands of a neoliberal shared mental model (Denzau and Roy, 2003). To the extent that they emphasized reducing inefficient government regulation, they were within the mainstream. With respect to ideas like "trickle down" economics, they were not. But if the popularity of deregulation is the criterion for defining the neoliberal era, it makes sense to credit Reagan and Thatcher with that particular accomplishment. In January 1981, Reagan took office with a plan for cutting double-digit inflation and creating new jobs. As it turns out, the plan to cut inflation through cuts in government spending on social welfare programs as well as through the Federal Reserve Board's tight monetary policy was much more successful than the plan to create new jobs through a "trickle down" effect in the early Reagan years.[3] The US interest rate hikes which banks passed on to debtor countries helps explain the sudden inability of Mexico, previously seen as a model debtor, to meet its debt payments. So, while the process of policy reform may have begun almost two years later in Latin America than in Britain and the US, the processes are interconnected. But the element of the "Reagan Revolution" that had real staying power was the change in budget policy that became known as the "New Federalism."

The Reagan administration believed that federal involvement both in state and local government affairs as well as private market affairs, was more likely to exacerbate problems than contribute to their solution. New Federalism not only moved greater policy-setting and financial responsibility to the state and local governments; it produced a large-scale deregulation effort, which together with the "Thatcherite Revolution" stood as a model for deregulation and privatization efforts world-wide (Yergin and Stanislaw, 1998: 124).

While in Europe and the United States the shift to neoliberal policy coincided with Reagan- and Thatcherism, not all advocates of neoliberalism agree that all of the policies adopted by Reagan and Thatcher necessary qualify as neoliberal. What does seem clear is that the rhetoric of the Reagan and Thatcher Revolutions played as significant a role in defining the neoliberal era as the actual policies that Reagan and Thatcher pursued. This explains why the perception persists that the deregulation revolution began with Reagan despite the fact that it actually began much earlier in the 1970s, with US airline and banking deregulation. What Reagan did was sell the political idea of a return to the free market to the general populace, in the process popularizing neoliberalism. This popularization of neoliberalism explains how aspects of neoconservative politics came to be seen as part of the neoliberal agenda. Certainly, deregulation counts as part of the Washington Agenda, as we shall see in the next section, but most proponents of the Washington Consensus-version of neoliberalism would not endorse supply-side economics. Yet, the widespread popularization of neoliberalism really is as much due to Reagan's catchy populism as it is due to the rational attraction of market reform. In short, market reformers benefited from the fact that Reagan and Thatcher opened the doors for market reform, but with that debt has come a price of being associated perhaps too closely with a more extreme form of economic populism.

Another sense in which Thatcherism, in particular, played more of a key role rhetorically than in terms of actual policy, is that despite a mixed record throughout the "neoliberal period" of actual neoliberal governments and policies among advanced industrialized countries, the period still reigns as one of overwhelming neoliberal dominance. But even defining the 1980s and 1990s as an era of neoliberalism, especially in Europe, as many scholars have, can be problematic. For example, left governments remained in power in Sweden, Austria, Australia, New Zealand, Greece, and Scandinavia throughout the 1980s and 1990s and made a substantial difference in the economic policy arena (Glyn, 2001). One could argue that Europe never moved away from "embedded liberalism" to a neoliberal model even when neoliberalism seemed to be most dominant. On the other hand, one could argue that even left-leaning governments like Clinton's Administration or Tony Blair's government tended toward neoliberal policies.

Globalization and the end of Bretton Woods

Another way to envision the age of neoliberalism is as a process of globalization, a characteristic of the international system. Especially if one has the globalization of financial markets in mind when referencing an age of neoliberal reform, the end of Bretton Woods makes sense as a starting point (Helleiner, 1993). Most directly, the collapse of Bretton Woods ended the world-wide pegged exchange rate system. After the closing of the US gold window in 1973, most advanced industrial countries chose to float their currencies on world markets. This alone constitutes a significant shift toward market reform. However, this did not necessarily constitute a move toward neoliberal policy, if neoliberalism is defined in the context of the Washington Consensus, because the Washington Consensus takes no position on the choice of exchange rate regimes, recognizing that international monetary theory shows that no one regime is best for all countries. The abandoning of capital controls in the wake of Bretton Woods, on the other hand, constitutes a central element of the neoliberal era. One by one, beginning with the US in 1974, advanced industrial countries removed capital controls. Britain followed the US lead in 1979, abolishing a capital controls regime that had been in place for 40 years (Helleiner, 1993). Throughout the 1980s, Australia, New Zealand, Denmark, and by 1988, the entire European Community, abolished capital controls. As capital controls were increasingly abandoned and technology further enhanced capital mobility, financial markets became increasingly globalized and interdependent, which further increased the cost of maintaining capital controls, or pegged exchange rates for that matter. Without question, the process of globalization had taken off, and was showing no sign of slowing. The level of acceptance of these processes as either inevitable and/or beneficial, however, would eventually wane. With the coming of the new century, neoliberal dominance and globalization more broadly met with renewed challenges: both political and intellectual.

A new century: the end of neoliberal hegemony

Regardless of the precise starting date, most would agree that the 1980s and 1990s constituted a period of neoliberal dominance, both ideologically and in terms of major policy changes, globally. This dominance, punctuated by dramatic events like the fall of the Berlin wall, led conservative observers like Francis Fukayama to perhaps prematurely declare "the end of history." Even before this, Thatcher declared that "there is no alternative" to liberal market economics, what scholars have since referred to as her "TINA" thesis. But contrary to these predictions and declarations, the pendulum has appeared to swing again, bringing in an era of challenges both in terms of policy shifts and critiques of neoliberalism from a variety of ideological sources. Some scholars point to a more dramatic shift, declaring that "the neoliberal wave has crested and broken," (Snyder, 2001: 3) while others simply point to a crack in the armor, demonstrated by the fact that "public officials now refer to the once widely accepted Washington Consensus as 'outdated'" (Helleiner, 2003: 686). Either way, the era of neoliberal hegemony is certainly being called into question.

Just as significant as the increasing intellectual challenges to neoliberalism is the emergence of leftist governments in Latin America that are challenging policy trends in place since the beginning of the 1980s Debt Crisis. With the election of Lula in Brazil, Chavez in Venezuela, Kirchner in Argentina, Morales in Ecuador, and Bachlet in Chile, pundits are asking "Is the Latin American Party Coming to an End?" (*Independent*, 2005) and predicting that "this series of Latin American elections is likely to completely change the political landscape" (Chang, 2005). The current political scene and popular economic ideology in Latin America is being deemed "the hour of the Left," (Montaner, 2005) suggesting a dramatic shift from a time when scholars addressed issues like "the neoliberalization of Latin American Populism," and "Latin American Political Economy in the Age of Neoliberal Reform" (Shifter and Jawahar, 2005).

Yet, despite the political significance of this shift to the left, opponents of neoliberalism continue to argue that pragmatically, not much of a shift has truly occurred. One such argument asserts that, regionally, Latin American economic policy cannot be classified as leftist because the new center-left is embracing "Third Way" economic policies much akin to neoliberalism. The claim is that despite differences in political discourses, the new left governments' macroeconomic policies are broadly similar, differing little from the policies of prior regimes (Vernengo, 2005). Whether one sees current policy trends as a substantive move away from neoliberalism, obviously depends on ones beliefs about what neoliberalism means.

In summary, not only is there not a clear consensus over when the neoliberal era began, there is even less of a consensus over whether it has ended. Part of the confusion follows from the ambiguous nature of neoliberalism as it relates to the global economy: is it a dominant set of policies or is it a characteristic of global markets? If it is a set of policies, then the neoliberal era has waned. If it is akin to globalization, that process is still moving full-steam ahead. Because this ambiguity exists, a historical treatment like the one offered in this section can only go so far toward furthering our understanding of neoliberalism. It now becomes necessary to seek a deeper, and perhaps more grounded, meaning of neoliberalism. The next section begins by identifying the major players in the debate over neoliberalism.

The meanings of neoliberalism

True believers

Neoliberalism has indeed inspired a plethora of fervently expressed anti-globalization and pro-globalization beliefs. The majority of anti-globalization movements have come to see neoliberalism as indistinguishable from globalization. Most neo-conservatives have also adopted a rhetoric that conceives of neoliberalism in broad ideological terms, equating its meaning with "freedom and liberty". Yet, actual neo-conservative policies have tended to look more like neo-mercantilism than anything else.

This is one reason that George Bush's neo-conservative approach to neoliberalism does not seem to be supported by many economists and neoliberal practitioners. Are these neoliberal reformers less ideological than Bush? One way to reconcile the meaning of neoliberal is to distinguish between the ideologues on the right or the left that use the term so generally and adhere to their pro or con positions so fervently that their ideas seem to rest more on faith than on evidence, on the one hand, and the practitioners who base their support for specific neoliberal policies on evidence and analysis. Perhaps the former can be described as true believers. From this perspective, the practitioners that form a middle camp can be described as rational, non-ideological analysts and policymakers who seek a positivist understanding of the way that markets operate and attempt to prescribe and implement policies that will increase the efficiency of economies, thus improving economic welfare. For most of the practitioners of market-oriented reform, defining neoliberalism in terms of a Washington Consensus allows for a more grounded, concrete and practical approach to policymaking.

The Washington Consensus

The Washington Consensus then gets situated in the middle of the debate over the merits of neoliberalism, with the more extreme ideological camps that define neoliberalism in polemical terms on either side. For those in the middle, the Washington Consensus is an attractive way to nail down the meaning of neoliberalism because this approach in providing a clear set of criteria seems to leave little room for confusion. And yet, there has continued to be considerable debate over what should be included in the Washington Consensus. This debate will be elaborated in the section that follows. But for now, we can define the Washington Consensus as this original list of ten policy objectives laid out by John Williamson (1990):

1. Budget deficits small enough to be financed without inflation tax.
2. Redirect public expenditure toward health, education, and infrastructure.
3. Broaden the tax base.
4. Financial liberalization-market determined interest rates.
5. Unified exchange rate/elimination of overvalued exchange rates.
6. Trade liberalization.
7. Abolish impediments to the entry of foreign direct investment.
8. Privatize state-owned enterprises.
9. Abolish impediments to competitive entry of firms.
10. Provide secure property rights, especially in the informal sector.

One benefit of the Washington Consensus is that attempting to say exactly what neoliberal reform is can serve as a first cut toward answering the question: What are the welfare effects of neoliberal reform? This is especially important in a debate where some people point to what they see as neoliberal reform to show that it works, and others point to what they see as neoliberal reforms to show that it fails. Part of the problem is the differing meanings of neoliberalism itself. That is, absent a clear consensus, opponents and proponents of market-oriented reforms tend to include different criteria in their definitions of neoliberalism. The point is that one can pick and choose one's evidence to demonstrate either case, so the idea with the Washington Consensus is to write down exactly what subset of reforms the community of mainstream economists agree on. In fact, John Williamson coined the term Washington Consensus in 1990 to refer to the lowest common denominator of policy advice being addressed by the Washington-based institutions, including the IMF and the World Bank, to Latin American countries (Williamson, 2000: 251). And yet, while the innovation of the Washington Consensus has served to diminish definition-based disagreement over neoliberalism, it has by no means ended debate even among economists and policymakers over the meaning of neoliberalism.

Mistaken identity

There is still internal disagreement among market reformers about the optimal set of policies, but to the extent that a major reason for the disagreements between reformers and their detractors is a case of mistaken identity, the Washington Consensus has helped to clarify rather than obscure. For example, many opponents of neoliberalism tend to throw everyone into the same pot, failing to make any meaningful distinction between neo-conservatives like Thatcher, Reagan, and Bush on the one hand, and economic liberals who support the Washington Consensus but would not associate themselves with these neo-conservatives on the other. The Washington Consensus also gets conflated with economic liberals like Milton Friedman and yet it clearly does not advocate monetarism. What can perhaps be said is that all monetarists are neoliberals, but not all neoliberals are monetarists. Proponents of the Washington Consensus agree that this reform prescription lays out a set of good and necessary policies, yet there is still disagreement about whether this package is sufficient.

Defenders of neoliberalism in the form of the Washington Consensus also point out that opponents tend to blame neoliberalism and neoliberal agencies like the IMF for bad outcomes even when those outcomes are the result of situations where the Washington Consensus was not actually followed. The value of being able to point to a concrete set of policies like the Washington Consensus is that under these kinds of circumstances it is relatively easy to point out the ways in which detractors are getting it wrong. For example, both sides can agree that a bad outcome happened like the most recent Argentine financial crisis. But it is also pretty straightforward to show that this particular crisis did not result directly from the Washington Consensus agenda since the Washington Consensus clearly does not advocate any particular type of exchange rate regime, let alone a currency board. This, however, has not prevented many countries from blaming the Argentina outcome on neoliberalism.

Another source of disagreement arises when agencies like the IMF, which are largely representative of neoliberalism in the form of the Washington Consensus, tend to be held responsible for all bad outcomes, whether those outcomes grew out of neoliberal policies advocated by the Fund or not. For example, often the IMF loans funds to countries for the purpose of supporting a market-oriented reform program and yet the country fails to make good on those reforms. If things go downhill, the IMF and the supposed reform program will get the blame and another example of failed neoliberalism will be cited, regardless of whether actual market-oriented reforms ever took place.

Similarly, misunderstanding between opponents and proponents of neoliberalism arise because while there is a Washington Consensus over a clear set of policies, certain aspects that have been agreed upon tend to get ignored during implementation. Sometimes this leads to incomplete reforms due to political resistance, even though the rhetoric continues to be pro-reform. South Korea in the 1980s is a perfect example of this. Korea has in reality implemented only some of these financial reforms, and where it has liberalized, its approach has been gradual and halting and not necessarily along liberal lines. Even after the supposed shift toward more comprehensive financial liberalization in the mid-1980s, Korean economic goals were being achieved through government institutions rather than by exclusive reliance on the price mechanism. But if the state retained control over financial prices, in what sense was finance liberalized in Korea? As of the end of the 1980s, it really was not. However, state policy makers went to great lengths in order to make it look as if it were. They accomplished this by significantly reducing inflation and setting high real deposit rates that more closely approximated the market price, a *de facto* financial liberalization of sorts (Auerbach, 2001: 81). The rather ambiguous nature of Korean financial liberalization in the 1980s allows neoliberal policy proponents to claim that the 1997 Asian financial crisis resulted from insufficient market reform while opponents argue that the crisis resulted from too much and too rapid liberalization. Both sides are correct in important ways – liberalization did lead to a series of perverse incentives, but partly because of the partial nature of liberalization.[4]

An incomplete model

However, not all disagreements can be adequately explained by pointing out that bad outcomes result only when the Washington Consensus is not followed closely enough. In fact, even the earliest proponents of the Washington Consensus have more recently declared the need to revisit and add to the original list of advocated reforms. In other words, the model as represented by the original Consensus may be incomplete. According to John Williamson, the originator of the term "Washington Consensus," a major reason why the "outcomes did not match the hopes of a decade ago is that reforms were incomplete" (Williamson, 2003: 5). The reforms were certainly incomplete in the sense that countries like South Korea neglected some "first generation" or original Washington Consensus reforms. But Williamson goes on to say that "there is a whole generation of so-called second generation reforms, involving the strengthening of institutions, that is necessary to allow full advantage to be taken of the first-generation reforms. . . ." Finally, Williamson suggests that a third reason for the disappointing performance of neoliberal reforms in the 1980s and 1990s "is that the main objective informing policy was excessively narrow . . . [in that] . . . policy remained focused on accelerating growth, not on growth plus equity" (Williamson and Kuczynski, 2003: 6).

For Williamson, the appropriate response to the incomplete nature of the original model is to lay out a series of new and progressive policymaking agendas for the future. These include: New Agenda I (crisis proofing); New Agenda II (completing first-generation reforms); New Agenda III (second-generation institutional reforms); New Agenda IV (income distribution and social sector). Other economists and high-ranking officials have gone even further than Williamson in declaring that "the Washington Consensus has been dead for years" (Wolfensohn, May 25, 2004). Nor is he the first to declare consensuses around new-and-improved, pseudo-neoliberal agendas. Joseph Stiglitz points to a post-Washington Consensus which includes the quality of institutions underpinning markets as well as a more far-reaching claim about the need for "voice and partnership" within countries and in terms of the interface between national economies and the international environment (Stiglitz, 2002: 106; Stiglitz, 1998). Some have referred to this continuing enlargement of the neoliberal agenda as a meta-narrative. According to one such study, the meta-narrative, also known as the Millennium Development Goals (MDG) "inevitably expands Williamson's ten bullet points to as many as twenty" (Maxwell, 2005: 1).

While this agenda adds considerably to the list of original policy prescriptions, the order of implementation remains consistent with the neoclassical assumption that growth can be pursued now while income can be distributed later. This assumption and the criticisms it has given rise to will be discussed in greater detail in the next section. For now, it may suffice to point out that the Washington Consensus has often failed to deliver all of the promised results, even according to its most committed proponents. One certainly could not expect opponents to jump through hoops to explain how, given the right new set of policy agendas, the original neoliberal agenda could work.

Incomplete or wrong?

While economic reform often fails for the reasons already cited (some vital parts of the program get left out), it can also fail because pre-existing market failures and complex political contexts make the statement "in theory it will improve efficiency" as applied to liberalization all but mute. Markets are deeply-embedded social structures and economic models rarely account adequately for this.[5] The problem becomes especially acute when these models are employed to lobby for certain reforms over others in the "real" world.

Some authors have questioned neoliberal analysis as it pertains to industrial policy, especially in Asia. The 1990s wave of neoliberalism with the fall of the Asian tigers gave occasion for widespread critiques of state interventionist policies in Asia. Proponents of neoliberal development strategies point to the performance of the Asian NICs to validate outward-oriented, market-led development models and simultaneously criticize dirigiste, state-centered development strategies in favor of a neoliberal approach based on policies supposedly reflecting the successful market-oriented development experience of the Asian NICs (Brohman, 1996: 108). Williamson himself goes to considerable lengths to exclude industrial policy from the list of much-needed second-generation institutional reforms that should be added to the original Consensus.

> One institutional reform that would seem a mistake is introduction of industrial policy, that is, a program that requires some government agency to "pick winners" (to help companies that are judged likely to be able to contribute something special to the national economy). There is little reason to think that industrial policies were the key ingredient of success in East Asia.
>
> (Williamson, 2003: 12)

There is no shortage of neoliberal interpretations of industrial policy as incoherent, subject to rent-seeking, and irrelevant to development success (Noland and Pack, 2003).

But others have demonstrated that a more nuanced micro-historical analysis of the state's interventions demonstrates that this oversimplification misses political elite objectives to overcome the pitfalls of weak-state ineffectual policies by using the power of the state and selective intervention to create a strong, integrated, diversified, and outward-oriented industrial economy. Korea certainly seems to have achieved this objective, but there is evidence to suggest that even Indonesia, which during the latter years of the Suharto regime came to resemble more of a predatory state, largely achieved this objective (Rock, 1999; Auerbach, 2001: 75–100). In short, critiques of the neoliberal interpretation have argued that industrial policy has been more important than the neoliberal argument permits. Other critics have gone further, arguing that neoliberal reforms themselves have created an incentive for corruption.

The net result is a "neoliberal paradox": financial markets demand that corporations achieve ever higher profits, while product markets make this result impossible to achieve. The neoliberal paradox helps explain the outbreak of financial accounting fraud in the late 1990s (Crotty, 2003). Needless to say, staking out a concrete middle-ground in the form a well-defined policy consensus has not served to mitigate the contentious debate over neoliberalism significantly, even among those who are largely on board with the notion of neoliberal reform. Given this, it is no wonder that observers who do not share a common worldview seem to talk past each other when it comes to debating the nature and impact of neoliberalism.

Bridging the neoliberal divide

Why do some observers look at the implementation of neoliberal policies all over the world and herald them as a triumph of economic efficiency, liberty, and welfare maximization while others are so moved in opposition to these policies that they are willing to fly hundreds and sometimes thousands of miles to protest their implementation? While mental models and ideology alone could certainly provide an answer, it may be more fruitful to try first to explain how this divide gets reinforced. That is, no ideology can survive long if the set of beliefs adhered to are total nonsense. Yet the notion on both sides of this debate, if one can call it that, is in fact that the other side makes no sense. Here it is argued instead that both the opponents and the proponents of neoliberalism have misunderstood and have been misunderstood when it comes to assessing the benefits and drawbacks of neoliberal economic policy.

There are several reasons why opponents and proponents of neoliberalism seem to come to such vastly different conclusions when assessing supposedly the same policies. The first question to ask is whether we are in fact talking about the same set of policies. One could make a case that a Washington Consensus around a coherent and identifiable set of policies did exist and in practical terms still does. Moreover, it is not unreasonable to assume that those critical of neoliberalism agree as to what those policies consist of. However, one of the first reasons for misunderstanding is that while there may be Washington Consensus over a clear set of policies, during the implementation stage, certain previously agreed-upon aspects of the agenda tend to get ignored, and more importantly, fail to be acknowledged. For example, in addition to calling for dramatic cuts in public expenditures otherwise known as fiscal discipline, the Washington Consensus calls for the public expenditures to be redirected toward health and education because market failures are thought to be particularly acute in these areas. In practice, only the cutting of public expenditures part of the neoliberal program seems to be consistently followed through on. So when the critics of neoliberalism blame "free market" policies for exacerbating poverty and deprivation among the most vulnerable in society, they are on solid ground. Unfortunately, proponents go back to the original program being called for and defend its soundness and they too are in a sense right.

It might help here to take a closer look at how neoliberalism gets justified rather than just attempting to nail down a concrete and agreed-upon set of neoliberal policies like the Washington Consensus. That is, neoliberalism and its predecessor classical liberalism constitute a worldview that is broader than just a set of policies. According to this worldview, economic analysis and policymaking is thought of as essentially separable from politics. Even when some economic policy analyses take politics into account as in some public choice models, it is usually as a force separate from and antithetical to sound economic policy. In other words, proponents of neoliberalism see liberalization itself as reaching an inherently apolitical end, whereas opponents of neoliberalism see the "neoliberal project" as inherently political in that it spells gains for the few, the powerful, at the expense of the poor. Both of these stances create an ideological divide across which it is all but impossible to engage in meaningful dialogue. Here an analogy can be drawn to C.P. Snow's "two cultures" and the ideological divide between the sciences and the humanities, though one need not point to even that extreme an example. Kuhn's writing on scientific revolutions points to the same ideological divide between shifting paradigms within science itself. Denzau and North's work illuminates how shared mental models facilitate and reinforce communication among each cultural community, and goes further to suggest that signals from outside that model will not even be heard or understood (Denzau and North, 1994).

One way to bridge this divide is to examine the usefulness of the way economics, economic policy, and markets are generally modeled. Equity issues are often not considered the purview of economics but rather as something separate from mainstream policy debates. Often the simplifying assumption is made that if we follow the path that leads to the most rapid growth despite resulting in a highly unequal income distribution, redistribution can take place afterwards without transaction costs or with minimal cost. In other words, economic models tend to prioritize growth over equitable structures. However, by doing so, the neoliberal agenda becomes anything but apolitical. It all but ensures in many cases that powerful and asset-rich elites will reap the benefits of neoliberalism at the expense of the poor who do not have the political weight to shape the policy implementation process. All the while, these same elites attempt to convince themselves and others that the reform program itself is unbiased and efficiency-promoting. Why does this outcome often result from the implementation of market-oriented reforms? It is not in theory and certainly does not have to be inevitable. To argue this would be to take the same ideological stance that the opponents of neoliberalism or globalization take in principle or as a reaction to capitalism itself. But essentially, this inequitable outcome is guaranteed because of a tremendously unequal asset distribution and political power base at the onset of most liberalization processes. Economists consider basic infrastructure (e.g. a functioning legal system and transportation and communications infrastructure), as an important a priori component to liberalization, but have tended traditionally to discount vast inequality as a key variable that can lead to very similar distortions.[6] In the belief that naming something and categorizing it at the very least attracts notice and even better focuses analytical attention on it, I have coined the term "justice infrastructure" or "infrastructure of justice" to refer to this a priori set of institutions or conditions that must exist before the promised benefits of neoliberalism can truly be realized. Meaningful land reform must constitute part of the "justice infrastructure" for the vast majority of developing countries. But some of this infrastructure involves simply prioritizing certain reforms already called for and agreed upon as part of the Washington Consensus.

As it happens, Washington Consensus reforms like "redirect public expenditure toward health, education, and infrastructure," and "broaden the tax base," tend to fall by the wayside as budget deficits get cut and taxes are cut for the wealthy. In this case, prioritizing the latter reforms actually exacerbates the problems associated with the former resulting in a narrowing of the tax base and cuts in primary services to the poor. There is of course a logical reason why "equity improving" reforms do not typically reach the implementation stage. Broadening the tax base, which directly and negatively affects the privileged elite, is nowhere near as politically viable as for example bank privatization, which directly benefits the elite.[7]

But perhaps the weight of the Washington Consensus could be used to exert pressure differently. After all, the reason for the inclusion of tax reform and redirection of public expenditures toward health and education in a very select set of ten policies that make up the Washington consensus is not because of fairness or justice per se, the reason is primarily that these reforms are considered efficiency enhancing. In other words, the market failure problems associated with these vital public services and the government's ability to provide them without deficit financing is likely to be particularly acute in developing countries. These policies are certainly consistent with microeconomic efficiency but rather less consistent with the likely political support of those who wield power in many developing nations. But there is no unsurmountable obstacle to the IMF for example using its considerable weight to pressure governments to prioritize reforms that redirect public expenditure toward health, education, and infrastructure or broaden the tax base over structural adjustment reforms that call for cuts to government spending in the form of social welfare policies. There is certainly reason for hope on this front if one looks at more recent attempts by economists to go beyond the Washington Consensus as it was originally formulated (Williamson and Kuczynski, 2003: 14–18).

The insistence on the positivist and hence non-ideological nature of economic modeling that undergirds the Washington Consensus for its proponents has given rise to a number of critiques of neoliberalism that focus precisely on the paradoxical belief that traditionally positive economics is free of value-laden outcomes that preference certain groups.[8] The feminist critique of neoliberalism points out that men and women participate in the economy in different ways.[9] Women tend to participate more in unpaid sectors of the economy such as household labor, subsistence agriculture and black markets. Even within the paid economy, women tend to concentrate their labor in export-processing zones in developing countries. Because of these differences, neoliberal reforms can have vastly different effects on women than they do on men and yet most of the economic models in their gender-neutral form, will not account for these differences. Moreover, neoliberal cutbacks to state expenditures like health care, childcare, or education, are likely to affect women disproportionately. Because neoliberal economic analysis focuses mainly on the paid private sector of the economy, it is subject to a key gender bias. Hence, there is a risk that what is perceived in conventional economic analysis as efficiency improvements may in fact be a shift in costs from the visible to the invisible economy. This might explain why economists can continue to herald the virtues of pro-market reforms based on what they perceive as solid evidence while opponents protest vehemently against such reforms secure in the knowledge that they have suffered real costs.

The majority of environmentalists engage in a Green critique of neoliberalism that follows a similar line of reasoning as the feminists. That is, they worry that free markets as well as neoliberal thinkers often fail to price ecological constraints accurately. The Greens see globalization and neoliberal reforms as a threat to local forms of knowledge and ways of living that have proven themselves ecologically sustainable for centuries. This belief has led the Greens to support initiatives for local economic autonomy like the creation of sub-national "local currencies," "buy local" campaigns, credit unions, and community shared agricultural schemes. These groups have been fierce critiques of neoliberalism and they have joined forces with the emerging transnational indigenous people's movements that are opposing neoliberalism on similar grounds (Helleiner, 2003: 691–692).

Finally, liberalization processes are extremely prone to capture by economic and political elites. While crony capitalism tends to be associated with statist policies, economists seem to be wearing blinders when it comes to seeing cronyism in the name of neoliberal policies. This type of cronyism is extremely pervasive, but because of the nature of markets and the extent of monopolization, this kind of corruption tends to take place without nearly the same degree of explicitness. This often leads economists to overlook not only sources of inequity associated with neoliberalism but sources of inefficiency as well. Though it is certainly true that public choice theory and some economic analyses are beginning to take greater account of this phenomenon, the majority of economic analysis concerning policy reform fails to do so.[10]

Take financial reform as a key example. It is not safe to assume, as economists and officials often have, that imperfect liberalization is better than no liberalization. This is not to support continued financial repression, but rather to argue that liberalization must be carried out carefully and with full attention to the dangers of "capture" of the liberalization process by special interests. Thus advocates of financial liberalization need to focus as much on political economy as on purely technical considerations.

Privatization of state-owned banks constitutes an important component of the financial reform process. Yet the privatization process itself can fall prey to perverse incentives. This can be viewed as an incompatibility between political motivations and economic incentives, or as political capture of the reform process. For example, privatization in principle should lead to greater overall efficiency as the private sector possesses some comparative advantage over government in making profit-maximizing economic decisions. However, the privatization process is particularly susceptible to political capture/rent-seeking given the stakes involved.

The charter of new merchant banks in South Korea prior to the financial crisis fell prey to rent-seeking behavior of this type. The government converted 24 financially weak short-term financing companies into merchant banks in two separate rounds: nine in 1994 and 15 in 1996. They proceeded to engage in risky foreign exchange transactions. Among the banks whose licenses were revoked in 1998, five were new entrants from 1994, and ten were from 1996. Thus, government reforms encouraged greater debt exposure in an already overexposed financial system (Auerbach, 2001: 208). The story behind both the incentives on the part of private market actors to buy up government-owned banks and the incentive to take on excessive risk is a relatively common story of market failure based on moral hazard. Because of the importance of the banking system to the economy as a whole, there exists at the very least an implicit and sometimes explicit guarantee against bank failure from the government. Ultimately the moral hazard problem in crisis ridden countries throughout the 1990s meant that the neoliberal privatization process essentially privatized profit while socializing risk or at least the costs associated with risk. Prior to every financial crisis of the 1980s and 1990s the rich got richer while after each of those crises the recessions, IMF restructuring, and neoliberal policy reforms implemented took the heaviest toll on the poor.[11] This is in part what leads opponents of neoliberalism to point out that "economic growth has proven inadequate to reduce poverty and policies to reduce income inequality did not form a part of the Washington Consensus."

All this suggests that politics is so central to any implementation of neoliberal reform that it is difficult to justify such a program without further attention to the political economy of the reforms. Only if an "infrastructure of justice" precedes the implementation of neoliberal reform could there be any agreement. Though this does beg the question, why if the answer is so straight-forward can we not figure out ways to do market reform better? The answer is not primarily ignorance but rather politics. Time and time again, it has proven nearly impossible to build a political consensus in developing countries around things like tax reform and improvements in health and education systems despite the obvious benefits in terms of overall social welfare. To see this we need only employ a simple public choice analysis which will tell us that tax reform in many Latin American countries for example would have wide-spread benefits and concentrated costs. This is a problem even in a semi-democratic setting because the political actors who face high concentrated costs have a real incentive to lobby against such policies. Needless to say, the situation is exacerbated considerably when economic and political power is concentrated in the hands of a relatively few elites. On the other hand, other neoliberal reforms like selling off state-owned banks and allowing the free movement of capital are reforms that can under preexisting conditions of market concentration enrich a few at the expense of the many. But because we can chalk this redistribution up to market forces rather than state-administered backdoor deals, the outcome is acceptable and the politics behind it not interpreted as self-serving as crony capitalism would be. One could reasonably conclude that neither situation is acceptable nor should one be treated as "natural" and the other as contrived.

Conclusion

Ideology can tend to blind or bias not just the globalization protestors on the left and hyper-capitalists on the right but also mainstream practitioners of the Washington Consensus in the middle. The most pervasive idea that supporters of the Washington Consensus buy into is that they are not ideological, whereas their critics are deeply ideological. They are rational and their detractors are not. Of course the very nature of ideology makes it very difficult to see and acknowledge one's own biases, especially coming out of a discipline like economics, which embraces positivism and the scientific method and devalues normative approaches as "soft" economics. Also, when elites are the beneficiaries of neoliberal reforms, which is often the case, (Auerbach and Willett, forthcoming), acceptance of the rational ideology of economics and its approach to economic reform serves elites not just materially but also psychologically in that neoliberalism attributes those material benefits to merit and describes them as efficient. Here one can think of economic liberalism or neoliberalism as the ideology that supports capitalism. This mental model tells members of society how an industrial market economy works. More importantly, the neoliberal mental model becomes a means by which dominant classes explain to themselves how their social system operates and what principles it exemplifies. Neoliberalism assumes market forces are not only efficient but also neutral or apolitical in their operation. Therefore, if the dominant class benefits from market reform, it is because they worked hard and are deserving of reward as they have contributed to the efficiency of the economy (Heilbroner, 1985: 107). This suggests that the supporters of neoliberalism have more to lose should neoliberalism fall from hegemonic status than just material gains. A move away from neoliberal ideology would challenge core beliefs and ultimately core identities.

Notes

1 Ravi Roy and Tom Willett offered insightful comments for which I am grateful. Special thanks go to Karen May for her editing expertise and comments.
2 For a more in depth treatment of neoliberalism as it relates to Latin America, see Anil Hira's chapter in this volume.
3 In the early 1980s, Paul Volker previously raised interest rates for a second time. Volker initially raised interest rates in 1979 which led in turn to US banks raising interest rates on syndicated loans to Latin America.
4 For a more detailed account of these perverse incentives see Auerbach and Willett (forthcoming).
5 There are thankfully a handful of economists who are beginning to recognize and work on this issue. See for example, Olsen (1988).
6 More recently an economics literature has emerged that has demonstrated a correlation between less unequal income distribution and faster growth rates.
7 For a detailed account of how the financial elite benefit form bank privatization and other forms of financial liberalization, see Auerbach (2001).
8 Almost every introductory economics text makes a distinction between positive and normative economics. Positive economics is simply the scientific study of "what is" among economic relationships while normative economics involves judgements about "what ought to be." Under this formulation, all policy prescriptions would be normative, but often policy prescriptions are presented in positivist terms. They claim that "these policy reform are pareto-improving," and thus leave the normative judgement that the policy should be implemented up to the policymaker (Gwartney and Stroup, 1995: 14).
9 See for example Marchland and Runyan (2000), Goetz (2000), Elson (1996), Kopinak (1995), and Waring (1988).
10 For an example of economic analysis that attempts to account for market-based cronyism, see Olsen (1988).
11 For a detailed account of how structural adjustment policies affect the poor in Latin America see Lustig (1995). She and her co-authors find extensive evidence that stabilization and structural adjustment policies yielded greater poverty and inequality than would have resulted in the absence of such policies. They also find that many stabilization and adjustment policies exacerbate rather than diminish the impact of economic crisis on poverty and economic inequality.

References

Auerbach, N.N. (2001) *States, Banks, and Markets: Mexico's Path to Financial Liberalization in Comparative Perspective*. Boulder: Westview Press.

Auerbach, N.N. and Willett, T. (forthcoming) "The political economy of perverse financial liberalization: examples from the Asian crisis."

Brohman, J. (1996) "Postwar development in the Asian NICs: does the neoliberal model fit reality?" *Economic Geography* 72: 2.

Chang, J. (2005) "Series of Latin American elections likely to completely change the political landscape," *International News*, December 2.

Crotty, James (2003) "The neoliberal paradox: the impact of destructive product market competition and impatient finance on nonfinancial corporations in the neoliberal era," *Review of Radical Political Economics* vol. 35, no. 3 (Summer), 271–279.

Denzau, A.T. and North, D.C. (1994) "Shared mental models: ideologies and institutions," *Kyklos*, vol. 47, no. 1.

Denzau, A.T. and Roy, R.K. (2003) *Fiscal Policy Convergence from Reagan to Blair: The Left Veers Right?* London: Routledge Press.

Elson, D. (1996) "Gender-aware analysis and development economics," in Jameson and Wilber (eds) *The Political Economy of Development and Underdevelopment.* New York: McGraw-Hill, 70–80.

Fukuyama, Francis (1992) *The End of History and the Last Man.* New York: Free Press.

Gilpin, R. (1987) *The Political Economy of International Relations.* Princeton, NJ: Princeton University Press.

Glyn, Andrew (ed.) (2001) *Social Democracy in Neoliberal Times: The left and Economic Policy Since 1980.* Oxford and New York: Oxford University Press.

Goetz, A.M. (2000) "The World Bank and women's movements," in O'Brien, R., Goetz, A.M., Scholte, J.A. and Williams, M. (eds) *Contesting Global Governance.* Cambridge: Cambridge University Press.

Gwartney and Stroup (1995) *Microeconomics: Private and Public Choice,* 7th edn. New York: Harcourt Brace.

Heilbroner, Robert (1985) *The Nature and Logic of Capitalism.* New York: Norton.

Helleiner, E. (1993) "When finance was servant: international capital movements in the Bretton Woods order," in Cerny (ed.) *Political Economy of International Finance.*

Helleiner, E. (2003) "Economic liberalism and its critics: the past as prologue?" *Review of International Political Economy* 10(4): 685–696.

Independent, "Is the Latin American party coming to an end?" July 2, 2005.

Kopinak (1995) "Gender as a vehicle for the subordination of women Maquiladora workers in Mexico," 30–48.

Lustig, Nora (ed.) (1995) *Coping with Austerity: Poverty and Inequality in Latin America.* Washington, DC: Brookings Institute.

Marchland M. and Runyan, A. (2000) *Gender and Global Restructuring.* London: Routledge.

Maxwell, S. (2005) "The Washington Consensus is dead! Long live the meta-narrative!" *Working Paper 243.* London: Overseas Development Institute.

McKenzie, R.B. and Lee, D.R. (1991) *Quicksilver Capital: How the Rapid Movement of Wealth has Changed the World.* New York: Free Press.

Montaner, Carlos Alberto (2005) *Latin America: fragmentation and forecasts.* Washington, DC: Heritage Foundation, vol. 2, June.

Norland, M. and Pack, H. (2003) *Industrial Policy in an Era of Globalization: Lessons from Asia.* Washington: Institute for International Economics.

Olson, James (1988) *Saving Capitalism: the Reconstruction Finance Corporation and the New Deal, 1933–1940.* Princeton: Princeton University Press.

Rock, M. (1999) "Reassessing the effectiveness of industrial policy in Indonesia: can the neoliberals be wrong?" *World Development,* vol. 27, no. 4 (April): 691–704.

Shifter, Michael and Jawahar, Vinay (2005) "Latin America's populist turn," *Current History,* vol. 104: 51–57.

Snyder, R. (2001) *Politics After Neoliberalism: Reregulation in Mexico.* Cambridge: Cambridge University Press.

Stiglitz, J. (1998) "More instruments and broader goals: moving towards the post-Washington Consensus." World Institute for Development Economics Research Annual Lecture, Helsinki.

Stiglitz, Joseph (2002) *Globalization and Its Discontents.* New York: Norton.

Vernengo, Matias (2005) "Latin America's left off track," *Dollars and Sense*, no. 259, 21–25.

Williamson, John (1990) "What Washington means by policy reform," in Williamson (ed.) *Latin American Adjustment: How Much has Happened?* Washington DC: Institute for International Economics.

Williamson, John (2000) "What should the World Bank think about the Washington Consensus?" *The World Bank Research Observer*, 15: 2.

Williamson, John and Kuczynski, Pedro-Pablo (eds) (2003) *After the Washington Consensus: Restarting Growth and Reform in Latin America*. Washington DC: Institute for International Economics.

Wolfensohn, J. (2004) Speech given in Shanghai, China, May 25, 2004. web.worldbank.org/wbsite/external/extaboutus/organizatioal/0,,contentMDK:2020669~menuPK:232083~pagePK:159837~PIPK:159808~theSitePK:227585,00.html.

Yergin, D. and Stanislaw, J. (2002) *The Commanding Heights: The Batttle for the World Economy*. New York: Simon and Schuster.

4 The genealogy of neoliberalism

Colin Hay

Introduction

The cultural political economy of the 'liberal market economies', as is widely noted, has been characterised in recent years by the rise and consolidation of neoliberal economic assumptions. This is reflective of a broader shift from a *normative* to a *normalised* neoliberalism. Such an ideational transformation provides an interesting test-case of the development, evolution, diffusion and institutionalisation of a new economic paradigm (Hall 1993) or set of 'mental models' (Denzau and North, 1994).

Whilst the former normative phase of neoliberalism was largely restricted to an anglophone enclave (centred on the US and the UK), the latter normalised phase has proved far more contagious. These phases are distinct but related neoliberal strands or mental models. They are thus components of an evolving neoliberal shared mental model. This chapter examines the role played by rationalist assumptions, in a variety of guises, in this extended process of normalisation and institutionalisation. In so doing it endorses Denzau and North's theoretical claim (1994: 27) that 'ideas matter and the way in which ideas evolve and are communicated is the key to developing useful theory which will expand our understanding of the performance of societies both at a moment of time and over time'. Building on this insight, this chapter considers the role of public choice theory, the time-inconsistency thesis, rational expectations economics and the business school globalisation thesis in the normative and normalised phases of neoliberal institutionalisation.

The argument proceeds in three stages and is summarised in Figure 4.1. The first of these provides a brief definition and stylised periodisation of transatlantic neoliberalism. In the following section, the focus turns to the role of rationalist assumptions in, first, the rise of neoliberalism out of the much-vaunted yet unevenly distributed 'crises' of the 1970s and, second, in the diffusion and consolidation of a normalised neoliberalism in and beyond this original anglophone core. The ascendancy of a spectacular and normative neoliberalism in the late 1970s and 1980s in the

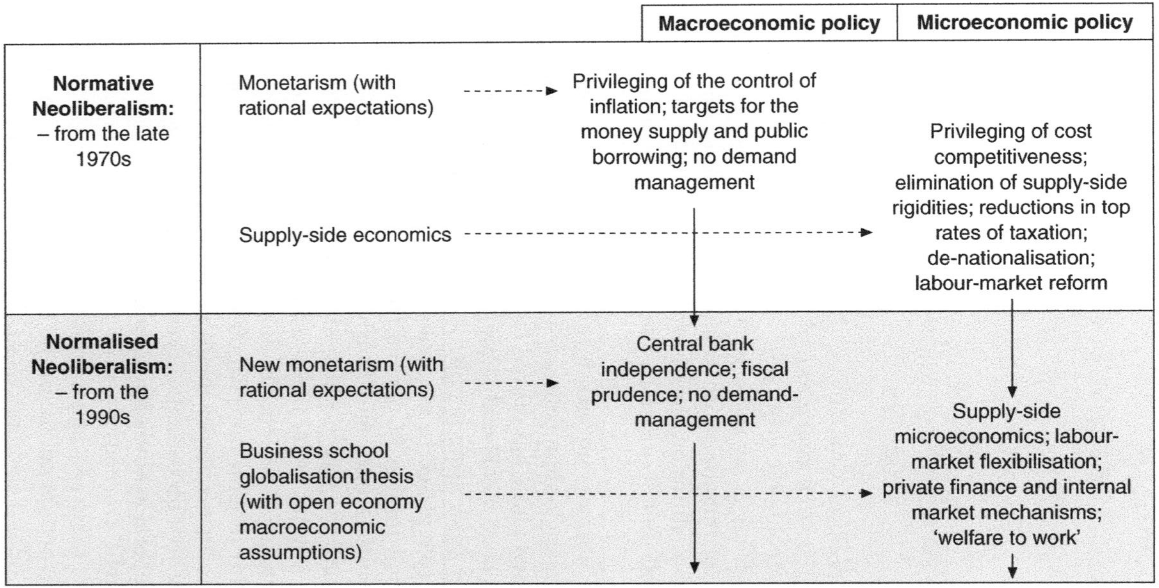

Macroeconomic policy
Microeconomic policy
Normative Neoliberalism: – from the late 1970s
Monetarism (with rational expectations)
Privileging of the control of inflation; targets for the money supply and public borrowing; no demand management
Supply-side economics
Privileging of cost competitiveness; elimination of supply-side rigidities; reductions in top rates of taxation; de-nationalisation; labour-market reform
Normalised Neoliberalism: – from the 1990s
New monetarism (with rational expectations)
Central bank independence; fiscal prudence; no demand-management
Business school globalisation thesis (with open economy macroeconomic assumptions)
Supply-side microeconomics; labour-market flexibilisation; private finance and internal market mechanisms; 'welfare to work'

Figure 4.1 From normative to normalised neoliberalism: the role of rationalist assumptions.

so-called 'liberal market economies', it is argued, was predicated on the success of the new right in mobilising widespread perceptions of a crisis of overload and ungovernability and that this narrative was, in turn, premised upon the stylised rationalist assumptions of public choice theory. This paved the way for a neoliberal offensive informed, to varying degrees, by monetarism/neo-monetarism and supply-side economics.

Yet it is the more recent process of normalising neoliberalism that has served to institutionalise neoliberal economic assumptions, placing them at the heart of contemporary modes of economic governance. Here too rationalist assumptions have played a crucial role in rendering necessary the capitulation of those not normatively wedded to neoliberalism to its core precepts.

I argue, more particularly, that in this broader normalisation of neoliberal economics, the time-inconsistency thesis (based on rational expectations assumptions) and the business school globalisation thesis (based on neoclassical open economy macroeconomic assumptions) have played an equivalent role to that played for the new right by monetarism and supply-side economics.

This second-generation neoliberalisation, associated with the international diffusion and dissemination of ideas such as the 'third way', is not normative but normalised and necessitarian. In other words, it is neither borne of, nor promotes, an ideological commitment to the sanctity, inviolability or infallibility of the market. Rather, it arises from a conviction that an ongoing agenda of neoliberal reform is a condition of sustained economic growth and competitiveness in an economically interdependent world in which market participants can be assumed to form their expectations in a rational manner. It is expressed in the so-called 'post Washington Consensus'.

Neoliberalism defined, neoliberalism periodised

If we are to chart the genealogy of neoliberalism as an economic policy paradigm or set of related strands that jointly comprise a shared mental model, it is imperative at the outset to provide a working definition of the term – against which to gauge the content of first and second-wave, normative and normalised neoliberalism. Yet this immediately raises a problem. For how does one encapsulate in definitional terms an evolving paradigm, ideology or shared mental model? The problem is one of fixing a moving target – for, as Denzau and North note, mental models are guides to learning, explanation and interpretation, not fixed and static sets of assumptions (1994: 13). Tempting though it is, then, to fashion a generic and trans-historical definition of neoliberalism, this will not do. For, arguably, in suggesting, say, that 'third way' political economy or the 'post-Washington Consensus' is neoliberal, it is less important to demonstrate some natural affinity with such a trans-historical definitional standard than it is to show how either or both can credibly be presented as part of an evolving neoliberal shared mental model. Yet there is an equal danger of a definition rendered so vague and imprecise as to be useless by virtue of the aim to recognise the temporal variability of the content of neoliberalism.

In what follows I deploy the following composite definition of neoliberalism. Neoliberalism is characterised by:

1 A confidence in the market as an efficient mechanism for the allocation of scarce resources.
2 A belief in the desirability of a global regime of free trade and free capital mobility.
3 A belief in the desirability, all things being equal, of a limited and non-interventionist role for the state.
4 A conception of the state as a facilitator and custodian rather than a substitute for market mechanisms.
5 A defence of individual liberty.
6 A commitment to the removal of those welfare benefits which might be seen to act as disincentives to market participation (in short, a subordination of the principles of social justice to those of perceived economic imperatives).
7 A defence of labour-market flexibility and the promotion and nurturing of cost competitiveness.
8 A confidence in the use of private finance in public projects and, more generally, in the allocative efficiency of market and quasi-market mechanisms in the provision of public goods.

Understood in this way, the political economy of many contemporary anglophone liberal democracies might be judged progressively more neoliberal in respect of each of the following:

1 In societies in which there had already been a phase of normative neoliberalism, a commitment to the maintenance and consolidation of the inherited public/private mix and to a variety of internal market mechanisms and new public management incentivising techniques (such as league tables and the competitive allocation of resources).
2 In societies not previously characterised by neoliberal economic governance, a commitment to the renegotiation of the public/private division in favour of the latter and to marketisation and commodification within a more residual public sector.
3 A commitment (rhetorical and/or substantive) to a global regime of free trade and free capital mobility.
4 An agenda of labour-market flexibilisation, designed to enhance cost competitiveness through the removal of labour-market rigidities.
5 A new monetarist commitment to a rules-bound (rather than discretionary) macroeconomic policy regime.

6 A commitment to fiscal prudence and passivity, an antipathy both to deficit financing and the use of fiscal policy as an instrument in the fight against inflation, and a commitment to lesson top rates of direct taxation.
7 A conception of unemployment as a primarily supply-side phenomenon, an effective acceptance of a 'natural' or 'equilibrium' rate of unemployment, a rejection of any notion of a long-term trade-off between inflation and unemployment, and an acceptance that there is no longer a role in macroeconomic policy for adjustments in aggregate or effective demand.

Having defined neoliberalism and having sought to state the prima facie case for the neoliberalism of much of the political economy of the OECD nations today, it is equally important to provide a simple periodisation of the development of neoliberalism. At the risk of some inevitable simplification, I split the period into three distinct phases – the pre-history of neoliberalism in the so-called Keynesian 'golden age' from the initial post-war years to the early 1970s; the phase of normative or spectacular neoliberalism arising first in the crisis period of the late 1970s and lasting until the early 1990s; and the contemporary period of normalised neoliberalism associated with the accommodation by previous opponents to the tenets of the neoliberal shared mental model (both in states that had earlier endured normative neoliberalism and in those that had not). My concern in this chapter is with these two most recent periods and, in particular, with the role of rationalist assumptions in the mobilisation and consolidation of the neoliberal shared mental model.

Spectacular neoliberalism

If we are to understand the spectacular and normative phase of neoliberalism, then it is important that we first locate its development in the context of the 'golden age' of supposed Keynesian ascendancy (see, for instance, Blyth, 2002; Marglin and Schor, 1990). In the self-understanding of the times, political and economic imperatives were seen to have been brought back into harmony after the persistent economic pathologies of the 1930s. The problem throughout the 1930s was one of a demand shortfall brought about by rapid technological innovation which generated for the first time the prospect of mass production for a (still as yet unrealised) mass market.

In the prevailing shared mental model's self-understanding (see Table 4.1), the post-war extension and development of the welfare state had served to generalise levels of demand sufficient to ensure both high and stable growth rates throughout the early post-war years. Such measures were counter-cyclical, injecting demand when it was most needed. They were also targeted on the most needy who were, in turn, most likely to

Table 4.1 Discourses of political and economic constraint in the rise of normative neoliberalism

		Economy–politics relationship (Diagnosis)	*Conditions of economic growth (Solution)*
Phase 0: Pre-history of neoliberalism	'Golden-age Keynesianism' (1940s–1960s)	Condition of economic and political synergy; political imperatives (legitimation) met by economic externalities; economic imperatives (demand management) met by political externalities.	Endogenous. Demand management ensures a flattening of the business cycle; possible danger of wage-push inflationary pressures arising from strength of labour.
Phase 1: Normative neoliberalism	'Overload' thesis (public choice theory)	Unsustainable disequilibrium; economic imperatives subordinated to narrow electoral interests or bureaucratic self-interest leading to fiscal crisis of the state.	Endogenous. Overload is a politically- or institutionally-induced logic of economic pathology; the spiral of escalating electoral expectations and fiscal burden must be broken; political discipline must be restored; bureaucratic autonomy must be checked.
	'Monetarism'	Political imperatives have compromised economic fundamentals; expansionary fiscal policy (assuming rational expectations) can only lead to inflation, indeed 'stagflation'; inflation is a monetary phenomenon; fiscal and budgetary policy must be subordinated to monetary policy.	Largely endogenous. Restoration of the price mechanism through control of inflation; unemployment must be allowed to find its natural rate; control of the money supply to end 'stagflation'; politicians must make firm commitments to MS targets to suppress inflationary expectations.
	'Supply-side economics'	Political imperatives have compromised economic fundamentals, impeding the efficient operation of the market mechanism; the supply-side has been sidelined due to an unhealthy preoccupation with the demand-side; high levels of taxation and a variety of labour-market rigidities impede market incentives and suppress entrepreneurialism.	Both endogenous and exogenous. Reductions in the burden of taxation to reward entrepreneurialism and raise revenue (Laffer curve); elimination of labour-market rigidities and union power to enhance (cost) competitiveness; marketisation and de-nationalisation to deliver more efficient provision of public goods.

spend (rather than save) such transfer payments as they received and to do so by purchasing domestic products as opposed to luxury imports. This served to ensure high levels of effective demand on the basis of comparatively modest rates of redistribution, helping in turn to establish a fortuitous synergy between economic imperatives and political priorities. In this stylised and popularised Keynesian account, economic imperatives were almost exclusively endogenous and were largely satisfied by social and political reforms (such as the extension of the welfare state) which were popular and which could be legitimated without appeal to a logic of economic compulsion. Economic imperatives (relating to demand management) were secured as a by-product of political goods and political imperatives (relating to legitimation) were secured from economic externalities.

This fortuitous situation was not to survive the 1970s. Moreover, the Keynesian paradigm or shared mental model which had provided the intellectual rationale for the growth phase was seen to offer no diagnosis or explanation of the affliction which now beset the European economies.[1] The problem which was now afflicting the advanced liberal democracies was one of 'stagflation' (see, especially Crozier *et al.*, 1975) – a condition of high and rising inflation combined with high and rising unemployment in a welfare state society whose citizenship contract had until this time been premised upon the commitment to full employment. In the context of a series of more or less widely-perceived crises, unevenly distributed between cases and arising at various points from the Yom Kippur War onwards, dominant economic understandings changed as the intellectual pendulum swung from left to right, from Keynesianism to neoliberalism. We enter the phase of spectacular neoliberalism.

The new right's diagnosis of the condition afflicting the advanced liberal democracies was elegant in its simplicity and in its simplicity lay its persuasive capacity. It was premised upon the crudest variants of public choice theory and, in turn, upon the assumed narrow instrumental rationality of bureaucrats (in maximising agency and bureau budgets), politicians (in maximising votes irrespective of the economic consequences of so doing) and electors (whose soul motivation for voting was assumed to be the blind pursuit of material self-interest). Given these parsimonious if unrealistic assumptions, the rest was merely a matter of logical deduction. Accept the assumptions, and neoliberalism was rationalised.

Two closely related but separable logics can be identified in neoliberal narratives of the crisis: the first, more influential in the US, sought to identify tendencies to bureaucratic overload and was a logical correlate of assuming public officials to be motivated solely by self-interest (see, for instance, Niskanen, 1971); the second, rather more influential in the UK, sought to identify tendencies to electoral overload and was a logical correlate of projecting precisely the same assumptions onto political parties (see, for instance, Brittan, 1975; Crozier *et al.*, 1975; Douglas, 1976; King,

1975). Given such assumptions, the logical was impeccable. Consider the electoral overload thesis.

Thinking merely of narrow electoral advantage, politicians would seek to accommodate themselves to the (rational, i.e. instrumental) preferences of the electorate for immediate material gain by sanctioning ever spiralling and ever more costly expectations. Consequently, in the run up to a general election, the parties (rationally maximising their electoral prospects) would seek to outbid one another in terms of the promises they made to the electorate and sectional interests therein. This served to establish a political competition for votes, yet one lacking the disciplining price mechanism of a genuine market – in which consumers are forced to bear the costs of their choices. Since the cost of each vote could effectively be discounted by politicians motivated only by short-term electoral advantage, and voters themselves would discount the long-term cumulative consequences of the parties' budgetary indiscipline that their greed encouraged, the effective price of a vote would spiral from one election to the next. Eventually demand would increase to the point of 'overload'. The result was a fiscal crisis of the state born of political irresponsibility or rationality (depending on one's audience). This, according to the new right, was the point that had now been reached.

The image was a simple one – a vicious political whirlpool from whose watery clutches parties could only escape at considerable cost to their electoral prospects. The solution, however politically unpalatable to an electorate that has come to conceive of government as a simple relay for its preferences, and however incompatible with the diagnosis of the affliction (a point to which we return), was simple: a severe bout of fiscal austerity, tight monetary control and a programmatic withdrawal of an overloaded, overburdened yet beleaguered state. Yet it is important to note that the substantive content of that response was not in any direct way deducible from the overload thesis itself (or, really for that matter, from public choice theory). In effect, the overload thesis provided a populist narration of the crisis capable of attributing responsibility to the then ascendant Keynesian paradigm or shared mental model, the parties that had internalised it and the sectional interests (principally the trade unions) that had exploited it. It opened the discursive terrain for both monetarism and supply-side economics which were to provide an alternative economic mental model, but which were perhaps less capable in and of themselves in providing a spectacular and populist narration of the crisis of Keynesianism.

Before turning to these more directly, it is worth first exploring the inconsistencies and obvious distortions of the overload thesis. For here two key themes of this chapter emerge for the first time: (1) the reliance of public legitimations of neoliberalism upon rationalist premises for which no substantiating evidence was provided; and (2) the sensitivity of such legitimations to variations in these undefended assumptions. Stated more boldly, the overload thesis (like other rationalist legitimations of neoliberalism) rests on fanciful assumptions; renders the assumptions more realistic and the 'rationalisation' of neoliberalism that it offers evaporates.

Though in many respects a simple, indeed simplistic, account – a simplicity, it might be suggested, making it all the more politically attractive – the overload thesis (bureaucratic, electoral or both) contains a number of profound internal contradictions and tensions. For reasons of brevity, I consider here only those relating to the electoral overload thesis, though the thesis of bureaucratic overload is no less problematic (see, for instance, Dunleavy, 1991; Goodin, 1982; King, 1987: 103–104).[2]

First, its proponents conjure the impression of a cynical and self-serving electorate looking to the state to satisfy its every whim and desire. Yet this depiction of the electorate as greedy, unprincipled and simply too stupid to consider the consequences of their actions stands in some tension to the rest of the analysis. It is also, of course, a product of the theory's most fundamental analytical assumption – for which no evidence is presented. The tension is well expressed by Anthony King in his influential essay on 'overload' published in *Political Studies* in 1975.

> It was once thought that governments would be extremely difficult to remove from office, given their ability to manage the economy. Now we are inclined to assume the opposite: that the tenure of governments is precarious and that for the foreseeable future it will be a lucky government that survives for more than a term.
>
> (1975: 282)

This implies – and the evidence clearly supports such a claim – that a (possibly *the*) principal factor determining success at the polls at the time was the perceived state of the economy and not the ability of parties to outbid one another in making irresponsible budgetary commitments to sectional interests. Ironically, both Thatcher and Reagan would rely on this very fact for their election in 1979 and 1980 respectively.

Second, in its call for a decisive break with the practices responsible for overload, the thesis's proponents appeal to precisely the good sense of the electorate that the assumption of instrumental rationality denies. Either the electorate is motivated solely by instrumental material self-interest or it is not. Ironically, the election of administrations designed to break the cycle of overload would appear to provide a compelling refutation of the overload thesis!

Yet, for opponents of neoliberalism there was little solace to be found in pointing to the internal inconsistencies of the overload thesis, however glaring these may have been. To assess its contribution in terms of intellectual cogency is to miss the point and to ignore altogether its most important contribution – to the political debate of the time. The thesis, as diluted and refracted by the think-tanks of the new right and the popular press on both sides of the Atlantic offered a spectacular, rhetorically-rich and ultimately persuasive narration and dramatisation of the events of the prevailing context. It would steer and mould perceptions not only of the nature of the condition afflicting the advanced liberal democracies, but of the necessary response to this crisis of an overextended state. When couched in these terms, its simplicity, its flexibility, its nostalgia for a deferential past that arguably never existed and perhaps even its internal contradictions, were a significant advantage.

Yet, as noted above, whilst capable of providing a public rationale and legitimation of neoliberalism, the overload thesis and indeed public choice theory more broadly, was not capable of animating a neoliberal 'project' or of providing an alternative economic paradigm or shared mental model to Keynesianism. That role was performed by monetarism and supply-side economics which were to become shared mental models for policy makers. It is to them that we must now turn. For reasons of brevity, I concentrate principally on the British case.

The neoliberal mental model: monetarist macroeconomics, supply-side microeconomics

Much has been written on the extent to which Thatcherism was predicated upon monetarism and supply-side economics, indeed, 'Reaganomics' (on the latter, see especially, Fink, 1982). It is certainly the case that the first Thatcher administration was monetarist in its general inclinations – and, perhaps more importantly, it was seen to be monetarist where previous administrations (and the Labour opposition) were not. This generic monetarism was expressed in its public subordination of fiscal to monetary policy, its resolute commitment to price stability (or, at least, the control of inflation) as the principal objective of macroeconomic policy, its rhetorical (if not always substantive) commitment to inflation as an exclusively monetary phenomenon and its (nominal) targeting of both the money supply (albeit in a variety of different forms) and the public sector borrowing requirement in its (eventually abortive) Medium Term Financial Strategy. Moreover, monetarism was certainly presented as the successor to a failed Keynesian paradigm or shared mental model and policy was couched in terms of the theory and its supporting assumptions (predominantly those of rational expectations). Nonetheless, despite the open advocacy of monetarism and the presentation of macroeconomic policy in monetarist terms, some caution is here required.

For whilst in general terms the Thatcher governments presided over the development of a new and distinctly monetarist macroeconomic mental model which arguably persists today (a point to which the analysis returns presently), in strict terms the first Thatcher government was characterised by its failure to produce an effective monetarist macroeconomic policy. For the targeting of both the money supply and the public sector borrowing requirement (the PSBR) was phenomenally ineffective, as has been widely documented, and it was eventually abandoned. Indeed, inflation was brought under control not through the effective use of monetarist policies (for these, in essence, failed) but by virtue of the strongly deflationary budgetary/fiscal stance that the government adopted between 1979 and 1981. In short, inflation was eventually controlled despite, and not because of, the conversion to monetarism. It might even be suggested that, at this point, monetarism was largely a rhetorical device and not an internalised and hence shared mental model amongst policy-makers. As Grahame Thompson has perceptively noted, 'monetary targets were a rather convenient, pragmatic and largely "presentational" device, behind which to conduct a familiar Keynesian deflation of the economy, without having the inconvenience of having to specify the likely real output and employment consequences' (1986: 30).

In fact, despite the emphasis placed upon monetarism by the Thatcherites, it was supply-side economics which was arguably more central to the agenda pursued in the first and subsequent terms. In contrast to the Reagan administration, only passing reference was made to the maverick Californian economist, Arthur Laffer who had famously predicted that a lowering of personal taxation would result in such a significant boost to economic activity that it would increase revenue (see, for instance, Laffer, 1981; Wanniski, 1978). Yet, this notwithstanding, much of the Thatcher government's microeconomic agenda was driven by the concern to eliminate a variety of supply-side and labour-market rigidities and to restore the incentivising and disciplining role of market mechanisms – here there is clear evidence of the existence of a shared mental model. The programme of de-nationalisation and welfare reform, the prioritisation of the cost competitiveness of British industry, the barrage of anti-union legislation, the introduction of internal markets within a residual public sector and the broader agenda of labour-market flexibilisation might all be seen as expressions of the new supply-side economics (see Table 4.1).

In sum, then, the neoliberal economic mental model in Britain was publicly predicated upon a public choice-inspired narration of the crisis of the 1970s as one of an over-extended state held to ransom by a combination of sectional interests (the unions) and the escalating expectations of the electorate. The Keynesian paradigm or shared mental model was pronounced obsolete and, with corporatism, held responsible for the pervasive and unsustainable condition of 'stagflation'. It was replaced by a combination of monetarist macroeconomics and supply-side microeconomics.

Having, albeit briefly, examined the initial rationalisation of normative neoliberalism, we can now turn to its subsequent normalisation. The argument here is simple. Though each has evolved significantly since the

1980s, the 'open economy macroeconomics' of the third way is a recognisable descendent of the monetarism of the earlier phase of normative neoliberalism, just as its labour-market and welfare reform agenda is a recognisable descendent of supply-side economics. In this way the current anglophone penchant for 'third way' political economy is decidedly neoliberal (see also Arestis and Sawyer, 2001; Thain, 2000; and for a comparison between the British and Irish cases, see Hay and Smith, 2005). Yet, whereas the neoliberalism of the first Thatcher term was normative and spectacular, that of the third way is normalised, necessitarian and vernacular. Nonetheless, just as rationalist assumptions and stylised models proved crucial to the popular articulation of normative neoliberalism, so rationalist assumptions – in the form of the rational expectations literature on the time-inconsistent inflationary preferences of governments and the stylised open economy macroeconomic assumptions of the business school hyperglobalisation thesis – have proved crucial in normalising neoliberalism in recent years. It is to the role of rational expectations and the hyperglobalisation thesis in the normalisation of neoliberal macroeconomics and microeconomics, respectively, that we now turn. Again, the British experience is instructive. In giving rise to the notion of the third way, packaged for export, it has also proved highly influential.

Rationalising neoliberal macroeconomics: rational expectations and the time-inconsistency problem

The new monetarism of New Labour's self-styled 'open economy macroeconomics', though not openly declared, is not very well hidden either (Balls, 1998; Balls and O'Donnell, 2002). It is expressed most clearly in the official justification for granting operational independence to the Bank of England in 1997. This was presented in terms of assumptions as to the time-inconsistent inflationary preferences of public authorities and the rational expectations of market actors. As this suggests, the British government's theoretical inspiration for operational independence came from a combination of public choice theory, Friedmanite monetarism and rational expectations economics (1998). Given the assumption of rational expectations, the logic is again simple and faultless. Governments cannot be trusted to stick to any inflation target they declare for themselves. For, given (the perception of) a short-term trade-off between inflation and unemployment, rational politicians will seek to orchestrate a political business cycle, trading inflation in the immediate aftermath of their anticipated re-election for growth and employment in the run-up to that election. This can only serve to dampen the aggregate long-term growth potential of the economy whilst, at the same time, driving up the natural or equilibrium rate of unemployment. It is, in short, rational for politicians to set for themselves inflation targets that they have no intention of keeping.

In a world of rational expectations, market actors will anticipate such defection, adapting their investment behaviour accordingly. In such a world, the consequences of anticipated inflation for the investment behaviour of market actors are just as severe as if that inflation were real. Accordingly, so long as control of monetary policy rests in the hands of public officials, unemployment, the aggregate rate of inflation and interest rates will all be higher than they need otherwise be.

If anti-inflationary credibility is to be restored, the public authorities need to be able to make a credible pre-commitment to a given inflation target (just as in the earlier monetarist account governments need to make strong and firm commitments to a money supply target). This entails an institutionally-guaranteed depoliticisation of monetary policy – in other words, an independent central bank mandated constitutionally to deliver a specific inflation target (typically in low to mid-single digits). In such a scenario (rational) inflationary expectations are diminished with consequent beneficial effects both upon the cost of borrowing and the equilibrium rate of unemployment.

The lineage of this new monetarist macroeconomics could scarcely be easier to trace. Though, in the strictest terms, post-monetarist (no emphasis is placed upon control of the money supply), such open macroeconomics is a clear and direct descendent of the monetarism of successive British governments since 1979. It is, moreover, a product of the internalisation of rational expectations assumptions (and the [shared] mental models they depict). The time-inconsistency problem is presented as a non-negotiable bind on elected officials, necessitating the institutionalisation of an independently-accountable new monetarist macroeconomic regime which guarantees the privileged status of price stability as macroeconomic objective number one. That status is seen to be inviolable and beyond political contestation – indeed, it is only because it is inviolable and beyond political contestation that any credible commitment to its delivery can be made (see Table 4.2).

In other words, 'open economy macroeconomics' is justified, not principally in its own terms, but as the only possible (and hence purely technical) solution to the time-inconsistency problem in a world of rational expectations. In this way rationalist assumptions normalise and institutionalise neoliberal policy such that no alternative is conceivable. Macroeconomic policy (certainly monetary policy) is thus relegated to a purely technical and entirely apolitical matter beyond the sphere of effective democratic scrutiny or accountability. The perpetuation of neoliberal macroeconomics is guaranteed.[3]

What makes this all the more remarkable is that the empirical evidence on the effects of central bank independence fails to lend much support to the rational expectations hypothesis. There is, for instance, no statistically significant correlation between the granting of independence and improved anti-inflationary performance (Posen, 1993). When it is

Table 4.2 Discourses of political and economic constraint in the normalisation of neoliberalism

		Economy–politics relationship (Diagnosis)	*Conditions of good economic performance (Solution)*
Phase 2: Normalised neoliberalism	'New monetarism' (rational expectations hypothesis)	Politicians cannot be trusted to make credible commitments to a given inflation target; they have time-inconsistent inflationary preferences; in a world of rational expectations any such commitments will be discounted leading to inflationary expectations.	Largely endogenous. A rules-based monetary policy regime is required; this must give responsibility for monetary policy to an independent public authority; only an institutional guarantee of monetary orthodoxy can quell inflationary expectations.
	'Third way' supply-side economics (stylised open economy assumptions)	Economic imperatives externally imposed; political autonomy subordinated to external economic constraints and imperatives.	Exogenous. Heightened mobility of capital exposes the welfare state, encompassing labour market institutions and other 'supply-side rigidities' as luxuries of a bygone era; the state must internalise the perceived interest of capital if it is not to precipitate capital flight.

considered that central bank independence tends to be seen as an institutional fix for administrations anxious to enhance their anti-inflationary credibility (who might, as a consequence, be expected to exhibit more hawkish attitudes than they had previously exhibited towards inflation), this is all the more troubling. If the suggestion is that the ability to control inflation is, and must be, the principal objective of macroeconomic policy, that this rests on anti-inflationary credibility, and that such credibility can only be maintained through operational independence, then the absence of compelling evidence that independence improves anti-inflationary performance is exceptionally damaging. It suggests that the necessitarian underpinnings of New Labour's neoliberal macroeconomics are profoundly misplaced. We return to a now consistent theme – the ability of stylised rationalist assumptions to deliver a spurious necessity to economic policy choices, rendering them purely technical.

Rationalising neoliberal microeconomics: the globalisation thesis

If neoliberal macroeconomics has been rationalised (and thereby normalised) through rational expectations assumptions, then a similar role in the rationalisation of supply-side microeconomics has been performed by the stylised open economy macroeconomic assumptions of the highly influential business school globalisation literature (see Table 4.2).

As has been widely noted, much of the distinctiveness of third way political economy rests on the sustained and systematic appeal to globalisation as an external economic constraint (Hay and Smith, 2005). Here, again, economic imperatives claim precedence over political discretion as, it is argued, heightened capital mobility serves to tilt the balance of power from immobile government and comparatively immobile labour to fluid capital. In such an inauspicious context for economic policy autonomy, the state (as fiscal authority) must adapt and accommodate itself to the perceived interest of capital (for labour market flexibility, a 'competitive' taxation environment and so forth) if it is not to precipitate a haemorrhaging of invested funds. The judgement of mobile assets (whether of invested or still liquid funds) is assumed to be both harsh and immediate, selecting for fiscal responsibility, prudence, a rules-bounded economic policy (as guarantor of credibility and competence), and both flexible labour markets and low levels of corporate and personal taxation. The appeal to globalisation thus conjures a logic of economic necessity and, indeed, compulsion driving a non-negotiable agenda for welfare retrenchment and labour-market reform – whilst further shoring up its open economy macroeconomics.

Once again, the justification for policy is presented not in its own terms, but as a necessary accommodation to the 'harsh realities' of new economic times in a (superficially) dispassionate, almost technocratic, manner. Appeal is again made to processes beyond the control of political actors which must simply be accommodated – and hence to a dull logic of economic compulsion which is non-negotiable.

The policy implications of such an account are painfully clear. As globalisation serves to establish competitive selection mechanisms within the international economy, there is little choice but to cast all regulatory impediments to the efficient operation of the market on the bonfire of welfare institutions, regulatory controls and labour-market rigidities.

Plausible, familiar and compelling though such a logic may well appear, it is important to isolate the parsimonious rationalist assumptions on which it is predicated. For it is these, rather than any inexorable process of globalisation, which ultimately summon the necessity of an accommodation with neoliberal (supply-side) microeconomics. They are principally five-fold, and each can be challenged on both theoretical and empirical grounds (for a more extended discussion, see Hay, 2005). They are summarised in Box 4.1.

Each of these premises is at best dubious, at worst demonstrably false. Such assumptions, it should perhaps be noted, are not justified in neoclassical economics in terms of their accuracy, but because they are convenient and make possible abstract quasi-mathematical modelling. That defence is simply not available to proponents of the hyperglobalisation

Box 4.1 Core assumptions of the 'hyperglobalisation' thesis as a shared mental model

1. That capital invests where it can secure the greatest net return on that investment and is possessed of perfect information of the means by which to do so.
2. That markets for goods and services are fully integrated globally and that, consequently, national economies must prove themselves internationally competitive if economic growth is to be sustained.
3. That capital enjoys perfect mobility and the cost of 'exit' (disinvestment) is zero.
4. That capital will invariably secure the greatest return on its investment by minimising its labour costs in flexible labour markets and by relocating its productive activities to economies with the lowest rates of corporate taxation; and, consequently . . .
5. That the welfare state (and the taxation receipts out of which it is funded) represent nothing other than lost capital to mobile asset holders and have no positive externalities for the competitiveness and productivity of the national economy.

thesis whose borrowings from neoclassical economics rarely extend past the assumptions to the algebra.

Consider each assumption in turn. Whilst it may seem entirely appropriate to attribute to capital the sole motive of seeking the greatest return on its investment, the political and economic history of capital provides little or no support for the notion that capital is blessed either with complete information or even with a relatively clear and consistent conception of what its own best interest is. Moreover, as the political economy of the advanced capitalist democracies demonstrates well, capital has a history of resisting social and economic reforms which it has later come both to rely upon and actively to defend (see, for instance, Swenson, 2002).

The second assumption is, again, a convenient fiction, used in neoclassical macroeconomics to make possible the modelling of an open economy. Few if any economists would defend the claim that markets for goods or services are fully integrated or clear instantly.

If the first two assumptions are problematic, then the third is demonstrably false, at least with respect to certain types of capital. For whilst portfolio capital may indeed exhibit almost perfect mobility in a digital economy, the same is simply not the case for capital invested in infrastructure, machinery and personnel. Once attracted to a particular locality, foreign direct investors acquire a range of non-recuperable or 'sunk' costs – such as their investment in physical infrastructure, plant and machinery. Consequently, their exit options become seriously depleted.

No less problematic are assumptions 4 and 5 – that capital can only compete in a more intensely competitive environment on the basis of productivity gains secured through tax reductions and cost-shedding and that the welfare state is, for business, merely a drain on profits. This is to extrapolate wildly and inappropriately from labour-intensive sectors of the international economy in which competitiveness is conventionally enhanced in this way to the global economy more generally. It fails to appreciate that foreign direct investors in capital-intensive sectors of the international economy are attracted to locations like the Northern European economies neither for the flexibility of their labour-markets nor for the cheapness of the wage and non-wage labour costs that they impose, but for the access they provide to a highly skilled, reliable and innovative labour force (Cooke and Noble, 1998). High wages and high non-wage labour costs (in the form of payroll taxes) would seem to be a price many multi-national corporations regard as worth paying for a dynamic and highly skilled workforce.

As the above paragraphs suggest once again, stylised rationalist and open economy assumptions deliver a spurious necessity to economic policy choices. Overly parsimonious rationalist assumptions have played a crucial role in consolidating, normalising and, above all, depoliticising a neoliberal shared mental model which is disingenuously presented as a simple and necessary accommodation to global economic realities.

Conclusions

Whilst the political economy of the advanced liberal democracies is by no means simply reducible to neoliberalism, its macro- and micro-economic agendas have been increasingly circumscribed by the presumed inviolability of neoliberalism. Yet, as I have sought to demonstrate, it rests on very shaky rationalist foundations, just as Thatcherism and Reaganomics rested on the logically inconsistent and empirically suspect overload thesis, to say nothing of the Laffer Curve (on which see Alt and Crystal, 1983; Henderson, 1981; Tobin, 1982).

As this suggests, however depoliticised, institutionalised and normalised neoliberalism has become it is, in the end, a political and economic choice, not a simple necessity. And it may not be a very good choice. This brings us naturally to the question of alternatives. A number of points might here be made which follow fairly directly from the above analysis.

First, our ability to offer alternatives to neoliberalism rests on our ability to identify that there is a choice and, in so doing, to demystify and deconstruct the rationalist premises upon which its public legitimation has been predicated. This, it would seem, is a condition of the return of a more normative and engaging form of politics in which more is at stake than the personnel to administer a largely agreed neoliberal reform agenda. Second, the present custodians of neoliberalism are, in many cases, reluctant converts, whose accommodation to neoliberalism is essentially borne of perceived pragmatism and necessity rather than out of any deep normative commitment to the sanctity of the market. Thus, rather than defend neoliberalism publicly and in its own terms, they have sought instead to appeal to the absence of a choice which might be defended in such terms. Consequently, political discourse is technocratic rather than political, normalised rather than normative. Moreover, as Peter Burnham has recently noted, neoliberalism is itself a deeply depoliticising paradigm (2001), whose effect is to subordinate social and political priorities, such as might arise from a more dialogic, responsive and democratic politics, to perceived economic imperatives and to the ruthless efficiency of the market. Finally, the institutionalisation and normalisation of neoliberalism in many advanced liberal democracies in recent years has been defended in largely technical and rationalist terms and in a manner almost entirely inaccessible to public political scrutiny, contestation and debate. The electorate, in recent years, has not been invited to choose between competing programmatic mandates to be delivered in office, but to pass a judgement on the credibility and competence of the respective candidates for high office to behave in the appropriate (technocratic) manner in response to contingent external stimuli. Is it any wonder that they have chosen, in increasing numbers, not to exercise any such judgement at the ballot box?

As this final point suggests, the rejection of the neoliberal shared mental model, the demystification of its presumed inevitability and the rejection of the technical and rationalist terms in which that defence has been constructed are likely to be a condition not only of the return of normative politics but also of the re-animation of a worryingly disaffected and disengaged democratic culture.

Notes

1 Whether monetarism and the new 'supply-side economics' fared any better in furnishing such a diagnosis is a moot point.
2 As I have elsewhere argued (Hay, 2004), the antipathy towards the state that characterises public choice theory is itself a logical correlate of the empirically dubious assumption that public officials are motivated solely by the narrow pursuit of self-interest.
3 To present this as a non-negotiable bind is in fact somewhat disingenuous, when other aspects of economic policy are considered. For, despite the rhetoric of economic compulsion, the Blair government is committed in principal to sacrificing the 'required' institutional solution to the time-inconsistency problem in arguing for membership of the Euro (albeit, only in the unlikely event of the Chancellor's five economic tests are met). On the implications of this, see Hay, 2003.

References

Alt, J.E. and Crystal, K.A. (1983) *Political Economics.* Brighton: Harvester Wheatsheaf.

Arestis, P. and Sawyer, M. (2001) 'The economic analysis underpinning the "Third Way"', *New Political Economy* 6(2): 255–278.

Balls, E. (1998) 'Open macroeconomics in an open economy', *Scottish Journal of Political Economy* 45(2): 113–132.

Balls, E. and O'Donnell, G. (eds) (2002) *Reforming Britain's Economic and Financial Policy.* London and Basingstoke: HM Treasury and Palgrave.

Blyth, M. (2002) *The Great Transformations.* Cambridge: Cambridge University Press.

Brittan, S. (1975) 'The economic contradictions of democracy', *British Journal of Political Science* 5(2): 129–159.

Burnham, P. (2001) 'New Labour and the politics of depoliticisation', *British Journal of Politics and International Relations* 3: 127–144.

Cooke, W.N. and Noble, D.S. (1998) 'Industrial relations systems and US foreign direct investment abroad', *British Journal of Industrial Relations* 36(4): 581–609.

Crozier, M.J., Huntingdon, S.P. and Watanuki, J. (1975) *The Crisis of Democracy: Report on the Governability of Democracies to the Trilateral Commission.* New York: New York University Press.

Denzau, A.T. and North, D.C. (1994) 'Shared mental models: ideologies and institutions', *Kyklos* 47(1): 3–31.

Douglas, J. (1976) 'The overloaded crown', *British Journal of Political Science* 6: 483–505.

Dunleavy, P. (1991) *Democracy, Bureaucracy and Public Choice.* Hemel Hempstead: Harvester Wheatsheaf.

Fink, R.H. (ed.) (1982) *Supply-Side Economics: A Critical Appraisal.* Frederick, MD: University Publications of America.

Goodin, R.E. (1982) 'Freedom and the Welfare State: theoretical foundations', *Journal of Social Policy* 11: 149–170.

Hall, P.A. (1993) 'Policy paradigms, social learning and the State: the case of economic policy-making in Britain', *Comparative Politics* 25/3: 185–196.

Hay, C. (2003) 'Macroeconomic policy coordination and membership of the Single European Currency: another case of British exceptionalism?', *Political Quarterly* 74(1): 91–100.

Hay, C. (2004) 'Theory, stylised heuristic or self-fulfilling prophecy? The status of rational choice in public administration', *Public Administration* 82(1): 39–62.

Hay, C. (2005) 'Globalisation's impact on states', in Ravenhill, J. (ed.) *Global Political Economy.* Oxford: Oxford University Press.

Hay. C. and Smith, N. (2005) 'Horses for courses? The political discourse of globalisation and European integration in the UK and Ireland', *West European Politics* 28(1): 124–158.

Henderson, D. (1981) 'The limits of the Laffer Curve as a justification for tax cuts', *The Cato Journal* 1: 45–52.

King, A. (1975) 'Overload: problems of governing in the 1970s', *Political Studies* 23(2/3): 284–296.

King, D.S. (1987) *The New Right.* London: Macmillan.

Laffer, A.B. (1981) 'Government exactions and revenue deficiencies', *The Cato Journal* 1: 1–21.

Marglin, S. and Schor, J. (eds) (1990) *The Golden Age of Capitalism: Reinterpreting the Postwar Experience.* Oxford: Oxford University Press.

Niskanen, W.A. (1971) *Bureaucracy and Representative Government.* Chicago, IL: Aldine-Atherton.

Posen, A. (1993) 'Why Central Bank independence does not cause low inflation: there is no institutional fix for politics', in O'Brien, R. (ed.) *Finance and the International Economy 7.* Oxford: Oxford University Press.

Swenson, P.A. (2002) *Capitalists Against Markets: The Making of Labour Markets and Welfare States in the United States and Sweden.* New York: Oxford University Press.

Thain, C. (2000) 'Economic policy', in Dunleavy, P. *et al.* (eds) *Developments in British Politics 6.* Basingstoke: Palgrave.

Thompson, G. (1986) *The Conservatives' Economic Policy.* London: Croom Held.

Tobin, J. (1982) 'The Reagan economic plan: supply-side, budget and inflation', in Fink, R.H. (ed.) *Supply-Side Economics: A Critical Appraisal.* Frederick, MD: University Publications of America.

Wanniski, J. (1978) 'Taxes, revenues and the "Laffer Curve"', *Public Interest* 50: 3–16.

5 When liberalisms change

Comparing the politics of deflations and inflations*

Mark Blyth

Introduction

The role of ideas or mental models as causal elements *in* institutional change, rather than as post hoc rationalizations *of* institutional change, is torturous ground for political economists. Rather than focusing upon ideas, agents' 'given' interests are the political economists ever ready tool of explanation. Thus when analysts seek to understand institutional change, many start with the reasonable assumption that agents have interests and act upon them. Given this, they conclude that if institutions no longer serve agents' interests, they will seek to change them; hence change is explained. But is this the whole story, especially in moments of crisis? Specifically, does it not matter that large scale institutional changes tend to occur against a backdrop of economic crisis which renders existing institutions unstable? And how does this matter? In a 'given' interest scenario it surely does not matter. In such a world, agents, the pursuit of whose interests are frustrated in such moments of institutional failure, should, knowing their interests, seek to change them; hence institutions change. But again, can this be the whole story given that it raises a rather thorny issue that such approaches neglect – how do agents know what institutions to construct if they do not know what futures to expect?

In 'Shared Mental Models', Denzau and North (1994) assert that uncertainty often shapes the choices that actors make. Under conditions of uncertainty, interests are often unclear. This suggests a role for economic ideas and mental models in the rather obvious sense of being a correspondence theory that tells agents what the crisis they are facing is a crisis of, and therefore what an appropriate institutional resolution should look like. There is however a problem with such a reading of the role of economic ideas and mental models. As Jonathan Kirshner points out, economic ideas are hardly unambiguous (Kirshner, 2003: 4–12). Any set of economic dislocations can be consonant with any number of economic ideas. Thus the stagflation of the 1970s could be the result of supply shocks, monetary imbalances, a positively-sloped Philips curve, a long term decline in profitability, or a host of other factors.[1] But perhaps just as important as the ambiguity of economic ideas is the politics such moments engender. If different mental models entail different distributional consequences, then the ability to 'set' the definition of a crisis, and thus its resolution, becomes a profound political resource. How then do agents 'choose' the 'right' mental models? Or, more appropriately, how does one group of agents get another group with orthogonal interests to accept their mental models, thus a shared mental model? For if we assume that ideas are causally powerful elements of institutional contestation and construction rather than simply being a correspondence theory of the world, how then do we better understand their role in the politics of institutional change?

This chapter examines macroeconomic regime change from 'embedded liberalism' to 'neoliberalism'. This regime change is rooted in a shift of shared mental models. In seeking to explain the shift from the 'embedded liberal' to the current 'neoliberal' macroeconomic regime among advanced industrial states, I have previously argued that an extension of Karl Polanyi's model of the 'double movement' provides a useful heuristic (Polanyi, 1944). Specifically, I questioned Polanyi's conclusion that having learned the lessons of the 'conservative twenties and revolutionary thirties', modern democratic governments would never again allow, as John Ruggie put it, the external financial balance to dictate the internal political balance of forces (Ruggie, 1982). For what seemed all too obvious during the 1970s and 1980s was that those agents who did not benefit from this re-embedding, namely, business interests, hardly sat back and accepted their role within this new regime (Blyth, 2002). Rather, the losers under this regime would seek to contest their status within it.

For example, the mental models that underpinned the embedded liberal institutional order of the 1940s–1970s portrayed consumption, as Keynes put it, as 'the sole end of economic activity' (Keynes, 1964: 104). Those who consumed (workers) drove the investment demand that made growth possible. In such a world, capitalists played second-fiddle to consumers. In contrast, the mental models that underpin the current neoliberal order portray innovation and the free movement of capital and the capitalists who make this possible, the engine of growth. Given the distributional non-neutrality of such ideas, it was hardly a surprise then that during the 1970s and 1980s disaffected business agents sought to reverse Polanyi's double movement and 'free' the market economy from its embedding institutions (Blyth, 2002: 152–251).

In my contribution to this volume I wish to revisit this issue of macroeconomic regime change and engage in a broader examination of the mechanisms through which such regime changes occur. I argue that while the broad contours of what might be called the 'Keynesian conversion' of the 1930s–1950s and the 'neoliberal convergence' of the 1970s to the present are, when seen from a Polanyian perspective, broadly similar, the precise mechanisms though which each regime emerged were different.

In brief, I argue that these regimes (and the mental models that underpinned them) emerged in large part due to the differential impacts of deflations and inflations on agents' conceptions of their interests and the politics of ideas these conditions engendered in each period.

To make this case, the first part of this essay reviews current theories of institutional change and explores certain absences in these theories; absences that suggest analysts should rethink how we view the relationship between uncertainty, interests, and crises. Specifically, in this section I build upon the pioneering work of Arthur Denzau and Douglass North on the role of ideologies in facilitating collective action and institutional construction (Denzau and North 1994). The second part of the essay contrasts the uncertainty engendered by the economic crises of the 1930s with the uncertainty actors faced in the 1970s and 1980s given the above. This comparison suggests that while understanding the effects of uncertainty on agents' interests is key, the mechanisms through which uncertainty is propagated and institutional change occurs differs across the two periods. Building upon this comparison, the third part of the essay suggests how 'political entrepreneurs' may have in fact caused, rather than resolved uncertainty, in an effort to alter other agents' concept of their own 'best interests' during the construction of the neoliberal order. Finally, and briefly, we return to Polanyi and re-examine the spread of neoliberal ideas or mental models through the lens of this reformulated 'double movement'.

Part 1: Institutions, reproduction, and change

Given that the point of invoking institutions is to explain the regularities of life, explanations of institutional change have typically relied upon exogenous factors as causes. Whether economic depressions, changes in factor prices, or technological shifts are invoked, the primary cause tends to be outside of the institutions themselves (Blyth, 1997). There are good reasons for this. First of all, as historical institutionalists have argued, if institutions give content to agents' preferences, then it makes little sense to identify the agents within such institutions as a source of change. Second, if institutions are path-dependent and exhibit increasing returns, then endogenous change arising from institutions themselves seems unlikely.

Recently however, several scholars have attempted to identify endogenous mechanisms of change within path-dependent institutions. Path dependence may seem an unlikely starting point for explaining institutional change given that its main purpose has been to explain institutional persistence (Mahoney, 2000).[2] This work has nonetheless sought to address how institutional change is possible without relying upon exogenous punctuations. These arguments typically focus on 'critical junctures' where 'initial steps in a particular direction induce further movement in the same direction such that over time it becomes impossible to reverse direction' (Mahoney, 2000: 512).[3] Such steps are said to be path dependent along two metrics.

Some events may begin 'self-reinforcing sequences' where initial steps along a path 'feed-back', making further path-switching unlikely (Mahoney, 2000). The mechanisms driving such 'positive feedback' can be factors such as high institutional set-up (sunk) costs; learning effects, and coordination effects (Pierson, 2000). Interestingly, cognitive factors are also credited with being able to create such positive (system maintaining) feedback. For example, adaptive expectations (co-properties of coordination effects) give rise to systematic cognitive biases among agents operating within institutions such that 'thinking off the path' becomes increasingly unlikely (Pierson, 2000a; Denzau and North, 1994). Such mechanisms do go a long way to explaining institutional continuity; but they do not tell us very much about institutional change.

The other metric of path dependence does more in this regard. James Mahoney refers to these as 'reactive sequences' – 'temporally ordered and causally connected events', where the order of events is key and backlashes against existing institutions set subsequent institutions on a new path (Mahoney, 2000: 509). In this case, the initial causes of, and designs for, particular institutions may bear little resemblance to their final output since 'events in ... [such a] ... sequence are often necessary or sufficient conditions for subsequent events' (Mahoney, 2000: 530). Thus, while initial conditions may be switch-points, subsequent events (and conjunctures with other sequences) shape the final outcome. Such an approach opens up greater possibilities for change 'off the path' with a focus upon the politics of institutional reproduction that attend these possibilities coming to the fore. For if such institutions are reproduced, then a failure of reproductive mechanisms such as who gets 'power' from an institution, can perhaps usefully account for institutional change.

Yet explaining change is perhaps not so easy. For example, while issues of power and legitimacy are clearly central to institutional change, such perspectives, just like their functional and utilitarian counterparts, run into some serious limits. At a basic level, the circularity issue that dogs functionalist (and utilitarian) explanations of change haunts power and legitimacy explanations too.[4] Specifically, power-centered perspectives of institutions tend to assume, 1) that there was (by definition) a 'powerful' coalition of interests around that wanted the institution (even if it was not designed by them) and 2) that since the institution in question changed/collapsed, this shows either that 3) the (assumed) coalition no longer supported the institution, or 4) (hypothesized) challengers usurped their position. One thus hypothesizes the existence of vested interests by virtue of institutional existence. Institutional persistence 'shows' that such interests are indeed 'powerful', while institutional failure shows, rather self-confirmingly, that such vested interests are no longer at play.

Such circularities of logic suggest perhaps that such explanations do not substantively improve upon existing theories. While there is obviously much in these accounts and mechanisms, particularly regarding institutional persistence and the importance of sequence, they are still of limited utility as a framework for understanding large scale institutional change. Clearly institutional change occurs and agents are implicated in it. However, the question remains of how best to conceptualize these moments when, as Ira Katznelson puts it, 'structurally induced unsettled times can provoke possibilities for particularly consequential purposive action' (2003: 274). In other words, far from institutional change being a simple function of declining interests or fading legitimacy, what may be of most importance is what happens in the moment of change itself, during the 'critical juncture' when paths are shaped (Collier and Collier, 1991).

Part 2: Rethinking institutional change

Critical junctures and constructed crises

Current concepts of 'critical juncture' are burdened by two commonly ignored conditions. The uncertainty faced by agents in such moments, and the set of ideas or mental models available to them for diagnosing what has gone wrong in the first place. This is indeed odd, since if 'critical junctures' signify anything, it is that the period in question is especially 'critical'. But critical in what way? If standard models of institutional change dictate that institutional supply follows from the 'need' for agents to realize their 'given' interests, then such periods may be a juncture, but there is little 'critical' – as in political – going on since the causal account tends to dissolve into a functionalist 'just-so' story (Elster, 2000).

What then is 'critical' in a critical juncture? In terms of the type of large scale institutional change that interests us here, critical junctures tend to be associated with moments of economic crisis, which is fair enough. But such a perspective tends to treat moments of institutional collapse in the same way that they treat the shift from one equilibrium to another; as a relatively unproblematic switching of statics where the 'reasons' for the collapse of the old order lead to new institutions that are 'designed' to overcome pathologies that are self-apparent to the agents involved (Blyth, 2001: 2–5). Yet what such a stance misses is the uncertainty over likely states of the world that such crises engender.

While observers of critical junctures such as Katznelson are correct to argue that agency is more prominent or possible in such moments, what they do not fully specify is why this is the case. That is, what are the 'environmental conditions' of such moments that make them so special? For if 'critical junctures' are seen as critical periods of politics, rather than simply (dis)junctures, then the notion of what a critical juncture actually is becomes much more problematic, and much more theoretically important, than is usually acknowledged.

The key idea I wish to introduce here is the notion that a particular type of critical juncture, economic crises, are political constructs as much as they are forces of nature, since what constitutes an economic crisis as a crisis is not a self-apparent phenomenon (Hay, 1996; Stone, 1989). While the destabilization of institutions may produce uncertainty, and while such uncertainty may manifest itself in effects such as currency collapses or rising and falling prices, neither the causes of, nor the solutions to such uncertainties, are given by the conditions of the collapse. Agents must argue over, diagnose, proselytize, and impose their notion of what a crisis actually *is* on others before collective action to resolve the uncertainty facing them can take any meaningful institutional form. In short, crises need to be constructed as crises of a certain type before meaningful collective action and institution building can take place.

As Colin Hay puts it, 'the mobilization of perceptions of crisis ... involves the formation and triumph of a simplifying ideology which must find and construct points of resonance with a multitude of individuated experiences' (Hay, 1999: 321). Crisis thus becomes an act of political intervention, where the sources of uncertainty are diagnosed and constructed. Given this, the set of available ideas with which to interpret the environment and make purposeful collective action possible becomes crucially important in determining the form of new institutions.

Such interventions are not, I stress, the discovery of objective truths. Rather, they are cognitive mechanisms (shared mental models aggregated into ideologies) that are used by agents to impose order in an institutionally unstable social world that has fewer fixed referents; an imposition that is fundamentally social, political, and contested (Greenfeld, 2001: 13–20; Denzau and North, 1994).

Such a notion, argues Leah Greenfeld, lies at the heart of Max Weber's notion of the 'rationalization of the social world'. Rather than rationalization being, in a positivistic sense, the ever greater conquering of the social by the technical/rational, Weber saw rationalization as the attempt by different social groups to enframe the world in such a way as to make intervention within it meaningful; for the more people that accepted these ideas, this 'rationalization', the more 'true' it became (Mitchell, 1988). In a similar vein, Denzau and North argue that such 'mental models are shared by communication, and communication allows the creation of ideologies' (Denzau and North, 1994: 20). Such ideologies then 'provide both an interpretation of the environment and a prescription as to how that environment *should* be structured' (Denzau and North, 1994: 4).

This is why attending to economic ideas in moments of crisis is key. Such ideas make institutional reconstruction possible by providing the authoritative diagnosis as to what a crisis actually is and when a given situation actually constitutes a crisis. They diagnose 'what has gone wrong' and thus 'what is to be done'. In short, the nature of a crisis is not simply given by its effects, dislocations, or casualties, nor are the actions of agents simply determined by their 'given' interests. Instead, the diagnosis of a situation as a 'crisis' by a particular set of ideas is a deliberate construction that makes the uncertainty agents perceive explicable, manageable, and indeed, actionable.

To anticipate the discussion to come, consider the 1930s. This was a period of shared experience among states, one of deflation – a sustained drop in the price level. However, despite this shared experience, the 1930s 'produced' Stalinism, at least four flavors of Fascism (Spanish, Italian, German and Japanese) and polar opposites types of reflationary social democracy (the USA and Sweden). What accounts for the variation? It can hardly be factor endowments or the specificity of assets given that the same cause of disruption (deflation) led the Germans to exterminate a minority while the Swedes invented social democracy. Nor can it be the simple 'fact' of deflation itself given that the same cause produced so many different outcomes. Material factors alone can tell us next to nothing about how interests are 'disrupted and recast' in such moments of crisis creation, or why in such moments economic ideas are so powerful. However, a perspective that takes the political construction of economic crises seriously can tell us more.

Economic ideas are generated to respond in a new way to new conditions and are a creative element in political economy, for better or worse. Such ideas do not 'come from nowhere' precisely because they arise out of confusion and uncertainty in times of instability. Yet because such ideas are a response to uncertainty, they are not simply reducible to a given and self-apparent crisis. Such ideas are generative, not correspondence theories.[5] Given this analysis, in periods of economic crisis it is imperative to attend to the economic ideas key economic agents have about what is going on around them. It is the set of available ideas and the specific nature of the uncertainties facing agents that make 'critical junctures' so critical in explaining institutional change.

Uncertainty, interests, and crises

How then do such 'unsettled times' engender institutional change? One way to answer this is to begin by noting that pretty much all economic crises engender uncertainty; an insight that is far more complex than is usually acknowledged. For those analysts who do take the notion of uncertainty seriously, but assume given interests, uncertainty tends to be seen as a computational problem. Douglass North, for example, views uncertainty as the result of 'the complexity of the problems to be solved ... the problem solving software ... possessed by the individual', and incomplete information between agents (North, 1990: 25). Given these problems, the 'institutional framework, by structuring human interaction, limits the choice set of the actors' (North, 1990: 25). Uncertainty, in this guise, is therefore a function of computational failings and environmental complexities that cause agents to devise institutions to help them cope by narrowing the choice set available to them.

Yet such a view of 'uncertainty as complexity' poses an interesting counterfactual. If agents could overcome their computational limitations, could they design optimal institutions, or better, would they even need institutions? If cognitive limitations were overcome then how ideas inform agency in moments of uncertainty would be irrelevant. Agents would be able to see the world as it really is. All ideas would be correspondence theories with zero ambiguity, and courses of action, interests, and choices, would be clear. In sum, politics would be unnecessary; which given its ubiquity suggests that there may be limits to viewing uncertainty as a problem of complexity. Luckily then, there is another way of viewing uncertainty.

As Jens Beckert argues, 'uncertainty is [commonly] understood as the character of situations in which agents cannot anticipate the outcome of a decision and cannot assign probabilities to the outcome' (Beckert, 1996: 804). Beckert further notes however, echoing Frank Knight, that uncertainty is much more than a probability distribution problem. Uncertain situations are qualitatively different from situations of risk because in situations of risk 'the distribution of the outcome in a group of instances in known ... [that is, probabilities can be assigned to possible outcomes] ... while in the case of uncertainty ... it is impossible to form a group of instances because the situation dealt with is in a high degree unique' (Knight, 1921, quoted in Beckert, 1996: 229). Denzau and North put it similarly, 'Knightian uncertainty ... [occurs] ... when a chooser can be viewed as capable of having even subjective probability distribution functions defined over a set of possible outcomes' (Denzau and North, 1994: 9).

Such situations of 'Knightian' uncertainty are therefore fundamentally different in kind from situations of 'uncertainty as complexity'. Under 'uncertainty as complexity' agents are sure of their interests, but unsure of how to realize them. Uncertainty is thereby reduced to risk.[6] 'Knightian' uncertainty does not reduce uncertainty to risk (Beckert, 1996: 807–809). Because the situation is 'in a high degree unique', agents have no clear conception as to what possible outcomes are likely, and hence what their interests in such a situation are beyond a very general level. This is not however to say that agents have no interests, they do. But in such situations agents may not merely be unsure about means–end calculations. Rather, they may be 'fundamentally' uncertain about which ends would best serve their perceived interests (Dequech, 2000; Davidson, 1991).

Thus, being unable to form 'a series of instances' of like-type events and project probabilities, agents' interests in such an environment cannot be given, either by assumption or structural location, and can only be defined in terms of the ideas agents themselves have about the causes of uncertainty. Again, as Denzau and North argue, interests only make sense in terms of the ideas agents have about their interests, since 'Humans . . . *construct explanations* in the face of ambiguity and uncertainty *and act upon them*' (Denzau and North, 1994: 12, my italics). They do not act upon some predefined and unambiguous materiality.

Economic ideas are obviously important in such moments; and *not* as a correspondence theory. Without having ideas as to how the world is put together, it would be cognitively impossible for agents to act in that world in any meaningful sense. As Denzau and North make clear, contra Bayesian models, individuals do not intervene in the world on the basis of ad-hoc generalizations distilled from randomly-gathered bits of information. Instead, complex sets of ideas – shared mental models – (such as ideas about the workings of the economy) allow agents to order and intervene in the world by bringing their beliefs, desires, and goals into alignment. Only then can agents diagnose, and thus collectively act upon, the 'crisis' they are facing (Denzau and North, 1994: 17, 22–23).

Furthermore, conditions of Knightian uncertainty such as those found in moments of economic crisis are complicated by another factor apart from their 'uniqueness'. If agents' interests in such situations can only be defined in terms of their ideas about their interests, then the outcomes such situations produce will also be a function of those ideas. Economic ideas do not simply help agents identify a given causal relationship in the economy in the manner of road maps or focal points (Goldstein and Keohane, 1993: 3–30). Such a view of ideas is to rob them of what makes them powerful in the first place. Rather, like Weber's 'rationalizations', such ideas serve to restructure causal relationships in the economy by altering the agents' own beliefs about the interests of others, upon which the realization of their own ideationally-derived interests depend.[7] This is what makes the assignment of probability values to outcomes, and hence the concept of 'given' interests producing institutions in such critical junctures impossible: the equilibrium set of institutions to resolve a crisis is a moving target pushed around by the beliefs of agents themselves.[8]

In sum, what is crucial in understanding agents' attempts to build institutions are the ideas held by agents, not their structurally-derived interests. Such a category has little meaning in moments of economic crisis. Because of these factors, the explanatory import of the ideas agents hold in moments of critical juncture cannot be appreciated as long as the analyst assumes interests that are constant and unproblematic. Instead, analysts should see agents' interests as being necessarily ideationally bound. When re-conceptualized in this way ideas are indeed intimately related to interests, but are not reducible to them, and moments of institutional change become much more fluid and open. Given these conceptual reformulations we can now begin to specify in detail how this discussion impacts our understandings of how embedded liberalism came about, and how neoliberalism replaced it.

Part 3: Ideas, uncertainties, and regime changes

Ideas and institutional change in the 1930s – deflation, uncertainty, statism

For the above discussion to have bearing, we need to show that the uncertainty facing agents in the 1930s was actually Knightian, otherwise the hypothesized causal effects of ideas in moments of economic crisis would be rather circumscribed. Evidence that the presence of this type of uncertainty led to the construction of the embedded liberal regime lies in the fact that the crisis of the period was a crisis of deflation. Although not limited to such situations, deflations, whether the result of monetary tightening, tariff wars, devaluations, or other dislocations, generate Knightian uncertainty. To see why, consider how agents were impacted by falling prices (regardless of their proximate causes) during this critical juncture, and how they could conceivably interpret their interests under such conditions.

On a macro level, continually falling prices lead to increased competition, which hits profits and thus lowers investment.[9] Growth slows, unemployment rises, and this in turn leads to a fall in demand, which reinforces the slump already underway. On a micro level then, such deflations have determinate effects on agent's perceptions of their interests; one which paradoxically makes their interests less, rather than more, certain. Consider for example, a hypothetical businessman's reaction to such an environment. A persistent deflation can signal two possible things. First, that the prices our businessman is charging for his goods, relative to the market prices, are too high. This may be a local event due to, for example, shifts in demand, and if this is the case, the appropriate response would be a price cut. Alternatively, the same businessman could realize that persistently falling prices were a global event over which he has no control. But such knowledge would hardly help. If our businessman is facing falling prices, and he has creditors, inventory to sell, and wages to pay, then regardless of the nature of the slump, the situation takes on the characteristics of a multi-person prisoner's dilemma. Our businessman's 'interest' is to 'sell first' at a discount and take market share in order to meet costs. But knowing this, his competitors will do the same thing, thus bringing about the deflation all of them are trying to avoid in the first place.[10] What was a locally rational choice was globally suboptimal, regardless of whether one knows what is 'truly' causing the deflation or not. And the more agents pursue such strategies, the worse off they will all be.

A similar situation faces labor. As Keynes pointed out, in a deflation labor cannot control its own supply price (its real wage), only its money wage (Keynes, 1964: 5–17). If prices fall, real wages increase without labor having done anything to increase them. In a deflation labor is in danger of constantly being priced above the market clearing wage rate. Labor can take a wage cut to obviate this, but this too is counter-productive. If labor's relative cost was determined by local events, then such wage cutting would restore equilibrium. But if price declines are global, then cutting wages would merely compound the deflation facing both labor and capital since it would cut into consumption and hence further the fall in prices.

The nub of the matter is this. Action by any one set of market agents to protect themselves tends to be zero sum against all others. This is how the downturn of the 1930s generated Knightian uncertainty. Actions undertaken to protect oneself (given one's perceived best interests) served only to worsen the overall situation, that is, cause greater uncertainty of a type which defied experience and created a situation that was indeed 'in a high degree unique'; Knightian uncertainty. Within such an environment one's own interests become increasingly uncertain since following them only seems to make things worse. Thus our hypothetical businessman may want higher profits and labor may want higher wages, but having such vague 'interests' would tell these agents nothing about how to realize these goals in such fundamentally uncertain conditions. Indeed, following 'the usual strategies' to achieve these goals would produce negative feedback, thus undermining the very institutions that sustain these interests in the first place.

In such a situation agents are not, in a probabilistic sense, sure of their interests but unsure of their strategies. Rather, following their first best interests (fire sales or wage cuts) produces the very dislocations that they seek to avoid. In such a context agents' interests become less grounded and more malleable, and hence the influence of ideas as interventions that diagnose the crisis facing such agents can become much more pronounced. This is precisely what makes this type of critical juncture critical. Absent ideas, and the uncertainty engendered by a deflation would make coherent patterns of collective action ever more problematic, and hence the downward movement of prices and the failure of institutions cumulative. To paraphrase Keynes, in the 1930s, what was individually rational proved to be collectively disastrous.

This is also why the state emerged as the key actor in this period, and why the economic ideas of the period took on the 'statist' cast that they did. If agents such as businessmen were unclear as to what their interests actually were, ('should we cut wages again if this means less people can buy our goods?'), and given that following what they thought were their first-best interests only made them worse off, then only the state had the breathing space (both politically and intellectually) to develop and deploy new ideas and narrate a way forward (Blyth, 2002: 49–126). Thus, regardless of the form taken, whether cartelistic then reflationary liberal (the USA), social democratic (Sweden), fascist (Germany), or even communist (the USSR), the common experience of the deflation of the 1930s produced narratives of intervention and control that stressed the role of the state in promoting stability, where the market was portrayed as an endogenously unstable environment in need of regulation.

This is not to say that this was an easy process where traditionally opposed interests suddenly (and painlessly) converted to a new way of viewing the economic world and adapted their interests accordingly. Rather, the process of building and acting upon alternative understandings of the crisis was intensely political, and local conditions mattered a great deal (Blyth, 2002: 77–86, 106–118). However, what did occur across countries was the ability of state actors to characterize the crisis as signifying that the old models of economics were redundant, and as such, pursuing one's interests had to be recast, as did the institutional order that made the realization of those interests possible. In sum, deflation produced statism and statist ideas produced the embedded liberal order.

Ideas and institutional change in the 1970s: inflation, uncertainty and entrepreneurship

How then do we explain the denouement of the embedded liberal order and the rise of neoliberalism; a set of economic ideas based upon antithetical principles? A rather obvious place to start is by first considering that the situation facing market agents in the 1970s was one of inflation rather than deflation, and then wondering if this makes a difference to the type of uncertainty generated. It is also noteworthy that it was business groups and their political allies, rather than the state, that took the lead in promoting institutional change in this period. These two factors are not coincidental. Let us examine the politics of inflation first and what this does to agents' conceptions of their interests, and then address why it was business rather than the state that took the lead during the 1970s in promoting institutional change.

What inflation does to interests and expectations, and the type of uncertainty it generates, should be treated differently from that which occurs in periods of deflation. First of all, unlike deflation, what inflation signals to agents varies by the assets they hold. As a consequence, the effects of inflation are at once less ambiguous, and yet more political. This is further complicated by the fact that what we think inflation is varies over time. As noted by Mathew Watson, every ten years or so economics develops a new theory of inflation (Watson, 2002). Each theory is held to be a 'general theory' that applies to all times and places. However, if each supposedly general theory changes every ten or so years, then one must question the extent to which the theory is actually general. If the causes, and hence diagnoses of inflation are historically variable, then the notion that one set of theories can diagnose all inflations as a correspondence theory of the world becomes impossible to sustain.[11] Therefore there can be no single optimal response to inflation, just as there was none for deflation. Given this, if we find a common response among states, it should once again alert us towards an examination of the ideas generated during this particular juncture.

Recognizing the historical specificity of such ideas allows us to see how particular theories become dominant interpretations precisely because they turn present uncertainties into transhistorical facts by appealing to generality. The narration of inflation made possible by the ideas of the 1970s (monetarism, rational expectations, public-choice theory's critique of 'big-government', and supply-side tax theory) was radically different both in terms of the understandings of inflation that preceded them, and in terms of the world such narrations portrayed. Only by reference to such ideas, and not to the fact of inflation itself, does the importance of such ideas for transforming the institutions of embedded liberalism become apparent.

Constructing an inflationary crisis

According to neoliberal ideas inflation has great costs associated with it and defeating it must become the overarching policy goal of the state. Such a target obviously has great distributional implications, not least of which is the cost of deflating. But what are the costs of inflation? And why was the 1970s perceived as such a serious crisis? After all, as Brian Barry argues, '[t]he orthodox interpretation of welfare economics has great difficulty in identifying a welfare loss from inflation at all commensurate with that often loosely attributed to it' (Barry, 1985: 282). For example, one recent survey of the literature on inflation finds that 'the costs of inflation, even rates of inflation as high as twenty percent a year, are extremely difficult to find' (Kirshner, 1999: 613). Indeed, attempts to find such costs by macroeconomists who have built their reputations on the dangers of inflation have reluctantly concluded that 'for inflation rates below twenty percent a year . . . the relationship between growth and inflation is not statistically significant' (Barro, 1995: 12). Nonetheless, the argument that inflation carries real identifiable economic costs was the core of neoliberal theory and became a totem of modern neoliberal practice. Yet such an understanding is far from uncontestable.

Again, as Barry notes, '[t]he assertion that inflation "can hardly be beneficial to anyone" is extraordinarily implausible. To the extent that inflation is purely redistributive, there are net gainers as well as losers' (Barry, 1985: 294). Moreover, if inflation is less than hyper-inflation, and if it arises over time, it can be fitted into indexing schemes that allow adjustment of expectations that can both help to stabilize the core rate and maintain the real value of money.[12] Indeed, some immanently respectable economists have argued that 'a little inflation may be a good thing' in terms of preventing zero-sum distributional conflict or in terms of encouraging, rather than discouraging, investment (Meidner, 1969; Tobin, 1972). The case of hyper-inflation seems to be what people have in mind when they think of inflation in general. Yet, there was never any theoretical reason given for any given level of inflation to spiral inexorably into hyper-inflation.[13] In short, there is no reason to expect increases in the rate of inflation to be exponential.

Another oft-noted objection of the time (and indeed today) was that inflation benefits lenders over debtors. Indeed it does, and this is perhaps a better explanation for why inflation became seen as a crisis. Inflation acts as a redistributionary tax on holding debt. Stock prices stagnate and bond prices increase as bond-holders demand a premium to guard against the effects of inflation. Investment returns slow as inflation eats away at yields. In response to inflation, investors move out of financial assets and into real assets such as property where the debt to be repaid falls over time. In short, inflation is a class-specific tax. Those with mortgages and consumer debt see the real costs of their debts diminish while those whose incomes depend upon stable prices and financial asset returns see those returns diminish. Those who credit suffer while those with debt, relatively speaking, prosper. Given that the benefits of inflation control (restoring the value of debt) are specific while the costs of inflation control (unemployment and economic recession) are diffuse, the reaction of business, particularly the financial sector, to inflation is perhaps best understood as the revolt of the investor class to what they saw as the long-run consequences of embedded liberalism. With this in mind, the apocalyptic pronouncements of the proponents of neoliberal ideas concerning inflation take on a more political meaning.

For example, at the height of the inflation of the 1970s Nobel Prize winning public choice theorist James Buchanan and his co-author Richard Wagner argued that 'inflation destroys expectations and creates uncertainty; it increases the sense of felt injustice and causes alienation. It prompts behavioral responses which reflect a generalized shortening of time horizons. "Enjoy, enjoy!" ... becomes a rational response ... where the plans made yesterday seem to have been made in folly' (Buchanan and Wagner, 1977, quoted in Barry, 1985: 284). Similarly, Milton Friedman argued that '[p]rudent behavior becomes reckless and "reckless" behavior becomes "prudent". The society is polarized; one group is set against another. Political unrest increases. The capacity of any government to govern is reduced at the same time that the pressure for strong action grows' (Friedman, 1991: 105).[14]

Why such hyperbole? Clearly these are exaggerations for the 1970s where the top eight OECD economies had an average annual rate of inflation of 8.8 percent. But what is the point of otherwise dispassionate commentators making such apocalyptic pronouncements? In short, what was the deployment of such ideas for? Given our prior discussion, such claims should not be seen as hyperbole but as a deliberate political intervention; as a necessary part of constructing an inflationary crisis in order to actively reconstitute agents' interests. If inflation directly affects only a small part of the population (and if it arguably benefits others), then convincing differentially-affected agents that what may seem to be in their interest (a continuing inflation, or at least no painful deflations) was in fact a general threat to all makes sense only as an attempt to recast interests.

This construction of inflation as an all encompassing social crisis that was explicable and treatable only in terms of neoliberal ideas that diagnosed the state as a pathology fits squarely with what we argued above concerning the importance of developing and deploying a dominant interpretation of a given crisis as a prerequisite of promoting institutional change. Inflation was a problem, for some more than others, but to maintain that inflation was in some sense a general social 'evil' and 'benefits no-one' was clearly a value judgment designed to promote action against it. Inflation is not an empirical given but a mediated social fact, as is the precise, or more accurately, vague understanding of what inflation is that people acquire.[15] Controlling the definition of inflation is therefore inherently political. Responding to inflation is no mere Pavlovian reaction by the public to a crisis. The inflationary crisis of the 1970s, just like its 1930s deflationary forebear, far from being self-apparent, had to be diagnosed, deployed, and debated before it could be institutionally resolved in any manner. Consequently, although the causes of the dislocation of the 1970s were multifarious and far from obvious to all agents, the fact that they impacted so disproportionately on business convinced business as a collective actor that they, rather than the state, needed to resolve this crisis (Blyth, 2002: 152–166, 209–219). However, admitting as much does not simply reduce the politics of the 1970s to the a priori material interests of business.

Creating (and then resolving) uncertainty

First of all, the causes of the crisis of the 1970s, like those of the 1930s, were far from obvious and had to be narrated. Similar to a situation of falling prices, there is nothing in the fact of rising prices that demands specific policies, especially given the ambiguity and historical specificity of ideas concerning the causes of inflation itself. Nonetheless, the fact that those dislocations affected business more than other groups lowered their collective action barriers. However, collective action is far from automatic and depends upon the representation of particular interests as universal interests. While the liberal market-conforming ideas of business had seemingly been delegitimated by the consolidation of embedded liberalism, the fact that such ideas were available for business to use 'off the shelf', so to speak, gave business a tremendous mobilization advantage when inflation opened a window of opportunity in the 1970s. Whereas the state, in its various manifestations during 1930s and 1940s, had to invent its own ideas to provide an institutional resolution to the deflation, business in the 1970s and 1980s was able to take these off-the-shelf ideas, which resonated with their identities as capitalists, repackage and deploy them as a narration of this new 'crisis'.[16]

Even then, such a usage, while instrumental, still does not reduce ideas to unproblematic material interests. The fact that a few conservative business elites wished to reestablish sound finance principles as the governing economic rationale of the state says nothing about how such beliefs were created among other agents, both labor and state, whose cooperation, or at least acquiescence in such a reformation, would be necessary.[17] While inflation may have been an unmitigated 'bad' for some sections of business, it had to be constructed as such for everyone else.[18] This is why business groups in a variety of states mobilized such extensive resources and mounted such lengthy ideological campaigns through think tanks, the media, and in funding politics in the 1970s and 1980s (Blyth, 2002: 152–166, 209–219). Just as occurred during the 1930s, other agents' interests had to be reinterpreted so that they became homologous with business, a homology that was neither obvious nor structurally determined (Blyth, 2003). The fact that such ideas effectively transformed elite opinion meant that, for example, American democrats could no longer argue for social spending and Swedish social democrats could argue for anti-inflationary policies, despite such policies directly hurting both parties' core constituencies. Absent the transformative effect of such ideas on agents' perceptions of their self-interest, and the policy choices of the heirs of embedded liberalism make little sense. In sum, while the 1930s was a clear example of Knightian uncertainty, the 1970s were 'made-Knightian'. While inflation's impact on business was relatively unambiguous, it was quite opaque to everyone else. Such parochial interests had to be transformed into a coherent picture of a general societal interest based around the notion of inflation as a social catastrophe. Given this, affected agents had to engineer uncertainty, rather than resolve it, in order to transform other agents' interests.

How then was this done? Unlike the 1930s where states came to the fore and developed and deployed transformative ideas, the dislocations of the 1970s demanded a response by new actors. I have covered how business groups mobilized around and proselytized neoliberal ideas empirically elsewhere. In this section I wish to revisit this issue more theoretically, as an issue of understanding agency and institutional change in a very different type of critical juncture; a constructed and attenuated juncture where agents, rather than being 'fundamentally uncertain' across the board, actually engineer uncertainty over what a particular economic crisis means, and indeed, when a given situation in fact constitutes a crisis. In this regard the work of Adam Sheingate on political entrepreneurs is particularly valuable.

Rethinking agency and critical junctures

Sheingate, in common with theorists such as Kathleen Thelen, argues that in order to understand institutional change we must shift attention from exogenous to endogenous causes (Sheingate, 2003; Thelen, 2003). This is fair enough, but it does beg a question; to what extent are phenomena such as 'deflations' or 'inflation' truly exogenous? For example, if the analysis of deflation laid out above is plausible, then while a deflation can be triggered by an exogenous cause such as the popping of a bubble or repeated competitive devaluations, the mechanism that produces deflation is, at base, agents' expectations. By 'expecting' falling prices agents act in such as way as to bring them about. Similarly, while periods of inflation may be caused by exogenous shocks such as oil price hikes, it is again agents' responses that either sustain or halt the inflation. Given this, Sheingate suggests that we focus upon 'political entrepreneurship' as the key element that shapes agents' responses, for without this 'creative element' the politics of inflations and deflations would produce a singular response, which the empirical record does not support.

For Sheingate, uncertainty is once again key, but this uncertainty is not generated by agents' 'best interests' failing them. Rather it is an ever present component of all complex institutional environments (Sheingate, 2003: 191). Given the institutional depth, fragmentation, and layering characteristic of modern political economies, 'it is impossible to tell how change in one component will impact other parts of the system' (Sheingate, 2003: 191). Minor changes within existing regimes can have far reaching consequences, so long as political entrepreneurs are attentive to these possibilities. Uncertainty over policy outcomes within institutions therefore 'makes possible the speculative entrepreneurial quality of ... politics' (Sheingate, 2003: 191). Speculative, since the policies proffered by political entrepreneurs can never offer a determinate picture of possible outcomes. Rather, such agents engineer uncertainty about likely future states of the world given present uncertainties, and press for a specific interpretation of how those changes will play out.[19] Political entrepreneurs play on institutional ambiguity to create uncertainty, and then use these uncertainties to generate possible alternative states of the world as 'probable' institutional outputs.

Political and economic regimes are inherently 'ambiguous' in so far as their institutional outputs are always subject to interpretation. For example, whether the Great Society produced a reduction in inequality or a dependency culture depends very much on the interpretation placed upon it. Given this, according to Sheingate, 'entrepreneurship will be more likely where institutional complexities generate uncertainty' (Sheingate, 2003: 193). In such an environment, 'rather than reduce uncertainty, institutions generate the uncertainties that lead to speculative opportunities for entrepreneurial innovation' (Sheingate, 2003: 194). I agree with Sheingate's assessment, but I would add something to it: the politics of losing and the very different type of critical junctures that such a politics engenders.

The politics of losing and gradualist transformation

As noted at the outset, if a given set of institutions enshrines different distributional outcomes, then there will be winners and losers. Embedded liberal institutions created winners among lower income groups and neoliberal institutions created winners among higher income groups, as a cursory glance at GINI coefficients over time demonstrates.[20] But as Thelen notes, 'losers do not necessarily disappear.... For those who are disadvantaged by prevailing institutions, adapting may mean biding their time until conditions shift' (Thelen, 1999: 385, quoted in Alexander, 2004: 9). Building upon this insight, Gerard Alexander argues that 'if an institution leaves intact ... losers' interests in contesting that institution ... it thereby leaves intact [the] necessary ... conditions for its own revision' (Alexander, 2004: 10).

Such losing groups did not disappear during the embedded liberal period, and when the opening provided by the inflation of the 1970s occurred, the losers struck back. By representing existing institutions and their outputs as 'unsustainable', 'perverse', or 'in crisis' – as much of the embedded liberal order was characterized in the 1970s and 1980s – neoliberal political entrepreneurs were able to engage in a politics designed to recast institutionally dependent interests in a new light. As neoliberal entrepreneur par excellence Milton Friedman once put it regarding his 'voice in the wilderness' during the embedded liberal era, the point of him remaining a dissident was precisely to wait for an opportunity to generate uncertainty in the existing order. His objective was;

> to keep options open until circumstances make change necessary. There is enormous inertia, a tyranny of the status quo, in private and especially governmental arrangements. Only a crisis – actual or perceived – produces real change. When that crisis occurs, the actions that are taken depend on the ideas that are lying around. That, I believe, is our basic function: to develop alternatives to existing policies, to keep them alive and available until the politically impossible becomes politically inevitable.
>
> (Friedman and Friedman (1982: viii))

In sum, rather than deflations defeating individual market agents' assessments of their own best interests and providing a statist response, inflations led to an empowerment of political entrepreneurs who were losers under the reflationary regime, which in turn suggests a rather different mode of institutional change from that which statism produced in the 1930s. Specifically, the institutional changes wrought by neoliberal ideas and entrepreneurs was to prove much more gradualist and attenuated than the institutional changes that brought about by the statist responses to deflation.

As noted already, the deflation of the 1930s brought forth three responses; fascism – where society was abolished and the market was preserved; communism – where the market was abolished and society repressed; and an 'embedded liberalism' – where the market was 're-embedded' so that economy and society could coexist through limits on the movement of capital and the redistribution of income. The first two were killed or died of natural causes. The latter regime remained and became the target of neoliberal political entrepreneurs who sought to narrate a crisis of inflation and institutional exhaustion. Such a 'crisis', once created, logically 'required' fundamental changes to existing distributional institutions, but the manner in which those changes occurred was much different from the changes that occurred during the 1930s.

Just as we saw in the differing responses to the 'fact' of deflation in the 1930s, the 'neoliberal critical juncture' was constructed out of different ideal components.[21] The inflation of the late 1970s and early 1980s effected states in different ways. Some states changed institutions immediately, some changed much later.[22] Local entrepreneurs, in Sheingate's terms, focused upon local institutional ambiguities and sought to generate uncertainty over what these institutions were in fact producing. In the Anglo-Saxon countries, the most financialized economies, a crisis of inflation was effectively constructed. Losses to the holders of financial assets were immediate and real. The trick was turning the crisis of the investor class into the crisis of society as a whole (Blyth, 2002: 156–165, 214–219). In the continental welfare states the inflationary crisis may have rendered past policies such as Germany's under-valued exchange rate or France's 'Keynesianism in one country' impossible, but the manner of institutional change undertaken was markedly more incremental than those of the Anglo-Saxon countries and occurred over a much longer time frame. In fact, most change occurred well after the inflation itself ended. It is worth recalling that EMU was constructed in the late 1990s to fight an inflation that ended in the mid 1980s. The neo-liberal turn in such states was legitimated not by the 'perversity' of existing institutions and the need for immediate reform, but by the need to create new (neoliberal) institutions that would guard existing distributions against the vagaries of globalization (Hay and Rosamond, 2000; Rosamond, 1999; Schmidt, 2002). In the Scandinavian countries different narratives of change were deployed. In Sweden a 'crisis of growth' was narrated as a way of disciplining labor's (supposedly) inherent inflationary demands through an external currency anchor, while in Norway, an oil rich state, 'Dutch disease' narratives were deployed to reign in welfare spending despite the Norwegians having the world's 'softest' budget constraint (Blyth, 2002: 238–244).

As well as creating uncertainty, and thus the imperative of reform through such ideas, political entrepreneurs must employ different institutional strategies to push their projects through. A frontal assault on a strongly institutionalized regime is extremely costly. In cases where a regime is weakly embedded, such frontal assaults (particularly in hierarchical political systems) may produce rapid change (Schmidt, 2002). In other more strongly embedded cases, a strategy of 'institutional salami-tactics' may work best. Kathleen Thelen and Wolfgang Streek detail possible mechanisms through which endogenous institutional change can occur over time (Streek and Thelen, 2004). Two of these seem particularly appropriate foci for examining the politics of entrepreneurship and neoliberal change: institutional layering and deliberate drift.

Institutional layering, where one set of institutions is grafted onto the jurisdictional and authoritative boundaries of another set, provides a clear example of how institutions can slowly change through political entrepreneurship. Jacob Hacker provides the example of 401k retirement provisions in the US (Hacker, 2002: 164–170). These tax-free individual retirement accounts were originally intended to promote private saving and were barely noticed by commentators at their inception. However, over time, the effect of these accounts was to residualize the constituency for publicly-funded pensions. As higher earning individuals funded their retirements through these accounts, which had a higher rate of return than social security, they delegitimated public provision by creaming-off the richest pool members and undermining the universalist support that social security had previously enjoyed. What was once seen as an unassailable public commitment was now portrayed as an expensive losing proposition in dire need of privatization.

Drift is a similar incrementalist strategy. As Paul Pierson and others have noted, frontal assaults on popular welfare institutions can be politically costly (Pierson, 1994). However, rather than assault such institutions directly, they can simply be deliberately underfunded. Again, Hacker provides an illustrative example in the realm of US health care. By failing to maintain coverage rates in the publicly funded system (Medicare), health care providers opted out of the system, coverage dropped, and the system as a whole came to be seen as failing. It was, but by encouraging drift between commitments and resources, it was being set up for a fall.

What all this suggests is that in terms of institutional politics, neoliberal regime change may occur in a fundamentally different manner to that which occurred in the prior embedded liberal era and demand a politics that relies upon incrementalism rather than all-or-nothing state action. As Streek puts it regarding (neo)liberalization as a political process;

> Nonliberal reforms in a market economy seem to require 'political moments' ... in which strong governments create and enforce rules that individual actors have to follow, even if they would ... prefer not to do so. Liberalization, by comparison can often proceed without political mobilization, simply by encouraging or tolerating self-interested subversion of collective institutions from below. To this extent,

liberalization ... may face far fewer collective action problems than the organization of capitalism, and much more than the latter, it may be achievable by default.

(Streek and Thelen (eds) (2004: 48))

I can only agree, but again would add the following caveat. Such institutional changes do not occur without political entrepreneurs using ideas to generate uncertainty and reconfigure interests. Only by attending to how reforms are constructed as necessary, as well as focusing upon how they are implemented, can the spread of neoliberalism in the developed states be explained. The spread of neoliberal ideas and policies demands that analysts focus upon a change as institutional incremantalism. A mode of change that depends upon the generation of a different type of uncertainty, and the construction of a different kind of critical juncture from that engendered by deflation. An uncertainty that is deliberately generated through the manipulation of ideas and institutional complexity.

Conclusion: the politics of inflation and deflation revisited

The politics of inflation and deflation are no simple Pavlovian responses to mono-causal environmental stimuli. The 'facts' of falling and rising prices have been interpreted in a multiplicity of different ways and have given rise to a variety of institutions solutions. Deflation demanded no obvious response and neither did inflation. This essay has sought to establish why this is the case, and to suggest why such very different institutional responses, and institutional politics, emerged from these uniform background conditions. At a most general level, I have sought to demonstrate that deflation produced statism and a particular associated set of governing ideas and institutions called 'embedded liberalism'. In response to these 're-embedding' institutions, those most affected by those institutional outputs, business agents, staged a revolt against the consequences of these institutions. That revolt's institutional manifestation, neoliberalism, is the world we find ourselves in today. At such a level of abstraction however, this 'Polanyi in reverse' explanation of the rise of neoliberalism perhaps does not go deep enough. Thus, in seeking to push our understanding of institutional change further, this essay has sought to emphasize the following points.

First, in contrast to the economic regimes developed during the deflation of the 1930s that sought immediate and rather all-or-nothing solutions to the problem of falling prices, the inflationary period of the 1970s onwards saw a variety of ideas deployed, problems identified, and reforms undertaken over a much longer time period. In order to explain this difference it was argued that we should attend to how the different background conditions of inflation and deflation sets boundaries on what type of uncertainty agents face, and indeed on which agents are actually empowered and disempowered during these moments. Both deflationary and inflationary conditions set limits upon the type of actors (state or private entrepreneurs) that respond to moments of dislocation, and each calls forth a particular politics of ideas. While deflation empowers the state, inflation empowers the losers under statist settlements. But while states in periods of deflation can command and control, political entrepreneurs in a democracy must be more circumspect, and work more creatively, over longer periods to effect fundamental changes.[23] Institutional change following inflations tends to be more incremental, with the politics here more attenuated and polyvalent – flickering in and out of prominence and working over time on multiple fronts. In this regard, two strategies of change – institutional layering and deliberate drift – seems particularly germane for analyzing the politics of neoliberal regime change.

Second, this essay sought also to problematize, both temporally and conceptually, the notion of 'critical junctures'. Rather than seeing them as moments where agency becomes more important and structures less important, it sought to conceptualize these moments of rupture as more contested spaces where uncertainty, either Knightian, or what might be termed 'Entrepreneurial Uncertainty', can be harnessed to recast agents' interests. In developing this notion of critical junctures, it was suggested that moments of economic crisis, far from being self-apparent, are in fact politically constructed. Such constructed crises suggests a strong role for agents who develop and deploy ideas that seeks to diagnose a period of dislocation as a crisis of a specific type. By locking-in specific notions of 'what has gone wrong', and crucially 'what must be done' in such moments of uncertainty, the path of institutional change is largely set in the moment of (dis)juncture itself.

In sum, Polanyi's notion of the double movement, once extended in this way, provides a useful heuristic for understanding macroeconomic regime change. The shift to embedded liberalism was in large part the revolt of those most affected by deflation against deflationary institutions (free trade, the Gold Standard, automaticity etc.). Similarly, the shift to neoliberalism was to a large extent a revolt of those most affected by reflation against reflationary institutions (collective bargaining, credit and capital controls etc). However, to leave the discussion there is to miss what is truly interesting – how periods of inflation and deflation empower different agents and engender different ideas about, and hence different tactics of, institutional transformation.

The spread of neoliberalism is not embedded liberalism in reverse, nor is it a simple reaction to some existential economic crisis transparent to agents on the ground (unless crises can credibly be seen to last 25 plus years, take a multiplicity of different forms, and yet have a single cause). The spread of neoliberalism was, and is, a political project. As Polanyi put it so well regarding a different era – 'laissez-faire was planned, planning was not' (Polanyi, 1944: 141).

Notes

1 On supply shocks as the cause of inflation see Blinder (1998); for monetary imbalances *and* positively sloped Philip's curves as possible causes see Friedman (1991); for a long term decline in profits view see Marglin and Schor (1990).

2 For example, as James Mahoney defines it, 'path dependence characterizes ... those historical sequences in which contingent events set into motion institutional patterns ... that have deterministic properties'. Mahoney 'Path Dependence ...' p. 507.

3 For an early example of such a logic see Hall (1986).

4 As Wolfgang Streek puts it 'Both rationalism and functionalism grossly exaggerate the capacity of human actors to know what they are doing before they have done it. As a result they project an image of the social world that is so unrealistically simplistic that it is not even useful as an abstraction' (2002: 7).

5 I thank Bill Connolly for this insight.

6 Which makes it tractable for modeling. Only in such a situation can ideas be usefully viewed as 'road maps' or 'focal points' as suggested by rational choice theorists. But only if one assumes interests themselves as unproblematic. See Goldstein and Keohane (1993: 3–30).

7 A contrast with the natural world is useful here. Causes in the natural world may be highly complex, but our understandings of those causes have no impact on the outcomes we observe. For example, what we believe about the motions of the planets has no impact whatsoever upon those motions. In the economic world however the problem is qualitatively different because the ideas that agents have about the impacts of their actions, and those of others, shapes outcomes themselves. If agents in the economy hold different ideas about how the economy works, this can lead to such agents taking a variety of actions, thereby producing radically different outcomes in the same circumstances. In contrast, agents can have a multiplicity of ideas concerning planetary motion, but such ideas will have no effect on those causal relationships in any way. I thank Robin Varghese for pointing out this lacunae in Knight's own conception of uncertainty to me.

8 For example, if agents believe that deficits cause inflation then deficits will cause inflation because like central bank watching, the belief becomes self-fulfilling. For a similar argument regarding movements on foreign exchange markets see Hopper (1997).

9 Even if the value of real money balances is increasing.

10 Hence why businessmen throughout the 1930s grumbled about 'ruinous competition'.

11 In the 1960s balance of payments disparities were the supposed source of inflation. In the 1970s technological obsolescence, the social limits to growth, money supply excess, and government largess were all to blame. By the 1980s labor market rigidities were to blame, whereas by the 1990s a lack of financial market credibility was the villain of the piece. Inflation, it seems, can be many things to many people. See Watson (2002).

12 Indeed, one of the few sets of employees to have realized this, and to have automatic indexing built into their contracts, are members of the US Congress.

13 Indeed, there was good reason to think that it would not do so given that the 'granddaddy' model of 'spiraling inflation', Friedman's refutation of the Philip's curve, assumes that agents have no money illusion regarding wages, but suffer a permanent money illusion regarding prices. Without such an assumption the model does not work (spiral), but with it, it is incoherent.

14 As Barry notes, '[t]he fact that academic economists accepted this sort of

diagnosis so readily reflects the tendency of positive economics to divide the social realm into one area where the deductive method can be put to work and another that is . . . open to uncontrolled speculation' (p. 285).

15 Especially when one considers that opinion poll data on public perceptions of inflation show a great deal of confusion about what inflation actually is. See Ben Bernanke *et al.* (1999: 17).

16 Indeed, when one strips away the math, there is little 'neo' about 'neoliberalism'. One need only compare the real business cycle theory of the 1990s with its 1920s equivalent to see this. Likewise, ideas such as Rational Expectations and Ricardian Equivalence are likewise very much 'old wine in new bottles'.

17 Since these ideas were far from being correspondence theories of the crisis at hand, it is far from clear why the policies that they demanded represented a universal interest, especially when one considers the short-term costs of deflation.

18 For example, labor has no obvious interest in deregulation, unless labors' interests are recast as those of consumers rather than as workers. Transforming identity, and thus interest, has no structural prerequisites. I thank Adam Sheingate for this observation.

19 For example, tax cuts are ever popular, but whether they will result in a huge deficit or endless prosperity depends entirely upon how agents react to those cuts, which is itself an entrepreneurial opportunity. If Ricardian equivalence were real, all tax cuts should be offset by saving, but the fact that they are not suggests that multiple possible outcomes are possible from the same policies.

20 See www.lisproject.org/

21 What sociologists refer to as bricolage.

22 For example, one might think of how rapidly collective bargaining institutions were reformed in the UK (early 1980s), in Sweden (early 1990s) and in Germany (if at all – 2004 onwards?).

23 Especially when the 'crisis' that brought them to prominence – inflation – has long since vanished from the developed world and shows no sign of returning anytime soon.

* I wish to thank Andrew Lawrence, Jeff Legro, Carol Mershon, Herman Schwarz, and Ravi Roy for their comments on earlier versions of this paper.

References

Alexander, G. (2004) 'Power, interests, and the causal effects of institutions', paper presented at the 14th bi-annual conference of Europeanists. Chicago, IL, March 11–13.

Barro, R. (1995) 'Inflation and economic growth', *Bank of England Quarterly Bulletin* 35(2): 1–14.

Barry, B. (1985) 'Does democracy cause inflation? Political ideas of some economists?' in Lindberg, L.N. and Maier, C.S. (eds) *The Politics of Inflation and Economic Stagnation: Theoretical Approaches and International Case Studies.* Washington, DC: The Brookings Institution.

Beckert, J. (1996) 'What is sociological about economic sociology? Uncertainty and the embeddedness of economic action', *Theory and Society* 25(6): 803–840.

Bernanke, B, Laubach, T., Mishkin, F., and Posen, A. (1999) *Inflation Targeting: Lessons from the International Experience.* Princeton: Princeton University Press.

Blinder, A. (1998) *Central Banking in Theory and Practice.* Cambridge: MIT Press.

Blyth, M. (1997) 'Any more bright ideas? The ideational turn of comparative political economy', *Comparative Politics* 29(2): 229–250.

Blyth, M. (2001) 'The transformation of the Swedish model: economic ideas, distributional conflict, and institutional change', *World Politics* 54(1): 1–26.

Blyth, M. (2002) *Great Transformations: Economic Ideas and Political Change in the Twentieth Century*. Cambridge: Cambridge University Press.

Blyth, M. (2003) 'Structures do not come with an instruction sheet: interests, ideas, and progress in political science', *Perspectives on Politics* 1(3): 695–706.

Buchanan, J. and Wagner, R.E. (1977) *Democracy in Deficit: The Political Legacy of Lord Keynes*. New York: Academic Press.

Collier, R.B. and Collier, D. (1991) *Shaping the Political Arena: Critical Junctures, the Labor Movement and regime Dynamics in Latin America*. Princeton: Princeton University Press.

Davidson, P. (1991) 'Is probability theory relevant for uncertainty? A post-Keynesian perspective', *Journal of Economic Perspectives* 5(1): 129–143.

Denzau, A.T. and North, D.C. (1994) 'Shared mental models: ideologies and institutions', *Kyklos* 47(1): 3–31.

Dequech, D. (2000) 'Fundamental uncertainty and ambiguity', *Eastern Economic Journal* 26(1): 41–60.

Elster, J. (2000) 'Rational choice history: a case of excessive ambition', *American Political Science Review* 94(3): 685–695.

Friedman, M. (1991) *Monetarist Economics*. London: Institute of Economic Affairs.

Friedman, M. and Friedman, R. (1982) *Capitalism and Freedom*. Chicago: University of Chicago Press.

Goldstein, J. and Keohane, R.O. (eds) (1993) *Ideas and Foreign Policy: Beliefs, Institutions and Political Change*. Ithaca: Cornell University Press.

Greenfeld, L. (2001) *The Spirit of Capitalism: Nationalism and Economic Growth*. Harvard: Harvard University Press.

Hacker, J. (2002) *The Divided Welfare State*. Cambridge: Cambridge University Press.

Hall, P.A. (1986) *Governing the Economy: The Politics of State Intervention In Britain and France*. Oxford: Oxford University Press, 1986.

Hay, C. (1996) 'Narrating crisis: the discursive construction of the "Winter of Discontent"', *Sociology* (30)2: 253–277.

Hay, C. (1999) 'Crisis and the structural transformation of the State: interrogating processes of change', *British Journal of Politics and International Relations* 1(3): 317–344.

Hay, C. and Rosamond, B. (2000) 'Globalization, European integration and the discursive construction of economic imperatives', IPSA XVIII World Congress of Political Science, Quebec City.

Hopper, G.P. (1997) 'What determines the exchange rate: economic factors or market sentiment?' *Federal Reserve Bank of Philadelphia Business Review*, Sept.–Oct., pp. 17–29.

Katznelson, I. (2003) 'Periodization and preferences: reflections of purposive action in comparative historical social science', in Mahoney, J. and Rueschemeyer, D. (eds) *Comparative Historical Analysis in the Social Sciences*. Cambridge: Cambridge University Press.

Keynes, J.M. (1964) *The General Theory of Employment, Interest and Money*. London: Harcourt Brace.

Kirshner, J. (1999) 'Inflation: paper dragon or trojan horse', *Review of International Political Economy* 6(4): 609–618.

Kirshner, J. (ed.) (2003) *Monetary Orders: Ambiguous Economics, Ubiquitous Politics*. Ithaca: Cornell University Press.

Knight, F.H. (1921) *Risk, Uncertainty and Profit.* Boston and New York: Houghton Mifflin Company.

Mahoney, J. (2000) 'Path dependence in historical sociology', *Theory and Society* 29: 507–548.

Marglin, S.A. and Schor, J.B. (eds) (1990) *The Golden Age of Capitalism: Reinterpreting the Postwar Experience.* New York: Oxford University Press.

Meidner, R. (1969) 'Active manpower policy and the inflation unemployment-dilemma', *Swedish Journal of Economics* 71(3): 161–183.

Mitchell, T. (1988) *Colonizing Egypt.* Cambridge: Cambridge University Press.

North, D.C. (1990) *Institutions, Institutional Change and Economic Performance.* Cambridge: Cambridge University Press.

Pierson, P. (1994) *Dismantling the Welfare State: Reagan, Thatcher and the Politics of Retrenchment.* Cambridge: Cambridge University Press.

Pierson, P. (2000) 'Increasing returns, path dependence, and the study of politics', *American Political Science Review* 94(2): 251–267.

Pierson, P. (2000a) 'Not just what, but when: timing and sequence in political process', *Studies in American Political Development* 14(1): 72–92.

Polanyi, K. (1944) *The Great Transformation: the Political and Economic Origins of Our Time.* Boston: Beacon Press.

Rosamond, B. (1999) 'Discourses of globalization and the social construction of European identities', *Journal of European Public Policy* 6: 4 (special issue), 652–668.

Ruggie, J.G. (1982) 'International regimes, transactions, and change: embedded liberalism in the postwar economic order', *International Organization* 36(2): 379–415.

Schmidt, V. (2002) *The Futures of European Capitalism.* New York: Oxford University Press.

Sheingate, A. (2003) 'Political entrepreneurship, institutional change, and American political development', *Studies in American Political Development* 17: 185–203.

Stone, D.A. (1989) 'Causal stories and the formation of policy agendas', *Political Science Quarterly* 104 (2): 281–300.

Streek, W. (2002) 'Notes on Complimentarily', paper presented for a CEPREMAP seminar, Paris, April.

Streek, W. and Thelen, K. (eds) (2004) *Institutional Change in Advanced Capitalist Economies,* manuscript.

Thelen, K. (1999) 'Historical institutionalism in comparative politics', *Annual Review of Political Science* 2.

Thelen, K. (2003) 'How institutions evolve: insights from comparative historical analysis', in Mahoney, J. and Rueschemeyer, D. (eds) (2003) *Comparative Historical Analysis in the Social Sciences.* Cambridge: Cambridge University Press, pp. 208–241.

Tobin, J. (1972) 'Inflation and unemployment', *American-Economic Review* 62(1): 1–18.

Watson, M. (2002) 'The institutional paradoxes of monetary orthodoxy: reflections on the political economy of Central Bank independence', *The Review of International Political Economy* 9(1): 183–196.

6 Evolution in macroeconomics

Principles, policy, and performance

*Graham Bird**

Introduction

In some kind of economic utopia, policy makers would be able to draw on a well-specified and accurate model of how the economy works. They would be able to forecast the economic future with precision and foresee deviations from an agreed set of policy objectives. They would possess an arsenal of policy weapons, knowing full well what the effects of these would be. And they would be able to design a package of policies to deliver the economic performance they desired.

Although there have been times when perhaps it seemed that this utopian ideal was being approached, these proved to be false dawns. The reality is that a process of trial and error, combined with changes in macroeconomic theory, which often occur when inherited models no longer seem to fit the facts, has brought about an evolution in macroeconomics. On some occasions changes have been more marked than on others, and the gradual process of evolution has been interspersed with periods of apparent macroeconomic 'revolution'.[1]

Policy makers do not inhabit an economic utopia. Their life is complicated by debates about what constitutes good economic performance. There may be competing macroeconomic models, with each claiming to offer a better representation of how an economy functions. No one model need necessarily be universally superior to all others. Not all economies are the same. And individual economies may change, meaning that a model that seems to work for a time may not work for ever. There may be disagreement about the efficacy of individual policy instruments, and economic forecasting may, at best, only give a broad indication of future performance. At worst, it may mislead. Moreover, policy makers may not have all the data they would like to have. On top of this, and since it will be politicians who make the final decisions about economic policy, it is not just a matter of calculating the effects of policies on economic performance, but also of calculating the political reaction to these induced changes in performance.

Policy design will not always, or even frequently, be the outcome of applying the 'scientific method', where an hypothesis is initially formulated on the basis of observation and is then rigorously tested against the evidence, in the light of which it is either rejected or accepted. Instead, economic policy may often be driven by political imperatives, or at least it may be limited by political constraints. Having said this, decision makers will possess what Denzau and North (1994) describe as shared mental models on the basis of which they design policy; even if the thought processes involved are to some extent subconscious. They need to believe that policies will have the effects that they want, and they need to have some basis upon which they can judge this.[2]

To understand the current status of macroeconomic policy – or indeed economic policy in general – it is helpful to consider how we arrived at it. How we got to be where we are depends on where we started and on the path we have taken.

This chapter traces out the interaction between mainstream macroeconomic principles, policy and performance over a protracted period of time. The interaction is multi-directional. For example, on occasions advances in economic theory lead to changes in policy that then affect performance. On other occasions, changes in performance lead to a reassessment of both underlying principles and policy design. Basically, any component of principles, policy and performance may affect, and in turn be affected by, any other component. The perspective of the chapter is panoramic and the interpretation subjective (hence the relatively small number of references). Rather than concentrating on any particular country, the article tries to identify a global pattern to evolution in macroeconomics. However, from time to time, country-specific examples will be used to illustrate more general points. The focus of the chapter is on macroeconomics, but this is not to deny the importance of the microeconomic foundations of many macroeconomic phenomena.

The layout is as follows. The next section briefly discusses the objectives of macroeconomic policy, and examines how the performance of economies can be evaluated by using them. Subsequent sections then look at particular time periods and discuss the connections between the dominant macroeconomic model, or shared mental model of the time, the policy direction that was derived from the model and the performance of economies. They also investigate why changes in policy direction occurred. A final section makes some general observations about the evolution of macroeconomics and conjectures about the future.

Macroeconomic policy objectives

Just as physicians have various criteria by which they judge whether a patient is healthy or not, so the health of an economy can be assessed in terms of whether certain objectives are being met. Conventionally these include operating the economy at full capacity, or, less ambitiously, avoiding mass unemployment, achieving low inflation, maintaining a rate of economic growth that allows living standards to rise, as well as having a sustainable balance of payments. In one sense, the last of these is more of a constraint than an objective in its own right.

There is much that can, and has been said about these objectives. Space limits our discussion here, but a few questions will illustrate the complexities. Is it always the case that unemployment is bad? Might it be, for example, that, in the short run, rising unemployment is associated with rising productivity? Is it always beneficial to reduce inflation? Or could a modest rate of inflation actually be preferable to zero inflation in the sense that it facilitates economic growth by allowing resources to be redirected to sectors where they are needed most? Does economic growth necessarily imply improved living standards or are there other issues that need to be examined, such as population growth, the composition and distribution of output, and the quality of the environment, before such an assumption can be legitimately made? These are difficult questions.

In addition to them (and other related questions), there is the matter of how the objectives may be combined to provide an overall indicator of performance. This will be particularly problematic if there are trade-offs between the policy objectives such as avoiding inflation and unemployment and if such trade offs differ over the short run and the long run. From the viewpoint of national welfare, is a specific reduction in inflation worth a related specific increase in unemployment? There are then the missing variables. Three or four macroeconomic aggregates will not give a complete picture of an economy's performance. But, this having been said, politicians may be looking for a broad rather than detailed picture, and, in this respect, information about unemployment, inflation, economic growth and the balance of payments may provide sufficient guidance. Large amounts of unemployment, rapid inflation, stagnant or falling living standards and an unsustainable balance of payments will all tend to be deemed unacceptable by policy makers. They will design policy with the intention of avoiding such problems or correcting them should they already exist.

Policy will not be plucked serendipitously out of thin air. Policy making is not a random process. Those making policy will need to have some basis upon which to believe that the policies they adopt will have the results they seek. But this basis need not come from objective and informed analysis; it may be relatively unscientific. Politicians may be influenced by lobby groups, or by advocates of a particular policy via the media. They may believe what it is politically convenient for them to believe, or what coincides with their own personal experience or prejudices. How have macroeconomic theory, policy and performance interacted over the last 100 years or so, and how have things evolved? It is to this question that the following sections turn.

Before the 1920s and 1930s. The classical model: is policy necessary?

Prior to the 1920s and 1930s, the dominant theoretical ideas were based on the 'classical' model. These ideas had stark implications for economic policy. With regards to unemployment, classical theory argued that the labour market would clear; giving an equilibrium real wage and an equilibrium level of employment. According to this model, anyone who was out of work was therefore voluntarily unemployed, believing that the real wage on offer did not compensate them adequately for the disutility of working. There was no such thing as 'involuntary' unemployment. Although frictions in the operation of the labour market might cause temporary unemployment for relatively few, mass unemployment would not be a problem. It would only be if the labour market was not allowed to operate freely that difficulties could arise. Thus, if for some reason the real wage was stuck at a level above its equilibrium level, then there would be an excess of labour supply over labour demand, i.e. unemployment; but this could be eliminated by simply restoring labour market flexibility. Unemployment was not a policy concern.

As its name implied, the so-called Quantity Theory of Money gave a similarly simple account of inflation. According to this theory, it would be increases in the stock of money that would lead to increases in the price level, i.e. inflation. There would be no real effects on output. So, in order to control inflation, all governments had to do was to prevent rapid growth in the money supply. While monetary growth was claimed to have no real effects, classical theory was relatively silent about what did affect output and economic growth. Instead, it preferred to take these as 'given', with them being determined by factors that lay outside the model.

Apart from preventing rapid monetary expansion, it is easy to see how classical theory supported a laissez-faire approach to economic policy. The message was basically not to intervene, but to allow markets to operate freely. Much the same message also applied to the balance of payments. Here, gold standard theory claimed that balance of payments disequilibria would be automatically eliminated by the gold flows to which they gave rise. A country with a balance of payments deficit and an excess of imports over exports would have to transfer gold to other countries to pay for its excess imports. Its domestic gold stock, and by assumption its domestic money supply, would decline. By the Quantity Theory of Money, the domestic price level would then also fall since, as already noted, permanent full employment was assumed. The fall in prices would improve competitiveness which would then eliminate the deficit. This course of events would be mirrored by what would happen in surplus countries where gold inflows would lead to an increase in the domestic money supply, a higher price level and a loss of competitiveness. The policy message for governments was not to intervene to offset the effects of the balance of payments on the domestic money supply. Adjustment would automatically occur and there was no need for a policy response.

In general, classical theory therefore vindicated a minimalist approach to macroeconomic policy. The classical model offered politicians an attractive prospectus since it suggested that any unemployment would be temporary and would not be large scale, that inflation could easily be avoided, and that balance of payments disequilibria would be automatically corrected. Economic growth would be what it would be; but was in any case beyond the control of governments. So, what was the need for macroeconomic policy? This comfortable state of affairs was rudely disturbed by the inter-war recession.

Inter-war depression: the Keynesian revolution

What went wrong? While the reasons might be open to debate, the reality was that the inter-war years of the 1920s and the 1930s saw an escalating number of severe economic problems, including mass unemployment, economic recession, balance of payments and financial crises, and falling world trade. Politicians were motivated to try and do something about this state of affairs, even though classical theory implied that they were relatively impotent. The mass unemployment of the Great Depression, in particular, generated dramatic political instability. Political leaders would have probably been unwise merely to inform those 'on the dole' that they were voluntarily unemployed! It seemed either that classical theory was right but that governments were not following its policy implications, or that the theory was wrong and was based on unrealistic assumptions.

Dissatisfaction with economic performance and a desire to do something about it coincided with, and may have helped cause, a reassessment of inherited macroeconomic theory. After all, a theory that predicted full employment sat uneasily alongside global recession. Keynesian economics was conceived and alongside it there was a recognition that more data about an economy's economic performance needed to be collected. Historians of economic thought will no doubt continue to debate just how revolutionary Keynesianism was.[3] It seemed to combine elements of both evolution and revolution. It was evolutionary in as much as it simply asked what would happen if money wages were in fact downwardly inflexible so that real wages could not be reduced by cutting money wages. It was also evolutionary in as much as it continued to assume that real wages moved counter-cyclically, rising during recessions and falling during economic expansions.[4] But it was revolutionary in as much as it attributed unemployment to a deficiency in aggregate demand. People were out of work because there was not enough demand for the goods and services they would produce. Previously, Say's Law had claimed that supply created its own demand. Keynes argued that, by raising aggregate demand, prices would tend to rise, real wages would tend to fall – a fall that would not be resisted by workers – and employment would increase.

However, the private sector could not be relied upon to increase aggregate demand; so, economies could settle – as they appeared to have done – in an unemployment equilibrium. The policy message was clear and in sharp contrast to that emerging from the classical model. According to Keynesian theory, governments had the responsibility to manage aggregate demand in a way that would deliver non-inflationary full employment. Macroeconomic policy needed to be discretionary, interventionist and aggressive. In circumstances of unemployment, measures should be taken to boost aggregate demand. With inflation, measures should be taken to reduce aggregate demand.[5]

But how should governments set out to manage aggregate demand? What policy instruments were at their disposal, and which should they use? Keynesian analysis was also quite clear on this. Monetary policy was deemed to be relatively ineffective, since Keynesians believed that the demand for money was unstable. This ruled out changes in the money supply having a predictable effect on the rate of interest. They also believed that the demand for money was highly elastic with respect to the rate of interest, meaning that the effect of changing the money supply on the rate of interest would only be small. Finally, they believed that even if the rate of interest could be changed in a relatively large and predictable way by manipulating the supply of money, this would not exert a significant effect on total expenditure. Investment, for example, was seen as being inelastic with respect to the rate of interest.[6] In these circumstances, Keynesians de-emphasised both the monetary sector, which was viewed as being relatively passive, and monetary policy. Instead, fiscal policy was heralded as the principal tool for managing aggregate demand. Keynesians advocated 'functional finance' with governments being encouraged to aim for fiscal deficits (an excess of government expenditure over tax revenue) when there was unemployment, and fiscal surpluses where employment was 'over full' and inflation was the problem. Keynesian economics empowered policy makers who believed that, armed with its policy advice, they would be able to run economies in such a way as to deliver full employment in the post-war world.

There are also interesting contrasts between Keynesianism and Marxism. The Great Depression appeared to be consistent with Karl Marx's prediction of a cumulative capitalist crisis in which the rich would be unable to spend all of their gains from exploiting the poor with the consequence that aggregate demand would not keep up with the growth of aggregate supply. But Keynes provided an answer to Marxism through the use of government spending to make good any shortfall in demand from the private sector. While many conservatives saw Keynes as a critic of capitalism, he saw himself as a defender of it against Marxism.

Keynesianism did not only influence views about domestic macroeconomic policy. Following the trials and tribulations of the inter-war years, policy makers set out to reform the international monetary system. The blueprint for a new system was laid down at Bretton Woods in 1944, with Keynes himself as one of the principal designers and negotiators. The Bretton Woods system was designed to help avoid the competitive macroeconomic and commercial policies that had characterised the 1920s and 1930s. Countries were encouraged to defend pegged exchange rates where balance of payments deficits were expected to be temporary and only adjust the exchange rate rather than the domestic economy if the disequilibrium was fundamental. This meant that macroeconomic policies in individual countries would, in effect, be co-ordinated. Countries with relatively rapid inflation would experience balance of payments deficits and would have to contract domestic demand. Those with persistent surpluses would be encouraged to expand demand. Consistent with Keynesianism, it was envisaged that the principal tool for managing demand would be fiscal policy; swings in the balance of payments would make it difficult to control the domestic money supply.[7]

As the world embarked on the post-war era in 1945, it therefore had a new approach to both domestic and international macroeconomic policy. The approach was informed by developments in macroeconomic theory and coincided with a strong political motivation to avoid returning to the global recession of the 1930s. The political climate of the time was favourable to a central role for governments in 'running the economy'.

The 1950s and 1960s: Keynesianism rules!

In the 30 or so years following the Second World War, Keynesian ideas dominated macroeconomic policy design. By the end of the 1960s, President Nixon was claiming that 'we are all Keynesians now', and few challenged his assertion. Advances in macroeconomic theory continued to occur that had an influence on policy, but these were seen as being largely consistent with basic Keynesian ideas. A.W. Phillips discovered an empirical relationship between unemployment and inflation which seemed to confirm that there was a trade-off between the two; lower unemployment implied faster inflation, and vice versa (Phillips, 1958). Although open to a number of theoretical interpretations, the Phillips Curve happily coexisted with the idea that the preferred combination of unemployment and inflation could be achieved by the appropriate pursuit of fiscal policy, designed to manage aggregate demand. Similar developments in international, or open economy macroeconomics, that culminated in the so-called Mundell–Fleming model, also supported the idea that, in a world with pegged exchange rates, fiscal policy should be assigned to achieve domestic macroeconomic objectives (Mundell, 1963).[8]

Indeed, provided policy makers were not too ambitious, it seemed that running an economy was not that difficult. To be over-ambitious would have been to target a particular combination of inflation and unemployment. Instead, policy makers seemed to settle for a range of combinations that were satisfactory. For as long as an economy performed within this range, there was little incentive to change policy. It was only when performance moved outside it that policy action was required. And, even then, theory seemed to be fairly unequivocal about the way it should change. After all, the Phillips Curve seemed to confirm that the problem would either be excess inflation or excess unemployment, and in either case Keynesian ideas provided the policy solution. If inflation (and related balance of payments deficits) were the problem, then contractionary fiscal policy was needed. If unemployment (and related low rates of economic growth) were the problem, then fiscal expansion was the solution. Economies exhibited a pattern of stop-go cycles.

Debates took place about the causes of inflation, with some economists claiming that it was 'pushed' by increasing costs rather than 'pulled' by excessive demand, and there was some experimentation with policies designed to directly control wage costs. But again, these ideas did little to challenge the dominance of Keynesianism. Similarly, this dominance served to focus policy attention on trying to stabilise economies. Less attention was paid to underlying economic growth. Theoretical advances in this area did not have a clear policy message and often appeared rather abstract. Indeed, neo-classical growth theory (neo-classical in the sense that it assumed 'full' employment) had more to say about what would not affect long run growth than about what would affect it. According to this theory, the driving force for growth was improving productivity, but this remained unexplained and was 'exogenous' to the model. Governments subsidised education and scientific research in an attempt to stimulate productivity growth, and there were some European attempts at 'indicative planning' as a way of trying to stimulate self-fulfilling expectations of faster growth. The idea here was that if governments said they expected faster growth to occur, businesses would invest more in anticipation of the greater demand for their products, and this investment would generate the economic growth that was anticipated. But such attempts largely failed and lacked credibility. At the same time, economic growth continued to occur at a rate that allowed living standards to rise and so policy-makers had little reason to be overly concerned about it. There was no political imperative to increase the rate of economic growth.

To some observers, the 1950s and 1960s are retrospectively seen as a 'golden age' in terms of global macroeconomic performance. It is easy to see why policy makers might have begun to suffer from hubris. Keynesian policy seemed to be working for domestic economies and the Bretton Woods system seemed to be delivering a satisfactory global economic environment, although there were some doubts about whether the system provided countries with enough liquidity to fend off occasional speculative attacks on currencies. But pride comes before a fall. And a fall was what was awaiting the global economy in the 1970s.

The mid-1970s: inflation, recession, unemployment and the shift in mental models

Globally, there was evidence of things starting to go wrong in the early 1970s. In practice, the Bretton Woods system placed too much reliance on countries being able to eliminate balance of payments disequilibria without altering their exchange rates. As a consequence, exchange rates were allowed to become seriously misaligned which, in turn, eroded confidence in the durability of currency pegs and led to speculative crises. The system eventually could not take the strain and collapsed in 1973, with industrial countries largely adopting flexible exchange rates.

Some notable economists had, for some time prior to the collapse of the Bretton Woods system, been making the case for flexible exchange rates (Friedman, 1966; Meade, 1955). Milton Friedman, and an expanding group of 'monetarists', had also been criticising Keynesian conventional wisdom and suggesting that macroeconomic policy should be based on the stable control of the money supply rather than on targeting an exchange rate and using discretionary fiscal policy (Friedman, 1968).[9] Although they had not fully persuaded policy makers of their point of view, a sharp global deterioration in economic performance in the mid-1970s created a situation where policy makers were forced to rethink the design of macroeconomic policy.

The deterioration affected the world economy as a whole and impinged on all the main indicators of performance. Inflation hit a post-war high and coincided with economic recession and rising unemployment. The coexistence of accelerating inflation and rising unemployment, so-called stagflation, seemed to be at odds with the Phillips Curve and transmitted a mixed signal to policy makers trained in a Keynesian tradition. High inflation argued for contractionary policy, whilst simultaneous recession and unemployment argued for expansionary policy. A challenge was laid down both for macroeconomic theory and policy to explain what was going on and to do something to improve economic performance.

Although a series of ideas were put forward in an attempt to explain events in the mid-1970s, such as the quadrupling of oil prices, it was monetarism that most effectively filled the vacuum created by the disillusionment with Keynesian economics. Although intellectually distinct, monetarism often formed part of a broader neoliberalist agenda that placed emphasis on the role of markets and de-emphasised the role of governments. There were three elements to the monetarist component of this agenda. The first was that it offered an explanation of the global economic crisis. According to monetarists, rapid global monetary expansion at the end of the 1960s and early 1970s had, with a long lag, resulted in rapid inflation in the mid 1970s.[10] Governments had then sought to counter this by pursuing contemporary contractionary policies that resulted in recession. The second element was that it offered a critique of

Keynesianism. According to monetarists, fiscal expansion merely resulted in rising interest rates (as governments borrowed to finance their budgetary deficits) and a decline in private sector expenditure, with this being 'crowded out' by increased government expenditure. The end result was not larger output but merely a larger government sector. Moreover, discretionary fiscal policy would only work after a lag. In practice, it could turn out to be destabilising rather than stabilising.[11] The third element was that monetarism offered an explanation of the disappearing Phillips Curve. To do this, it re-processed the classicists' idea about voluntary unemployment in the form of the 'natural' rate of unemployment; a rate which was dictated by workers' preferences as between work and leisure, and by the general efficiency of labour markets. Attempts to reduce unemployment below this natural rate by conventional Keynesian policies would, so monetarists claimed, lead to accelerating inflation. For a time, this would catch workers by surprise. Money wages that had been negotiated on the assumption that inflation would be lower would, as a result, fall in real terms, and given that labour was now cheaper, there would be a temporary increase in employment, and a fall in unemployment. But, after a lag, workers would realise that their real wages had fallen and that their money wages would not buy as much as they thought they would. They would then adapt to the higher rate of inflation. Real wages would be restored to their old equilibrium level and unemployment would return to its natural rate. In the long run, there would be no trade-off between unemployment and inflation. Keynesian fiscal expansion would lead to no long term fall in unemployment, but merely an enduring increase in inflation.

But, third, the monetarists' message was not just negative. Unlike Keynesians, they believed that the conditions necessary for effective monetary policy, based on controlling the supply of money, did hold. They believed that the demand for money was stable, that, since money had few substitutes as a medium of exchange, the demand for it was insensitive to changes in the rate of interest, and that expenditure decisions were responsive to changes in interest rates. Monetarists placed the monetary sector and monetary policy centre-stage. However, they remained acutely sceptical of discretionary monetary policy, and favoured a monetary 'rule' as the basis for macroeconomic policy. By always allowing the money supply to increase at an annual rate based on the trend growth in the demand for money, they believed that the economy would be stabilised automatically. During a recession, the supply of money would grow faster than the demand for it, and the rate of interest would fall, inducing a movement out of recession. During a period of inflation, the demand for money would grow more rapidly than the supply of it, and the rate of interest would rise, dampening down the inflation.

In summary, the mid-1970s witnessed poor economic performance, dissatisfaction with previous policy design, and an apparently simple and coherent explanation of why things had gone wrong and what could be done to put them right. Policy makers who had previously pursued Keynesian policies began to pay more attention to monetary aggregates. But it was not really until the turn of the decade that political leaders opted to pursue a 'monetarist experiment'.

The 1980s: the monetarist (and neoliberal) experiment

Monetarism offered newly-elected conservative politicians the world over pretty much what they wanted; key figures were Ronald Reagan in the United States and Margaret Thatcher in the United Kingdom. It focussed on inflation which was seen as the major problem to be overcome. It was easy to comprehend, and carried with it a clear policy message. And it argued for a more limited role for government and against fiscal deficits as a way of stimulating aggregate demand. In this respect it co-existed happily with the broader neoliberal approach to economic policy which political leaders at the time were keen to implement. The only potential political downside was that the notion of adaptive expectations suggested that a period of relatively high unemployment (above the natural rate) would have to be endured in order to break built-in inflationary expectations; this was politically unattractive. The political clincher for monetarism came in the form of the theory of rational expectations, which was an extension of older monetarist ideas. This theory claimed that people formed their expectations about future inflation rationally, by looking forward rather than by learning from, and adapting to, previous errors. Thus, if governments announced policies that people believed would reduce inflation, and seemed unswervingly committed to them, workers would immediately adjust their wage claims downwards to allow for the lower inflation they expected. This would mean that real wages would not rise and that higher unemployment could be avoided, even in the short run. Rational expectations theory offered politicians a prospectus of reducing inflation without increasing unemployment. It is hardly surprising that it proved appealing.

To go along with this, new classical macroeconomics, of which rational expectations and the assumption of wage flexibility were key aspects, seemed to confirm the impotence of discretionary macroeconomic policy. The 'Lucas critique' claimed that policy designed on the basis of observed previous behaviour would be ineffective because it would alter that behaviour in a way that neutralised the effects of the policy (Lucas, 1976). With such theoretical justification, politicians enthusiastically embraced a 'hands off' approach to macroeconomic policy.

If fiscal policy was left with any role, it was as a microeconomic supply-side tool designed to influence the incentive to work through changes in tax policy. Politicians rejoiced in the prospect that they could both stimulate economic growth and increase tax revenue by reducing tax rates.

According to the so-called Laffer Curve, if taxes were too high, the additional incentives associated with reduced tax rates would so stimulate economic activity that lower taxes would indeed raise tax revenue, allowing fiscal deficits to be reduced or eliminated. However, not all monetarists subscribed to the more radical elements of supply-side economics, (on this issue see the chapter by Denzau and Roy in this volume).

Did monetarism work? Certainly inflation fell, and generally speaking has continued to fall to relatively low levels ever since. The snag is that the trick was not really to reduce inflation. The trick that new classical macroeconomics claimed it could perform was to reduce inflation without causing recession and rising unemployment. This it failed to deliver. The world economy moved into a sharp recession at the beginning of the 1980s and unemployment rose.[12] On top of this, a number of other things undermined the monetarist experiment. First, it proved very difficult to define, let alone control, the supply of money, with the result that monetary targets were almost always missed. Second, as the stock market crash in 1987 confirmed, financial markets seemed to be relatively unstable. Ironically, and in part as a result of financial innovation, the degree of historic stability in monetary relationships that monetarist researchers had discovered began to break down at approximately the same time as monetarist policies began to be adopted. Third, monetarism implied that governments needed to be relatively unconcerned about interest rates and exchange rates; their focus was on the quantity rather than the price of money. As it turned out, governments were not indifferent about either interest rates or exchange rates because these have political repercussions.[13]

Monetarism was therefore gradually abandoned, more quickly in some countries than others, but generally without the razzamatazz that had surrounded its adoption. Continuing success at maintaining low inflation also made it easier to sideline monetarism. When the stock market crisis came in the 1987, governments responded to their anxiety that it could lead to a sharp recession by relaxing fiscal policy; this was an essentially Keynesian response.

Macroeconomic policy after monetarism

The demise of monetarism created an interesting dilemma and raised an important question. What model would now provide the theoretical framework for the design of policy? The classical model had been tried and deemed to fail. The Keynesian model had similarly been the basis for policy during the post-war period but encountered problems. Now monetarism and new classical macroeconomics had not delivered what had been promised. There was no fundamentally different alternative model that remained yet to be tried. In essence, economic disequilibria are corrected either by a change in prices or by a change in quantities. The macroeconomy is no different. Classical and new classical macroeconomics claimed that disequilibria would lead to changes in prices but not quantities whereas Keynesians claimed that quantities would change. Who was right?

Perhaps they both were. The answer to the above dilemma was to look for something in between the two extremes. A more eclectic model has therefore emerged. This emphasises the importance of time. Thus, over the long run, it is suggested that classical and new classical macroeconomics is basically correct. It is prices rather than quantities that change as a result of attempts to manage the economy. In the long run, an economy's output depends on the determinants of economic growth and largely on productivity growth. In the short run, however, quantities may be affected by macroeconomic policy. Economies may be Keynesian in the short run and classical in the long run. This 'new Keynesian' approach once again opened the door to active macroeconomic policy.

But, at the same time, policy makers have learned from experience and have been anxious not to repeat their previous mistakes. What lessons have been taught? First, that it probably helps to have a central focus for macroeconomic policy. Second, that the scope for fine tuning an economy via discretionary macroeconomic policy is limited. Third, that although running fiscal deficits on a quasi permanent basis is likely to lead to problems one way or another, they may be appropriate in some sets of circumstances. Fourth, that it is extremely difficult, if not impossible, to tightly control monetary aggregates, but that rapid monetary expansion should be avoided. Over the long run, high inflation is likely to hinder rather than help economic growth.

Having absorbed these lessons, policy makers have either demonstrated enhanced skill or have experienced good fortune. In broad global terms, and on average, mass unemployment has been avoided, inflation has been kept low, and economic growth has been sustained. Macroeconomic performance has been satisfactory and there has been no incentive to fundamentally rethink issues surrounding macroeconomic theory and policy. There have, however, been notable deviations from this overall picture. For example, many European countries have encountered relatively high unemployment and Japan struggled during the 1990s and early 2000s to escape from protracted economic stagnation.

How have the lessons described above permeated the design of macroeconomic policy since the end of the 1980s? For many, the central focus for macroeconomic policy has been sought either by managing exchange rates or by inflation targeting. For example, many Latin American economies experimented with exchange rate-based stabilisation under which they used the policy of pegging the value of their currencies as a means of showing a commitment to reducing their formerly rapid rates of inflation. Many European economies followed similar policies although they did not have the same inflationary history as Latin America. For a short time in the early 1990s, the UK joined Europe's Exchange Rate Mechanism. Again the idea was to use the announced intention of defending the value of the currency to exert counter-inflationary pressure.[14] Europe as a whole moved towards full monetary integration as a means of co-ordinating macroeconomic policy and keeping inflation low.

Where countries have adopted flexible exchange rates, they have gone for an alternative focus as a way of keeping inflation low. The control of monetary aggregates which, in principle, could have been an option had of course been shown to be problematic; hence there has been a move to inflation targeting. This is based on monetary policy but, unlike monetarism, focuses on the price of money (and in particular the real rate of interest) rather than on the quantity of money. Interest rates are set in order to help achieve targeted inflation rates. In terms of the issues that divided Keynesians and monetarists, a compromise view has developed. Although it is accepted that the demand for money may be unstable and that the supply of money is difficult to tightly control, it is still assumed that expenditure decisions can be significantly influenced by changes in interest rates. Even in the US, where inflation targeting has not formally been adopted, counter-inflationary policy has rested largely on the manipulation of real interest rates. Furthermore, concerns that politicians would exploit monetary policy for political ends by relaxing it shortly before elections and tightening it after them, creating a 'political cycle', have been mitigated by a trend towards granting central banks greater independence.

While monetary policy has been resuscitated in the context of inflation targeting, fiscal policy has regained some of its former prominence as an instrument for aggregate demand management, but only subject to strict constraints. These were informally spelt out as part of the Washington Consensus which, at the beginning of the 1990s, sought to capture broad areas of agreement in terms of economic policy. Avoiding large fiscal deficits was an important part of the consensus. Since its zenith the Washington Consensus has evolved in various ways, but the commitment to 'sound' macroeconomic policy remains a central element (see Bird, 2001, for a discussion of this evolution). In Latin America where there has been a reassessment of some components of the Consensus, the eschewal of lax fiscal and monetary policies that were previously associated with a heterodox approach to economic policy seems to have remained broadly intact, (see, for example, Bird and Helwege, 1997 for a brief description of the evolution of economic policy in Latin America). In the UK, the Chancellor of the Exchequer imposed a 'golden rule' upon himself not to allow fiscal deficits to persist over complete economic cycles; thereby permitting himself to run deficits in economic downturns. More formally, the Eurozone countries adopted the Growth and Stability Pact which sets out to constrain their ability to run fiscal deficits. However, frustration with the rigidity of the pact resulted in some European economies breaking the rules to enable the automatic stabilisers built into fiscal policy to have their full effect. During a recession, tax revenue tends to automatically fall and government expenditure to rise. Whether the right balance between discretion and constraints relating to fiscal policy has been achieved remains an open question.

Concluding remarks: the future for macroeconomic policy

Over the years, the debates about and experiments with macroeconomic policy have led to a form of global consensus concerning what can and cannot be expected from it, and how it should be operated. A more balanced, nuanced and expedient eclecticism has replaced the earlier extremist dogmas. In part, this reflects changing currents of thought in terms of mainstream theory, where extreme classical and Keynesian ideas have been replaced by an analytical hybrid. From a policy perspective the ideas that at one end of the spectrum saw macroeconomic policy as unnecessary or impotent, and at the other end saw it as capable of fine tuning an economy have been superseded by a view that it can help to deliver policy objectives but that there are also limits on what it can achieve.

There is agreement that inflationary expectations need to be anchored in sound monetary policies, but that against this background there is some scope for using interest rates as a way of manipulating aggregate demand. In terms of fiscal policy there is broad agreement over the claim that fiscal deficits should not be allowed to become excessive, but rather less agreement over what constitutes 'excessive'. Thus in the US in the mid 2000s the debate continued about the effects of the fiscal deficit, and in Europe a debate raged over whether fiscal constraints were too binding given levels of unemployment.

Since the mid 1970s, and recognising that there are exceptions, one of the key macroeconomic successes has been the reduction in inflation. While, again, unemployment has been a non-trivial problem in some countries, the success in reducing inflation has not been bought at the cost of mass unemployment. For the countries where unemployment has remained unacceptably high in political terms, the challenge has been to devise policies to help lower it without reverting to over-expansionary macroeconomic policies. These may involve labour market and 'structural' policies. However, unlike the 'structuralism' found in Latin America prior to the 1990s this newer type of structural policy is seen as a complement to, rather than a substitute for policies of macroeconomic stabilisation. There have also been suggestions that the world needs to find an efficient mechanism for internationally co-ordinating macroeconomic policy.[15]

Amongst theoreticians the attention bias has appeared to shift towards gaining a better understanding of economic growth, which after all has the largest impact on economies' ability to deliver improved living standards. Macroeconomics has come a long way, but challenges still remain.

Notes

1 'Apparent' in the sense that, although the changes have sometimes been presented as 'revolutionary', they have also sometimes been interpreted as involving relatively minor modifications to what has gone before. We shall not pursue the question of how much change there has to be in order to justify the claim that it is revolutionary as opposed to evolutionary.

2 Keynes famously observed that there may be lags in the influence of economic theory on policy, with contemporary decision makers being the slaves of defunct theory. The idea here is that it takes time for people to get into a position where they can make policy decisions. Although their decisions will be based on the theory that was the conventional wisdom at the time they were trained, things may have subsequently moved on. Current policy will therefore be based on old theory. Intriguing as this idea is, it assumes that theory does indeed make progress and that policy makers lack a mechanism for keeping up to date (or choose not to use it). Both of these claims could be open to some degree of debate.

3 In this chapter, we shall make no distinction between the economics of Keynes and Keynesianism, although the latter may have been a simplification, or even a caricature, of Keynes's ideas. Those readers who are interested can consult Keynes (1936), Hicks (1937) and Leijonhufvud (1968).

4 Macroeconomic theory has subsequently sought to explain why, in practice, real wages appear to move pro-cyclically. Ironically, such a pattern is not inconsistent with the basic idea that, in the short run, output is relatively flexible and prices relatively rigid.

5 In the aftermath of the 1930s recession, the focus of Keynesianism was on unemployment rather than inflation.

6 Keynesian theory also tended to relate consumption and saving much more to variations in the level of income than to those in the rate of interest. In this respect, Keynesians again differed from classicists.

7 This was because the monetary authorities needed to buy and sell the domestic currency in order to defend its price relative to other currencies. If they were seeking to control the price of the currency, it meant that they would be unable at the same time to control its quantity.

8 Although Keynes expressed considerable interest in international monetary affairs, the basic Keynesian model had little to say about the balance of payments. Its focus was on a 'closed' economy.

9 From a monetarist perspective, a key argument against pegged exchange rates was that they largely eliminated a government's ability to control the money supply. There was therefore a logical consistency in advocating flexible exchange rates.

10 Monetarism claimed, in Friedman's words, that inflation was 'always and everywhere a monetary phenomenon'. It also claimed, however, that money would influence inflation after a long and variable lag. Apart from anything else, this ruled out the possibility of using monetary policy as a discretionary tool.

11 There were, however, 'automatic stabilisers' built into fiscal policy since, as an economy expands, tax revenue tends to rise, and government expenditure tends to fall, and vice versa.

12 To some extent, the Third World debt crisis that occurred at the beginning of the 1980s was associated with the strict monetary policies being pursued in advanced economies. These not only drove up world interest rates and the cost of borrowing, but also generated recession which made it more difficult for indebted developing countries to earn foreign exchange by exporting.

13 Home owners, for example, find it distasteful to see interest rates and the costs

of their mortgages rise. Meanwhile, an appreciating exchange rate makes imports cheaper and can result in deindustrialisation and a loss of domestic jobs. Governments will not be indifferent about the loss of political support that may result.

14 In the case of the UK, it seemed to turn out that defending the exchange rate carried a high cost in terms of unemployment and recession. It is surely not coincidental that the UK withdrew from the ERM in 1992 when living standards in the UK were falling. This was another example of unsatisfactory macroeconomic performance leading to a change in policy. In the UK's case, the change in policy was to move, initially informally but then formally, to inflation targeting.

15 For example, in the early 2000s, the echoes of competitive macroeconomic policies were heard with the US accusing Asian economies in general, and China in particular, of maintaining under-valued exchange rates and of pursuing insufficiently expansionary fiscal and monetary policies. The reluctance of Asian economies to accept a weakening in their current account balance of payments, according to the US, constrained its ability to reduce its own increasing current account deficit. Some observers have seen the stand off as constituting a threat to future global macroeconomic stability.

* I am grateful to Tom Willett and Pierre Siklos for their helpful comments on an earlier version of this chapter. The usual disclaimer applies.

References

Bird, Graham (2001) 'What happened to the Washington Consensus?', *World Economics* 2(4): 33–51.

Bird, Graham and Helwege, Ann (1997) 'Can liberalisation survive in Latin America?', *Millennium: Journal of International Studies* 26(1): 31–56.

Denzau, Arthur T. and North, Douglass C. (1994) 'Shared mental models: ideologies and institutions,' *Kyklos* 47(1): 3–31.

Friedman, Milton (1966) 'A case for flexible exchange rates', in *Essays in Positive Economics.* University of Chicago Press, 157–203.

Friedman, Milton (1968) 'The role of monetary policy', *American Economic Review* 58: 1–17.

Hicks, John (1937) 'Mr. Keynes and the classics: a suggested interpretation', *Econometrica.*

Keynes, John Maynard (1936) *The General Theory of Employment, Interest and Money.* Macmillan.

Leijonhufvud, Axel (1968) *On Keynesian Economics and the Economics of Keynes: A Study in Monetary Theory.* Oxford.

Lucas, Robert (1976) 'Econometric policy evaluation: a critique', *Carnegie Rochester Conference Series,* 1.

Meade, James E. (1955) 'The case for variable exchange rates', *Three Banks Review* 27: 3–27.

Mundell, Robert A. (1963) 'Capital mobility and stabilisation policy under fixed and flexible exchange rates', *Canadian Journal of Economic and Political Science* 29: 475–485.

Phillips, A.W. (1958) 'The relation between unemployment and the rate of change of money wage rates in the United Kingdom, 1861–1957', *Economica* 25: 283–299.

Part II

National and regional experiments with neoliberal mental models

7 The neoliberal shift in US fiscal policy from the 1980s to the 1990s

A shared mental model approach to understanding coalition-driven policy shifts

Ravi K. Roy and Arthur T. Denzau

This chapter applies Denzau and North's (1994) "Shared Mental Models" framework to examine the influence of neoliberal ideas in shaping deficit reduction in the US from Reagan to Clinton. We argue that distinct fiscal strategies pursued by the Reagan and Clinton administrations were informed by the distinct strands of the neoliberal shared mental model that each adopted. We further explore the influence of these mental models in providing the coalitional glue that brings like-minded actors together in support of common policy agendas and strategies. In that regard, we examine the mental models and associated coalitions that were involved in shaping deficit reduction agendas and strategies in the 1980s and 1990s.

Policy trajectories and strategies pursued by policy actors are often informed by the mental models they possess about policy environments and how actors will behave in them.

Policy environments structure behavior by providing formal institutional rules, as well as informal incentives and disincentives that encourage certain behaviors and discourage others. The mental models that actors hold about these environments help guide them in their policy decisions and political maneuverings. Mental models help shape actors' beliefs in those environments about which options will maximize their interests and which will not. Coalitions are made up of individuals and groups that have adopted a shared view of the policy environment and helped them identify their related interests in it. It is therefore, mental models that provide the coalitional glue that brings interests together in the first place.

Neoliberals composed of Laffer-curve supply-siders, traditional conservatives, and monetarists were aligned in their general criticism of excessive growth in what John G. Ruggie (1996a) refers to as the "New Deal State" shared mental model that became associated with the expansion of "big government" in the 1960s under President Johnson and "The Great Society" programmatic initiatives.

Neoliberal ideas developed salience in the political mainstream in the US in the early 1980s with the election of Ronald Reagan. The Reagan administration offered sharp criticism of government's capacity for "waste, fraud, extravagance, and abuse" (Niskanen, 1988: 25). Reagan demonized the "Great Society" and the growth of "Big Government" for creating conditions that resulted in excessive taxation and high levels of government deficit spending. Reagan identified both of these factors as the culprits that had led to America's entrepreneurial decline. In order to reinvigorate entrepreneurial energies, in 1981 President Reagan pursued a neoliberal agenda that sought to cut taxes, restrain domestic spending (except in the area of defense), and balance the budget. According to William Niskanen (1988), "The new Reagan administration recognized that the President's overall economic plan could not succeed without a sharp reduction in the growth of spending that was built into current law and policy" (p. 25). Increasing numbers of policymakers came to share Reagan's policy views. According to Michael Boskin (1987), by the mid-1980s, policymakers in the United States were growing increasingly concerned "that deficits contribute to high interest rates, both directly through government borrowing in credit markets, and indirectly through uncertainty over their likely economic effects" (p. 171).

Deficit reduction under Reagan

During the Reagan era, distinct neoliberal mental models were adopted by contending political coalitions. Reagan's fiscal policy initiatives were largely informed by the Laffer-curve supply-side strand of the neoliberal shared mental model. Friction within Reagan's own cabinet arose out of distinct supply-side camps. Laffer-curve supply-siders such as Ronald Reagan, George Gilder, Arthur Laffer, Robert Mundell, Richard Rahn, and Jude Wanniski along with Norman Ture, Craig Roberts, and Steve Entin believed that supply created its own demand and that cutting marginal tax rates would create the investment incentives required to boost private economic output sufficiently to take care of the deficit (McClure and Willett, 1983: 60). As a result, this group's first commitment was to reduce marginal tax rates and as a secondary commitment, to reduce the rate of increase in federal spending. Monetarists and Conservatives such as Michael Boskin and Martin Feldstein asserted that tax cuts were important, but that spending cuts should be the administration's first concern. In the short-term, this group believed that tax cuts alone would not be sufficient to balance the budget (ibid.). Others such as David Stockman, Murray Weidenbaum, and Alan Greenspan regarded tax cuts as a necessary ingredient for growth but viewed them operating over the long term and focused instead on reducing government spending as their top priority (Niskanen, 1988: 5).

Michael Boskin (1987) brings out that Reaganomics was a complex mix of neoliberal ideas and policy positions containing preferences that sometimes coincided with one another and sometimes ran counter to one another (p. 2). Although Laffer curve supply-siders were the front-runners to reduce marginal tax rates, monetarists and conservatives were not far behind. They were concerned however, about how proposed tax cuts would affect the deficit. In the end "none of the schools got exactly what they wanted" (ibid.). Boskin asserts that monetarists such as Milton Friedman complained that the Federal Reserve Board's control of the money supply was too erratic, whereas Laffer-curve supply-siders such as Paul Craig Roberts complained that the tax cut agenda was not pursued aggressively enough from the very beginning and was ultimately offset by subsequent tax increases (ibid.). Meanwhile, fiscal conservatives, such as Martin Feldstein, who lauded the administration's efforts to cut domestic spending and reform America's antiquated tax structure, simultaneously expressed grave misgivings about the enormous growth in deficit spending (ibid.).

Mental models and intra-partisan coalitions in the Reagan era

At least five significant intra-partisan coalitions were apparent in the US fiscal policy subsystem in the early 1980s. Two of these coalitions followed policies, programs and procedures that appeared to be sympathetic with the logic of the New Deal State shared mental model. The other three of these coalitions however, shared a mutual dislike for the notion of "big government" that had become associated with the New Deal State shared mental model. These three coalitions adopted distinct aspects of the neoliberal shared mental model. All three shared similar views about the need for promoting private initiative and limiting government predation and expenditure. Partisan politics however, would play a significant role in explaining the mixed success of neoliberalism during the 1980s, particularly in the area of deficit reduction. The first coalition included the traditional Democratic spenders – adherents of the New Deal State shared mental model who strongly believed in the merits of government-led strategies and programs for promoting economic growth and full employment. Second were the traditional Republican spenders – a gradually waning group of Nixon-like Republicans who were moderate adherents of the New Deal State shared mental model who simultaneously supported politically popular tax cuts proposed by the president. Next came Republican tax cutters – Laffer-curve supply-siders led by Ronald Reagan – a faction of neoliberals who regarded tax cuts as the best means for restoring private incentives and entrepreneurial initiative. Although viewed as important, fiscal prudence and deficit reduction initiatives were ultimately sacrificed to build the necessary political support for their tax cut plan.

Republican tax cutters were able to forge a political compromise with Republican spenders in a manner that enabled them to become the dominant faction in the party at the time. Fourth, Republican deficit cutters composed of traditional conservatives and monetarists represented a distinct faction within the party and believed first and foremost in the need for fiscal prudence and a balanced budget as well as tax reform as a secondary issue. They vigorously pursued policy changes that would limit uncontrolled spending. As a relatively smaller voice in the party, they experienced many setbacks in this area in the 1980s. (They nevertheless pressed forward with their cause into the 1990s and were ultimately successful in elevating the position of deficit reduction in the Party's political discourse.) Last, Democratic deficit cutters composed mainly of conservatives represented a small but cohesive faction of deficit-reduction neoliberals who included a group of conservatives within the party. Their conservative views made them, in many ways, indistinguishable from their Republican deficit-cutter counterparts (e.g. the partisan crossover of Congressman Phil Gramm, TX). Their views on public spending ran counter to the Democratic Party's more leftist beliefs at that time. By the 1990s, their neoliberal views on fiscal discipline would be championed by the more conservative leadership of Bill Clinton and the "New Democrats."

Game tree illustration of contending coalitions and mental models in the Reagan era

Table 7.1 identifies the executive leaders and each of the coalitions and organizes them according to their broad normative core (New Deal State or neoliberal) belief systems and policy preferences. Figure 7.1 provides a chart of the significant coalitional players in the fiscal policy subsystem during the Reagan era (1982). The policy preferences for the five intrapartisan coalitions are presented using a non-cooperative three-player sequential game tree in Figure 7.2. As both Republican and Democrat deficit cutters shared critical core policy beliefs regarding the need for fiscal prudence, we have included both under the category of Player 1. Republican tax cutters I are represented as Player 2. Because Democrat and Republican spenders demonstrated little or no significant commitment to deficit reduction, we have placed them jointly in the category of Player 3. The equilibrium path for the players in this game is indicated by large bold type in the figure. Whenever possible, each coalition in a policy subsystem will pursue strategies that will enable them to realize their respective core as well as secondary policy preferences (Sabatier and Jenkins-Smith, 1993). That said, deficit cutters in the 1980s sought to pursue cuts in spending as their core objective and tax cuts as their secondary objective. Tax cutters, by way of contrast, would be expected to pursue tax cuts as their core objective and spending cuts as their secondary objective. A coalition is likely to abandon secondary objectives if

Table: 7.1 Executive leaders and different dimensions of the neoliberal shared mental model

	Core beliefs	*Secondary beliefs*	*Core policy issue*	*Secondary policy issue*
Reagan & core partisan supporters: (Laffer-Supply-Side Tax Cutters)	Government is inefficient; government predation leads to poor economic performance.	Monetary and fiscal stability is necessary for economic growth.	Seeks to restrict the extent of predation through minimal taxation.	Seeks overall stability through deficit reduction and spending restraint.
Clinton & core bipartisan supporters: (Traditional Conservatives-Deficit Cutters)	The purpose of government is to provide an economic environment of fiscal and monetary stability; key for growth is investment in human and financial capital.	Government can encourage economic growth through investment in human and financial capital by reducing the tax burdens on certain kinds of economic behavior.	Monetary stability encourages investment. Seeks overall stability through deficit reduction and spending restraint.	Seeks to offer tax credits and tax relief for investment in research and development, small business, and education.

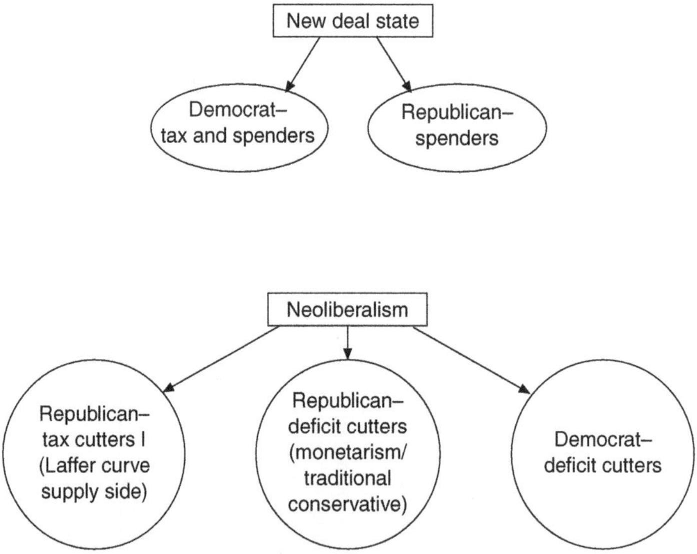

Figure 7.1 Contending shared mental models and related subsystem coalitions in the Reagan era.

they come in conflict with core objectives. The conflict that existed between tax cutters and deficit cutters in the 1980s illustrates this point and is reflected in our game tree model. Disagreement over core objectives between tax cutters and deficit cutters led each to pursue divergent fiscal approaches.

The game tree model illustrates that the highest utility for deficit cutters (Player 1) was to pursue strategies that enabled them to enact tax and spending policies consistent with producing a balanced budget. Where that was not possible, the next best option for deficit cutters was to pursue cuts in spending even at the expense of compromising their (secondary) tax cut objective. If they failed in their main objectives to cut spending rates, deficit cutters could make mild gains if their (secondary) tax cut objectives were realized. Finally, deficit cutters gained nothing if neither core nor secondary objectives were realized.

Given the ambitious size of the tax cuts sought by Reagan and other tax cutters, reaching a consensus with core deficit cutters was very difficult. The best case for tax cutters (Player 2), therefore, was to cut taxes and leave spending patterns unchanged. If tax cutters were to pursue a genuine deficit reduction strategy, they would have no choice but to compromise over the size and structure of their preferred tax cut agenda. If tax cutters failed in their core objective to cut taxes to the degree they desired, the next best strategy for them was to pursue spending cuts,

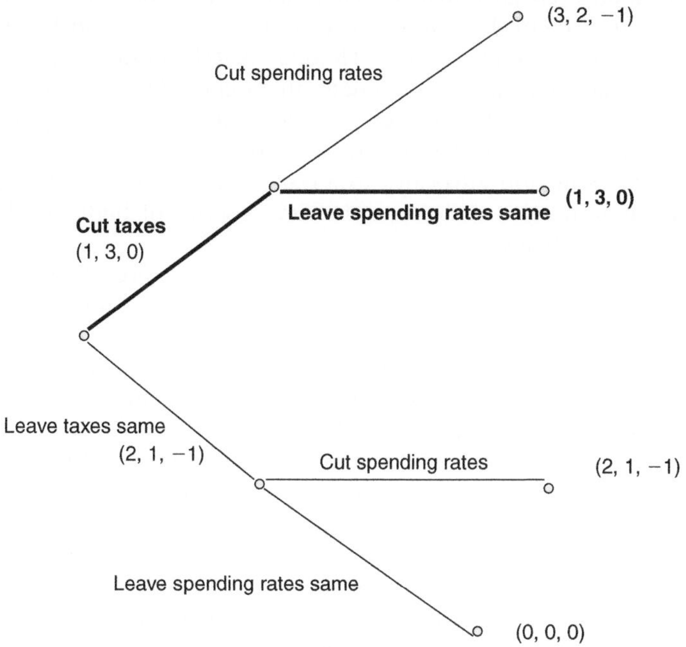

Figure 7.2 Non-cooperative sequential game tree illustrating preference options of significant coalition players in the fiscal policy subsystem during the Reagan era (1982).

which represented a secondary objective of their policy agenda. Finally, tax cutters, like deficit cutters, gained nothing if tax and spending policies remained unchanged. Therefore, the Nash Solution is that "cut taxes" and "leave spending the same" wins.

Explaining what happened under Reagan

The Reagan administration was able to make gains in bringing down real federal spending during its first term in office. Despite this success however, spending remained substantially higher than initially projected. According to Niskanen (1988) "by FY 1985, moreover, real federal spending was 15 percent higher than the initial forecast, about 120 billion in 1985 dollars, and this difference between actual and forecast real spending was almost identical to the increase in the real deficit" (p. 26).

As spending continued to increase throughout the 1980s, Reagan's Laffer-curve supply-side agenda came under intense fire by deficit cutters who were not satisfied with Reagan's efforts on achieving a balanced budget. Deficit cutters were important partners in the Reagan-led neoliberal consensus and were a group that the administration could not ignore.

Deficit cutters sponsored an initiative that would compel both Congress and the president to control spending. The Balanced Budget and Emergency Control Act, or Gramm–Rudman–Hollings (GRH), outlined spending reduction goals that would eliminate the deficit by 1991. GRH institutionalized the core beliefs of deficit cutters. Although the original deficit reduction targets were ultimately abandoned, GRH provided a forum for deficit reduction advocates to advance their views and bring greater public awareness to their issue through a series of high profile public hearings and debates.

Disagreements between members of Congress and the president persisted over how much should be cut from domestic programs versus defense and whether taxes should be lowered or increased. A major point of contention for the administration and Congress was the law's provision demanding across-the-board cuts in military and social spending. Deficit reduction was the core issue championed by staunch fiscal conservative deficit cutters, such as Senators Phil Gramm (R-TX) and Warren Rudman (R-NH). They believed first and foremost that tax cuts should be matched with cuts in public spending; they were opposed to tax cuts that would negatively affect the deficit.

Reagan and other Laffer-curve supply-siders in the other offices of government supported the president's tax reduction plan. The source of tension between the two conservative groups was based on distinct neoliberal mental models. These differences led to a rift in the broader neoliberal consensus. Hard-core deficit cutters hoped that GRH would compel Reagan and other Laffer-curve supply-siders, along with traditional "tax-and-spend" members in Congress, to begin serious work to reduce the deficit.

Critics belonging to both the left and right of center raised serious concerns about GRH and its lack of flexibility in allowing increased spending during a recession that might be necessary to initiate a government-led economic recovery. Alas, these differences led to political conditions that made the adoption of GRH in its original form politically unfeasible. In the initial budget that was to be submitted in 1986, Congress passed a resolution that enabled it to attain the GRH deficit target for FY 1987 at $144 billion. President Reagan and his other ardent tax cutter coalition allies rejected the 1986 budget because key provisions contained within it called for a significant tax hike as well as cuts in defense spending. Democrats in Congress, however, would not allow defense spending to be exempted from the budget cuts, especially when domestic programs were not. This led to a budget standoff between the White House and Congress that continued into the next fiscal year.

According to Harry Havens (1986), "several years of frustration over the deficit, rising constituent concern, and the absence of any other apparent way to break the stalemate combined to stimulate a ground swell of support for [GRH]" (p. 9). Havens brings out that Senators Bob Dole,

Pete Domenici, Bob Packwood (then chairman of the Senate Finance Committee), and Lawton Chiles (ranking Democrat on the Budget Committee) built a consensus to institute the high profile deficit reduction bill. Havens further reveals that this group "committed themselves to making [the bill] technically workable, predictable in its effects, and perhaps most important, acceptable to the House Democratic leadership" (p. 9). Although the Reagan administration and the Democrat-led Congress were able to reach a consensus on social spending that enabled them to come close to the prescribed spending limits in the late 1980s, the recession of the early 1990s rendered the original targets virtually unobtainable.

When analyzed within a larger context, GRH marked a critical point in the deficit reduction effort (James Miller, III 1994: 34–35). GRH institutionalized the core values of deficit cutters and provided a platform for legitimizing cuts in social spending. The shift in the policy discourse that GRH initiated in the 1980s paved the way for the Budget Enforcement Act of 1990 (BEA). The BEA was finally enacted as the Omnibus Budget Reconciliation Act of 1990 (OBRA 1990)" (Kosters, 1992: ix). It amended enforcement procedures for budget discipline laid out in both Gramm–Rudman (1985) and the Congressional Budget Act (1974) (Kosters 1992: ix). The OBRA called for tax increases, cuts in projected increases in expenditures under entitlement programs, and a $500 billion reduction in budget deficits over fiscal years 1991 to 1995 (Kosters, 1992: ix). According to James Edwin Kee and Scott V. Nystrom, "the negotiations leading to this agreement considered the status of the deficit and led to a philosophical shift from 'no new taxes' to 'fair taxes'."

Deficit reduction in the Clinton era

Gramm–Rudman–Hollings helped reshape the fiscal policy subsystem in the United States. The first phase of the deficit reduction initiative in the United States began in the 1980s and was characterized by a targeted criticism of the New Deal State shared mental model and the enormous tax-and-spending engine that supported it. The second phase of the deficit reduction effort reemerged in the policy agendas of the "New Democrats" led by Clinton and deficit cutter Republicans.

Convinced by the arguments of deficit cutters, Clinton and "New Democrats" came to believe that fiscal prudence was the best means for encouraging new investment in the private sector and, hence, higher growth overall. The rise to power of Clinton and the "New Democrats" such as Al Gore, Al From, Dave McCurdy, Will Marshall, Ed Kilgore, Joseph Lieberman and others, sought to redefine the party's basic policy ideas in line with neoliberal thinking. Clinton adopted a conservative-based deficit reduction focus that distinguished his neoliberal agenda from Reagan's Laffer-curve supply-side-based tax reduction approach. The expectations of financial markets and, more precisely, the bond market came to occupy a central concern in Clinton's overall economic strategy (Woodward, 1994: 69). The administration was acutely concerned about the unprecedented gap between short-term and long-term interest rates.(Woodward, 1994: 69). Clinton and deficit cutters in the administration came to believe that the best way to bring long-term interest rates down was to control growth of the federal deficit (Woodward, 1994: 69.)

Clinton was impressed with Greenspan's assessment that without sizable and credible deficit plan, another recession would rear its head in less than two years (Walker, 1996: 169). Clinton abandoned the economic stimulus package to "jump start the economy" that he had been peddling throughout the 1992 election when it was initially defeated in Congress. Deciding not to press the issue further, he adopted a deficit reduction-focused fiscal strategy instead. Clinton's commitment to the deficit reduction issue was visible through his appointments of such deficit "hawks" as Alice Rivlin, Lloyd Bentsen, Robert Rubin, Lawrence Summers, and Leon Panetta to key economic policy positions in his cabinet (Pierson, 1998: 144).

Mental models and intra-partisan coalitions in the Clinton era

The conflict between tax cutters and deficit cutters in the Reagan era carried over into the 1990s. Figure 7.3 illustrates the intrapartisan coalitions in the US fiscal policy subsystem from Clinton to Reagan. The fiscal policy subsystem during the Bush and Clinton eras was, therefore, shaped by the conflict between Laffer-curve supply-side tax cutters and a new bipartisan coalition of monetarist/traditional conservative deficit cutters. This new coalition of deficit cutters (which included many Republicans) was willing to abandon secondary objectives of their own tax relief (in some cases even conceding to tax increases) to alleviate deficit spending that had skyrocketed to nearly $300 billion. Three significant intrapartisan coalitions had evolved by 1992. First, Republican deficit cutters, now a larger voice in the party, had successfully established deficit reduction as a central issue within the party. Second, Democratic deficit cutters included a group of neoliberals collectively known as New Democrats led by Tim Roemer (IN), Calvin Dooley (CA), and Jim Moran (VA), and a more conservative group known as "Blue Dog Democrats" led by Gary Condit (CA), Collin Peterson (MN) and John Tanner (TN), as well a number of House members belonging to the DLC-affiliated caucus known as the "Mainstream Forum." By the early 1990s, these neoliberal groups had managed to capture their Party's mainstream agenda under the leadership of Bill Clinton. Third, Republican tax cutters II emerged, composed of a combination of those who saw tax cuts as the main vehicle for restoring private incentive and entrepreneurial initiative as well as those who supported them because they were politically popular.

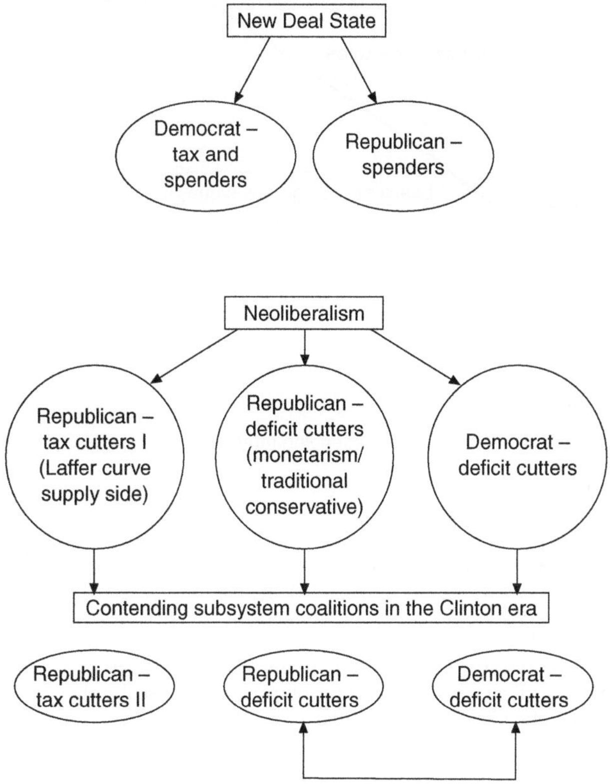

Figure 7.3 Contending shared mental models and related subsystem coalitions from the Reagan and Clinton eras compared.

Game tree illustration of contending coalitions and mental models in the Clinton era

The preference rankings regarding distinct fiscal strategies for the three intrapartisan coalitions are presented using a non-cooperative three-player sequential game tree in Figure 7.4. When Clinton and the "New Democrats" took power in 1993, partisan politics initially kept Republican deficit cutters from cooperating with Democratic deficit cutters despite the fact that they shared core policy beliefs. After the Republicans won the House and Senate in the 1994 election, however, Clinton found the Republican deficit cutters far more willing to cooperate with his administration than they had been when they were in the minority. The game tree illustrates that both groups had an incentive to cooperate on the basis of their shared core policy beliefs. We place Republican deficit cutters as Player 1

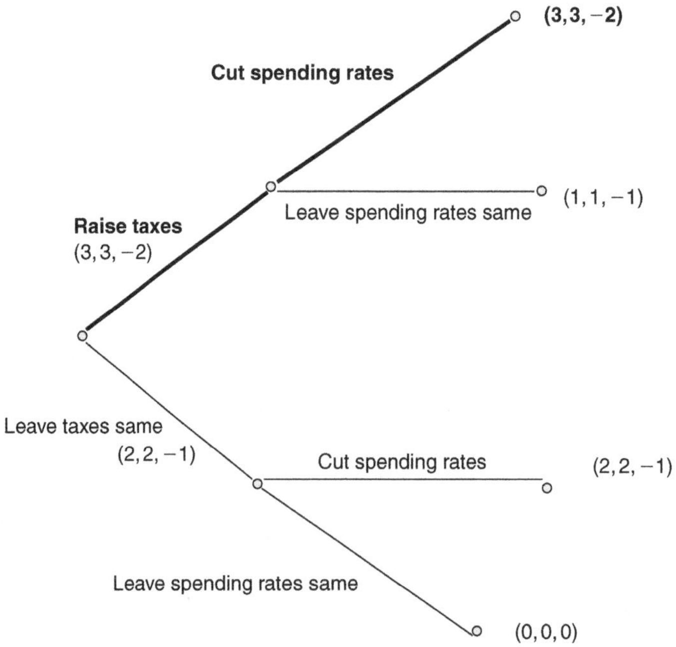

Figure 7.4 Non-cooperative sequential game tree illustrating preference options of significant coalition players in the fiscal policy subsystem during the Clinton era (1990s).

and Democratic deficit cutters as Player 2. Republican tax cutters II are assigned as Player 3. In the changed policy subsystem, the game tree model illustrates that the best scenario for both Republican and Democratic deficit cutters was to pursue spending cuts while actually supporting some increases in taxes. This put them at direct odds with Republican tax cutters II, whose best expected outcome under the changed structure of the fiscal policy subsystem could only be "Leave taxes the same." The equilibrium path for the players in this game is indicated by large bold type in the figure. The model illustrates that the Nash solution "raise taxes" and "cut spending" wins.

What happened under Clinton

Having committed to a balanced budget, Clinton was able to build support among a critical group of disenchanted Republican voters who agreed with Ross Perot on the urgency of bringing down deficit spending. Having gained control of both houses of Congress, Republican Party deficit hawks, such as John Kasich (who asserted that "there is no compromise with a balanced budget") and Senate Budget Committee Chairman Pete Domenici, exhibited a stronger willingness to work with the Clinton administration on the deficit-reduction issue.

Clinton found that he had to make tough political choices regarding entitlements and taxes. In fact, conflicts between the president and Congress over contending budget proposals led to two government shutdowns before Congress and the president reached a compromise in April 1996 (Meeropol, 1998: 1). Clinton found himself in a political conflict involving how much revenue would come from cuts in existing entitlements versus how much would come from new taxes. The administration ultimately pursued cuts in discretionary spending in areas such as housing, transportation, and defense but wanted to protect funding for entitlements, the environment, and education. Protecting entitlements was the defining issue in the conflict over deficit reduction strategies between the White House and opponents in Congress. Paul Pierson reiterates that disagreements revolving around this issue led to two budget impasses in 1995 and FY 1996 (Pierson, 1998: 128).

The conflict between deficit cutters and tax cutters in the Republican Party was heightened in 1996 in the Senate as ardent tax cutters, such as Trent Lott (R-MS), were sharply divided against deficit cutters, such as Pete Domenici (R-NM). Tax cutters in the House proposed and mobilized support for substantial tax cuts while the Senate plan, by contrast, did not call for any additional tax cuts until it could be assured of a balanced budget by 2002. Once it was balanced, deficit cutters in the Senate reasoned, Congress could then enact as much as $170 billion in tax cuts over seven years (*Congressional Quarterly*, June 17, 1995: 1718). Tax cutters, such as Bill Archer (R-TX) stated that they wanted all the unanticipated surplus of FY Budget 2000 to be applied to an even larger tax cut than Republicans had initially planned. Acting in accord with Democratic deficit cutters, such Republican deficit cutters as Budget Committee Chairmen Rep. John R. Kasich (R-OH) and Sen. Pete Domenici (R-NM) refused to commit to further tax cuts until a viable solution was reached for shoring up Social Security and Medicare.

New Democrats, along with members affiliated with the Mainstream Forum and the Blue Dog Democrats cooperated with moderate Republicans belonging to groups such as the Tuesday Lunch Bunch, led by Fred Upton (R-MI), Nancy Johnson (R-CT), Mike Castle (R-DE), and Christopher Shays (R-CT) and the Mainstream Conservative Alliance headed by W.J. Tauzin (R-LA), in bringing about critical budget compromises. In cooperation with their allies in the Senate, such as John Breaux (D-LA) and Senator John H. Chafee (R-RI), who headed the bipartisan centrist coalition, House deficit cutters worked with the Clinton administration in bringing about a deficit reduction compromise that represented a shift in social spending politics. The Clinton administration insisted that tax cuts should not jeopardize the established deficit reduction targets. Naturally, disputes arose between ardent tax cutters in Congress and the administration (and other deficit cutters) over the size and structure of the tax cuts. The Administration sought to pay for its tax cut proposal by making substantial spending cuts in the Department of Urban Housing and Development (HUD), the Department of Energy, the Department of Transportation, the General Services Administration, and the Office of Personnel Management ("The Clinton budget: the impact on key agencies," *Wall Street Journal*, February 6, 1997: A12–A13).

In addition, Clinton cut deeply against the grain of traditional Democrats by levying new taxes on Social Security benefits for affluent retirees to raise more revenue to relieve pressure on the deficit (Pierson, 1998: 145–146). Paul Pierson brings out that when "combined with smaller cuts made elsewhere, and reductions in interest payments resulting from the smaller anticipated deficits, however, these changes in entitlements meant that spending cuts would roughly match the tax increases in contributing to a lower deficit while leaving significant funds for the administration's domestic agenda" (Pierson, 1998: 145–146). In taxing the Social Security benefits of America's wealthier individuals, the Clinton administration demonstrated that it was even prepared to sacrifice the sacred cow of Social Security to balance the country's budget.

Within less than a year after the 1996 election, disproportionate majorities in both houses passed a budget and a tax agreement that had been designed jointly by the Clinton administration and the Republican majority in Congress (Meeropol, p. 1). The cuts represented a breakthrough compromise between the Clinton administration and tax cutters in the Republican-led House. This "historic compromise" paved the way for similar bipartisan budget agreements in the later years. The sustained economic boom largely facilitated these historic tax compromises in 1996 and 1997. Economic prosperity meant that the amount of spending reductions necessary to achieve a balanced budget by 2002 could be much smaller than when Congress had passed a bill with the same goal in 1995.

By committing the nation to a course of fiscal discipline, the economic boom of the 1990s and the tax receipts derived from it (about $150 billion of personal income tax receipts from stock options and capital gains) would go to balancing the budget rather than support new spending on political popular and expensive programs. And despite the fact that the NASDAQ broke an historic 5,000 points, Washington continued to restrain spending and followed a course to reduce the deficit rather than use the surplus for new programs.

The FY 2000 budget represented a revolution in US fiscal policy whereby the discretionary side of the budget was balanced without drawing on entitlements. According to Bob Reichauer, former director of the Congressional Budget Office, in the FY 2000 budget "politicians changed the aim of fiscal policy from balancing the unified budget to balancing the budget without counting on the Social Security surplus" (*The*

Economist, November 20, 1999: 30). This was a hallmark achievement for deficit cutters, who finally got the overall balanced budget they were seeking.

Conclusion

This bipartisan coalition did not last long however. Not surprisingly, once the budget was balanced and historic surpluses occurred, political divisions surfaced among the parties over what should be done with the budget surplus. The sense of urgency over fiscal discipline naturally diminished and as a result the broad bi-partisan deficit reduction consensus dissolved. The Budget Committees in Congress, which establish the spending limits in Congress and had grown enormously powerful in the Clinton years, lost their preeminence in the budget arena. Clinton and other deficit cutters felt strongly that the surplus, which many hoped would be long-lasting, should be used to pay down the nation's overall public debt and shore up Social Security. Others felt strongly that the surplus should be returned to the tax payers as it was "their money" in the first place.

When President George W. Bush was elected, concerns about the public debt and fiscal discipline have not appeared to be a top priority for the administration or the majority in Congress. There are several reasons for this. The nation in general has become preoccupied with other areas of domestic and foreign policy. Leaders in Washington have focused the nation's political and economic resources on dealing with the tragic events of 9/11 and the aftermath, bolstering the nation's security, as well as committing large budgetary resources to Afghanistan and Iraq. On the domestic front, the President and bi-partisan groups in Congress together enacted ambitious and very expensive social programs such as the prescription drug benefit for seniors. In addition, President Bush and Democrats in Congress enacted the No-Child Left Behind which called for an additional 40 percent increase in the size of Department of Education's budget. Additionally, Congress has enacted massive amounts in pork spending over the past six years. And during this time, the Administration has not vetoed one spending bill. In 2006, the nation's budget deficits have now returned to record highs and the prospect of achieving a balanced budget despite the presence of a strong economy appears a long way off.

References

Boskin, Michael J. (1987) *Reagan and the Economy: the Successes, Failures, and Unfinished Agenda.* San Francisco: ICS Press.

Business Week (1980) "A guide to understanding the supply-siders: resurrecting classical theories on supply, demand, and tax cuts [ideas underlying President-Elect Ronald Reagan's economic program]," pp. 75–78, December 22.

Clarke, Harold D., Stewart, Marianne C., and Zuk, Gary (eds) (1989) *Economic Decline and Political Change: Canada, Great Britain, the United States.* Pittsburgh: Pittsburgh University Press.

Cohen, R.E. (1997) "Special report: the splintered congress", *National Journal* January 25.

Congressional Quarterly, December 31, 1994, p. 3601.

Congressional Quarterly, June 3, 1995, p. 1563.

Congressional Quarterly, June 17, 1995, p. 1718.

Congressional Quarterly, December 17, 1995, p. 3560.

Congressional Quarterly, August 3, 1996, p. 2175.

Congressional Quarterly, September 21, 1996, pp. 2705–2706.

Congressional Quarterly, October 5, 1996, p. 2826.

Congressional Quarterly, February 8, 1998, pp. 332–333.

Cranford, J.C. "Economic policy: Bush's plan consolidates, recycles old ideas," *Congressional Quarterly Weekly Report* 50: 2705.

Denzau, A.T. and North, D.C. (1994) "Shared mental models: ideologies and institutions," *Kyklos* vol. 47.

The Economist, "What now," 331: 57, May 14, 1994.

The Economist, March 21, 1998, p. 41.

The Economist, November 20, 1999, p. 30.

The Economist, "The hardest act to follow," 355: 62 no. 8172, May 27, 2000.

The Economist, June 9, 2001, p. 10.

The Economist, "Fiscal policy: a decade of deficits," 363: 27–28, no. 8278, June 22, 2002.

The Economist, "George Bush: the disappearing presidency," 364: 27–28, no. 8283, July 27, 2002.

The Economist, "A tale of two legacies: why are the heirs of Ronald Reagan doing so much better than Margaret Thatcher's," 365: 64–66 no. 8304 December 21, 2002.

Edwin Kee, James and Nystrom, Scott V. (1991) "The 1990 budget package: redefining the debate," *Public Budgeting and Finance*, Spring: 3–24.

Evans, Gary R. (1997) *Red Ink: The Budget Deficit, and Debt of the US Government.* San Diego: Academic Press.

Fenno, Jr., Richard (1991) *The Emergence of a Senate Leader: Pete Domenici and the Reagan Budget.* Washington, DC: CQ Press.

Financial Times, March 27, Thursday, 1980, p. 1.

Financial Times, "Dramatic gains for the rich," Wednesday, March 16, 1988, p. 23.

Financial Times, March 18, 1998, p. 22.

Furner, Mary O. and Supple, Barry (1990) *The State and Economic Knowledge: The American and British Experiences.* Washington, DC: Woodrow Wilson International Center for Scholars and Cambridge University Press.

Gamble, Andrew (1996) *Hayek: The Iron Cage of Liberty.* Boulder: Westview Press.

Greenberg, Stanley B. (1995) *Middle Class Dreams: The Politics and Policy of a New American Majority.* New York: Times Books.

Havens, Harry S. (1986) "Gramm–Rudman–Hollings: origins and implementation," *Public Budgeting and Finance.* Autumn: 4–24.

Kosters, M.H. (1992) *Fiscal Policies and the Budget Enforcement Act.* Washington, DC: AEI Press.

McClure, Harold J. and Willett, Thomas D. (1983) "Understanding the supply-siders," in Stubblebine, Craig and Willett, Thomas D. (eds) *Reaganomics: A Midterm Report.* San Francisco: ICS Press.

McLarty, Thomas (1995) *Preparing Our Country of the 21st Century: The Official Transcript of the United We Stand America Conference.* New York: Harper Pernnial.

Meeropol, Michael (1998) *Surrender: How the Clinton Administration Completed the Reagan Revolution.* Ann Arbor: The University of Michigan Press.

Miller, Daniel J. (1990) "The grim truth about Gramm–Rudman: the deficit law is working," *Policy Review* Spring.

Miller, James III (1994) *Fix the Budget: Urgings of an Abominable No-Man.* Stanford: Hoover Institution Press.

Mills, Gregory B. and Palmer, John L. (1983) *The Deficit Dilemma: Budget Policy in the Reagan Era.* Washington, DC: The Urban Institute Press.

Nell, Edward (1984) *Free Market Conservatism: A Critique of Theory and Practice.* London: George Allen and Unwin.

Niskanen, William (1988) *Reaganomics: An Insider's Account of the People and Policies.* New York: Oxford University Press.

Penner, Rudolph G. (1992) "The political economics of the 1990 budget agreement," in Kosters, Marvin H. (ed.) *Fiscal Policies and the Budget Enforcement Act.* Washington, DC: AEI Press.

Pierson, Paul (1994) *Dismantling the Welfare State: Reagan, Thatcher, and the Politics of Retrenchment.* Cambridge: Cambridge University Press.

Pierson, P. (1998) "The deficit and politics of domestic reform," in Weir, Margaret (ed.) *The Social Divide: Political Parties and the Future of Activist Government.* Washington, DC: Brookings Institution Press.

Rein, Martin and Schon, Donald (1993) "Reframing policy discourse," in Fischer, Frank and Foster, John (eds) *The Argumentative Turn in Policy Analysis and Planning.* Durham: Duke University Press.

Ruggie, J.G. (1982) "International regimes, transactions, and change: embedded liberalism in the postwar economic order," *International Organization* 36(2): 379–415.

Ruggie, J.G. (1996a) "Globalization and the embedded liberalism compromise: the end of an era," MPIfG Lecture Series Economic Globalization and National Democracy, lecture given on October 24.

Ruggie, J.G. (1996b) *Winning the Peace: America and world order in the New Era.* Columbia University Press.

Sabatier, Paul A. (1993) "A policy change over a decade or more," in Sabatier, Paul A. and Jenkins-Smith, Hank C. (eds) *Policy Change and Learning: An Advocacy Coalition Approach.* Boulder: Westview Press.

Singer, Otto (1993) "Knowledge and politics in economic policy-making: official economic advisers in the USA, Great Britain, Germany," in Peters, B. Guy and Barker, Anthony (eds) *Advising West European Governments: Inquiries, Expertise, and Public Policy.* Pittsburgh: University of Pittsburgh Press.

Stein, Herbert (1986) "The chief executive as the chief economist," in *Washington Bed Time Stories: the Politics of Money and Jobs.* New York: The Free Press, a division of Macmillan, Inc.

Stockman, David (1986) *The Triumph of Politics: How the Reagan Revolution Failed.* New York: Harper and Row.

Stoesz, David (1996) *Small Change: Domestic Politics Under the Clinton Presidency Small Change: Domestic Politics Under the Clinton Presidency.* New York: Longman Publishers.

Thomas, Norman C. (1989) "Adapting policy-making machinery to fiscal stress," in Clarke, Harold D., Stewart, Marianne C., and Zuk, Gary (eds) *Economic Decline and Political Change: Canada, Great Britain, the United States.* Pittsburgh: Pittsburgh University Press.

U.S. News and World Report (1982) "Economic theories that vie for dominance: Keynesianism, monetarism – and now 'supply side' ideas; the course the nation chooses can have a major impact on pocketbooks," 92: 55–56, April 26.

Walker, Martin (1996) *The President We Deserve, Bill Clinton, His Rise, Falls, and Comebacks.* New York: Crown Publishers, Inc.

Weaver, R. Kent (1986) "The politics of blame avoidance," *Journal of Public Policy* 6: 371–396.

Weiner, A.J. and Kahn, H. (1968) "Crisis and arms control," (Harmon-on-Hudson, NY: Hudson Institute, 1992) cited in Sills, David L. (ed.) *International Encyclopedia of the Social Sciences*, vol. 3. The Macmillan Company and the Free Press.

Woodward, Bob (1994) *The Agenda: Inside the Clinton White House.* New York: Simon and Schuster.

8 Shared mental models and active labor market policy in Britain and Ireland

Ideational coalitions and divergent policy trajectories*

Nigel Boyle

In 1997 a Labour government was elected to office in Britain. Its flagship initiative was a neoliberal welfare-to-work policy. There was a striking continuity with the mental models that informed the policies pursued by the Thatcher governments. The 1997 Irish general election resulted in a Fianna Fáil-Progressive Democrat coalition government: the most right-wing outcome possible. Between 1997 and 2006 this Irish government merely tweaked a labor market policy that was one part Scandinavian-style activism and one part Irish clientelism. Why has active labor market policy in Britain and Ireland taken such different paths? How did these two distinctive ideological syntheses come about? Why have they prevailed across changes in government?

Both public choice and political-institutionalist approaches to understanding policymaking and economic performance have each wrestled with how to incorporate the role of ideas. For economists and other rational choice models, getting inside the problematic "black box" of the substantive rationality assumption has led to an interest in cognitive systems. For institutionalists, figuring out how ideas are used by institutions has led to an interest in the dynamics of policy learning. Denzau and North's seminal essay (1994) on "Shared Mental Models" provides two critical insights for these approaches. First, decisions made in institutional settings have to be explained in terms of the shared perceptions and understanding of the environment that the relevant actors share. Second, uncertainty rather than risk is the problem that confronts actors. In this chapter the significance of these insights is set out for analysis of national continuities and cross-national divergence in active labor market policy in Britain and Ireland since the 1980s.

Answering questions about national continuities and cross-national convergence requires that one (1) examines the institutional setting in which policy was formed, (2) looks at the shared understandings of policy that were forged in key episodes and (3) considers the uncertainty that confronted policymakers in these episodes/settings. The 1981 and 1987 shifts in Britain and Ireland were, depending on one's disciplinary vocabulary, dramatic third-order (Hall, 1986), equilibrium-punctuating (Eldredge and Gould, 1972) or representational redescriptions (Clarke and Karmiloff-Smith, 1995).[1] Subsequent adaptations of policy reflected the mental model of a dominant policy coalition.

Empirically, the chapter is organized around two key policy episodes in each country: the creation of the Youth Training Scheme in 1981 and the "New Deal" in 1997 in Britain and the creation of *An Foras Áiseanna Saothair* (FÁS) in 1987 and the Community Employment scheme in 1994 in Ireland. Each of these four episodes is examined to identify the source of policy ideas, the ideational contestation that took place and the forging of a "winning" policy consensus. In both cases there were a variety of alternative policy options available, some neoliberal, some not. Why did some options remain "beyond the pale"[2] whilst others were implemented? The Thatcher government in 1981 undertook a counter-intuitive shift away from laissez faire to an interventionist, though neoliberal active labor market policy. The Blair government's "New Deal" in 1997 represented a repackaging of neoliberal interventionism, stressing the needs of individual clients over employer needs, but maintaining the neoliberal trajectory. The Irish government's creation of FÁS in 1987 (by then Minister of Labour, since 1997 Taoiseach, Bertie Ahern) introduced a Scandinavian-inspired comprehensive active labor market policy that repudiated any "coercion" of the unemployed. The 1994 introduction of Community Employment (by a Fianna Fáil – Irish Labour Party government) greatly expanded ALMP, creating a program that employed up to 5 percent of the workforce on voluntary community work projects sponsored by community organizations.

The competition state, mental models and the active labor market policy sub-system

Much of the literature on neoliberalism and/or globalization has suggested an inexorable international policy convergence. For some, the international integration of markets and capital mobility has dramatically eroded national autonomy: the end of the nation-state is at hand as international markets become the effective economic policy maker, with governments reduced to a vestigial, dignified role.[3] Policy options are narrowed to a single, neoliberal path resituating the state "into a subordinate relationship with global economic forces."[4] Other political-economists have maintained that globalization, far from mandating one-size-fits-all neoliberalism, leaves the social democratic alternative as viable as ever.[5] Comparativists have been able to demonstrate that there are distinctive types of advanced capitalist economies,[6] and there has been particular interest in the question of whether the "Anglo-American," "residual" or "liberal" world of welfare capitalism enjoys a comparative institutional advantage over other "worlds."[7]

There are two problems with this literature. First, neither "globalization," nor "neoliberalism" nor even "Anglo-American welfare capitalism" simply means "less state." Philip Cerny has argued that economic globalization has led not to a decline of state intervention but rather to an increase in intervention and regulation in order to promote competitiveness and marketization.[8] This involves microeconomic intervention rather than macroeconomic intervention, responsiveness to international markets, and a focus on enterprise, innovation and profits rather than social cohesion: the "welfare state" metamorphosizing into the "competition state." Second, at the same time that globalization gives rise to an intensification of certain sorts of intervention it also increases the level of uncertainty about the course of action that needs to be followed (Hemerijck and Schludi, 2000)[9]: competitiveness in an uncertain international environment requires states and other policy actors to engage in more "puzzling" and less "powering."[10] This explains the recent interest in policy ideas and how they are communicated across a wide range of intellectual traditions. From a Gramscian–Marxist perspective, a concern with socially-constructed political discourse,[11] from new institutionalist political analysis a new interest in the role of actors beliefs about governance traditions,[12] from a policy analysis framework a concern with mental models[13] and advocacy coalitions.[14] Scholars working on globalization itself are increasingly tending to distinguish between the economic outcomes of globalization and the effects of the discourse about globalization.[15]

These two observations are particularly important for the analysis presented here: the utility of the concepts of "the competition state," and the importance of "mental model-based politics" and ideational contestation at the sub-system level. Contemporary Britain and Ireland are exemplars of the "competition state" where social policy is subordinated to the needs of the economy and recalibrated to address international competitiveness rather than domestic égalité. But "puzzling" is not a benignly technocratic process. It also involves strategic manipulation: the heresthetics[16] of policy change, manipulation of the framing of issues by political leaders in order to deconstruct alternative coalitions and construct a new winning coalition, is particularly important. For analysis at the sub-system level the "Advocacy Coalition Framework" (Sabatier, 1988; Sabatier and Jenkins Smith, 1993) which views policy subsystems as central in bringing about policy change is of particular utility. A policy subsystem encompasses a large and diverse set of actors that attempt to translate their beliefs pertaining to a particular political issue or set of issues into governmental policies and programs.[17] According to Sabatier, most subsystems contain only a few politically significant advocacy groupings, usually ranging from "two to four important coalitions."[18] The "Advocacy Coalition Framework"

(ACF) sees the policy process and policy change as involving competing coalitions of policy actors[19] within sub-systems mediated by policy brokers.[20] Coalitions form around different "policy core" ideas: mental models.[21]

This sort of analysis is brought to bear in the empirical parts of the chapter. In the second part, an analysis of the British case first examines the development of the Youth Training Scheme in the early 1980s, including its evolution towards a work-welfare program in the 1985–1989 period, and the development of the Blairite "New Deal" 1995–2000. In the third part, the Irish case is examined with a focus on the creation of FÁS in 1987 and then the emergence of the Community Employment program in 1994.

British labor market policy 1981–2004: Thatcherite interventionism and Blairite neoliberalism

The 1981 Youth Training Scheme was the principal response to the labor market crisis in the first Thatcher administration. The Blair administration's "New Deal for a lost Generation" was the "Third Way" policy flagship. The triumph of an interventionist neoliberalism in 1981 and a welfare-to-work neoliberalism in 1997–1998 resulted from the construction of advocacy coalitions that neutralized opposition without compromising core neoliberal beliefs. Ideas about national competitiveness among certain Thatcherite actors in 1981–1983 and New Labour actors in 1995–1998 were crucial.

Thatcherite interventionism: the YTS departure

> We all know that there is no prospect of getting unemployment down to acceptable levels within the next few years (consequently) we must show that we have some political imagination, that we are willing to salvage something – albeit second best – from the sheer waste involved.
>
> (Prime Minister's Central Policy Review Staff, February 1981 report)

Despite coming to power in 1979 disliking what little there was of Active Labor Market Policy (ALMP)[22] in Britain, the 1979–1990 Thatcher governments developed a set of ALMP programs[23] which involved a quintupling of expenditures and which, by the late 1980s, had over one million people a year occupied on Manpower Services Commission (MSC) schemes. This spending came close to rivaling that on "passive" unemployment and welfare programs, and was high in comparative perspective. ALMP 1979–1990 was the most spectacular, and counter-intuitive, aspect of Thatcherite labor market policy.

ALMP underwent a "qualitative" shift in mental models under the

Thatcher governments. The pre-1979 ALMP mental model, which had been corporatist but essentially non-interventionist, was shattered 1979–1981 whilst being contested by a new set of "flexibilist" neoliberal ideas promoted by the Thatcher government and its supporters. ALMP 1979–1990 involved a prolonged struggle between the MSC's "developmentalist" or "Rhenish"[24] alternative and that of the Thatcherites. The MSC was the quasi-autonomous agency, appointed and funded by the government but operating under a corporatist employer/union Board, responsible for ALMP. That the incoming Thatcher government did not abolish the MSC was a small surprise. That the government worked through the MSC to create a startling policy departure was startlingly counter-intuitive. The MSC's "house philosophy" was based on an analysis that saw Britain's relative economic decline as being rooted in a flawed social ethic, a cultural constraint on economic modernization: a constraint that had to be challenged. The key actors involved in the development of MSC ideas and programs shared these views.[25] The MSC saw its task as involving the transformation of entrenched social values that separated education from training and detached education from questions of economic development. This "new vocationalism" regarding education was to be accompanied by an effort to change the national psyche regarding wealth creation (what would become, in Thatcherite rhetoric "the enterprise culture," embraced by New Labour).[26]

Mass unemployment allowed the MSC to build a fire-fighting empire on the basis of its ability to "get things done," but it had to tailor its shared mental model to suit the ideological predilections of the government. In doing so different aspects of its shared mental model had different sorts of attractions. Whereas the Thatcher government's rhetoric increasingly came to emphasize "the enterprise culture," with a stress on maximum feasible competitive flexibility ("pricing people into jobs"), the MSC's House Philosophy was rooted in a desire to end the distinction between mental and manual labor, increasing qualitative flexibility. The two versions of the shared mental model are set out in the simultaneously produced "New Training Initiative" documents by the government and the MSC in 1981.[27] They jointly embraced the same mental model and were induced by the common realization of the political and institutional opportunities available, but their versions of the shared mental model were distinct: parallel, they would never meet. The critical distinction between the two variants of the new shared mental model concerned the question of "compulsion" (or "conditionality" of benefits as it later became known): should people be forced into training programs, on pain of loss of benefits, or should training be entirely voluntary? This distinction came to have considerable resonance in all cases of ALMP in the 1980s. The Youth Training Scheme initiative of 1981 involved the introduction of a comprehensive post-educational training system and a mental model-breaking shift to a mental model focused on labor flexibility. With other political priorities driving macroeconomic policy, it was ALMP that bore the brunt of labor market problems in the 1980s.

The Youth Training Scheme was proposed in the May 1981 MSC consultative document,[28] accepted by the government in 1982, and became fully operational in 1983. Participation on the scheme was voluntary (unemployed youths were not obliged to join). However, the proposal stated "we must move towards a position where all young people under the age of 18 have the opportunity either of continuing in full-time education or of entering training or a period of planned work experience combining work-related training and education."[29] The document's key assumptions were that policy change should be dictated by the needs of the economy (rather than the educational needs of the individual); that the need was for a more versatile, multi-skilled workforce; and that though the provision might "reduce the vulnerability of individuals to unemployment", the reforms were designed to improve training and only indirectly to reduce unemployment.[30] Given the government's earlier laissez faire views about training this was a remarkable policy departure. Furthermore, despite the government's distaste for the Trades Union Congress (TUC) and its contemporaneous efforts to "disestablish" the unions in other policy subsystems, the government had no alternative to working with the TUC (and the employer's Confederation of British Industry, CBI) on the Commission itself and allowing the unions at the level of the Area Manpower Boards an effective veto over the use made of MSC schemes locally. TUC cooperation was seen as especially vital in developing YTS, as the government feared that if the TUC opposed it so would large numbers of private employers who had much less to gain from the scheme than they had to lose in needless conflict with the unions.[31] Not only was the TUC able to ignore opposition from some left-wing unions and union factions,[32] it was also perfectly willing to side with the CBI and "double-team" the voluntary sector (whose cooperation in delivering many YTS places was important[33]) in internal MSC politics.

In addition to assembling a broad "advocacy coalition," the MSC was remarkably effective in the rapid formulation and implementation of policy. Among policy makers it swiftly acquired the reputation of having the "ability to get things done."[34] David Young, first as MSC chair then later as Department of Employment Secretary of State, was forever tagged with a quote from Mrs. Thatcher that "other people come to me with their problems, David comes with solutions."[35]

The YTS case involved a sub-system coalition between "Thatcherites" and interventionist elements of the "corporatist" MSC. Propagating the "deep core" policy shared mental model that youth had to be made to adapt to changing market forces, the Thatcherites nonetheless were able to win the support of MSC administrators and business and union "stakeholders" for a strategy that committed the government to substantial public expenditures and an activist agenda. Although officials and business and union leaders within the MSC shared a reformist perspective about the youth labor market that was decidedly "Rhenish" – looking to the German model of high quality apprenticeships within a "social partners" ideational framework – they were manipulated into overseeing a policy that effected a very different "flexibilist" model.

In 1986–1988 the MSC's spectacular programmatic growth reached its zenith, but its "Rhenish" version of the shared mental model was emasculated as ALMP itself became more closely linked with the benefits system.

> We will now guarantee a place on the YTS to every school leaver under 18 who is not going directly into a job. . . . We will take steps to ensure that those under 18 who deliberately choose to remain unemployed are not eligible for benefit. . . . We will improve the Community Programme [the main program focused on the long term unemployed] to make it full time and better able to help those with families. We shall pay those working on the programme an allowance giving a premium over and above their social security payments.
>
> (1987 Conservative Party Manifesto)[36]

After reelection on this manifesto in 1987 the government announced its plans for a new "Employment Training" (ET) program, the central element of an incipient workfare system.[37] Together with a "guarantee" of an ET place being made to all those aged 18–24 (and it was hoped to extend this to all the unemployed after a while) and eligibility rules being tightened so as to make refusal of an ET place likely to result in benefit loss, compulsion was effectively introduced. Much of the most important meat put on the skeletal ET originated outside the MSC: the Restart initiative had been the brainchild of David Young in his time as Employment Secretary[38]; and the main "ideas merchant" influential in the development and ancillary reforms was not MSC House Philosopher Geoffrey Holland but Kay Stratton, an American advisor brought into the DE by new Employment Secretary Fowler. A former Massachusetts Secretary of Economic Affairs for Employment and Training, Stratton was parachuted into the DE to promote school compacts, local training councils and a workfare system.[39] A revolt by member unions forced the TUC to withdraw support for ET in September 1987. The Government moved immediately to abolish the MSC and all tripartite mechanisms in ALMP.[40]

It was only after the TUC's forced withdrawal from ET and the abolition of the MSC that the pattern regarding business involvement in ET (and thus in post-MSC ALMP) became clear. The fireworks over the TUC's role had obscured the fact that the CBI had become marginalized. Plans for a network of employers groups (which were to become the Training and Enterprise Councils) had been drawn up in the summer of 1986.[41] This involved abandoning the last vestiges of macro-corporatism and attempting to foster a more localized micro-level clientelism: the new

TECs received the bulk of ALMP revenues from government; their chairpersons communicated directly with the Employment Secretary; and their membership was skewed towards smaller, service sector, and politically "Thatcherite" employers.[42] The emergence of work-welfare in the 1985–1989 period involved the triumph of policy ideas imported from the US and the demise of the "Rhenish" approach favored by MSC interventionists. The period of the Major government 1990–1997 witnessed the dominance of Thatcherite interventionists now ensconced in the TEC network: employer-dominated but dependent on central government for resources and direction (a meso-level version of the "free economy and the strong state"). This new, neoliberal advocacy coalition marginalized the MSC-based coalition that had predominated since 1981. The Labour Party and the unions continued to articulate the "Rhenish" alternative in impotent opposition. However, by the time the Labour party looked like returning to power it had explicitly abandoned this alternative and adpted a new, neoliberal policy.

New Labour, New liberalism, New Deal[43]

> New Labour is a party of ideas and ideals but not of outdated ideology ... we have liberated these values from outdated dogma or doctrine, and we have applied these values to the modern world. I want a country in which people get on, do well, make a success of their lives.... We will give under-25s opportunities for work, education and training. Four options will be on offer. Rights and responsibilities must go hand in hand, without a fifth option of life on full benefit.
>
> (1997 Labour Party Manifesto, *Britain will be better with New Labour*)

Tony Blair's emergence as Labour leader in 1994 precipitated an ideological refoundation of the party. Although "Third Way" rhetoric usually stressed that New Labour was transcending traditional social democracy, a shift in shared mental models affecting all aspects of economic and social policy was undertaken that abandoned core social democratic goals. The 1997 manifesto guaranteed a conservative macroeconomic stance (which turned out to include central bank independence), a commitment not to raise income tax, and a promise to serve the interests of business. Labor market policy involved retaining the main institutional architecture created by the Thatcher governments and the commitment to get a quarter of a million young people off benefit and into work. This stance reflected both the policy review launched in 1987 after three crushing electoral defeats, and the 1994–1997 founding of "New Labour," heavily influenced by the example of the Clinton administration in the US.

Although Labour adhered to the "Rhenish" model in the 1976–1987 period, after both the 1987 and 1992 election defeats the Party embarked on policy reviews during which it began to accept two important modifications to its traditional welfare collectivist position and incrementally proceeded in a "competition state" direction. First there was the formal acknowledgement that the role of the state should be limited.[44] The only form of intervention now considered feasible was "market management" through medium-term supply-side policies, the aim being to promote long-term economic stability above all else. Second, this recognition of the "efficiency and realism that markets can provide" found an echo in the acceptance of individual liberty and responsibility as opposed to social equality as the primary goal of social policy. The 1992 Labour Party Manifesto, *Meet the Challenge, Make the Change* made it clear that citizens "had to take responsibility for their own lives and fulfill their obligations to others". After the 1992 defeat the Party appointed the Commission on Social Justice to rethink social and labor market policy. Employment flexibility was established as a core policy value and a new welfare ethic based on a redefinition of individual rights and responsibilities was identified. However, these incremental shifts were radically superceded by the emergence of the Tony Blair/Gordon Brown leadership team and "New Labour" thought in 1994.

"Blairism" was rooted in the notion of individual rights being inextricably linked to individual responsibility. New Labour "modernizers" believed that labor market policy would be designed in accordance with these core beliefs. New labour sought to establish tight eligibility criteria with time limits on traditional welfare benefit in an effort to dramatically reduce "welfare dependency." This core policy belief was supported by think-tanks[45] such as the Demos Institute, founded in 1993, and allied scholars such as Anthony Giddens. The influence of Demos and its neoliberal ideas is evidenced by the appointment of Geoff Mulgan (co-founder of the Demos) to head Number 10's Social Exclusion Unit in 1997.[46]

The US model looms large at this point for Tony Blair, Gordon Brown and the New Labour modernizers. Shared neoliberal ideas regarding the need to reform labor markets in order to make them more internationally competitive was rooted in the common struggles experienced by both the Labour and Democratic Parties in the era of globalization. Whereas in 1990 political strategists and electoral commentators were asking what the Democratic Party could learn from its British counterpart,[47] by 1993 the US was the model. Clinton championed the cause of economic growth through entrepreneurial initiative over government-led redistribution and strongly advocated substituting a policy of "workfare" in place of traditional welfare dependency.[48] New Labour had strong intellectual ties with key figures in the Clinton Administration.[49] Gordon Brown frequently met senior officials in the Clinton administration (such as then US Deputy Treasury Secretary Larry Summers and Hilary Clinton) to discuss fundamental aspects of economic policy strategy, often placing the issue of welfare and employment at the top of the list.[50]

The New Deal initiative was part of a broader strategy aimed at fostering a partnership between individuals and government through a labor market mental model based on the principle of helping individuals move from welfare-to-work.[51] This "individualized" or "client-based" (rather than provider-based) idea was a significant departure from the earlier YTS model: the language of "conditionality" replaced that of "compulsion", but the underlying goal was much the same. As shadow Chancellor, Gordon Brown sought to aggressively promote this agenda by raising more money for youth training by placing austere limits on welfare benefits for the long-term unemployed.[52] Brown set out the main elements of New Deal in a 1995 speech. The policy document, entitled "New Deal for a Lost Generation," was presented on May 16, 1996.[53] A one-off Windfall Tax that would fall on privatized utilities would pay for the scheme.[54]

Corporatist labor market institutions central to the Rhenish model and to the MSC in the 1980s were seen by the Blair government as too rigid and interventionist to deal with dynamically-changing labor market conditions. Most importantly, their corporatist genealogy was embedded in the traditional welfare state apparatus that had become too expensive and therefore, unsupportable given new fiscal imperatives.[55] The Blair government believed that bringing about monetary and fiscal stability would draw increased investment that would in turn produce higher growth and productivity: the competition state.[56]

In 1997, having served less than six months in office, Brown and Blair sought £3.1 billion to address youth unemployment.[57] In 1998 Employment Minister Andrew Smith issued a classically Blairite speech that formally launched New Deal into action. Ministers directly involved with "New Deal" were determined that the scheme should not be run exclusively by the Education Service, in an effort to curb its direct power over the distribution of benefits.[58] The result is a complex pattern of arrangements in each of the 136 Education Service districts. It is important to emphasize that each district possesses its own unique institutional arrangements that involve various public–private partnerships. This is viewed as critical for ensuring the flexibility required to respond to regional needs.[59]

"New Deal" was meant to be fundamentally different because it is based on local partnerships between employers, local authorities, training providers, Training and Enterprise Councils (TECs), Local Enterprise Companies, Jobcentres, environment groups, voluntary organizations and others. The TECs inherited by the Blair government were utilized during the first two years of "New Deal," but were then abolished as the government found the flexible mixture of different local agencies preferable to the employer-dominated TECs. Thus these relics of 1980s Thatcherism went the way of the relics of 1970s corporatism before them. Initially they assisted in winning the support of employers who might otherwise have refused cooperation that was deemed necessary for the success of the initiative. Once the advocacy coalition had facilitated the initiative these institutions were superfluous to New Labour.

Policy change did not consist of a center-Left government being forced to abandon partisan preferences to toe an exogenously determined line. There is a striking continuity in mental models that informed the youth labor market policies pursued by the Thatcher governments (1979–1990) and the Blair government (1997–2001). Thus, each represented distinct but related strands of a neoliberal shared mental model. Primacy is accorded to market forces and policy intervention is predicated on the idea of promoting flexibility and adaptation to promote national competitiveness. Cerny's notion of the "competition state" certainly applies. There is a strong rhetorical continuity in the British case that distinguishes it from the "Rhenish" or European social model, and policy borrowing from the US was a prominent feature of policy in both the late 1980s and late 1990s. The Labour government elected in 1997, starting from a policy document *New Deal for a Lost Generation* issued in opposition in 1996, was able to craft a policy once in power that maintained the "deep core" normative belief about the necessity of youth to adapt to the labor market (and not vice versa) whilst forging a coalition out of "New Labor" modernizers and the training policy network of TECs that had been bequeathed them by the Thatcher and Major governments.

Irish labor market policy 1987–2004: social partnership, FÁS, and community employment

The creation of FÁS (An Foras Áiseanna Saothair) as an all-encompassing labor market agency in 1987 (by a Fianna Fáil government) represented the most concrete institutional instantiation of the Irish version of "social partnership." The creation of the Community Employment program in 1994 represented a significant deepening of a pragmatic, part social democratic and part clientelistic approach to combating unemployment and social exclusion. Although the "Bostonian"[60] rhetoric of one wing of the Fianna Fáil Progressive Democrat government since 1997 has been distinctly neoliberal, this government has not tampered with the corporatist, interventionist shared mental model it inherited in the area of labor market policy. Ideas about national competitiveness among the Irish political elite, formulated as a shared mental model of "social partnership" have shaped labor market policy in a way that has excluded features of the Anglo-American neoliberal model.

The economic transformation of the "Celtic Tiger" is astonishing.[61] The employment data indicate the extent of the boom. With minor cyclical variation, the number of people in jobs in Ireland hovered at just over one million for the first 70 years of independence: half of all people born in Ireland 1922–1972 emigrated.[62] Between 1991 and 2001 the number of jobs rose to from 1.1 to 1.8 million. Despite the slowdown in the Irish economy in 2002–2003, employment growth continued and it is now expected that the Irish labor market will consist of two million jobs by

2010.[63] According to one authoritative measure, Ireland is the most globalized country in the world (Foreign Policy, 2003).[64] Ireland has some markedly neoliberal features: "passive" social protection spending in Ireland was by far the lowest in the EU and only half the EU average (14.1 percent of GNP compared to 27.3 percent for the EU-15).[65] Ireland also has a low tax regime: 25 percent of GNP compared to 40.5 percent for the EU-15.[66] Irish rates of poverty, social exclusion and inequality are high: thirteenth out of 18 OECD countries on exclusion and twelfth out of 18 on poverty as measured by the UNDP Human Poverty Index (UNDP, 2000) and seventeenth out of 18 on income inequality.[67] But the tiger's "golden" neoliberal fiscal stripes are arranged alongside the black stripes of "social partnership."[68]

Economic policy since 1987 has revolved around a comprehensive "social partnership." This includes centralized wage bargaining coordinated with government social policy,[69] but it also involves a much broader political and economic consensus on economic strategy negotiated by the social partners and political elites: "Social partnership has strong cross party political support . . . [it] has in effect been elevated to a *shared political ideology*, which infuses all aspects of public policy-making and with minimal dissent."[70] For some this is a novel model of "problem-solving," negotiated economic and social governance (O'Donnell, 2000a). The framing documents for social partnership in Ireland have been four national partnership agreements that have formed the basis for four national development plans: the 1987 Programme for National Recovery (1987–1989), the 1989 National Development Plan 1989–1993, the 1994 National Development Plan (1994–1999) and the 2000 National Development Plan 2000–2006.[71] These plans receive broad support from all political parties.

A key element of the social partnership model has been active labor market policy. General Irish social spending as a percentage of GDP is half the EU average[72] but spending on active labour market programs is almost double the EU average.[73] Of those 1.8 million in employment in 2004 well over half have participated in FÁS training and/or employment programs.[74] The bulk of the job growth has been in sectors that have drawn heavily on FÁS programs and trainees.[75]

FÁS programming, which ranged from modernized apprenticeship schemes for trades such as carpentry, electrical and plumbing, to "make-work" direct employment projects sponsored by community organizations (the latter often "heritage" based projects, restoring sites of historical interest, creating hiking trails, etc.). This latter generated a legacy not unlike that of the WPA and CCC in the New Deal era. FÁS programs employed a large number of youth who would otherwise have emigrated (emigration was substantial in the 1981–1994 period but much less than the dire macroeconomic circumstances would have suggested). About 100,000 people were on FÁS training and employment programs each year through the 1990s.[76] Nearly 5 percent of the workforce was on FÁS direct employment schemes.[77] In the period 1990–1995 only Sweden spent a greater proportion of its GDP (3 percent) on active labor market policy than Ireland (2 percent).

The creation of FÁS: political consensus; social partnership and the EU

FÁS was created in 1987 and introduced by Minister for Labour (Taoiseach since 1997) Bertie Ahern who set out its mission as:

> Firstly ... Government policy on boosting competitiveness in the wider economy calls for special intervention through training.... Secondly the scale of the unemployment problem and particularly the high levels of long term and youth unemployment and emigration must be the immediate focus.... Thirdly, we need a radical rethink about making manpower schemes more effective at local level ... the government has confirmed its commitment to a regional structure [that] will entail greater devolution of decision making to the regions.[78]

An earlier labor market agency AnCO, with a narrow remit focused on the apprenticeship system had existed in Ireland since 1967. After Ireland's accession to the EEC, AnCO gained access to limited European Social Fund resources but more importantly European ideas about manpower policy. An AnCO ethos developed in the 1970s that was very similar to the contemporaneous MSC ethos in Britain: flaws in the apprenticeship and education systems were perceived as fundamental and a "Rhenish" alternative posited. However, unemployment and wider social–economic crisis in the 1980s saw AnCo politically marginalized. A 1985 National Economic and Social Council Report[79] and then a government-commissioned consultants report[80] made a series of policy recommendations, including radical neoliberal ideas such as a voucher system. However, the main proposals centered on institutional reform: amalgamating all labor market agencies and giving a stronger strategic role to the Department of Labour. These were taken up by the Minister for Labour Ruairi Quinn (a leading Labour politician) who drafted the September 1986 White Paper on Manpower Policy. The defeat of the Fine Gael–Labour government and the emergence of a Fianna Fáil government after the 1987 elections did little to interrupt the new policy. Ahern secured the passage of the Labour Sevices Act 1987 that created FÁS. The "social partner" Board of FÁS appointed in September 1987 and the organization came into being January 1, 1988. This institutional reform placed AnCo's ethos within a more politically responsive institutional entity. A period of administrative reorganization led to a shrinkage of the "head office" of the new agency and the installation of a politically well-connected (and anti neoliberal) CEO John Lynch.

It was the 1987–1992 Fianna Fáil-led government that, contrary to most expectations, introduced both fiscal austerity and social partnership in the face of an enormous fiscal deficit. The party, under Charles Haughey, had been populist and expansionist, both in government 1979–1981 and in opposition 1982–1987. Social Partnership secured a corporatist bargain. Fiscal austerity secured the support of the main opposition party, Fine Gael, whose leader Alan Dukes committed to support the governments economic program. The startling outbreak of social peace (in an industrial relations system long renowned for conflict) and an end to adversarial party politics provided the context for the emergence of a powerful new coalition in the ALMP subsystem, a coalition that has held firm ever since. Whereas in other policy areas extreme fiscal austerity placed severe limits on policy innovation, the ALMP subsystem encountered a sudden windfall: the new European regime for cohesion funds aka "Delors 1" and "Delors 2."[81] Delors 1 channeled IR£3.1billion to Ireland, one-third of it through FÁS. Delors 2 channeled IR£4.6 billion into Ireland. Over one third of this went through FÁS.

The importance of the funding has been somewhat exaggerated. More important were the ideational and administrative strings that came with the funding. In some areas European Commission goals such as gender equality were imposed on a reluctant Irish state. A rigorous monitoring system was implemented as a check against misuse of funds. Such misuse was a major issue in Italy and Greece. However, in Ireland the administration of program funds, which obviously have pork-barrel potential, was punctilious. This despite the wider disrepute that Irish politicians were falling into regarding corruption and crony capitalism. At a broader level, the European Commission as an important actor in Irish ALMP reinforced the concept of social partnership and highlighted European models (both Social and Christian Democratic) for Ireland.

The Finance ministry and FÁS had a joint interest in maximizing the Irish "take" from the EU. Within the Commission the Irish were viewed as the most solicitous and determined of grant seekers. At the same time they earned a reputation for being tremendously responsive to the Commission and very effective users of funds.[82] The direct contacts that FÁS had with the Commission were crucial in giving FÁS autonomy from government departments. FÁS was able to horse-trade with the Commission and its interactions were unmediated by any government department.[83]

Irish state institutions are usually caught between the rock of powerful, centralized state (especially the Finance Ministry) and the hard place of a party system highly responsive to local political pressure. In the case of FÁS, European money and the ability of Finance to calculate the net cost of programs gave FÁS leverage with Finance that sustained support for FÁS programs even in times of extreme fiscal austerity. The breadth of local support for FÁS programs provided further political insulation that extended across party political boundaries. The regionalization of FÁS furthered its ability to nurture and mobilize alliances with local community groups.

Community employment: FÁS, local activist networks and the politicians

The Delors windfall was important for FÁS training programming. However, employment programs without a large training component, such as the Community Employment program, were not supported by EU funds. These soon became the largest part of the FÁS budget, and the most beloved by community organizations. As Exchequer funding represented 100 percent of the cost of these programs, domestic support was crucial. FÁS was able to be very entrepreneurial and responsive to political directives.[84] It also now enjoyed autonomy from government departments, extensive resources and effective insulation from critics. When savings from the social welfare budget due to participation in a FÁS scheme are calculated in FÁS was always able to make the case to Finance that the net cost of exchequer support was only 10p in the punt.[85] This net-cost calculus was important for Finance, which was particularly concerned to make savings from the social welfare budget. Finance always had a representative on the FÁS Board and in a climate of fiscal austerity it was keen to make savings. The 1992 general election occurred with the prospect of 300,000 unemployed (approaching 20 percent of the workforce). Taoiseach Albert Reynolds made policy to counter unemployment his chief priority (his battle cry "get the feckin' numbers down"). In July 1992, a parliamentary report called for the rapid expansion of employment programs. Fianna Fáil sustained heavy losses in the November 1992 elections but, after tortured coalitional negotiations, a new Fianna Fáil–Labour Party Coalition took power. This coalition was based on a "Program for Government" that among other things created a Community Employment Development Programme (CEDP) in the office of the Taoiseach. The coalition also created an additional "social partnership" body – the National Economic and Social Forum (NESF) to consider the unemployment problem and to include the "voluntary and community sector" as a third pillar alongside business and the unions. The CEDP and the NESF introduced new sources of policy ideas, but at this point FÁS was able to take the initiative and it was FÁS's policy development division that devised Community Employment. CE was developed as a program that would employ supervisors to ensure a relatively high quality program, largely sponsored by the community sector. Labour Minister Quinn announced the program in January 1994, with a budget double that of existing employment program budgets designed to more than double the number of placements to 40,000 per year.

Substantial as this was, more radical proposals emerged from other sources. A June 1994 NESF report made the case for a large program outside FÁS. In September 1994 a Taskforce on Long Term Unemployment was announced which was to report in early 1995.[86] FÁS was confronted from the left by an alternative coalition involving key actors at the center, the voluntary sector, and parts of the political left. In December 1994 the Fianna Fáil–Labour government collapsed (over an unrelated scandal) and was replaced by a "Rainbow Coalition" of Fine Gael, The Labour Party and the leftist Democratic Left. However, the change of government did not alter the development of CE.[87] The challenge from the left dissipated in 1995 and Community Employment as designed by FÁS was implemented.

Dr John Lynch, FÁS CEO 1991–2000, stresses the extent to which he and the leadership of FÁS were looking to European models rather than Anglo-American models for labor market policy.[88] Labour Minister Ruairi Quinn also cites Sweden (as well as Hungary) as inspiration. Minister FÁS officials visited Britain, Germany, France and Sweden, and the Swedish model was the one that was preferred. This is particularly interesting given the explicit copying of the US model being undertaken in Britain in the late 1980s. CE involved a particularly striking mobilization of the community sector as sponsors of CE projects. FÁS here played a proactive role in searching out, cultivating and training activists: often people who were very alienated from "the system." FÁS created courses and diplomas in community work for the purposes of cultivating such social entrepreneurs. This was particularly important in the most deprived areas where local civic activism was often absent: churches and unions were absent in the most dysfunctional urban communities; professionals such as doctors and teachers did not live locally, community activism had to start from a tabula rasa.

The bulk of the credit for the strong support FÁS received and the success of FÁS programs is attributed to elected politicians.[89] Politicians, including serving ministers, are highly responsive to constituents (the Irish STV electoral system punishes not just parties but individual politicians who lose touch with constituents). The partisan complexion of governments did not matter either. All politicians had FÁS schemes in their constituencies. It was also the case that any coalitional permutation would contain a party or party faction that was populist and strongly pro-FÁS: this applied to the populist wing of the Fianna Fáil party (Bertie Ahern being the best example) and to the Labour Party and the Democratic Left.

In addition to a challenge from the "Left," FÁS and CE faced a challenge from a rival coalition on the right. This rival coalition had the sympathy of the two Employment Ministers who oversaw FÁS and active labor market policy from 1994–2004: Richard Bruton, Fine Gael politician and Employment Minister in the 1994–1997 Rainbow coalition, and Mary Harney, leader of the neoliberal Progressive Democratic Party and Employment Minister (and Deputy Prime Minister) in the Fianna Fáil–PD government 1997–2004. However, despite a decade of such leadership, and the complete transformation of the labor market from mass unemployment to labor shortage, neither FÁS nor CE have been fundamentally tampered with.

Richard Bruton had, while in opposition, been a vocal critic of FÁS programming and had also become sympathetic to a growing chorus of opposition to FÁS programming from employers. Regarding policymaking, Bruton sought to reverse the pattern of FÁS dominating the Department of Employment and sought to work with Departmental officials in crafting a new policy. Bruton and his officials crafted the 1997 *Human Resource Development* White Paper that drew on three distinct sources of criticism of FÁS: expert and/or consultant opinion on the effectiveness of FÁS programs; criticism of FÁS from employers; and criticism of FÁS's independence from Departmental control.

The influence of mental models over the *Human Resource Development* White Paper was not the rhetorical neoliberalism of the new right but the "triangulating"[90] neoliberalism of Clinton and, especially, Tony Blair. Bruton was much enamored of the Small Business Administration model in the US for "enterprise-led" intervention. Officials were much influenced by Blairite[91] thinking, and were especially prone to borrowing code words for more vigorous enforcement of client obligations: "robustness" and "conditionality" (code words for a connection between work and social welfare benefits); "targeting"; and "early interventions" were cited by Department officials as Blairite euphemisms for a harsher regime. The *Human Resource Development* mental model fuses a Blairite neoliberalism originating within the DEE which drew heavily on expert analysis of policy, together with an employer call for employer-centered and employer-led active labor market policy. It was not, however, a backdoor route to workfare. The mental model represented a modified and heavily coded form of Irish neoliberalism: a "new economy" approach that viewed training as a vehicle through which Irish firms could become more strategic, "thinking organizations."

The proposals set up a major confrontation with the FÁS coalition. FÁS's allies in the cabinet, especially Ruairi Quinn, were able to exercise a "pocket veto," in effect consigning it to post-election limbo. Had the Rainbow government been re-elected in 1997, the White Paper might have been revisited, as it was the election of a Fianna Fáil-led government resolved this political problem. However, it wasn't just elite-level opposition that undermined Bruton's initiative. Grass-roots opposition was channeled through the clientelistic political system: it is striking how the clients shaped the views of patrons. The evidence that politicians cite is largely drawn from their constituency service caseload rather than an "expert" analysis – in short, Irish politicians are arguably more fluent in "anecdote" than in "regression."[92] These proposals were successfully resisted. One disadvantage that this coalition had was that it was seen as a "Thatcherite" solution to which there was a widespread aversion in Ireland.

The defeat of the "Blairite" Human Resource Development coalition demonstrated the strength of the FÁS-based coalition. This was to be put to the test again by (a) the disappearance of mass unemployment and (b) the tenure of Mary Harney as Minister responsible for employment policy 1997–2004. With the end of mass unemployment, was not FÁS's raison d'être gone? Au contraire. Not only did FÁS not fold indeed, its mental model was reaffirmed and its organization was enhanced and given the opportunity to undergo an internally-driven restructuring. And not only did CE not wither away, in fact, relative to the number of long-term unemployed, it remained as large a program as ever, and was increasingly asked to address an even larger array of policy problems.

In a letter sent to the newly-appointed FÁS Board in June 2001, Tánaiste Harney set out an agenda for FÁS, ending a three-year interregnum during which active labor market policy had continued as before with little or no changes.[93] Although this agenda was couched in a different terminology it did not reflect the kind of robust neoliberal rhetoric the Tánaiste is renowned for.[94] Its fundamental theme was that the changed labor market situation, including the significantly shrunken CE clientele base offered FÁS the opportunity to reorient itself as an organization. In terms of the existing active labor market shared mental model, the letter stated nothing that the 1985 NESC report, John Lynch or anyone at FÁS could fundamentally disagree with, and the FÁS 2002–2005 Statement of Strategy duly replicates. However, even mild efforts to cut CE back, in light of the elimination of long term unemployment, generated fierce resistance, again channeled through elected politicians. Backbench Fianna Fáil T.D.s, especially those representing rural constituencies, were particularly unnerved.[95]

Conclusions: ideational coalitions and divergent policy trajectories in Britain and Ireland

Thatcher's YTS and Blair's New Deal youth strategy demonstrates that in Britain the shift in shared mental models in labor market policy was based upon a qualitative shift from a core belief that governments can and (in cases of structural unemployment) should intervene in the labor market to a core belief that market mechanisms should determine the structure of labor markets. The broad underlying ideas each government embraced were remarkably similar, though framed for different audiences. Each initiative relied upon governments that were able to build broad support among potential ideational allies in the policy subsystem for their agenda.

Tony Blair's ideological refoundation of the Labour Party in concrete policy terms involved the marginalization of the "Rhenish"/corporatist synthesis. In terms of rhetoric the importance of education and training for social and economic progress was maintained: "equal opportunity in the enterprise culture." However, the ideas emanating from the new

Blairite think tanks such as Demos, increasingly influenced by the experience of the Clinton administration with "welfare reform," involved an acceptance of the neoliberal premises already guiding active labor market policy – stressing the responsibility of the unemployed to render themselves employable, the primacy of private sector employment, and the proactive role of government in using the benefit system to "move people into work."

In Ireland the creation of FÁS and the expansion of active labor market policy in the 1987–1994 period established a very different policy trajectory. All programmatic efforts to pressure people who were in receipt of benefits into employment/training schemes were resisted. Irish versions of "Blairite" policy initiatives were blocked by an anti-neoliberal policy coalition, even when the Ministers responsible were sympathetic to such initiatives.

In both Britain and Ireland policymakers were focused on labor market problems that were viewed as central to the competitiveness of the economy. In Ireland neoliberal options were repudiated and a part-social democratic and part-Irish clientelist system became entrenched. In Britain a particular sort of interventionist neoliberalism was adopted in 1981, repackaged in 1997 and has also become entrenched. In both cases the mental models shared by members of dominant policy coalitions were crucial in determining the path that was followed.

Notes

1 Political institutionalist Hall (1986), paleobiologists Eldredge and Gould (1972), and Cognitive Psychologists Clarke and Karmiloff-Smith (1995).
2 A term coined by English colonists to describe the territory beyond Dublin's hinterland inhabited by the "wild Irish." Here referring to policy options that were politically unacceptable.
3 A popular version of this is Kenichi Ohmae's (1993). Among political scientists the strongest claims are often made by those working on capital mobility: David Andrews and Thomas Willett (1997).
4 Richard Falk (1996: 15).
5 Geoffrey Garrett (1998).
6 P. Pierson (1994); D. King (1995); Gosta Esping-Andersen (1990).
7 Peter Hall and David Soskice (2002).
8 Philip G. Cerny (2000: 122).
9 Anton Hemerijck and Martin Schludi (2000). Their argument parallels that of Denzau and North (1994).
10 A formulation borrowed from Peter Hall (1986: 18).
11 Bob Jessop (2002).
12 Mark Bevir, R.A.W. Rhodes and Patrick Weller (2003).
13 Arthur Denzau and Douglass North (1994).
14 P.A. Sabatier, "Policy change over a decade or more" (1993).
15 C. Hay (2002) and Mark Blyth (2003).
16 W. Riker (1986). Heresthetics is the art and science of political manipulation. Heresthetics involves the strategic manipulation of issues so as to bolster one policy coalition and fracture rival coalitions.

17 "Advocacy coalitions are composed of elite actors from a variety of institutions – interest groups, agency officials, legislators, executive overseers, intellectuals – who share a general set of normative and causal beliefs concerning the policy area." P. Sabatier and N. Pelkey (1987: 237).
18 Ibid. p. 26.
19 Actors' organizational affiliation is not primordial, members of different coalitions come from different organizations.
20 Coalitions may attempt to map their goals into policy by, among others means, "venue shopping."
21 These are distinct from system-level "deep core" beliefs, more broadly applicable and less directly relevant to the policy domain. They may also be regarded as distinct components of a broader neoliberal shared mental model.
22 "Active" labor market policies (ALMP) involve government action to shape the demand for labor by creating jobs and/or increase the supply and quality of labor through training programs.
23 41 schemes altogether between 1979 and 1990.
24 Continental European models, particularly the West German Vocational Education and Training model were widely admired.
25 Geoffrey Holland was an early planner of the Training Services Agency and he subsequently became director of the MSC and, after its abolition, permanent secretary at the Department of Employment. In an interview with Peter Hennessy (*Independent* February 2, 1988) he aligned himself directly with the cultural constraint thesis.
26 Gordon Brown, *Wall Street Journal*, June 14, 2001.
27 MSC (1981a and 1981b).
28 MSC (1981b).
29 Ibid. para. 23.
30 Ibid. para. 30.
31 Lord David Young stresses this view on the pusillanimity of employers and the resultant fear for the implementability of YTS. Lord Young (1990: 138).
32 This proved to be an enduring capacity: even when the government began violating tripartite norms in the later 1980s the TUC had little difficulty in bypassing union dissent.
33 Lord David Young, *The Enterprise Years* (1990: 78).
34 A phrase used by one of the TUC Commissioners in evidence to the House of Commons Employment Committee, 1981–1982 (HC 221, The Work of the Department of Employment Group HC 348-I, HMSO).
35 *Financial Times*, April 5, 1986.
36 Conservative Party Manifesto, 1987 *The Next Moves Forward.*
37 Another element was the "Restart" scheme. Its perceived success (stressed by both Young (1990: 174) and Fowler (1991: 187) did much to set the terms of the debate over the extent of work-shyness on the part of the unemployed.
38 Lord David Young, *The Enterprise Years* (1990: 165).
39 Norman Fowler, *Ministers Decide*, 1991: 298–299.
40 The government announced this on September 15, 1988 *Financial Times*, September 16, 1988, and carried this through, despite last minute pleas by the TUC in its December 1988 White Paper *Employment for the 1990s*, Cmnd 540, HMSO December 1988.
41 *Financial Times*, July 31, 1986 and August 11, 1986, MSC chairman Bryan Nicholson being instrumental here.
42 Report by Apex Trust in the *Financial Times*, May 2, 1991.
43 According to a textual analysis of 53 of Tony Blair's speeches, "New Deal" (70 instances) was second only to "New Labour" (72 instances) as the most frequently used phrase. Norman Fairclough (2000); *Guardian*, March 3, 2000.

44 Neil Kinnock commenting in the Review's main published document that "there is a limit to what the modern state can do."
45 Interview with Richard Warner, General Manager, *Demos Institute*, July 18, 1999.
46 Ibid.
47 D. King and M. Wickham-Jones (1999) 64.
48 Ibid.
49 Ed Balls, the special adviser to Gordon Brown who was most intimately involved in creating New Deal, studied under Larry Summers (Secretary of the Treasury) and Lawrence Katz, (who served under Robert Reich in the Department of Labor), whilst at Harvard. They co-authored a paper that analyzed British unemployment by region and skill and concluded that long term unemployment was largely the result of "skill mismatches and a loss of the culture of work...." Ed Balls points out that both the Clinton and Blair governments' welfare reform strategies have been forged in accordance with this basic logic. Interview with Ed Balls, Special Adviser to the Chancellor of the Exchequer, HM Treasury, November 18, 1998.
50 "New Labour's Gurus: The American Connection," *The Economist*, November 8 (1997) 63.
51 Interview With Mr Bill Wells, DFEE, July 26, 1999.
52 Interview with Luke Bruce, The Labour Party Policy Unit, Millbank Tower, July 21, 1999.
53 Interview with Andrew Maugham, Special Adviser to the Secretary of State for Social Security, July 27, 1999.
54 "Labour's Training Policy," *The Economist*, May 18 (1996) 58–59.
55 S. Driver and L. Martell (1998: 63).
56 Interview with Andrew Kilpatrick, Head of Macroeconomic and Fiscal Policy, HM Treasury, November 16, 1998.
57 "New Deal Special Report," *New Statesman*, April 3 (1998: 52–58).
58 Jobs for the Boys and Girls, *New Statesman*, February 13 (1998: 22–23).
59 Interview with Mr Bill Wells, DFEE, July 26, 1999.
60 In Ireland the Left–Right debate has become known as "Boston versus Berlin," a phrase coined by Deputy Prime Minister Mary Harney. The fact that the Irish microeconomy is so heavily tied to US FDI and its macroeconomy so tied to the EU gives this debate added sharpness.
61 See Walsh, Brendan "The transformation of the Irish labour market: 1980–2003" *Statistical and Social Inquiry Society of Ireland Presidential address* 6th May, 2004. The OECD *Employment Outlook 2004* highlights the Irish case. Looking at labor market performance across all dimensions (employment/population ratios, activity and long and short term unemployment rates across gender, age group, level of educational attainment for the period 1990–2003), Ireland outperforms all 30 OECD countries in every category except growth in female participation rates, where the Netherlands performs better – though even here, the Dutch figure reflects that it has double the proportion of part-time female workers that Ireland has.
62 Allen, 1998, 13.
63 FÁS *The Labour Market Review* 2003
64 Foreign Policy magazine's Globalization Index ranked Ireland as the most globalized economy of 62 in its survey for both 2001, 2002 and 2003. A.T. Kearney (2003).
65 Spending on health, disability, old age, widows and widowers, families and children, unemployment, and housing CORI "Priorities for Fairness" April 2004
66 CORI Justice Commission Annual Report "Priorities for Fairness" April 2004. OECD figures for 2003 on taxation show Irish taxataion as 28 percent of GDP compared to the EU 15 average of 40.5 percent. 2000 European Commission

figures show that National Social Protection Expenditures ("passive" spending on healthcare, housing and benefits for the disabled, elderly, families and children) as 14.1 percent of GDP for Ireland, compared to 27.3 percent for the EU 15.

67 World Development Report 1998/9 Table 5, p. 198.

68 The color coding is derived from the neoliberal "Golden Straitjacket" identified by Thomas Friedman (2000) and the black of European Christian Democracy (clerical by origin), the ideological underpinning concepts of social partnership and subsidiarity.

69 Interestingly this is a system that has broken down in Scandinavia itself in the early 1999s.

70 Walsh, Craig and McCafferty (1998, 15–16).

71 The first three relied on labor market programs to counter social exclusion, the 2000 has a broader strategy for "social inclusion."

72 Eurostat (2003).

73 OECD (2003).

74 Between 1987 and 2001 FÁS throughput on its training and employment schemes averaged about 100,000 per year (FÁS annual reports 1987–2001). MacSharry and White note that 500,000 participated in EU supported training 1989–1993, though they characteristically omit to mention that all of this operated through FÁS (MacSharry and White, 2000: 156).

75 70 percent of the job growth has been concentrated in five sectors: construction; sales; hospitality; transport and communication; and financial. These figures are for the 1994–2000 period, Quarterly National Household Survey, November 2000. All of these sectors recorded growth of more than 30 percent.

76 FÁS Annual Reports 1988–2001.

77 OECD (1995).

78 Focus (Newsletter of the Youth Employment Authority) no. 24, October 1987.

79 The National Economic and Social Council (NESC) is the Irish government's semi-detached think tank for policy reform.

80 Report by Danaher, Frain and Sexton (consultants) – mandate to review current measures and make recommendation. Noted inability of education system to respond to labor market. Need for an (HEA) for ED noted. Need for a stronger DoL and a merged agency (FÁS). Need to reform apprenticeship. Problem of YEA levy and ESF money being restricted to the young. Concern over AnCO's External Training budget (O'Reilly's fief). Levy grant system should be abolished – need is for a "strategic" identification of kill areas. Need to drop "manpower" for "labor market." Need to shift from "industrial" to broader sectors. Suggest voucher system. Goal of creating an oversupply of skilled labor is established. Goal of more modular delivery of educ and training established. Need for a research unit outside DoL.

81 *The Economist*, February 27, 1988: 41.

82 Interview with Terry Stewart, senior official in the Social Affairs Directorate General of the European Commission 1985–1991, 1-16-02.

83 Interview with Pat O'Toole, FÁS Head of European Union Affairs 1987–present, 1-10-02.

84 One principal actor recalled, "I remember going to a National Consultative Committee meeting, which monitored progress on the partnership programme, and being asked if we could increase the Social Employment Scheme (later, the Community Employment Scheme). To the horror of our parent civil service Department, I said that we could double it to over 30,000 participants (representing nearly 3 percent of the labour market). We were subsequently asked to double it. This would not have occurred in the normal liaison between FÁS and its parent Department." Correspondence with Henry Murdoch, Assistant Director General of FÁS 1987–1999.

85 Interview with Pat O'Toole, FÁS Head of European Union Affairs 1987–present, 1-15-02.

86 Headed by Julie O'Neill (in Tanaiste Spring's office). An interdepartmental committee also at work on this. The Taskforce report came out in February 1995.

87 1996: Dissension within coalition over whether the 1995–1996 Taskforce report represents the definitive response to ltu. Finance fearful of 40,000 public sector low paid.

88 Interview with Dr John Lynch, FÁS Chairman 1988–1991 and FÁS Director General 1991–2000, 1-15-02.

89 Interview with Dr John Lynch, FÁS Chairman 1988–1991 and FÁS Director General 1991–2000, 1-15-02.

90 The political strategy of casting a "progressive" agenda as equidistant from the new right and the old social democratic/liberal Left.

91 In the area of active labor market policy this involved both an emphasis on the "duties" of benefit recipients and an "individualized" approach to addressing skill needs.

92 Irish clientelism is a self-abasing sort, according to Collins and O'Shea (2003) in which clients view patrons as being beholden to them, not vice versa.

93 This letter was delivered June 6, 2001, the day before the Board were to become involved in the strategic review.

94 Although some actors in ALMP see Mary Harney as a neoliberal ideological zealot, others see her as cautious (4, 64), and others as being little interested in policy (as opposed to politics).

95 This applied to TD's from rural Ireland across the political spectrum, for example PD Mae Sexton (Roscommon-Longford) was vocal in calling for extra provision for older unemployed people in rural Ireland. *Irish Times*, December 4, 2003. Local newspapers played a particularly important role in making CE cuts a hot electoral issue. For example *Roscommon Champion*, March 16. 2003.

* The research that this chapter is based on is reported more fully in Boyle (2005), Boyle (2006) and Boyle and Roy (2003). The various iterations of this research have benefited greatly from Ravi Roy's advice.

References

Andrews, David and Willett, Thomas (1997) "Financial interdependence and the State: international monetary relations at century's end," *International Organization* 51: 479–511.

Balls, E. (1998) Interview with Ravi Roy, November 1998.

Bevir, Mark, Rhodes, R.A.W. and Weller, Patrick (2003) "Traditions of governance," *Public Administration* vol. 81, No. 1.

Blyth, Mark (2003) "The political power of financial ideas: transparency, risk and distribution in global finance," 2002, in Jonathan Kirshner *Monetary Orders: Ambiguous Economics, Ubiquitous Politics.* Ithaca: Cornell University Press.

Boyle, Nigel (2005) *FÁS and Active Labour Market Policy 1987–2005.* Dublin: the Policy Institute.

Boyle, Nigel (2006) *Crafting Change: Labor Market Policy under Mrs. Thatcher.* New Orleans: University Press of the South.

Boyle, Nigel and Roy, Ravi (2003) "National politics and globalization: varieties of neo-liberal youth labour market policy under Thatcher and Blair," in Cohen, M. Griffin and McBride, S. (eds) *Global Turbulence: Social Activists' and State Responses to Globalization.* Aldershot: Ashgate.

Cerny, Philip G. (2000) "Restructuring the political arena: globalization and the paradoxes of the competition state," in Germain, Randall D. (ed.) *Globalization and its Critics: Perspectives from Political Economy*. Basingstoke: Macmillan – now Palgrave, p. 122.

Clarke and Karmiloff-Smith (1995) "The cognizer's innards," *Mind and Language* 8: 487–519.

Collins, Neil and O'Shea, Mary (2003) "Clientelism: facilitating rights and favours," in Adshead, M. and Millar, M. (eds) *Public Administration and Public Policy in Ireland*. London: Routledge.

Conservative Party (1987) Manifesto. *The Next Moves Forward*.

Denzau, Arthur and North, Douglass (1994) "Shared mental models: ideologies and institutions," *Kyklos* vol. 47: 1994.

Driver, S. and Martell, L. (1998) *New Labour: Politics After Thatcherism*. Cambridge: Polity.

Eldredge, N. and Gould, S.J. (1972) "Punctuated equilibria," in Schopf, T. (ed.) *Models in Paleobiology*. San Francisco: Freeman.

Esping-Andersen, Gosta (1990) *The Three Worlds of Welfare Capitalism*. Princeton U.P.

Eurostat (2003) *Basic Statistics of the Community*. Office for Official publications of the European Community, Luxembourg.

Fairclough, Norman (2000) *New Labour, New Language*. London: Routledge.

Falk, Richard (1996) "An inquiry into the political economy of world order," *New Political Economy* vol. 1, no. 1, p. 15.

FÁS (2003) *The Labour Market Review* 2003. Dublin: FÁS.

Fowler, Norman (1991) *Ministers Decide*. London: Chapmans.

Friedman, T. (2000) *The Lexus and the Olive Tree*. New York, Anchor Press.

Garrett, Geoffrey (1998) *Partisan Politics in the Global Economy*. Cambridge: Cambridge University Press.

Hall, P. (1986) *Governing the Economy*. London: Polity.

Hall, Peter and Soskice, David (2002) *Varieties of Capitalism: The Institutional Foundations of Comparative Advantage*. Oxford: OUP.

Hay, C. (2002) *Political Analysis*. Basingstoke: Palgrave Macmillan.

Hemerijck, Anton and Schludi, Martin (2000) "Sequences of policy failures and effective policy responses," in Scharpf, F. and Schmidt, V. *Welfare and Work in the Open Economy* vol. 1 (OPU, 2000).

Jessop, Bob (2002) *The Future of the Capitalist State*. Cambridge: Polity.

Kearney, A.T. (2003) *Foreign Policy Magazine Globalization Index*. Foreign Policy, Washington, DC.

King, Desmond (1995) *Actively Seeking Work*. Oxford: Oxford University Press.

King, Desmond and Wickham-Jones, M. (1999) "From Clinton to Blair: the democratic party origins of welfare to work," *Political Quarterly* 70.

Kurzer, Paulette (1993) *Business and Banking*. Ithaca: Cornell.

Labour Party Manifesto (1997) New Labour: Because Britain Deserves Better (London: Labour Party).

Manpower Services Commission (1981a) *A New Training Initiative: A Consultative Document* (Sheffield: MSC May 1981).

Manpower Services Commission (1981b) *A New Training Initiative: A Consultative Document* (London: MSC, May 1981).

MacSharry, Ray and White, P. (2000) *The Making of the Celtic Tiger*. Dublin: Mercier.

O'Donnell, R. (ed.) (2000) *Europe: The Irish Experience.* Dublin: Institute of European Affairs.

OECD (1995) *Employment Outlook,* July 1995, Paris: OECD.

OECD (2003) *Employment Outlook,* Paris: OECD.

Ohmae, Kenichi (1993) *The End of the Nation State: the Rise of Regional Economies.* New York: Free Press.

Pierson, Paul (1994) *Dismantling the Welfare State.* New York: Cambridge University Press.

Riker, W. (1986) *The Art of Political Manipulation.* New York: Yale University Press.

Sabatier, P.A. (1988) "An advocacy coalition framework of policy change and the role of policy-oriented learning therein," *Policy Sciences* 21: 129–168.

Sabatier, P.A. (1993) "Policy change over a decade or more," in Sabatier, P.A. and Jenkins Smith, H.C. *Policy Change and Learning: An Advocacy Coalition Approach.* Boulder: Westview Press.

Sabatier, P.A. and Jenkins Smith, H.C. (eds) (1993) *Policy Change and Learning: An Advocacy Coalition Approach.* Boulder: Westview Press.

Sabatier P.A. and Pelkey, N. (1987) "Incorporating multiple actors and guidance instruments into models of regulatory policymaking: an advocacy coalition framework," *Administration and Society* XIX.

Walsh, B. (2004) "The transformation of the Irish labour market: 1980–2003," *Statistical and Social Inquiry Society of Ireland Presidential Address.*

Walsh, J., Craig, S. and McCafferty, D. (eds) (1998) *Local Partnerships for Social Inclusion?* Dublin: Oak Tree Press.

World Bank (1999) World Development Report 1998/9. Washington, DC: World Bank.

Young, Lord David (1990) *The Enterprise Years.* London: Headline.

9 Neoliberalism isn't enough

On the interaction of the neoliberal and Europeanist shared mental models in the European Union

Craig Parsons

Today's European Union is commonly viewed as one of the great concrete triumphs of the neoliberal shared mental model – or at least it should be. A fair number of observers describe the EU as a 'Fortress Europe' of protectionist agricultural policies, rigid regulations, and onerous bureaucracy, when in fact these facets are best understood as secondary elements or side-payments in a fundamentally neoliberal enterprise. There remain many things for neoliberals to complain about in Europe, of course. But especially with the 'Single Market 1992' and monetary union projects launched in the 1980s and 1990s, Europe has been reorganized to more closely reflect neoliberal principles of competition, price arbitrage, and public policies that favour background economic stability over active intervention in markets.

Why has neoliberalism gone as far as it has in Europe? This chapter tries to answer this question, and in particular to understand the role of neoliberal ideas in driving the process of change since the 1980s. Existing scholarship offers two main kinds of responses. Probably the most widely-accepted interpretation of recent EU-related change in European political economy can be called a 'structural rationalist' one (Moravscik, 1998). As of the 1970s, major trends in the underlying structure of markets and production – notably expanding international capital flows and increasing foreign competition – signalled to European businessmen and policymakers that their relatively interventionist, nationally-oriented economic policies were unlikely to deliver prosperity in the future. Not without reluctance, Europeans gradually recognized that broad liberalization and anti-inflationary monetarist policies were the rational response to their changing structural landscape. Thus the 1980s brought a gradual convergence in national-level economic policies around these principles, paralleled by attempts to institutionalize them collectively in the Single Market and monetary union projects.

The other major interpretation of recent political-economic change in Europe echoes the theme of this book, emphasizing neoliberal ideas as causal factors in their own right. For scholars like Peter Hall or Kathleen McNamara as well as Denzau and North, the European convergence on neoliberal principles in the 1980s flowed from an ideational shift in 'paradigms' or shared mental models, not a straightforward, rational reaction to changing structural constraints (Hall, 1989, 1992; McNamara, 1997). The elaborate conceptual frameworks that guide economic policy-making have their own dynamics, distinct from objective reality. Objective reality can undercut certain ideas – as it did in the 1970s, when poorly-understood crises undermined the postwar European consensus on Keynesianism – but never clearly dictates new ideas. Thus the turn to neoliberalism and monetarism in the 1980s resulted from the intellectual coherence, political resonance, and simple 'availability' of these ideas more than from their objectively functional solutions to real problems. The Single Market and euro were the European manifestations of this policy consensus.

These two interpretations differ on the fundamental nature of political action, but agree on one major historical point: both portray the EU's major projects as flowing from a consensus on neoliberalism. Some see this consensus as a rational reaction to reality, others as built on new ideas – but either way, once Europe's major states moved toward neoliberal policies, the Single Market and euro apparently followed. The core argument of this chapter is that this common historical view is substantially wrong. The Single Market project was not launched or supported consistently by convinced neoliberals; the euro was not launched or supported consistently by convinced monetarists. Certainly the convergence on neoliberalism and monetarism was a necessary prerequisite to these liberal and monetarist European projects, but a partial convergence in domestic economic policies was never the same thing as the endorsement and implementation of an immense deregulatory and monetarist programme within centralized European institutions. Only because neoliberal ideas intersected with 'Europeanist' ideas – a distinct agenda about the appropriate institutional locus of authority in postwar Europe – did the EU become the locus of a strong neoliberal programme.

Furthermore, it was the distinct impetus from this 'Europeanist' institutional agenda that allowed the neoliberal shift to have such revolutionary effects across Europe. When neoliberalism and monetarism were fused with the Europeanist agenda, they acquired a legitimate institutional framework that gave them unlooked-for power. Even more striking, within this fusion, Europeanist ideas tended to trump substantive policy preferences. Neoliberals like Margaret Thatcher actually preferred to limit substantive liberalization rather than accept European centralization, and relatively illiberal Europeanists like François Mitterrand accepted much more liberalization and monetarism than they preferred in order to strengthen the EU. In other words, the neoliberal revolution in Europe is more a story of neoliberalism as vehicle for Europeanism than the other way around. This observation leads to the broadest point of the chapter, which is relevant even to readers of this book who care little about the EU. Neoliberal ideas themselves rarely, if ever, dictate the political-institutional framework within which their substantive policy agenda can be enacted. Their influence will always be conditioned by their intersection with conceptually distinct ideas about the locus of political authority. Those who seek to spread or oppose neoliberal policies elsewhere – or who simply seek to understand their success or failure – had best pay close attention to the broader politics of institution-building.

This argument obviously fits well with the work by Denzau and North that inspires the volume. Though the European politicians and bureaucrats I have interviewed and studied are trying hard to be rational, they confront such a complex and ambiguous environment that their interpretive 'mental models' play a major role in determining their choice of actions. Two points here can be seen as extensions, or perhaps sympathetic qualifications, to the Denzau and North approach. First, my emphasis on the intersection of two logically and historically distinct shared mental models adds even more complexity to their general picture. I strongly suspect that even the most top-down, elite-crafted outcomes tend to reflect more than one idea – both within the head of any given person (with people mixing logically distinct ideas) and in interaction (with collective actors like governments choosing strategies through compromise between several ideas distributed unevenly across their members). Second, expanding on the latter point, my story of debates cross-cutting European governments places more emphasis on the potentially discontinuous distribution of ideas. Denzau and North note that even culturally-similar individuals may 'learn' different things over time, and that the construction and maintenance of shared mental models depend on fairly continuous communication. I would stress that even such communication does not necessarily lead to homogeneous views, and that we cannot expect a priori that any particular group will share a certain mental model. Just how broadly and deeply seemingly similar people share a given idea is an empirical question.

Far from discouraging us to follow Denzau and North's advice to look for shared mental models, the potential for overlapping and messily-distributed ideas makes this kind of approach all the more important. It magnifies the risks that in overlooking ideas, conventional rationalist scholarship may impose overly simple, acontextual, and perhaps demonstrably wrong plot lines onto patterns of action. Whether we want to investigate the causal power of certain ideas or to show the power of alternative explanations, we have no scientific choice but to undertake the kind of interpretive, process-tracing research necessary to evaluate how actors reached their decisions.[1] Thus the study of mental models can no longer be seen as an optional elaboration on structural or institutional approaches. It is an unavoidable part of any serious attempt at explanation.

Neoliberalism and Europeanism in the Single Market project

Consider first the story of the 'Single Market 1992' project. This package of liberalizing regulatory reforms was bundled with institutional changes in the 'Single European Act' (SEA) of 1986 that modified the basic treaties of what was then called the European Economic Community (EEC). The SEA laid out a series of goals of liberalization and modified formal decision rules to signal a shift from unanimity rules to majority voting among the member states (in the EEC's Council of Ministers). Though perceived as relatively modest at the time, all now agree that the SEA inaugurated a massive, concrete wave of change across Europe. Thousands of pages of legislation harmonized national regulatory regimes; capital movements were freed of restriction; eventually even mostly-nationalized sectors like electricity were pried open. In political terms this substantive agenda shifted substantial power to Brussels, turning the EEC's enhanced customs union into what Giandomenico Majone labelled a 'regulatory state' in 1994 (Majone, 1994). By the early 1990s a majority of legislation in Europe's national parliaments was being passed simply to enact decisions by the EU.

How do scholars explain this huge new European project of liberalization? At a basic level, any explanation of the SEA departs from a series of figures about rising economic interdependence. If we look at French figures, for example, international trade rose from 14.5 per cent of GDP in 1960 to 23.9 per cent in 1985 (OECD, 1990: 126–129). Intra-EEC trade accounted for an increasing part of French exports, growing from 30 per cent to 47.6 per cent in the same period. For the EEC as a whole, intra-EC trade grew from 34.5 per cent of total exports to 52.1 per cent from 1960 to 1985 (De la Torre and Kelley, 1992: 20; Sapir, 1992; Lawrence, 1996: 59). By the 1970s financial ties were expanding even more quickly. International banking markets increased at almost twice the rate of trade growth (21.4 per cent annually, versus 12.7 per cent for trade) from 1972 to 1985. Capital flows in exchange markets grew exponentially, from a few billion dollars per day in the early 1970s to $100 billion in the late 1970s, and $650 billion by the late 1980s (Goodman and Pauley, 1993). All these trends increased European incentives and pressures to cooperate economically. Cross-border trade limited fiscal autonomy because domestic expansion swelled imports, particularly if neighbours were practising fiscal austerity. The availability of international finance to domestic firms undercut monetary autonomy, as national finance systems were essentially forced to compete to lend. Combined with a growing sense of economic failure – most painfully showcased by a steady rise in unemployment that did not occur in America or Japan – this restructuring of international markets deeply threatened Europe's national economies.

For structural thinkers like Harvard's Andrew Moravcsik, these underlying changes led to national-level liberalization, which led to the SEA's changes in EEC. Britain's deregulatory turn under Thatcher, German abolition of capital controls in the early 1980s, and the famous 1983 'U-turn' of the French Socialists from Keynesian expansion to fiscal austerity reflected a 'pan-European trend' to freer markets (Moravcsik, 1998). As the last major country to effect the shift, France's U-turn made European bargains possible. The key intermediate step was the 1984 French programme of financial liberalization. After the U-turn, the Socialists began to worry that French firms were disadvantaged by capital controls and other limits on domestic finance. In liberalizing domestically, they simultaneously signed on to the Single Market plan to bolster this agenda. Moravcsik writes that they pushed EEC institutional change – majority voting, mutual recognition – to facilitate a neoliberal policy agenda: 'Backed by business leaders, the French government committed to international liberalization, for which Europe served as a technocratic means and as a source of political legitimation' (Moravcsik, 1998: 332). Similar processes in other European states made the '1992' programme the substantive centrepiece of the SEA. The French also tried to introduce less neoliberal projects into the deal – calling for tighter EEC coordination in monetary policy, industrial policy, and social affairs – but these were vetoed by the British and Germans. The structural situation ultimately meant that the one agenda Europeans could agree on was liberalization, with some institutional changes to make it work.

The contrasting ideational account of the SEA appears in two guises. The first is implicit, appearing not in scholarship directly on the SEA but in the work of Hall and others on the shift from Keynesianism to neoliberalism in the late 1970s.[2] The basic argument of this large literature is summarized above: by the early 1980s a new neoliberal consensus had spread across Europe. Certain European elites lagged behind this general shift, especially on the Left and even more so if they had not been in government in the 1970s. The French Socialists were the pivotal example, and their ignominious alignment in 1983 is generally seen as the key moment in the consolidation of the new consensus. From this point, the implicit account of the '1992' project and the SEA would follow the same lines as that of the structuralists. These scholars imply that Moravcsik is right that around 1984 we see EEC reform and liberalization because of a 'pan-European trend' to neoliberalism, but wrong to see this trend simply as a rational adaptation to structural imperatives.

The second, more direct kind of partly-ideational scholarship on the SEA looks more closely at how the neoliberal consensus spread within the EEC. The most immediate focus of scholars like John Zysman and Wayne Sandholtz or Neil Fligstein is on the role of the European Commission in persuading national governments to endorse a major European program of liberalization. These authors allow that a neoliberal consensus was spreading, and particularly that European business was pushing governments in this direction, but emphasize that it was only when the Commission crafted the clever '1992' package of reforms that the member-states began to perceive interests in such an ambitious neoliberal agenda (Sandholtz and Zysman, 1989; Fligstein and Mara-Drita, 1996). In 1983 and 1984, they note, the Commission assembled a wide array of directives – some long blocked by certain governments – into a new package deal that eventually appealed to almost everyone. The plan was presented unobjectionably as '*completing* the Single Market,' though it went far beyond earlier EEC ambitions. Behind the slogan of 'Europe 1992' (the proposed deadline), Commission President Jacques Delors created an 'élite social movement' of politicians, bureaucrats, and businessmen (Fligstein and Mara-Drita, 1996). This version of the story introduces some separation between a neoliberal consensus in European governments and the specific shape and extent of a liberalizing initiative at the EEC level, and so takes a step in the direction that I will emphasize below. But the basic storyline here still runs almost entirely through a consensus on neoliberalism and substantive reforms, from which European institutional and substantive developments follow. The EEC assigned itself these new tasks and procedures because national actors became convinced that a neoliberal agenda was desirable; these authors add that the Commission did some of the convincing.[3]

The common problem of all these accounts is that they see an EEC-level project of liberalization following from neoliberalism, when in fact there is a major historical disconnect between the two. Even a superficial glance at the negotiating positions on the SEA underlines that no amount of enthusiasm for neoliberalism generated the desire to empower European institutions to lead a regulatory revolution. On the one hand, the main champions of deregulation tended to oppose new European powers. The British were the most consistent advocates of liberalization, but led the opposition to revising the EEC treaty or even questioning the 'Luxembourg Compromise' that kept EEC decision-making within formal rules of unanimity. They preferred simply to endorse the Single Market plan, leaving governments free to accept or reject liberalization in the system of unanimity. On the other hand, the champions of EEC institutional reform were reluctant or indifferent vis-à-vis the '1992' liberalization plan. The French and Italian governments led the institutional charge, but preferred a European industrial policy and tighter monetary coordination as collective responses to the economic crisis.[4] In the middle, the Germans and Dutch supported both the liberalization programme and institutional reform, but the former did not lead to the latter. Both had called for various 'supranational' EEC reforms and for ending the Luxembourg Compromise throughout the 1970s. It was their support for liberalization that was new – and in the German case, this was hesitant (Ross, 1995; Haywood, 1989). Overall, no one in the SEA process moved from support for neoliberalism to enthusiasm for European institutions charged with deeper political-economic responsibilities. The actual pattern of action that gave European institutions both a new neoliberal agenda and new institutional authority to enact it was a deal between liberalizers who did not want institutional reform, and reformers who were indifferent to liberalization.

Liberalization push meets Europeanist institutional reform

The remainder of this section traces the origins of the two distinct movements that became the SEA, and how they came together. From 1983 to 1985 the European Commission began to assemble a new liberalization package, with some modest support from business actors. In 1984, French President Mitterrand launched a crusade for EEC institutional reform. In 1985, bargaining among the EEC member-states fused them into a single deal.

The liberalization programme that became the guts of the SEA had humble beginnings. In 1981, the European Commissioner for the Internal Market, Karl Heinz Narjes, began to gather a set of existing proposals into a package of 30 directives that would decrease intra-EEC trade barriers. Although free trade in the Internal Market was ostensibly the main business of the EEC, at this point there were not even regular Council of Ministers meetings on Internal Market issues (as opposed to the regular 'Councils' that existed in other areas: the Council of Agriculture Ministers, Council of Health Ministers, etc.). In 1982 Narjes persuaded his colleagues to create an Internal Market-focussed Council, but mostly for political and personal reasons: he 'wanted to have his own Council – just like the other Commissioners' (Cowles, 1994: 208). These meetings began in January 1983 and attracted very little attention. The French were represented by junior Minister for Consumption Catherine Lalumière, who was chosen to attend precisely because she was the least important member of the government (Lalumière interview, April 1997). German officials endorsed the notion of Internal Market discussions but 'without great enthusiasm' (Moravcsik, 1998: 330). A Narjes proposal that Internal Market directives be given a special 'fast-track' process received little support and was officially blocked by the French.

In 1983 and 1984 Narjes's office continued to elaborate a broader package of barrier-reducing measures, hoping that a wider deal would allow member states to trade off the various barriers they defended. Narjes and other actors at the Commission also established stronger contacts with European big business – most notably the European Roundtable of Industrialists (ERT). Formed in 1983 under the chairmanship of Pehr Gyllenhammer of Volvo, the ERT aimed to coordinate big-business initiatives to stimulate the European economies. While the formation of the ERT certainly reflected the Zeitgeist of calls for activism to overcome 'Eurosclerosis,' the group did not focus spontaneously on the kind of liberalization agenda Narjes was envisioning. Several major firms, especially those from

France, had joined the ERT specifically because they saw it as committed to lobbying for European industrial and research policies instead of Thatcherian-style deregulation (Cowles, 1994: 231). The ERT's first written proposal to the Commission in June 1983 called for initiatives that were tied to longstanding French calls for more dirigiste-style transnational 'grands projets.' They put the greatest emphasis on funding for collaborative infrastructural, research, and venture-capital projects and R&D tax credits. While they also mentioned deregulatory elements – more open public procurement, lowering of barriers to transnational mergers and acquisitions, industrial standardization – most of the ERT members found the notion of an initiative focused around liberalization measures 'dull and boring' well into 1985 (Cowles, 1994: 244; Moravcsik, 1998: 355).

It was not until early 1985, with the installation of a new European Commission, that the broad notion of a 'Single Market 1992' proposal emerged. The new Commission President was Jacques Delors – previously the powerful French Finance Minister, and a strongly pro-EEC figure. Eager to take an activist role in Brussels, Delors took a tour of EEC capitals in late 1984 to measure national leaders' support for various EEC 'big ideas.' Delors's personal preferences (like those of most French policymakers) were for enhanced monetary cooperation and industrial and social policies. But he was discouraged by reactions outside of France to these priorities, and found that the one substantive area to which there was no violent opposition was 'completing the Internal Market.' Once in Brussels, he worked with Narjes's successor, British Commissioner Lord Cockfield, to rapidly assemble a more grandiose Internal Market package. In the space of a few months Cockfield drew up the now-famous White Paper on Completing the Internal Market, with an Annex setting out a timetable for passage of 279 directives by the end of 1992. The White Paper was submitted to the national governments on June 14, 1985 and approved with little discussion at the outset of the European Council meeting in Milan ten days later.

The much more acrimonious issues at the Milan meeting – and in the SEA negotiations that followed – concerned EEC institutional reform. To understand these debates and their relationship (or lack thereof) to the Single Market proposal, we need to back up and trace their historical thread forward.

The early 1980s saw a modest upsurge in the perennial proposals from Europhiles to give more power and authority to the EEC institutions, but no serious intergovernmental negotiations. In the background since the 1970s were occasional calls from a variety of actors for greater use of majority voting in the EEC's Council of Ministers – the body where the member states' governments were directly represented. While formal EEC rules provided for qualified majority voting (QMV) on many issues (especially those relating to the Internal Market), the Luxembourg Compromise of 1966 had established an informal right to national vetoes that effectively maintained unanimity. Pro-EEC actors thus called periodically for at least living up to the letter of the treaties. The EEC business association UNICE (Union des Confédérations de l'Industrie et des Employeurs de l'Europe), for example, reiterated its support for greater use of majority voting at a few points early in the 1980s. Still, there was no sense of a serious business push for institutional reform; the QMV issue was ignored in the substantive proposals of the ERT. More ambitiously, in 1980–1981 the Italian Euro-federalist Altiero Spinelli initiated discussions in the European Parliament to redraft the EEC treaties entirely. The Parliament approved an ambitious (many said utopian) treaty in February 1984 and called upon the member states to ratify it. But the toothless EP was not taken seriously by any national government, and its call was initially ignored except for an approving resolution in the Italian parliament. The closest that governments came to discussing EEC reform prior to 1985 was in reaction to the 'Genscher–Colombo' proposal of 1981. The German and Italian foreign ministers called for treaty reforms that included more majority voting (though they focused more directly on stronger cooperation in foreign policy). They received a lukewarm reception from the other governments, however, and the plan was shunted into an hortatory 'Solemn Declaration on European Union' in 1983. While the declaration suggested that member states should informally limit their recourse to the Luxembourg Compromise – invoking vetoes only over very important issues – the French, British, Danish, Irish, and Greeks immediately issued statements reaffirming their right to use the veto as they saw fit.

Institutional reform only became a serious possibility in 1984, when French President Mitterrand surprised everyone by shifting several of his country's longstanding positions. Mitterrand was a lifelong advocate of European integration, but had shied away from any strong opinions on the EEC since the 1970s because they tended to split his hard-won coalition of the Left (Haywood, 1993; Parsons, 2003). In the aftermath of his painful economic U-turn in March 1983, however, Mitterrand seemed to turn to European ambitions to help recast his political identity. His public and private European rhetoric escalated steadily in 1983. Upon his return from the stalemated Athens European Council of December 1983, he announced to his aides that he had decided to 'pull Europe out of the mud' during the French EEC presidency in the first half of 1984 (Favier and Martin-Roland, 1990: 198).

Mitterrand's decision to refocus his ambitions around a stronger EEC reflected his own Europeanist predilections, not widely-perceived imperatives in policy-making or electoral politics. Economically, while the 1983 U-turn was certainly a prerequisite to turn Mitterrand's priorities away from the Socialist domestic agenda, he did not draw its economic lessons and then consider European ways to implement them. When Mitterrand decided to pursue a major European initiative in late 1983, his government was still hesitating between its electoral incentives (which were massively for staying the Socialist course) and a broad shift to liberalization (a very different thing from the fiscal austerity adopted with the 1983 U-turn). A serious programme of financial deregulation was not yet on the horizon. Thus even the economically-focused Moravcsik writes, 'true to the European idealism he had espoused since the 1940s ... Mitterrand, without being entirely sure where the initiative was leading, became the primary spokesman for relaunching Europe' (Moravcsik, 1991).

Electorally, while Mitterrand was certainly in need of a new agenda once the U-turn ended his major domestic projects, his decision to focus on Europe was unrelated to the counsels of his domestic–political strategists. Literally none of his political advisors or Socialist Party allies advised him in late 1983 or early 1984 to consider a new focus on Europe (Védrine, 1996: 295, and interviews of all Mitterrand's major advisors). They all perceived that European initiatives were unlikely to produce any electoral benefit. They were correct: Mitterrand's European activism after 1983 did nothing to halt the Socialists's electoral slide through a series of defeats to a landslide loss of their majority in 1986. Moreover, the constituency to which Mitterrand's subsequent European push is often argued to have appealed – international business, as suggested in the Moravcsik quotation above – was the last part of the electorate that was ever going to vote for the Socialists. As Elizabeth Haywood concludes, to see Mitterrand's turn to Europe as electorally motivated, we must assign him a 'maladroitness' atypical of his political career (Haywood, 1989: 134; Stevens, 1986).

'Relaunching' the EEC in 1984 meant not just grandiose rhetoric and long-term plans, but immediate concrete concessions on several distributive conflicts that had empoisoned intra-EEC discussions for several years. Margaret Thatcher insisted that Britain contributed too much to the EEC budget and wanted a 'rebate.' The British and Germans sought limits to spending in the Common Agricultural Policy (CAP) that the French and Italians had heretofore resolutely refused. The French also stood as the main obstacle to the stalled EEC accession of Spain and Portugal, which French farmers opposed for fear of competition. In early 1984, Mitterrand deblocked the EEC agenda with new French concessions and launched serious discussions of EEC institutional reform. By the European Council in Fontainebleau that concluded the French presidency in June 1984, all the major issues were resolved, 'in each case largely owing to an unexpected French willingness to compromise' (Moravcsik, 1991: 28). Mitterrand agreed to pay Thatcher a sizeable permanent 'rebate,' accepted limits on CAP subsidies, and ended French stalling on the Iberian enlargement. In parallel, Mitterrand introduced EEC institutional reform as a constant theme in the 30-odd meetings he held with national EEC leaders during these six months. (One advisor called it his 'new political utopia': Attali, 1993.) In May 1984 the President even proclaimed that France was favorable to the European Parliament's Draft Treaty – shocking his

Socialist Party leadership, which had already distributed materials opposing the treaty. At the Fontainebleau summit, Mitterrand proposed at the last second to create a new committee on EEC institutional reform and treaty revisions, modeled explicitly on the 'Spaak Committee' that had launched the EEC negotiations in 1955–1956.[5]

Much like the choice of the supranationally-minded Spaak to chair discussions on European proposals in 1955, Mitterrand's suggestion of a 'Spaak Committee II' was a conscious attempt to set the EEC agenda in a supranational direction. As his personal representative in the committee he appointed Maurice Faure, the aging ultra-Europeanist who had negotiated the EEC Treaty for France. Though this body became known as the Dooge Committee after its Irish chair (under the Irish EEC presidency in the second half of 1984), Faure informally dominated the meetings (De Ruyt, 1987; Meenan, 1985; Keating and Murphy, 1987; Faure interview, March 1998). To the horror of the British, who had expected the French to help *block* any major proposals for institutional reform, Faure soon endorsed the 'maximalist' position supported by the Benelux, Germans, and Italians, calling for a clear shift to majority voting and expanded powers for the European Parliament. He also proposed and won majority voting within the committee itself, leaving the 'minimalist' British, Danish, and Greek minority to register objections in footnotes. When the 'Dooge Report' was circulated, a high-level committee of the French Foreign Ministry agreed with British reservations and argued against treaty revisions (Haywood, 1993; Moravcsik, 1998: 362; interviews, several senior French diplomats and Mitterrand advisors, 1997–1998). But Mitterrand approved the report anyway, and so a call for substantial institutional reform came before the European Council at Milan in June 1985.

In the approach to the Milan meeting, the White Paper on the Internal Market and the institutional discussions of the Dooge Committee were widely perceived as entirely separate. A few days before Milan Jacques Delors hinted in a press conference at linking the two, but he continued to worry that a connection to the bitter fights over institutional reform might kill the Single Market plan (Moravcsik, 1998: 362). In the clearest manifestation of the perceived disconnect, at the Milan meeting itself, there was initially confusion over whether the Dooge Report majority (France, Germany, Italy, Benelux) were proposing their institutional reform plan as an *alternative* to the Single Market initiative (Ross, 1995: 73; Haywood, 1989: 140). After reassurances to the effect that the two plans were in no way incompatible – but were conceptually distinct – the Italian chair called a vote on opening negotiations on treaty revisions. Mitterrand, German Chancellor Helmut Kohl, and the Benelux and Italian leaders supported the idea. The British, Danes, and Greeks complained that a vote by majority was 'illegal' and political 'rape,' but opted to participate because the pro-reform majority hinted that they would proceed without any hold-outs (De Ruyt, 1987; Keating and Murphy, 1987;

Moravcsik, 1998: 360–363). The separation between liberalization and institutional reform was complete. The French, Italians, and Germans – all relatively ambivalent to the Internal Market plan and sharing no other substantive preferences (on industrial, monetary, or social policies) – had opened treaty revisions by threatening to exclude the British, who favored liberalization and little else.

These two historical threads only connected in the rapid 'intergovernmental conference' on treaty revisions from September to December 1985. The Commission set the agenda for the policy-focussed aspects of the negotiations by quickly submitting texts of treaty revisions on the Internal Market, research and technological development and the environment, cohesion and cultural policy, and monetary policy. The initial broad treaty framework was submitted by Luxembourg, which held the EEC Presidency for the second half of 1985. The main bargaining essentially sorted into overlapping and counterbalancing deals on policy substance versus institutional reforms. In terms of substantive policies, the French (with mainly Italian support) generally found themselves blocked by an Anglo-German front. The French submitted texts for a stronger EEC role in social policy and monetary coordination, and offered an Internal Market proposal that was designed to cut back the Commission's plan. But the British and Germans opposed any significant steps in social or monetary policies, and defended stronger versions of the Internal Market programme. The French basically lost this battle, as was prefigured in an internal memo to Mitterrand in preparation for the final bargaining in Luxembourg in December 1985:

> An Anglo-German front has formed against French positions on three essential subjects: the Internal Market, monetary policies, social policies. At Luxembourg, you are not certain to be able to count on German support, as has been the case so far.... In terms of the creation of a great Internal Market, our positions in favor of a *rapprochement* of policies in all areas – fiscal, monetary, social – are still running into the free-trade approach of our British and German partners.
>
> (Élysée documents cited in Favier and Martin-Rolandm 1991: 216)

With minor modifications, the contents of the Commission's White Paper ended up as the sole major substantive engagement to survive the negotiations.[6] On institutional reform, however, a Franco-German-led coalition imposed a broad extension of majority voting, upgraded powers for the European Parliament (giving the EP 'co-decision' veto rights in many areas), and the inclusion of all the issues in a single treaty document (rejecting British attempts to hive off a codification of foreign-policy cooperation to keep it entirely distinct from the supranational Community). The British continued to fight to limit the scope of majority voting – including within the Internal Market (De Ruyt, 1987: 74) – with agreement reached only in last-minute redrafting by Mitterrand, Kohl, and Thatcher themselves.

With the partial exception of the swing-voting Germans, then, it was clear to all participants through the end of the SEA negotiations that they were working out a trade-off between a liberalization agenda and reforms to transfer more authority to the European level. Only for the very small subset of actors who wanted both – some individuals at the Commission, and some minoritarian officials and politicians scattered across the various national delegations – was the notion of a functional link between the two remotely persuasive. For the much larger and more powerful sets of actors who had pushed for only one of these elements, the functional link of treaty reform to help implement liberalization was a myth invented post-hoc to help sell the final product. Liberalizers could downplay their private misgivings about majority voting and suggest that it was a necessary price to pay to make liberalization work. Euro-reformers who were hesitant about liberalization could find virtue in giving the Community new regulatory authority, even if it tended in a deregulatory direction.

But did institutional reform matter?

In terms of historical process, the EEC only empowered itself to undertake a major new liberalizing mandate in the SEA because separate pushes for deregulation and European institutional reform met in an intergovernmental deal. But did process really matter for the outcome of deep continental liberalization? We have seen that irrespective of the distinct debates over treaty revisions, all EEC governments agreed by 1985 to endorse the 'Single Market 1992' programme. Even if this endorsement came with varying degrees of enthusiasm (and a preponderance of indifference), why should we think that the eventual implementation of the '1992' programme depended on concomitant changes in the institutional rules?

This counterfactual objection to my argument – that even had there been no push to reform EEC institutions, the underlying convergence on neoliberal ideas would have brought massive liberalization anyway – is made explicitly by some EU scholars. Jonathan Golub has shown that the SEA's supposed shift to more majority voting produced little change in how long it took to pass directives. Golub's statistics further suggest that the SEA's expansion of EP powers slowed down decision-making (since most legislation now had to pass through the 'cooperation' or 'codecision' procedures). Pointing also to the collective determination to liberalize flowing from the convergence on neoliberal ideas, and to the informal shift in the '1992' programme to a streamlined 'new approach' of mutual recognition to harmonize national standards, Golub speculates that liberalization might have proceeded at least as well without institutional reform:

> If it were not for the institutional drag exerted by the cooperation and codecision procedures – in other words, if there had been no reforms at all – this determination [to liberalize], along with the member state decision to pursue a 'new approach,' might have allowed the Council to accommodate legislation (including 'important' legislation) as well as, if not more successfully than, it actually did.
>
> (Golub, 1999)

Moreover, it is widely known that even since the SEA, consensual processes have continued to dominate in the Council of Ministers. Formal votes are simply not called very often. Tracking available information on votes from 1996 to 2002 (which unfortunately only tracks successful legislation), Dorothée Heisenberg estimates that votes occur in only about 25–30 per cent of cases where QMV would apply (based on my extrapolation of her figures in Heisenberg, 2005). She concludes, echoing Golub, that formal voting rules in the Council matter little in EU politics.

Golub and Heisenberg deserve credit for qualifying a simple view of EU institutional mechanisms, but their thin quantitative studies miss some obvious reasons why most real actors and academic observers think that implementation of much of the '1992' programme depended on the SEA's formal shift to majority voting. Taking time-to-passage as a proxy for decision-making effectiveness has problems, but here I will focus on less quibbling issues.

First, even if academics had robust evidence that voting rules seemed unimportant, real political actors seem to think the rules matter a great deal. As noted above, the main fight over revising the treaties at all in 1985 was over voting rules. The same was true at a more detailed level in the SEA negotiations, and is generally true of negotiations across EU history. Heisenberg's weak attempt to account for this – speculating that these actors cared about the rules not because they were important but because they might someday become important if informal norms broke down – does not match up to the way these issues dominated the actors' substantive positions.

Second, it is well known that a superficially 'consensual' process of decision-making may operate in the shadow of non-consensual decision rules. As a senior official at the Council of Ministers told me, 'Nobody wants to call a vote; everybody looks for a compromise, and we usually find one. But who compromises is obviously influenced by the potential for a vote. The players do calculate how votes would go' (Interview, November 2003). In other words, despite strong norms of 'getting everyone on board,' QMV has generated leverage for substantial compromise and shifted the locus of compromises. This is a point made repeatedly not only by theorists of collective choice like Fritz Scharpf, but by some of the most concrete and well-informed EU-watchers, such as Helen and William Wallace, Wolfgang Wessels, and Philip de Schoutheete (Scharpf, 1997:

191–193; Maurer and Wessels, 2003: 48; Wallace and Wallace, 1996: 139–140).

Third, the record of the '1992' liberalization agenda after the SEA was not a highly consensual process in which states sat down consensually to collaborate on a series of regulatory changes. There were a significant number of explicitly contested votes (about 40 of the 260 directives in the '1992' programme, and about 20 per cent of successful decisions in the Council of Ministers overall in the past 15 years, or somewhere between 750 and 1,000 decisions[7]) and well-known instances where contestation only turned into 'consensus' when it was clear that major actors were going to be outvoted (such as the French surrender to the hugely important capital liberalization directive in 1988; see Védrine, 1996: 419). Far from suggesting an easy convergence that would have produced deep liberalization regardless of institutional mechanisms, the now-extensive literature on the '1992' programme tends to suggest that few (if any) actors understood the full extent of the initial rhetorical commitment in 1986, and that its implementation has been a hard-fought political battle in which the EU's institutional authority mattered a great deal (Crouch and Marquand, 1990; Woolcock *et al.*, 1991; Swann, 1992; Smith and Ray, 1993; Dreyfus *et al.*, 1993; Keeler and Schain, 1996; Katzenstein, 1997; Armstrong and Bulmer, 1998; Wessels *et al.*, 2003).

In sum, this chapter is not being revisionist in suggesting that the depth and scope of implementation of the neoliberal '1992' programme depended on the SEA's institutional reforms. That view is advanced by the vast majority of real actors and well-informed observers in the EU arena. This chapter is quite revisionist, however, in highlighting that these institutional reforms did not flow from a substantive neoliberal agenda. The pushes for liberalization and a stronger EEC had distinct political roots, and were only bound together in the SEA by the political logic of bargaining, not the functional logic of instrumental institutions. Without the separate push for institutional reform, the EEC of the mid-1980s would have only achieved a weak, erratically-supported rhetorical commitment to a list of liberalizing goals – much like a large number of other declarations that litter EU history. Some liberalization would certainly have occurred in Europe in the 1980s, but in a much more incoherent, scattered way that varied hugely across national programs. As it was, neoliberalism was bound into a reinvigorated institutional framework with newly-extended authority. In the decade that followed, the neoliberal flag was staked at the core of the European project, and carried to many of the dark corners of the European landscape.

Monetarism, Europeanism, and the euro

The remarkable story of Europe's single currency is just as important as the '1992' project for the neoliberal revolution in Europe. The push to the euro focussed monetary policies across Europe on anti-inflationary goals and eventually placed monetary policy beyond the reach of governments, closing off some of the long-important channels of discretionary intervention in European economies. Monetary union also generated major pressure on profligate fiscal policies: to meet the deficit criteria enacted to encourage confidence in the single currency, European countries underwent a round of spending cuts that looked extremely unlikely in the absence of a large political justification. Although today these 'Stability Pact' rules for fiscal discipline are under severe challenge, this does not change the fact that monetary union has diminished the space in Europe for active government interventionism and added broad pressure on all government spending. Moreover, the euro is more irrevocable than any particular piece of liberalization. Monetarism is bound into the heart of Europe for good.

As with the Single Market project, scholars fight over many of the details of the monetary-union story, but tend to agree that it flows through a consensus on the monetarist economic principles evidenced in the Maastricht Treaty. Some structural thinkers emphasize objective economic imperatives to such a consensus. They focus mainly on how rapidly expanding capital mobility (together with some of the other structural pressures noted above for neoliberalism) made a monetarist single currency the most rational substantive policy option for most European states. Thus for Moravcsik, EMU was 'driven primarily by [governments'] enduring structural economic interests [from] increased capital mobility and macroeconomic convergence' (Moravcsik, 1998: 381). Other structural thinkers trace the imperatives to EMU more to objective geopolitical conditions. The Cold War's end and German unification provoked fear of a Franco-German split in the 'new Europe,' driving both countries' leaders to bind the EC together more tightly through EMU (Baun, 1996; Middlemas, 1995; Grieco, 1995). Probably the most common interpretation of the euro combines these two structural logics, with geopolitics creating the need for a project at this time and capital mobility defining its monetarist content.

The most prominent ideational account of EMU, by Kathleen McNamara, disputes the sources of European monetarism rather than challenging the idea that monetarism led to EMU. While being careful to note a variety of conditions that fed into the EMU process, her core argument characterizes the euro as a 'currency of ideas.' The ideas in question are neoliberalism and its monetarist component; the basic story is that 'the EU governments had a strong enough policy consensus to reach agreement at Maastricht on a low-inflation, German-model style EMU' (McNamara, 1997: 170). European elites converged on similar new policy-making ideas, wanted the same economic policies, and so were encouraged to fuse a major aspect of their economic sovereignty into a new collective institution. There are also other partly-ideational arguments about EMU, like about the SEA, in which entrepreneurial action by the European Commission is seen as the key mechanism by which national actors became convinced to support EMU. Jacques Delors and his team played up EMU as the solution to EMS asymmetries (which worsened as a consequence of capital liberalization from the Commission's '1992' programme), notably drawing reluctant Germans into the discussion by convincing them that EMU would only happen under the most rigorous conditions (Ross, 1995; Sandholtz, 1996; Gros and Thygesen, 1992). But like the other approaches, most such arguments still arrive at EMU mainly through a policy consensus; their novelty is in highlighting the role of the Commission in constructing this consensus.[8]

As with the Single Market project, all sides of this debate miss some of the fundamental lines of political mobilization around EMU, and so fail to see how much the monetarist project depended on connection to a distinct Europeanist agenda. This is easier to forgive than in accounts of the SEA: all these scholars are more right that European states shared a consensus on monetarism by the late 1980s than they were that European states shared a consensus on liberalization around 1985. Moreover, the patterns of action that display a distinction between supporting monetarism and supporting EMU were sometimes more private than the open break between pro-liberalization and pro-EEC reform in the SEA negotiations. That said, the historical case that the implementation of EMU depended on a separately-motivated institutional agenda is even stronger than the parallel case for EU liberalization.

The notion of near-term monetary union came onto the European scene with the creation of the 'Delors Committee' of central-bank governors in 1988, which produced a three-stage plan for creation of a European Central Bank and single currency. Importantly, the Delors Report did not mention explicit dates for the later stages; without a dated commitment, the plan was not terribly different from earlier unimplemented proposals for monetary union (most notably the Werner Plan of the 1970s). But in 1989 – well before the fall of the Berlin Wall – the French pushed hard to open an Intergovernmental Conference (IGC) for concrete negotiations based on the Delors Report. At the European Council meeting in Strasbourg in December 1989, German Chancellor Helmut Kohl accepted this French proposal. Britain's Margaret Thatcher did not, but much like at Milan in 1985, a majority vote bypassed the British to convene an IGC for the end of 1990. The negotiations ran from late 1990 through the European Council meeting in Maastricht in December 1991, where Mitterrand, Kohl, and most other EU leaders committed to fuse their currencies together by 1999. Any particular states' participation was contingent on fulfillment of restrictive criteria – low inflation, low interest rates, currency stability, and most famously keeping budget deficits below 3 per cent of GDP – but whichever countries were ready would create the euro by 1999 in any case. The British and Danish, however, chose to 'opt out.'

How can we evaluate the relative importance of neoliberal ideas, structural pressures, and other factors in this story? Consider first the basic national negotiating positions. The Germans held Europe's dominant currency, and had little to gain in policy terms from fusing their perennially-strong, non-inflationary Deutschmark with weaker European currencies. Most of the convinced monetarists in the German economic bureaucracy (and in particular at the German Bundesbank) were thus opposed to full monetary union. But some German elites – including Chancellor Helmut Kohl – favoured monetary union for ideologically Europeanist reasons (Heisenberg, 1999; Kaltenthaler, 1998). Still, broader German reluctance to give up the Deutschmark ensured that at most, Kohl could accept, not demand, monetary union – and he could only accept a union that imitated the anti-inflationary mandate of the German Bundesbank.

The other major European government that was thoroughly won over to neoliberal and monetarist thinking – the British – was more hostile to the idea of monetary union. In 1989 the pound was still not participating in the European Monetary System's (EMS) exchange-rate mechanism, which had sought to dampen intra-EU currency volatility since 1979. The financial giants of the City in London and British big business more generally were increasingly favourable to joining the EMS and even considering EMU, and by 1989 a rebellion was emerging within the Conservatives to reverse Thatcher's opposition to such steps. But if Thatcher would eventually be forced out of office in 1990 over these issues, she never wavered in her opposition to giving up the pound. Nor did her weak successor, John Major, come close to considering the option. At most the British were willing to discuss a 'common currency' – issued alongside national currencies rather than in place of them. This alternative was seen as potentially inflationary by devout monetarists in Germany and elsewhere, however, and never made much headway.

Thus it is quite simple to show that in the German and British cases, leaders' stances on Europeanism trumped any linkage between substantive commitments to neoliberalism and preferences for a single currency. Even some ostensibly structural accounts, like that of Moravcsik, admit something similar in caveats and footnotes.[9] It is more revisionist, however, to make the same claim about France. Just as the best-known accounts of the SEA place great weight on the French U-turn of 1983 as completing an economic-policy convergence that led to the '1992' project, the best-known accounts of EMU give much attention to either the structural circumstances or spreading ideas that ostensibly made the French the main champions of full EMU. Structural accounts point out that the French alignment on monetarist rigour in the 1980s had not brought the expected payoff of a strong franc. Even when French inflation fell below that of Germany, financial markets continued to demand higher interest rates to keep money in francs, and threatened capital flight into the

D-mark unless the French actually pursued even stricter economic policies than those across the Rhine. Thus EMU appeared preferable to a situation in which French policies were effectively forced to shadow German ones. The rapid process of Germany's reunification in early 1990 added the additional motivation of using EMU to bind a reunified Germany more tightly into western Europe. Ideational accounts trace the same French views to the spread of monetarist ideas into France, either directly or through the entrepreneurship of the European Commission.

But just as a close look at French decision-making around the SEA highlights a disconnect between economic goals and European projects, so the same is true of EMU. President Mitterrand began his push for EMU in summer 1988, after his narrow reelection. Although all French policymakers were concerned with the pressure through the EMS to shadow German policies, few were drawing the conclusion that a single currency was the appropriate solution. Gaullist leaders like Édouard Balladur and Jacques Chirac called in 1988 for new monetary coordination to fix the EMS, but later strongly opposed the EMU project for sacrificing sovereignty and enshrining German dominance (Balladur, 1989; Bauchard, 1994: 115; Aeschimann and Riché, 1996: 268; Balleix, 1994). French business did not demand any particular policy; the most detailed study of their attitudes through 1992 concludes, 'there is no evidence of strong private sector preferences in favour of or against EMU' (De Boissieu and Pisani-Ferry, 1998). Leaders in Mitterrand's Socialist Party rightly considered EMU an electoral loser, and avoided the subject almost completely in European Parliament elections in 1989 (Balleix, 1994; Cole, 1996). Most importantly for immediate policy decisions, Mitterrand faced strong opposition to his EMU plans within his own government and administration. His long-loyal Socialist Finance Minister, Pierre Bérégovoy, echoed the skepticism of many of the officials at the Banque de France about a German-dominated single currency. They preferred to focus on the British idea of a 'common currency,' or failing that to fall back to coordination among national central banks. In a series of bitter private confrontations, Mitterrand ordered his recalcitrant Finance Minister to negotiate for a successful treaty (Aeschimann and Riché, 1996: 89; Favier and Martin-Roland, 1996: 162).

The French government was so divided over EMU that Mitterrand's immediate advisors were unsure if the President would insist on a dated commitment when he went to Maastricht in December 1991 (Interviews, Mitterrand's major advisors, 1997–1998). Thus Mitterrand's decision to ask for a dated EMU at Maastricht was not unlike Kohl's decision to accept it; both stepped well beyond their economic-experts' preferences and electoral incentives. The weakness of support for EMU among Mitterrand's electorate was then displayed in the French referendum on the treaty in September 1992, which passed by the razor-thin margin of 50.9 per cent to 49.1 per cent. The 'yes' vote 'was built on the votes of [Mitterrand's] opponents' on the Right, with 'no' majorities from 51 of the 78 departments that Mitterrand had carried in 1988 (Criddle, 1993; Appleton, 1992). The trouncing of the Socialists in the 1993 legislative elections, like those in 1986 after the SEA, showed that European projects still delivered no electoral payoff.

Thus it does not make sense to say that any of the major governments at Maastricht derived their positions on EMU from an underlying commitment to neoliberalism. The point is not to dispute that European policy-makers had largely adopted such a commitment by 1989 or 1990; it is simply to note that convinced neoliberals and monetarists were themselves quite divided over EMU. Political actors were even divided within each country (and in France and Germany, even within the governing political coalitions and economically-focused administrations): Kohl and Mitterrand's choices were distinctly unrepresentative of their immediate political allies, and of their polities more broadly. To put it in other terms, Kohl and Mitterrand were representative in favouring neoliberal policies (at least of their national policy-making elites, if not broader populations) but much less directly representative in favouring supranational European projects. The decision at Maastricht required both commitments, and again seemed to require a bit more Europeanism than neoliberalism; EMU was supported across Europe by just as many Europeanists scattered across the Left as scattered across the Right, and opposed by just as many nationalists on the Right as on the Left.

My claim that the binding of Europe into monetarism depended on European institutional reform stands on its own more easily than my similar claim about liberalization in the '1992' programme. While it makes some sense to wonder if liberalization might have gone just as far without the SEA reforms of majority voting, it does not make much sense to wonder if such binding European commitments to monetarism would have emerged without the new institutions of a European central bank and a new currency. More than any element of the '1992' programme, EMU was obviously about removing the authority for future policy choices irrevocably from national governments' control. It is very difficult even to imagine a similarly powerful and far-reaching substantive commitment to anti-inflationary rigour without EMU's creation of new institutions. There was no chance that European governments were all going to reform their national systems to imitate the German Bundesbank, and even this scenario would have retained much more potential for national-government influence over monetary policies than does an independent ECB. Thus if the euro obviously institutionalized and extended the neoliberal aspects of European political economy, this does not mean that the prior spread of neoliberal policies comes close to explaining EMU. Neoliberal ideas have gone as far as they have in Europe largely because they benefited from a fortuitous political connection to the distinct project of Europeanist institution-building.

Conclusion

This chapter has argued that existing accounts, whether structural or ideational, are wrong to see the development of the European Union since the 1980s largely as an offshoot of a convergence on neoliberal economic policies. Those who are attempting to explain European integration simply cannot get very far if they try to trace mobilization around the SEA or EMU to commitments to certain substantive economic goals. More importantly for this book, the same is true for those who are interested in explaining not the EU but the extent of substantive shifts to neoliberal policies in recent decades. Since the European institutions became such powerful levers for substantive commitments to neoliberalism, any robust account of the substance of policy outcomes must be able to explain these institutional commitments as well. To explain these institutional commitments, we must pay attention to the distinct ideational agenda of supranational Europeanism.

Two qualifications are important to limit potential misreadings of my argument. First, it is important to understand that when I write of Mitterrand or Kohl making unrepresentative decisions out of personal Europeanism, this is not just a story of 'great men' making up history as they go along. Mitterrand and Kohl and other 'Europeanist' leaders are part of a concrete historical movement of people who share similar ideas about supranational institutions as solutions to a wide variety of problems in postwar Europe. These people frequently say quite explicitly that they espouse these ideas, and are often denounced by people with other ideas (like Margaret Thatcher) in similar terms. They have been a minority in all European countries in the past 50 years, however, and they appear highly scattered politically because their defining ideas cross-cut the Right/Left principles that continue to organize the European political landscape (especially among electorates). Their agenda only moves forward when several of their proponents arrive in power for other reasons – typically being elected for their Right/Left agenda, but thereby gaining the authority to pursue their European ambitions as well. But again, this is not a story of leaders using the autonomy of their office to act on their whims of the moment. Just as proponents of neoliberal ideas pursue a long-term program, these Europeanists' choices in the SEA or EMU follow the lines of a conscious institutional agenda laid out in the 1950s (Parsons, 2003).

To restate my argument, then, I claim that the choices for the SEA and EMU were made by politicians who directly represented minority elites in their countries who favored Europeanism, with weaker and much more erratic support from the gestating majority of elites who favoured neoliberalism. It is in this sense that these cases are somewhat more about Europeanism using neoliberalism as a vehicle than the other way around. But my second qualification is to note that if neoliberalism has gone much further due to Europeanism, the same is obviously true of Europeanism. Neoliberalism and monetarism turned out to be enormously effective vehicles for the project of building strong European institutions. The language of the market legitimized the delegation of national sovereignty in ways that would have been hard to sell otherwise. Reregulation provided a formula to reconstitute that power at the European level without requiring massive bureaucracies or spending. The language of monetarism convinced many Europeans that central banks should be independent anyway, making it much easier to swallow the shift of power from national banks to the ECB (Jabko, 1999).

With respect to the broader goals of this book, I hope that it is easy to see how these claims display the conceptual value of Denzau and North's shared mental models. To understand the major patterns of economic change in contemporary Europe we must recognize the importance of not just one but two packages of ideas that have reconfigured the continent. This makes the notion of mental models all the more important in this setting – though it qualifies the impact of the particular mental model of neoliberal ideas. I also submit that the same qualification will extend beyond the European setting: neoliberal agendas everywhere will be dependent on other ideas about institutions and political authority. Neoliberal principles certainly tend to favour large-scale political units over small ones, but they tend to be ambiguous about whether and how large-scale units should be regulated by coordination between units or by centralized institutions (especially as policy-makers get into the nitty-gritty of any particular situation). As many have noted, even if neoliberalism itself advocates a relatively 'weak state,' reform of existing economies in a neoliberal direction typically requires a 'strong state' of some sort – and so the justification for the central capacities to implement neoliberal principles tend to come from other foundations. If we lived in a world where economic benefits defined action, this might not be the case. But we live in a world of political economies, in which actors care not just about the distribution of resources but the distribution and justification of authority and power. In such a world, neoliberal ideas alone are not enough. Their success or failure will always depend heavily on the political institutions and ideas that enact and justify them.

Notes

1 Except for those who effectively abjure explanation to focus on prediction, as defended in Friedman, 1953. For a larger philosophy-of-science defence of this assertion, see Parsons, 2003.

2 Thus I should emphasize that I am extracting an argument from this literature that is somewhat distant in time and focus. In so doing I should highlight a distinction between tracing out an implication of this literature and claiming that these authors endorse this implication. Their arguments about the 1970s and early 1980s suggest that a neoliberal consensus was established, but if they

looked directly at EEC processes they might well allow that other things were going on as well (as I argue). See Hall, 1989, 1992.

3 The strongest versions of this kind of argument, however, increase the separation between national-policy convergence and European developments – emphasizing more distinctly political processes that connected the former to the latter – and so come closer to my argument. See especially Jabko, 1999.

4 Moravcsik (1998: 332) puzzles, 'The French position in the SEA negotiations was characterized by a curious combination of caution about the single market project and enthusiastic support for European reforms.'

5 There was actually no time for discussion of this proposal, and it was included in the meeting conclusions 'on the authority of the Presidency' (Pryce, 1984).

6 Minimal references to monetary and social policies were included in the final text, and then only at the price of further French and Italian concessions on exchange-control liberalization and a rhetorical pledge to complete capital liberalization.

7 The first figure is from De Schoutheete, 2000; the latter is a rough estimate drawn from figures from Maurer and Wessels, 2003 and Heisenberg, 2005.

8 As with the SEA, the strongest arguments about EMU in this vein (above all Jabko, 1999) come close to my argument in emphasizing that 'Europeanist' political action actually played a key role in rallying many actors who were skeptical of EMU – though Jabko and I disagree slightly about the relative influence of Delors versus national leaders (Mitterrand and Kohl).

9 Moravcsik (1998: 416) allows that ideology played a 'secondary but significant role' in French preferences and an even stronger role in Germany.

References

Aeschimann, E. and Riché, P. (1996) *La guerre de sept ans.* Paris: Calmann-Lévy.

Appleton, A. (1992) 'Maastricht and the French party system: domestic implications of the treaty referendum', *French Politics and Society* 10: 1–18.

Armstrong. K. and Bulmer, S. (1998) *The Governance of the Single European Market.* Manchester: Manchester University Press.

Attali, J. (1993) *Verbatim.* Paris: Fayard.

Balladur, E. (1989) *Passion et longueur du temps.* Paris: Fayard.

Balleix, C. (1994) 'La banque centrale européenne dans le discours politique français', *Revue politique et parlementaire* 96: 38–45.

Bauchard, P. (1994) *Deux ministres trop tranquilles.* Paris: Belfond.

Baun, M. (1996) *An Imperfect Union: The Maastricht Treaty and the New Politics of European Integration.* Boulder, CO: Westview.

Cole, A. (1996) 'The French Socialists', in Gaffney, J. (ed.) *Political Parties and the European Union.* New York: Routledge, pp. 71–85.

Cowles, M.G. (1994) *The Politics of Big Business in the European Community*, unpublished dissertation, American University.

Criddle, B. (1993) 'The French referendum on the Maastricht Treaty', *Parliamentary Affairs* 46: 228–239.

Crouch, C. and Marquand, D. (eds) (1990) *The Politics of 1992: Beyond the Single European Market.* London: Basil Blackwell.

De Boissieu, C. and Pisani-Ferry, J. (1998) 'The political economy of French economic policy in the perspective of EMU', in Eichengreen, B. and Frieden, J. (eds) *Forging an Integrated Europe.* Ann Arbor: University of Michigan Press, pp. 49–90.

De la Torre. A. and Kelley, M. (1992) *Regional Trade Arrangements*, International Monetary Fund Occasional Paper no. 93. Washington, DC: IMF.

De Schoutheete, P. (2000) *The Case for Europe.* Boulder, CO: Lynne Rienner.

De Ruyt, J. (1987) *L'Acte unique européen.* Brussels: Université de Bruxelles.

Dreyfus, F.-G., Morizet, J. and Peyrard, M. (eds) (1993) *France and EC Membership Evaluated.* London: Pinter.

Favier, P. and Martin-Roland, M. (1990) *La décennie Mitterrand I: Les ruptures (1981–1984).* Paris: Seuil.

Favier, P. and Martin-Roland, M. (1991) *La décennie Mitterrand II: Les épreuves (1984–1988).* Paris: Seuil.

Favier, P. and Martin-Roland, M. (1996) *La décennie Mitterrand III: Les défis (1988–1991).* Paris: Seuil.

Fligstein, N. and Mara-Drita, I. (1996) 'How to make a market: reflections on the attempt to create a single market in the European Union', *American Journal of Sociology* 102: 1–33.

Friedman, M. (1953) *Essays in Positive Economics.* Chicago: University of Chicago Press.

Golub, J. (1999) 'In the shadow of the vote? Decision-making in the European Community', *International Organization* 54: 733–764.

Goodman, J. and Pauley, L. (1993) 'The obsolescence of capital controls? Economic management in an age of global markets', *World Politics* 46: 50–82.

Grieco, J. (1995) 'The Maastricht Treaty, economic and monetary union and the neo-realist research programme', *Review of International Studies* 21: 21–40.

Gros, D. and Thygesen, N. (1992) *European Monetary Integration.* New York: St Martin's.

Hall, P.A. (ed.) (1989) *The Political Power of Economic Ideas: Keynesianism across Nations.* Princeton: Princeton University Press.

Hall, P.A. (1992) 'The movement from Keynesianism to monetarism', in Thelen, K., Steinmo, S. and Longstreth, F. (eds) *Structuring Politics: Historical Institutionalism in Comparative Analysis.* New York: Cambridge University Press, pp. 90–113.

Haywood, E. (1989) 'The French Socialists and European institutional reform', *Journal of European Integration* 12: 121–149.

Haywood, E. (1993) 'The European policy of François Mitterrand', *Journal of Common Market Studies* 31: 269–282.

Heisenberg, D. (1999) *The Mark of the Bundesbank: Germany's Role in European Monetary Cooperation.* Boulder, CO: Lynne Rienner.

Heisenberg, D. (2005) 'The institution of "Consensus" in the EU: formal versus informal decision-making in the Council', *European Journal of Political Research* 44: 65–90.

Jabko, N. (1999) 'In the name of the market: how the European Commission paved the way for monetary union', *Journal of European Public Policy* 6: 475–495.

Kaltenthaler, K. (1998) *Germany and the Politics of Europe's Money.* Durham, NC: Duke University Press.

Katzenstein, P. (ed.) (1997) *Tamed Power: Germany in Europe.* Ithaca, NY: Cornell University Press.

Keating, P. and Murphy, A. (1987) 'The European Council's Ad Hoc Committee on Institutional Affairs', in Pryce, R. (ed.) *Dynamics of European Union.* London: Methuen, pp. 217–237.

Keeler, J.T.S. and Schain, M. (eds) (1996) *Chirac's Challenge: Liberalization, Europeanization, and Malaise in France.* New York: St Martin's.

Lalumiere, C. (1997) Interview with author, Brussels, April 22, 1997.

Lawrence, R. (1996) *Regionalism, Multilateralism, and Deeper Integration.* Washington, DC: Brookings.

Majone, G. (1994) 'The rise of the regulatory state in Europe', *West European Politics* 17: 77–102.

Maurer A. and Wessels, W. (2003) 'The European Union matters: structuring self-made offers and demands', in Wessels, W., Maurer, A. and Mittag, J. (eds) *Fifteen into One? The European Union and its Member-States.* Manchester: Manchester University Press.

McNamara, K. (1997) *The Currency of Ideas.* Ithaca, NY: Cornell University Press.

Meenan, K. (1985) 'The work of the Dooge Committee', *Administration* 33: 580–589.

Middlemas, K. (1995) *Orchestrating Europe: The Informal Politics of the European Union, 1973–95.* London: Fontana.

Moravcsik, A. (1998) *The Choice For Europe: Social Purpose and State Power from Messina to Maastricht.* Ithaca, NY: Cornell University Press.

Moravcsik, A. (1991) 'Negotiating the Single European Act: national interests and conventional statecraft in the European Community', *International Organization* 45: 19–56.

Organization for Economic Cooperation and Development (OECD) (1990) *OECD National Accounts, vol 1: Main Aggregates, 1960–88.* Paris: OECD.

Parsons, C. (2003) *A Certain Idea of Europe.* Ithaca, NY: Cornell University Press.

Pryce, Roy (1984) 'Relaunching the European Community', *Government and Opposition* 19: 486–500.

Ross, G. (1995) *Jacques Delors and European Integration.* London: Polity.

Sandholtz, W. (1996) 'Membership matters: limits of the functional approach to European institutions', *Journal of Common Market Studies* 34: 403–429.

Sandholtz, W. and Zysman, J. (1989) '1992: recasting the European bargain', *World Politics* 42: 95–128.

Sapir, A. (1992) 'Regional integration in Europe', *Economic Journal* 102: 1491–1506.

Scharpf, F. (1997) *Games Real Actors Play: Actor-Centered Institutionalism in Policy Research.* Boulder, CO: Westview.

Smith, D. and Ray, J.L. (eds) (1993) *The 1992 Project and the Future of Integration in Europe.* New York: ME Sharpe.

Stevens, A. (1986) 'France', in Lodge, J. (ed.) *Direct Elections to the European Parliament 1984.* London: Macmillan, pp. 92–116.

Swann, D. (1992) *The Single European Market and Beyond: A Study of the Wider Implications of the Single European Act.* New York: Routledge.

Védrine, H. (1996) *Les Mondes de François Mitterrand.* Paris: Seuil.

Wallace, H. and Wallace, W. (1996) *Policy-Making in the European Union.* Oxford: Oxford University Press.

Wessels, W., Maurer, A. and Mittag, J. (eds) (2003) *Fifteen into One? The European Union and its Member-States.* Manchester: Manchester University Press.

Woolcock, S., Hodges, M. and Schreiber, K. (1991) *Britain, Germany, and 1992: The Limits of Deregulation.* New York: Council on Foreign Relations Press.

10 Neoliberal reform in the post-communist world

Mental models in the transition from plan to market

Shale Horowitz

Across the developing world, a democratic consensus in favor of neoliberal or market-oriented economic policies does not easily form without an authoritarian period in which such policies produce a long period of high growth. This pattern can be seen in East Asia, and in a kind of reverse image, in Latin America – where Chile seems to be the only clear analogue to the market-oriented East Asian democracies. Only in the post-communist world has this rule been widely defied. Following the collapse of the communist regimes, much of Eastern Europe embarked on ambitious market reforms, and then stuck with them through significant economic difficulties and many democratic changes of government. What accounts for these anomalous levels of ideological and political consensus in favor of neoliberal reform? What explains the lack of such consensus and the more limited reforms in other post-communist countries?

This chapter explores economic reform from communism to neoliberalism through what Denzau and North refer to as shared mental models (1994). The post-communist cases of consensus reform involved democratic processes in which high, sustained levels of mass ideological support went along with elite-level shared mental models that endorsed the need for rapid, thorough transitions to market economies. These reform-oriented mental models were often referred to as "Big Bang" models, because they argued for introducing the elements of market economies quickly and fully. Their main rivals were most often called "Gradualist," as they sought to avoid anticipated negative consequences of market reform by delaying and compromising key reforms at the macroeconomic and microeconomic levels. This chapter focuses mainly on explaining why strong consensus sometimes developed in favor of "Big Bang" reforms, while, in other cases, resilient old regimes stuck by various "Gradualist" formulas, or, in still other cases, successive governments have moved back and forth between agendas of rapid reform and gradualist compromises. The literature on positive political economy has tended to focus on the expected struggles among strongly affected, well-organized economic interest groups (e.g. Frieden, 1991; Olson, 1971; Rogowski, 1989). Here it is argued that cultural factors – particularly the presence of strong national identities oriented towards reviving "golden pasts" – played the most important role in creating consensus support for post-communist neoliberal reform.

The logic of this cultural explanation is consistent with the theory offered by Denzau and North (1994), and by Roy, Denzau, and Willett in the introduction to this volume. Rapid transitions from planned to market economies were highly complex and had not been previously attempted. They involved collective choices under uncertainty: complex environments with limited information and, for pivotal numbers of actors likely to benefit from neoliberal reforms, relatively limited incentives to invest in information and organization. In such cases, shared cultural backgrounds may support convergence of ideologies and mental models in a matter that might not otherwise take place. Across different collective choice settings, this is likely to produce divergent, path-dependent policy outcomes, rather than consistent "learning" and policy convergence. Such cultural biases can explain sustained support for suboptimal policies. They can also lock in more optimal policies by counteracting resistance that would otherwise arise due to individual economic interests, myopia, or policy implementation errors.

The next section lays out the main mental models – the Big Bang versus Gradualism – that characterized the post-communist debate over the transition from planned to market economies. The following sections turn to the main explanations of variation in policy choices: differences in ex ante economic development, which predict variation in economic interest group support and opposition; and "frustrated national ideals," shared collective identities predicting variation in hostility to the old communist regime and in support for democratic capitalism, the most obvious alternative. Case studies of Poland and Russia offer preliminary assessments of these explanations. More systematic evidence is then provided by a statistical analysis of the full set of post-communist countries. Both the case studies and the statistical evidence provide strong support for the hypothesized cultural explanation, and weaker support for the hypothesized interest group explanation.

Mental models of the transition: Big Bang versus Gradualism

The main issues of transition economics involved making the leap from plan to market. Planned economies relied primarily on state rather than market allocation of resources. At the inter-firm level, a state-determined central plan determined the flow of inputs from state-owned producers to next-stage users. International trade was limited to a small number of transactions, to make hard currency available for the hardest-to-produce inputs, or to engage in barter with other planned economies. Capital-intensive industry and agriculture were heavily subsidized at the expense of light industry and services. Cheap energy and energy-intensive inputs were a particularly important form of subsidy.

Apart from systemic inefficiencies and rigidities, this allocative system created perverse incentives at the firm level. Firms placed less emphasis on consumer-relevant quality and innovation, and more emphasis on meeting quantitative state output targets. Managers had an incentive, not to maximize efficiency gains that would be mostly captured by the state, but to make sure that sufficient slack existed to make it easy to meet quantitative targets and, increasingly, to divert resources informally into the hands of managers' personal networks.

Prices did not convey information about relative scarcity of inputs and outputs, but reflected political decisions about how to distribute incomes. Hence firm balance sheets did not measure ability to add value. Paper "losses" were covered by open-ended state credits – the so-called "soft budget constraint" – while "profits" went into state coffers. At the macroeconomic level, the resulting large fiscal deficits were covered by expanding the money supply. Consumer prices were fixed at artificially low levels, so that inflation was repressed and goods were allocated by queuing or, in many cases, using political criteria and personal connections (Kornai, 1992; Nove, 1986).

What was necessary to transform a planned economy into a market economy? In the early approaches, three dominant policy dimensions were identified: liberalization of prices and entry; macroeconomic stabilization; and privatization of state-owned enterprises. Liberalization of prices would allow prices to carry information about relative scarcities of inputs and outputs. Liberalizing entry, by both domestic and foreign firms, would create competitive pressures to increase efficiency and respond to consumer preferences. Macroeconomic stabilization would be achieved by imposing "hard budget constraints" on both state-owned enterprises and the government. Apart from achieving macroeconomic price stability, this would force state-owned firms to compete rather than rely on state subsidies. Privatization would give owners control over production and residual profits, thus increasing incentives to respond to market opportunities and competitive pressures. To create accurate price signals and strong market-based incentives, most economists believed that these reforms should be implemented as quickly as possible as elements of a single "Big Bang" program (World Bank 1996).

Such a systemic transition involved a high level of uncertainty. The biggest worry was that large ex ante structural inefficiencies, confronted all at once with market prices and hard budget constraints, would yield a massive wave of bankruptcies and unemployment. This might create a Great Depression-scale effective demand failure, with downwardly spiraling second-order effects. Particularly given that people would generally lack experience with a market economy, it was not clear how quickly market actors would respond to new opportunities, channel newly available inputs into more productive uses, and thus generate compensating aggregate demand. A related worry was that much salvageable specific capital would be wasted in a rapid transition, as financial constraints became binding before agents could figure out how to adapt to market conditions.

These worries were the basis of the "Gradualist" alternative. Liberalization, stabilization, and privatization should be implemented gradually. Delaying components of liberalization that threatened large sectors would brake their decline, so that the gradually rising market economy could keep pace and thus limit the initial demand shock. Similarly, selective delays in introducing hard budget constraints and privatizing would allow state-owned firms sufficient time to learn how to adapt, thus preserving valuable specific capital.

Big Bang supporters argued that the supposed virtues of gradualism were serious or even deadly flaws. "Gradual" macroeconomic stabilization would allow high inflation to continue, which would distort price signals and increase investor uncertainty. At the firm level, more promising new or old firms would be starved for capital to prop up inefficient state-sector firms. Moreover, it was not clear how the firms with the most valuable specific capital would be identified, or that providing such firms with soft budget constraints or more formal subsidies would more certainly conserve their specific capital. At the same time, the old system generally would still be suffering from substantially reduced subsidies and increased competition. Thus, gradualism might not significantly blunt the initial demand shock, but it would more certainly retard and distort the rising market economy. Supporters of Gradualism pointed to China's success in implementing phased market reforms during the 1980s. Critics argued that China's economy was largely based on family-plot, subsistence agriculture, with a relatively small urban, plan-based sector. They argued that phased reform would not work in highly urbanized, industrialized economies with dominant state sectors. Hungarian, Yugoslav, and late Soviet experiments with hybrid economic systems arguably showed that Gradualism did not prevent transitional shocks, but did seem to guarantee subsequent stagnation (Åslund, 2002; World Bank, 1996).

The Big Bang and Gradualist mental models were not complete policy blueprints, but rather interdependent lists of necessary or facilitating conditions – as with the much-discussed "Washington Consensus" policies. It is sometimes argued, for example, that these mental models ignored the need to establish the rule of law. More accurately, they underestimated the difficulty of establishing the political, legal, and civil society institutions necessary to a well-functioning rule of law. Similarly, there was no initial consensus on the most efficient means of privatizing large numbers of medium and large state firms; on when and how to privatize the commercial banking system; or on what type of exchange rate regime was best suited to the various strategies and stages of transition. There is no space here to discuss these important issues.

Political feasibility and sustainability: interest groups and institutions

Such optimal policy debates did not address whether either of the broad approaches would be politically feasible in the short run, or politically sustainable in the longer run. What patterns of economic interest group support could be expected for rapid and thorough Big Bang reforms, as opposed to slower and partial Gradualist reforms? State-dominated heavy manufacturing and agriculture – the most heavily subsidized sectors under the old economic regime – would be expected to form the core of opposition to Big Bang reforms. The main support base would be the under-capitalized service sector, and generally, the more educated, flexible workforces of the big cities, which were in the best position to take advantages of market opportunities.

What can be said about the likely balance of power between these conservative and reformist coalitions? The manufacturing and agricultural sectors had all or most of the advantages of "concentrated" interest groups: the costs of market reform were high, direct, and immediate; relatively homogeneous products made it easier to mobilize around specific policies; and large productive units and regional concentration, particularly for heavy industries, facilitated political mobilization. By contrast, the service sector was a more "dispersed" group: the benefits of market reform were more uneven, indirect, and back-loaded, i.e. much more uncertain; products were heterogeneous, and productive units were small and relatively scattered. Thus, one would expect concentrated group opposition to Big Bang reforms to be strong and constant, and dispersed group support to be weaker and less constant.

Related points can be made about expected inter-temporal and cross-national variation. Across time, even if dispersed group support suffices to allow initially ambitious market reform, it should tend to erode more quickly when confronted with the initial shock of transition and the relatively slow, market-based recovery (Przeworski, 1991). Across countries, the relative size of the concentrated and dispersed groups should vary with the level of ex ante economic development. Richer countries have more skilled workforces and more urbanized economies. Thus, their heavy industries are likely to be more competitive under market conditions, their agricultural sectors smaller, and their urban service sectors larger. In contrast, poorer countries should have larger uncompetitive heavy industries and agricultural sectors and smaller urban service sectors.

Such microfoundations of support and opposition, of course, must operate through political institutions and leaders. The main political alternatives were maintaining communism, or some suitably adapted authoritarian variant controlled by the incumbent communist party elite;

or adopting a democratic system, in which communist elites and anti-communist opposition groups would engage in structured competition for popular mandates. If incumbent communist elites maintained authoritarian systems, they could be expected to favor traditional clients in the state-dominated economic system, both in propping up non-competitive sectors and in using patron–client networks to allocate opportunities in the new market economy. Under democracy, it would more feasible for pro-market groups to organize and influence the government. One would expect, though, that they would be hampered by weaker, more inconstant preferences. In the post-communist world, then, the initial political conditions made democratization a necessary but not a sufficient condition for rapid, thorough market reforms.

Post-communist neoliberal reform: sources of ideological consensus

Tracing political process developments, it is clear that post-communist neoliberal reform tended to follow democratization, and to be implemented initially by new center-right, non-communist governments (Fish, 1998). Where there was no democratization, there was no rapid, thorough market reform. Where there was democratization, the initial center-right successor governments usually lost power to center-left parties or coalitions after one or two election cycles. However, the second, typically reformed communist-dominated governments, did not attempt to role back neoliberal reforms. More frequently, they continued with the reforms, while pushing for a more generous social safety net. In the intermediate cases where there was democratization, but where reformed communist parties won the first set of elections – as in Bulgaria, Romania, and Ukraine – neoliberal reform was implemented more gradually, and later-stage reforms were more sporadic and unpredictable.

In other words, the trajectories of short- and longer-term neoliberal reforms exhibit marked path dependence. Where market reforms were implemented quickly and thoroughly, they were always deepened rather than rolled back over time. Market-oriented mental models of reform commanded consensus support. Where market reforms were implemented very slowly and inconsistently, as in the authoritarian cases, they never managed to stage strong later-stage recoveries. In the intermediate cases, there was more later-stage variation, with some converging toward the fast reformers, others toward the slow reformers, and others continuing to muddle through with partial, inconsistent reforms.

How is this variation to be explained? Three main approaches will be examined here. First, as discussed above, more economically developed post-communist countries should have a stronger interest group basis of support for neoliberal reform. It may be that a critical mass of interest group support suffices to create a lasting, pro-market ideological consensus.

Hypothesis 1: More economically developed post-communist countries should have smaller uncompetitive manufacturing sectors and agricultural sectors and larger urban service sectors, and hence weaker opposition and stronger support for neoliberal reform.

Second, it may be that broader cultural factors played an important role. As discussed by Denzau and North (1994), this is particularly likely where complex decisions require simplifying mental models to structure their policy preferences and choices. Such cultural variation is here evident in the political roles played by "frustrated national ideals." In countries where rapid, thorough market reforms occurred, anti-communist Popular Front movements with overwhelming mass support challenged incumbent communist regimes based on ideologies of national independence and revival. Neoliberal reform was part of a larger package of policies that aimed not only to improve economic conditions, but also to throw off foreign (Soviet or Yugoslav) domination, secure political, cultural, and economic freedoms, and reorient foreign military and economic policies toward the West. All of these goals were viewed as desirable in themselves, but what tied them all together and provided the overarching goal was the cause of national revival or renaissance. Where such national revival movements were strong, their ideologies were also internalized by reform-oriented communists. This facilitated smooth transitions to democracy, as well as market-oriented policy consistency across changing post-communist governments. Where such movements were weak, incumbent communist parties tended to retain authoritarian power, re-label themselves as reformers, and preside over cronyist partial reforms.

How would such cultural sources of support be expected to interact with interest group sources of support and opposition? Cultural sources of support would be expected to be more effective in stiffening service sector support than in neutralizing or reversing heavy industry and agricultural sector opposition (Horowitz, 2001). This is because interest group opposition is more grounded in direct, immediate experience with large costs, in contrast to the more indirect, back-loaded, and uncertain benefits accruing to supporters. Figure 10.1 summarizes the interest group and cultural sources of support for post-communist market reform.

Why did such national revival movements have so much more influence in some countries than others? The pattern seems to be that countries that had experienced greater pre-communist economic development and more independent and prominent pre-communist political attainments, tended to view communism as a significant setback to greater national potential (Horowitz, 2004). Countries with stronger frustrated national ideals were more likely to make a sharp break with the communist past and to have a strong political consensus on adopting the most obvious alternative model for success – market-oriented democracy with strong economic and geopolitical links with the larger community of such coun-

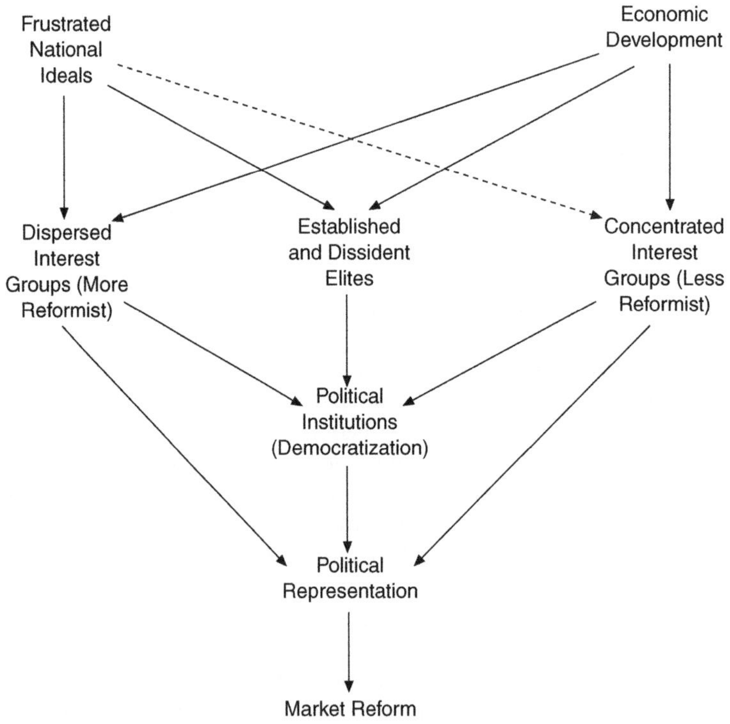

Figure 10.1 Sources of post-communist neo-liberal reform.

Note
Dashed line indicates *weaker* influence.

tries. Notably, this logic is based primarily on correlation rather than causal theory, and is historically conditional. Not only were state-controlled economic models associated with the most recent, illegitimate period of foreign domination, but their market-oriented rivals were branded by no such "scarlet letter" in the more distant past. Moreover, the transitional period was one in which market-oriented economic models were ascendant, both in the West and in the developing world.[1]

Hypothesis 2: Countries with greater pre-communist economic and political achievements ("golden pasts") should be more likely to break sharply with communism and support market-oriented democracy.

Many of the post-communist countries had restive internal minorities, often patronized by neighboring countries; or were involved in disputes over the status and treatment of ethnic kin living as minorities in neighboring countries. These disputes often erupted into full-scale inter-ethnic wars. Such wars functioned as external shocks that tended to distract, delegitimize, and overthrow reform-oriented democratic governments. On the other hand, the wars did not tend to displace partial, patronage-oriented economic reforms, even where they did destabilize less reformist governments.

Hypothesis 3: Countries at war for longer periods of time should experience slower and more incomplete neoliberal reforms.

Poland and Russia

Do the examples of Poland and Russia shed any light on these hypotheses? In 1989, Poland was the first adopter of rapid, thorough neoliberal reforms. Prices, along with private sector entry and international trade, were almost completely liberalized. Macroeconomic stabilization was achieved through fiscal restraint, and at the banking sector level, hard budget constraints. Although medium and large state enterprise privatization was largely blocked by firm-level vetoes until late 1996, state subsidies to firms were slashed and regulations strictly limited new credit to firms with non-performing loans. This kept outstanding credit and non-performing loans at low levels. Falling state sector output was balanced mostly through growth of new start-ups, rather than that of newly-privatized firms. Since 1996, medium and large privatization has gone forward slowly but steadily. Foreign investment also grew rapidly from 1996, soon putting most of the commercial banking sector into foreign hands. Corruption has been relatively well controlled, through a combination of legal and civil service reforms, mass media coverage, active NGOs, and political oversight initiatives. In the initial shock from 1990–1991, GDP fell by 11.6 percent and 7 percent. A sustained recovery followed, accelerating from 2.6 percent in 1992 to a range of 5–7 percent in 1994–1997, and slowing to around 4 percent per annum thereafter. Unemployment shot up from 0.1 percent in 1989 to a peak of 16.4 percent in 1993. It then fell to 8.6 percent in 1997, before rising again to 17.3 percent in 2001. Overall, Poland adopted neoliberal reforms much faster than most other post-communist countries (EBRD, 1994, 32–33, 165; EBRD, 1998, 182–183, 223; Karatnycky *et al.*, 2002, 306–311; Sachs, 1993).[2]

Now consider the hypothesized predictors of neoliberal reform. At the time of transition, Poland's agricultural sector employed 27 percent of her workforce, as compared to a mean of 23 percent and a median of 21 percent for the 28 post-communist countries. Poland also had large uncompetitive heavy industries. On the other hand, Poland had high levels of pre-communist economic and political achievement (see Table 10.1 and the appendix later in the chapter). Poland was also not diverted from internal reform by war. Poland's large agricultural sector and uncompetitive heavy industries predict greater-than-average resistance to neoliberal reform by losing economic sectors, along with a correspondingly large transitional recession likely to erode service sector support for market reform. But resistance from economic interest group losers should be counteracted by stronger, more persistent service sector support, based on a stronger perceived collective interest in breaking with communism to secure national independence and revive national greatness.

Poland was the first place where the incumbent communist party allowed elections, in June 1989, that led to a turnover of power to a non-communist government. The anti-communist opposition was organized as the Solidarity popular front movement. Although Solidarity originated as a trade union, it rapidly mutated into a broad national resistance movement, including participation by the Catholic Church, urban intellectuals, and farmers. Once Solidarity took power, Poland's communist party transformed itself into a western European-style social democratic party. The early Solidarity governments, as mentioned, were the first to implement rapid, thorough market reforms. The reforms were explicitly represented as a part of a difficult but necessary process of restoring the nation by adopting western political and economic institutions. The reformed communist party supported this worldview, including the need for rapid, thorough market reforms, and differed mainly in supporting a stronger social safety net. Solidarity successor parties won the October 1991 elections, before the transitional recession had ended. But in September 1993, the reformed communist party along with an allied center-Left agricultural party retook power. Since then, the center-Left led by the reformed communist party (Democratic Left Alliance), and the center-Right led by various Solidarity successor parties, have exchanged power in every election. Throughout, there has been no significant deviation from the neoliberal reform path laid out by early Solidarity governments.

Poland's frustrated national ideals were crucial in generating a well-led, overwhelmingly supported reform movement dedicated to a program of national revival, in which market reform was viewed as having a central place. This worldview was internalized by the Left, which facilitated a peaceful transition to democracy and secured economic policy consistency over time. On the other hand, Poland's losing economic interest groups – heavy industry and agriculture – did not put up the resistance that would be expected from their size. This is because their opposition was heavily diluted by their loyalty to the cause of national revival. Again, Solidarity itself originated as a trade union in an uncompetitive heavy industry – shipbuilding. The trade union elements of Solidarity were extremely well organized, and it would have been quite difficult to implement thorough neoliberal reforms against their unified opposition. But these elements were instead largely supportive of the overall market reform process. Only in medium and large privatization, where trade union elements long wielded firm-level veto power over privatization proposals, were significant delays imposed. Similarly, heavily agricultural regions were initially strongly supportive of Solidarity, and even over time, remained divided between the center-Right and center-Left parties. In a manner somewhat exceeding expectations, then, Poland's frustrated national ideals not only bolstered the service sector for market reforms, but also blunted opposition from heavy industry and agriculture (Balcerowicz, 1995; Raciborski, 1996).

Relative to those of Poland, Russia's neoliberal reforms were slower, more compromised, and more incomplete. In 1992, most prices and private sector entry were liberalized. However, significant energy price controls remained in place, and more varied price controls were imposed by local authorities. Trade controls were largely eliminated in 1992, but high tariffs (averaging about 50 percent) were imposed from 1994. Macroeconomic stabilization has been, to put it kindly, a work in progress. Soft budget constraints remained in place until late 1993. Banks remained poorly regulated thereafter, failing to uphold basic standards of loan quality and diversification, and routinely lending based on personal connections. Through 1998, fiscal deficits were generally in the unsustainable range of 6–9 percent per annum. Combined with a pegged, increasingly overvalued exchange rate, this produced a financial crisis and a massive devaluation in late 1998. Subsequently, high oil prices have generated small fiscal surpluses in most years. Significant numbers of medium and large state enterprises were privatized by late 1994, through a mass voucher distribution that left incumbent managers in control of most firms. In the mid-1990s, many of the most valuable firms, especially in the energy sector, were privatized to allies of the government at artificially low prices. These corrupt privatizations often formed the core of business conglomerates controlled by the so-called "oligarchs." At the microeconomic level, corruption imposes significant constraints on competition and investment. Officials have extensive formal and informal ties to private businesses they are supposed to regulate. Those in less strategic positions are underpaid and routinely extract bribes. Local "mafias" use threats and violence to extract "taxes" and monopolize lucrative lines of business. The net effect is to choke off competition and investment at both the federal and local levels. GDP fell rapidly from 1991, falling 14.5 percent in 1992, 8.7 percent in 1993, and 12.7 percent in 1994. GDP then fell more slowly until the 1998 crisis, and has since recovered rapidly. Unemployment rose rapidly, and has remained at around 10 percent since 1996 (Åslund, 1995; EBRD, 1994, 34–35, 167; EBRD, 1998, 186–187, 225; Karatnycky *et al.*, 2002, 339–344).[3]

Consider again the hypothesized predictors of neoliberal reform. At transition, the agricultural sector absorbed 14 percent of Russia's workforce – well below the mean level of 23 percent. There were sizeable uncompetitive heavy industries, but also an underdeveloped and promising energy sector. Russia's pre-communist economic development was near the average. Its pre-communist political prominence, while considerable, was eclipsed by her superpower status under communism. Russia should therefore have had relatively weak resistance to market reform from uncompetitive heavy industry and agriculture. On the other hand, frustrated national ideals would not be expected to generate much additional service sector support for reform. Russia did not see war until 1994, when her pattern of economic reform was already well established. Moreover, the Chechen wars were on a small scale relative to the size of the Russian state. Therefore, these wars would not be expected to have a diverting effect comparable to the other major wars in the former Soviet Union and Yugoslavia.

Russia's reform movements and parties have always been much weaker than those of Poland. To begin with, Russia's first president, Boris Yeltsin, only came to power as a result of a failed, hard-line communist military coup. This occurred when crucial segments of the Red Army resisted the coup and shifted their allegiance from the Communist Party of the Soviet Union to the elected, Yeltsin-led government of the USSR's Russian Federal Republic. Yeltsin's support in the Russian legislature was shaky. First, Russia's anti-communist opposition was weaker and more divided than that of Poland. Moreover, the Communist Party of Russia remained ideologically unreformed while still retaining considerable popularity. After an initial honeymoon period in which Yeltsin was delegated decree power, opponents of market reform controlled the legislature. Divided government particularly undermined macroeconomic stabilization efforts. Yeltsin's conflict with the opposition-controlled legislature became increasingly embittered, leading Yeltsin to use force to end the deadlock in late 1993. The December 1993 and December 1995 elections returned a strong opposition bloc of communists and xenophobic nationalists, a weak group of reformist center-Right parties, and a pivotal group of populist parties. Yeltsin governed in cooperation with these populist parties. Neoliberal reform efforts continued to be compromised. Most significantly, Yeltsin presided over widespread insider transfers of lucrative natural resource assets to political clients. Although this provided short-term financial support, it permanently hobbled the transition. The public increasingly came to see market reforms, not only as producing few benefits, but as driven by corruption. By concentrating such huge resources in the hands of a small group with strong political connections, it further entrenched clientelism and monopoly power in the economy. In 1999, Yeltsin handed over power to Vladimir Putin. After the 1999 and 2003 elections, Putin governed with the support of populist parties, particularly his own Unity Party. The communists and xenophobic nationalist parties have declined, and the reformist center-Right parties remain weak (Handelman, 1997; Marsh, 2002). Although Putin campaigned on a platform of restoring the rule of law and attacking corruption, his policy reform record is mixed. Despite effective tax reforms, clientelism and corruption remain entrenched. Putin has gone after "oligarchs" only when they dared to oppose him politically – as with Mikhail Khodorkovsky – while reimposing greater state control in the crucial energy sector. Experts now debate whether Russia is still a democracy, and few are optimistic about the political and economic future.

Russia's relatively weak frustrated national ideals can be seen in the weakness and internal division of the opposition in the late communist period, and after the USSR's collapse, in the widespread nostalgia for the economic security and geopolitical prominence of the communist period. Politically, the correlates are an unreformed Communist Party and weak moderate reform parties. On the other hand, Russia's relatively high level of economic development predicts weak economic interest group opposition. However, heavy industry and agriculture have been quite effective in lobbying for subsidies. In this context, the energy sector has, paradoxically, played an important role in holding back neoliberal reforms. Russia's level of economic development is highly dependent on its huge oil and gas output. The energy sector would be expected to be a significant beneficiary of market reforms, which would allow sales at high, international market prices, and thereby generate significant capital inflows and sectoral increases in incomes and employment. However, the political process derailed this ideal trajectory. The energy sector has either remained in state hands, or has been turned over to political cronies. "Oligarchs" have used energy sector resources to burrow into a variety of industries, while stashing huge sums abroad. Largely to compensate for weak political legitimacy, energy is made available to domestic industry and agriculture at subsidized prices. The energy sector's corruption, apart from stunting its own growth, thus props up already uncompetitive sectors and undermines competition and growth in still others.

In Poland, frustrated national ideals seem to have greater-than-expected predictive power, while economic interest group opposition is weaker than expected. In Russia, absence of strong frustrated national ideals seems to have the predicted effects, while economic interest group opposition is stronger than expected. To obtain more precise estimates of the effects of frustrated national ideals and economic interest groups, while controlling for the impact of war, we turn now to statistical analysis.

Cross-national data and findings

Using ordinary least squares regression, the three hypotheses above are tested on the full set of 28 post-communist countries – Albania, Armenia, Azerbaijan, Belarus, Bosnia-Herzegovina, Bulgaria, Croatia, the Czech Republic, Estonia, Georgia, Hungary, Kazakhstan, Kyrgyzstan, Latvia, Lithuania, Macedonia, Moldova, Mongolia, Poland, Romania, Russia, Serbia-Montenegro, Slovakia, Slovenia, Tajikistan, Turkmenistan, Ukraine, and Uzbekistan.

Neoliberal reform is measured over shorter and longer time-spans.

Market reform efforts approximately two years after the transition – at the end of 1991 for Poland, at the end of 1992 for Bulgaria, Czechoslovakia, Hungary, Mongolia, Romania, and at the end of 1993 for Albania and the successor states of the former Soviet Union and former (Socialist Federal Republic of) Yugoslavia – are measured by the World Bank's Liberalization Index (LI). This is a yearly index for each country based on a weighted average of liberalization of internal markets (abolition of price controls and state trading monopolies – 30 percent), external markets (convertibility, and replacement of export and import controls with moderate tariffs – 30 percent), and private sector entry (privatization and banking reform – 40 percent). The LI ranges from zero (no progress towards a market economy) to one (full transition to market institutions).[4] To measure market reform approximately ten years after the transition – eight years after the LIs are measured – the Nations in Transit Economic Liberalization Index (ELI) is used. The ELI has three equally-weighted components: privatization, macroeconomic policy, and microeconomic policy. It ranges from one (maximum market reform) to seven (minimum market reform). To facilitate comparison of results across time, the ELI is here reversed and rescaled – so that higher scores indicate more complete market reforms and, like the World Bank Liberalization Index, scores vary from zero to one.

Economic development at the time of transition from communism should ideally be measured as per capita GDP at purchasing power parity. Since this data is not available for many countries, the share of the population working in agriculture is used as a proxy. The share of time at war is the percentage of time (in months), from the transitional election through the year in which market reform is measured, that a country has been involved in large-scale military conflict. Frustrated national ideals are measured as the average of pre-communist economic and political achievements. Pre-communist economic achievements are measured by a five-point scale, based on the share of the workforce employed in agriculture at the time of transition to communism. Similarly, pre-communist political achievements are measured by a five-point scale, which ranks the level of pre-communist geopolitical prominence, independence or autonomy relative to attainments under communism. Economic and political rankings are shown in Table 10.1. The appendix offers a detailed explanation of the rankings.

The World Bank Liberalization Index is given in De Melo, Denizer and Gelb (1994: 6–7). The Nations in Transit Economic Liberalization Index is taken from Karatnycky *et al.* (2001a) and Karatnycky *et al.* (2001b; 2002). For data on agricultural share of the workforce, see World Bank (1996: 194–195). Information on the incidence and duration of warfare can be found in Horowitz (2004). See the appendix for additional sources.

Model 1 of Table 10.2 shows estimated relations between the independent variables and market reform two years after the transition from

Table 10.1 Sources of national economic and political expectations in the post-communist context

	Index of past economic achievement	*Index of past political achievement*
Very Strong	Czech Republic, Hungary, Slovenia	Baltic States (Estonia, Latvia, Lithuania), Hungary, Mongolia, Poland
Strong	Croatia, Estonia, Latvia, Poland, Slovakia	Bulgaria, Croatia, Czech Republic, Serbia, Slovenia
Moderate	Albania, Armenia, Azerbaijan, Bosnia-Herzegovina, Bulgaria, Georgia, Lithuania, Macedonia, Romania, Russia, Serbia	Armenia, Georgia, Romania, Slovakia
Weak	Belarus, Moldova, Tajikistan, Ukraine, Uzbekistan	Albania, Moldova, Russia, Tajikistan, Ukraine, Uzbekistan
Very Weak	Kazakhstan, Kyrgyzstan, Mongolia, Turkmenistan	Azerbaijan, Belarus, Bosnia-Herzegovina, Kazakhstan, Kyrgyzstan, Macedonia, Turkmenistan

Note
For the early period in which a unified Czechoslovakia still existed, its rankings are the same as for its dominant Czech part.

communism. Economic development at the time of transition – proxied by the share of the workforce employed in agriculture – is not a statistically significant predictor and has little substantive impact. On the other hand, frustrated national ideals are highly significant, both statistically and substantively. Share of time at war has a strong negative impact, although it is significant only at the 10 percent level. Model 2 of Table 10.2 shows estimates for predictors of market reform ten years after the transition. The results are quite similar to the two-year results. Again, agricultural share of the workforce at transition is not statistically significant and has little substantive impact – and the direction of impact is here estimated to be positive. The estimated effect of frustrated national ideals is virtually identical. As compared to the two-year interval, share of time at war has stronger predictive power and higher statistical significance over a decade.

Conclusions

It was hypothesized that the negative interest group effects of having less developed economies might be counteracted by positive ideological effects of frustrated national ideals. However, it seems that economic initial conditions had little systematic effect, while predictors of strong reform nationalist ideologies and movements had an overwhelming

Table 10.2 Predictors of post-communist neo-liberal reform: two-year and ten-year time spans

	Model 1: Market reform (Liberalization Index) 1991–1993	*Model 2: Market reform (Economic Liberalization Index – Adjusted Scale) 1999–2001*
Agricultural Employment	−0.045	0.051
Share at Transition	(0.295)	(0.257)
Frustrated National Ideals	0.122***	0.150***
	(0.026)	(0.023)
Share of Time at War	−0.142*	−0.284**
	(0.075)	(0.131)
Constant	0.226*	0.105
	(0.129)	(0.111)
R-Squared	0.612	0.735
Adjusted R-Squared	0.561	0.702
F	12.095***	22.183***
N	27	28

Notes

Model 1 has one less observation because Czechoslovakia had not yet split apart into the Czech Republic and Slovakia.

*** p<0.01, ** p<0.05, * p<0.10.

impact. There is extensive case study evidence that organized interest groups, particularly the losers, lobbied to retain traditional subsidies and protection (e.g. Fidrmuc, 2000). It is just that this lobbying did not have systematically predictable effects. This was mainly because two very different political paths tended to be marked out in advance. Either reform nationalist movements with overwhelming mass and elite support shifted the political and economic system abruptly onto a democratic capitalist path, or communist-era elites did not face serious opposition, maintained authoritarian control, and transformed collapsing planned economies into patron–client-based market economies. A few cases – including Russia – fall in between, with violent or delayed transfers of power and more varied, intermediate levels of market reform. These results support the idea that elite-level shared mental models along with consistent mass-level ideologies may lead to strongly divergent, path-dependent policy outcomes. The policy trajectories of the consensus reforming countries were so strong as to swamp evidence of underlying patterns of resistance by organized interest group losers. Moreover, divergent political and economic choices made immediately after transition proved remarkably stable over time.[5]

Returning to the theoretical debates between the Big Bang and Gradualism mental models, there is little evidence to support the main gradualist arguments. Compromising macroeconomic stabilization and microeconomic budgetary and competitive reforms did not limit the size of the initial output shock. If anything, such policies seem to have worsened the shock by delaying and weakening the market-based recovery – as in Russia. There were many efforts to salvage valuable specific capital by subsidizing state-owned firms or newly privatized firms, whether directly or through soft credits, trade protection, and the like. Usually this delayed rather than facilitated the process of separating the salvageable assets from the non-salvageable ones. By failing to concentrate new investment in the most promising areas, capital was wasted on a net basis. This can be seen in the huge non-performing loan burdens piled up by the state-owned commercial banks across most of Eastern Europe. In Poland, where unusually strict regulations prevented such soft lending, there is little evidence of greater wastage of valuable specific capital, and strong evidence of a rapid recovery propelled by new start-ups. The argument for using subsidies to salvage specific capital was often used to justify restrictions on foreign investment, both in banking and in heavy industry, on the grounds that foreign "bean counters" lacked the requisite local knowledge for the job. Yet foreign capital and knowledge was precisely what was most needed for rapid and relatively efficient restructuring of legacy firms.[6]

APPENDIX: INDICES OF FRUSTRATED NATIONAL IDEALS

The relative economic and political achievements of the pre-communist period are ranked on a scale of one to five, with five indicating highest achievement. The idea behind the first, economic ranking is that countries with greater pre-communist economic achievements will look more unfavorably upon the consequences of planned or socialized economic regimes. The best available quantitative index of development at the onset of the communist period is share of the workforce employed in agriculture.[7] In the former Soviet Union, it is the titular ethnic group's share that is used in the ranking. This was often higher than the total share, due to predominance of ethnic Russians in the big cities. The units fall into six distinguishable groups, Czechoslovakia at the bottom with 34.6 percent, Hungary and Slovenia at around 50 percent, Croatia, Estonia, Latvia and Poland at around 60 percent, Albania, Armenian, Azerbaijan, Bosnia-Herzegovina, Bulgaria, Georgia, Lithuania, Macedonia, Romania, Serbia-Montenegro, and Russia at 70–85 percent,[8] Ukraine, Belarus, Uzbekistan and Tajikistan at 85–95 percent, and Kazakhstan, Kyrgyzstan, Turkmenistan and Mongolia at 95–100 percent (Clem, 1976: 278; Mitchell, 1980, series C1; Rothschild, 1974: 37, 39, 91, 167, 204, 285, 359, 367, 369; Socialist Federal Republic of Yugoslavia, 1987).[9]

The second ranking refers to past political power and prestige for states having independent juridical and administrative status under communism, and to past independence and political achievement for states not having such independence under communism.[10] Thus, Russia, Mongolia, Poland, and (somewhat more ambiguously) Hungary were all once centers of greater empires. However, this standard would not have been violated during the communist period for Russians, the dominant ethnic group of the former USSR. Czechoslovakia, Bulgaria and Romania were once truly independent states that were reduced to satellite status after World War II. Under Nicolae Ceausescu, Romania was able to carve out a limited autonomy from Soviet control. Hence Romanians would not be expected to feel the same level of resentment towards the communist political order per se. Newly independent Slovaks, emerging from the shadow of the more numerous and economically advanced Czechs, would not be expected to feel the same level of political hostility towards the period of communist rule. Albania was able to maintain an independent national communism, while Russia, again, provided the ethnic core of the USSR.

Among states that did not have separate juridical status under communism, the Baltic States had the most recent and most popularly legitimate period of independence. Here the Soviet political yoke was felt most strongly. The Caucasian States had a few brief years of independence after the end of World War I, but only in Armenia and Georgia did this involve an influential mass mobilization process aimed at securing a self-consciously held national identity. Nor is this surprising, given that Armenia and Georgia both had broken but consistently recovered histories of political independence and regional prominence going back over a millennium. Given the dominant role of Serbia within the interwar Yugoslavia, and the preceding decades of Serbian independence following the collapse of Ottoman power in Europe, Serbia-Montenegro could plausibly be placed in between the Baltic and Caucasian States. While Serbs were numerically preponderant in the Yugoslav state and army, they increasingly viewed Josep Broz Tito's federal system as artificially marginalizing them relative to the smaller ethnic groups. Slovenia and to a somewhat lesser extent Croatia had strong traditions of regional political autonomy within larger territorial units. Both would have preferred independence after World War I, but felt compelled to unify with Serbia in order to protect themselves from Italian and Hungarian territorial ambitions. They too viewed Tito's system as one that marginalized them. Ukrainian political independence developed in the ninth through the eleventh centuries, but the region was then partitioned among different empires until its consolidation under Soviet rule after World War II. Over time, a majority of the Ukrainian population came to identify closely with the Russian nation. In Moldova there was a distinct pre-communist national identity, as in the Baltic States violated in more recent memory. However, this identity was as part of the Romanian nation. The Persian-speaking Tajiks and Turkic-speaking Uzbeks were jointly at the core of a number of medieval Islamic empires and civilizations centered on

Bukhara and Samarkand. But their distinct national identities only developed during the Soviet period. To this day, there is dispute over which people has the "correct" claim to Bukhara, Samarkand and their historical legacies. None of the other Soviet successor states had a prior independent political existence. The same can be said for Bosnia-Herzegovina. Macedonian Slavs are ethnically closest to Bulgarians, and were subjected to Serbianization during the interwar period. A sharply distinct Macedonian political identity did not develop until the Yugoslav period.

These political rankings can of course be debated at the margins. For example, as compared to Bulgaria, the Czech Republic arguably achieved more and had greater popular legitimacy during the interwar period of independence. Arguably, Croatia and Slovenia had somewhat weaker traditions of political independence than Serbia. But making limited adjustments, such as moving the Czech Republic up one level and/or moving Croatia and Slovenia down one level, do not significantly affect the overall rankings.

Notes

1 An alternative cultural explanation is that countries with Catholic or Protestant pluralities or majorities tended to have a reform-oriented consensus, while those with Christian Orthodox or Muslim pluralities or majorities did not. It is less clear why this pattern should exist, especially because, in other historical contexts, Catholicism has been viewed as inimical to democracy and market reform. Some have argued that fast-reforming countries were motivated primarily by a desire to gain entry into the European Union and the North Atlantic Treaty Organization. Two points can be made here. First, membership in these organizations was not a realistic short-term option in 1989–1991. Second, it is not clear why some potential members of these organizations were more decisive in making the reforms necessary to position themselves to join them at a later point in time. For more discussion of these issues, see Horowitz (2004).

2 Poland's two-year Liberalization Index score was 0.72, as compared with a mean for the 28 post-communist countries of 0.55; and Poland's ten-year Economic Liberalization Index score was 0.89, as compared with a mean of 0.52. For details of these measures, see the next section.

3 Russia's two-year Liberalization Index score was 0.59 and her ten-year Economic Liberalization index score 0.51 – both quite close to the mean for all the post-communist countries.

4 LIs are not available for Bosnia-Herzegovina and Serbia-Montenegro. Rather than dropping these data points, the LIs for Yugoslavia in 1990 are used. Given that little further market reform had been attempted in Bosnia and Serbia by the end of 1992, this is a close approximation.

5 In this context, war sometimes intervened as an adverse shock. Wartime distractions, emergencies, and disruptions tended to divert countries that showed significant prewar ideological impetus toward democratization and market reform toward authoritarianism and more state-centric economic policies. Important examples are Armenia, Croatia, Georgia, and Serbia.

6 There may be sound political reasons for slowing the decline of selected large firms in strategic locations, such as capital cities. But such subsidies are motivated by political feasibility rather than economic efficiency.

7 Data are not available to compare levels of economic development in significantly earlier periods. Hence, comparisons of pre-communist development in earlier periods tend to focus on comparative political status. On this, see below.
8 Slovakia alone also falls into the 70–85 percent category.
9 Czechoslovakia is grouped with Hungary and Slovenia in order to use five-level rankings for both economic and political dimensions. Allowing a sixth level for past economic achievement has no significant effect on the results.
10 The classifications in this and the following paragraph reflect the discussions in Bremmer and Taras (1997), Dyker and Vejvoda (1996), Katz (1975), Rothschild (1974), and Tomasevich (1955). Why isn't political achievement measured only for the immediate pre-communist period? Because collective memory and formal cultural and educational institutions tend to emphasize the periods of greatest achievement without "discounting" for time. Mongolians look back to Genghis Khan and his immediate successors, French to Napoleon, Louis XIV, and Charlemagne, and so on.

References

Åslund, A. (1995) *How Russia Became a Market Economy.* Washington, DC: Brookings Institution.

Åslund, A. (2002) *Building Capitalism: The Transformation of the Former Soviet Bloc.* Cambridge: Cambridge University Press.

Balcerowicz, L. (1995) *Capitalism, Socialism, Transformation.* Budapest: Central European University Press.

Bremmer, I. and Taras, R. (eds) (1997) *New States, New Politics: Building the Post-Soviet Nations.* Cambridge: Cambridge University Press.

Clem, R.S. (1976) "The changing geography of Soviet nationalities and its socioeconomic correlates, 1926–1970," unpublished thesis, Columbia University.

De Melo, M., Denizer, C., and Gelb, A. (1994) *From Plan to Market: Patterns of Transition.* Washington, DC: World Bank.

Denzau, A.T. and North, D.C. (1994) 'Shared mental models: ideologies and institutions," *Kyklos* 47: 3–31.

Dyker, D.A. and Vejvoda, I. (eds) (1996) *Yugoslavia and After: A Study in Fragmentation, Despair and Rebirth.* London: Longman.

EBRD [European Bank for Reconstruction and Development]. (1994, 1998) *Transition Report.* London: EBRD.

Fidrmuc, J. (2000) "Political support for reforms: economics of voting in transition countries," *European Economic Review* 44: 1491–1513.

Fish, M.S. (1998) "The determinants of economic reform in the post-communist world," *East European Politics and Societies* 12: 31–78.

Frieden, J. (1991) *Debt, Development, and Democracy: Modern Political Economy and Latin America, 1965–1985.* Princeton. NJ: Princeton University Press.

Handelman, S. (1997) *Comrade Criminal: Russia's New Mafiya.* New Haven, CT: Yale University Press.

Horowitz, S. (2001) "The persistent liberalizing trend in foreign economic policies: coalitions and institutions in East Asia, Latin America, and Eastern Europe," in Horowitz, S. and Heo, U. (eds) *The Political Economy of International Financial Crisis: Interest Groups, Ideologies, and Institutions.* Lanham, MD: Rowman and Littlefield.

Horowitz, S. (2004) "Structural sources of post-communist market reform: economic structure, political culture, and war," *International Studies Quarterly* 48: 755–778.

Karatnycky, A., Motyl, A., and Piano, A. (2001a) *Nations in Transit 1999–2000: Civil Society, Democracy and Markets in East Central Europe and the Newly Independent States.* New Brunswick, NJ: Transaction.

Karatnycky, A., Motyl, A., and Schnetzer, A. (2001b) *Nations in Transit 2001: Civil Society, Democracy and Markets in East Central Europe and the Newly Independent States.* New Brunswick, NJ: Transaction.

Karatnycky, A., Motyl, A., and Schnetzer, A. (2002) *Nations in Transit 2002: Civil Society, Democracy and Markets in East Central Europe and the Newly Independent States.* New Brunswick, NJ: Transaction.

Katz, Z. (ed.) (1975) *Handbook of Major Soviet Nationalities.* New York: Free Press.

Kornai, J. (1992) *The Socialist System: The Political Economy of Communism.* Princeton, NJ: Princeton University Press.

Marsh, C. (2002) *Russia at the Polls: Voters, Elections, and Democratization.* Washington, DC: CQ Press.

Mitchell, B.R. (1980) *European Historical Statistics, 1750–1975.* New York: Facts on File.

Nove, A. (1986) *The Soviet Economic System,* 3rd edn. London: Allen and Unwin.

Olson, Mancur Jr. (1971) *The Logic of Collective Action: Public Goods and the Theory of Groups,* revised edn. New York: Schocken.

Przeworski, A. (1991) *Democracy and the Market: Political and Economic Reforms in Eastern Europe and Latin America.* Cambridge: Cambridge University Press.

Raciborski, J. (1996) "An outline of the electoral geography of the Polish society," in Wiatr, J.J. (ed.) *Political Sociology and Democratic Transformation in Poland.* Warsaw: Wydawnictwo Naukowe Scholar.

Rogowski, R. (1989) *Commerce and Coalitions: How Trade Affects Domestic Political Alignments.* Princeton, NJ: Princeton University Press.

Rothschild, J. (1974) *East Central Europe between the Two World Wars.* Seattle, WA: University of Washington Press.

Sachs, J. (1993) *Poland's Jump to a Market Economy.* Cambridge, MA: MIT Press.

Socialist Federal Republic of Yugoslavia (1987) "The non-agricultural population," *Yugoslav Survey* 28: 3–24.

Tomasevich, J. (1955) *Peasants, Politics, and Economic Change in Yugoslavia.* Stanford, CA: Stanford University Press.

World Bank (1996) *From Plan to Market: World Development Report 1996.* Washington, DC: Oxford University Press.

11 The clash of mental models in the Middle East

Neoliberal versus Islamic ideas

Lewis W. Snider

Introduction: Why Do They Hate Us?*

After the suicide attacks of September 11 Americans were asking "Why do they (Muslims/Arabs) hate us?" The short answer is that the terrorist groups responsible for the crimes of 9-11 draw strength from "in-groups" whose values and beliefs legitimate the use of extreme and indiscriminate violence against the civilian populations of "out-groups." As a consequence of globalization, the values and beliefs of "in-groups" in the Arab/Muslim world are increasingly clashing with the liberal values and beliefs of "out-groups" in market economies. These clashes, in turn, produce extreme socioeconomic disruption and intense antimarket rage that Muslim terrorist groups and their supporters have successfully exploited. They have succeeded, in part, because of the long standing belief in Muslim societies that it is truly evil for infidels to rule over true believers. This state of affairs is unnatural and even blasphemous, since it leads to the corruption of religion and morality in society, and to the flouting or even the abrogation of God's law (Lewis, 1990: Part 2:2). Seen from this perspective, the "war on terror" is a mental war involving not so much a clash of civilizations but one of mental models.

If the anti-western anti-liberal values espoused by al-Qaeda, Islamic Jihad, Hizbollah and similar organizations were confined solely to such organizations, then the "war on terror" would simply be a matter of locating and destroying these groups. However, if al-Qaeda and its associated groups represent the values and beliefs of substantial numbers of people – and all signs suggest that they do – then defeating the terrorist groups will not end the struggle against terror. That objective can be accomplished only by changing the values and beliefs of supporters of terrorist groups. In this chapter I argue that the social origins of international terrorism in the Middle East are rooted less in poverty or in the growing discontent with American foreign policy and more in the collective autocratic values and beliefs associated with the clientalist economies that persist in most of the Middle East. Muslim hostility toward the West is intensified by a profound sense of rage and injustice as a result of Muslim communities that are ruled by non-Muslims in a globalizing world. This conflict can be thought of as a clash of mental models: one based on neoliberal values and capitalist economics, the other based on Islamic fundamentalism and clientalist economies. The source of the conflict is the social anarchy produced by globalization and the disruptions attending the transition to a market economy.

This chapter is organized as follows. After briefly reviewing the literature on rational and cultural explanations of terror, I describe how market democracies constitute a global civilization based not so much on international trade, but on common liberal values and beliefs that thrive in market economies. I then discuss how neoliberal values and beliefs clash with values and beliefs embraced in much of the Middle East and other parts of the developing world. The clash of mental models is represented as a clash of economic and political orientations in which the much of the Middle East perceives itself to be under an attack by the West, led by the United States. This perceived threat has been used very skillfully by the leaders of al-Qaeda and similar groups to attract and mobilize as many members of the *umma* or universal Islamic community by casting the U.S. as the arch enemy of that community and portraying the leaders of the Arab and Islamic world as idol worshippers cowering behind America, the most powerful idol ever worshipped.

I next show how clientalist values arising from very illiberal institutional settings are a necessary condition for resorting to terrorist violence. Another necessary condition is the rage and sense of humiliation that Muslims have experienced over the last 300 years, based on the infiltration and domination of Christian civilizations of Europe and North America that have overshadowed them militarily, economically and culturally. These conditions – particularly the idea of infidels ruling over believers – totally contradict Qur'anic scripture. I conclude with some recommendations for developing a political strategy to win the war on terror that in essence works to erode the mental model that under-girds global terror. These recommendations, however, may only be valid for the long term. In the interim a deeply embedded clash of mental models lies just beneath the surface – market civilization versus the clientalist and patronage-driven forms of social and political organization that still predominate in the Middle East.

Why do they want to provoke us?

Rational versus cultural explanations for terrorism

If we want to understand why some societies support terrorism we have to move from asking why they hate us to the question of "why do they want to provoke us?" A partial answer lies in the nature of terrorism itself. As far back as 1975 David Fromkin noted that terrorism is not simply violence used against civilian populations in order to create fear; "but it is aimed at creating fear in order that the fear, in turn, will lead somebody else – not the terrorist – to embark on some quite different program of action that will accomplish whatever it is that the terrorist desires" (Fromkin, 1975: 693). When a terrorist kills, the goal is not the victim's death itself but to provoke something else (such as a police crackdown on the population) that will lead to changed political conditions (and perceptions) favoring the terrorist group's ultimate objectives.

The academic literature offers two explanations – one rational, the other cultural – to account for why some societies support terrorism. "Rational" simply means that people are assumed to have goals that they attempt to realize through their actions.[1] In so doing, they will do what they believe is in their own best interest given what they know at the time of choosing. Rational actors will do what leads to the best achievable outcome under the circumstances. In the context of this discussion a rational actor is assumed to prefer life over death.

The rational view holds that terrorism is a reasoned strategy for addressing particular socioeconomic grievances in societies where "paths to the legal expression of opposition are blocked" (Crenshaw, 2003: 95). The rational perspective identifies the root causes of terrorism as "lack of opportunity for political participation (ibid.) and "those of economic exclusion, poverty and under-development" (Wolfensohn, 2002). "We [the United States] can no longer afford to allow states to fail" wrote Jessica Stern, a specialist on terrorism at Harvard University's Kennedy School of Government. If the U.S. does not devote a higher priority to health, education and economic development in the Muslim world, "new Osamas will continue to arise" (Stern, 2001: A.27). Samuel Huntington has argued that governments that "fail to meet the basic welfare and economic needs of their peoples and suppress their liberties generate violent opposition to themselves and to Western governments that support them" (Huntington, 2001).

There are, however, no arguments in print that I have seen that provide a persuasive explanation of how poverty causes terror, but there are some that debunk it. Daniel Pipes, for example makes a persuasive case that the forces that cause militant Islam to decline or flourish appear to have more to do with issues of identity than with economics (Pipes, 2002: 14).

One problem with assuming poverty is the root cause of terrorism is that it overlooks an inconvenient fact: "the Al Qaeda terrorist network is not made up of the poor and dispossessed" (Zakaria, 2003: 136). Suicide bombers clearly are not motivated by the prospect of their own individual economic gain. Further, those who back militant Islamic organizations tend to be financially well off, coming more often from the richer city rather than the poorer countryside (Pipes, 2002: 17). In fact the main breeding grounds of terror, starting with Saudi Arabia, have seen the greatest influx of wealth over the last 30 years. Recall that 15 of the 19 hijackers who attacked the World Trade Center and the Pentagon on September 11, 2001, were from Saudi Arabia. Most of them were well educated and appeared to have had ample opportunities for building materially rewarding lives.[2] Even the lower level al-Qaeda recruits appear to have been educated middle-class men.

Nor is there any empirical evidence to support the position that a reduction in poverty or an increase in educational attainment would, by themselves, significantly reduce the incidence of international terror. Indeed, the available empirical evidence from the Middle East suggests quite the opposite. Nasra Hassan, a United Nations relief worker, interviewed nearly 250 people involved in terrorist attacks from 1996 to 1999. The subjects included failed bombers, families of deceased bombers and trainers. Her conclusion as reported by Kruger: "None of them were uneducated, desperately poor, simple-minded or depressed" (Krueger, 2001: C2).

Professor Ariel Merari, director of the Political Violence Research Center at Tel Aviv University concurs: "All information that I have also indicates that there is no connection between socioeconomic indicators and involvement in militant/terrorist activity in general and in suicide attacks in particular, at least as much as the Palestinian case is concerned" (ibid.).

Other empirical evidence from polling data of Palestinians in the West Bank and Gaza and the composition of Hezbollah's militant wing in the late 1980s and early 1990s in Lebanon suggests that there is little direct connection between poverty, education and participation in or support for terrorism (Krueger and Maleckova, 2002). Based on the evidence he has examined, Alan Krueger, professor of economics and public affairs at Princeton University, flatly asserts, "the common stereotype that they [the terrorists] come from the ranks of the most uneducated and economically deprived is a myth." (Krueger, 2001: C2). The profile of the 19 hijackers who carried out the September 11 attacks – many of whom were college-educated and hailed from middle class families – may not be so atypical after all.

In short, a rational choice approach – in terms of costs, benefits and probability of success – does not explain the social origins or the social support for terrorism. The hijackers of September 11 were motivated by something deeper, something that fundamentally distinguished them from their victims. Simply put, terrorists and their supporters do not think like their victims. From a cultural perspective, terrorists are engaged in much more than a rational strategy of the weak. Rather there may be something ingrained in the social habits and historical traditions that sanctions terrorism as a socially acceptable option for addressing grievances in some societies, but not in others (Crenshaw, 2003: 94). When these traditions are combined with social, economic and political grievances, individuals can be socialized into violence from early childhood, particularly when they experience violence in their early years (Mousseau, 2002/2003: 8).

Cultural explanations of terrorism begin with an examination of the terrorists' values and beliefs. If the hijackers of September 11 were motivated by something deeper that fundamentally distinguished them from their victims, then what was it? Since all of the September 11 hijackers were from Muslim countries and all expressed strong religious motivation, a cultural explanation would suggest that there is something inherent in Islamic beliefs and values that elicits social approval of terror. The explanation is reinforced by the fact that all of the suicide bombers who have attacked Israeli populations have been Muslim and not Christian. However, as the eminent Middle East scholar, Bernard Lewis, observes, "At no point do the basic texts of Islam enjoin terrorism and murder. At no point – as far as I am aware – do they even consider the random slaughter of uninvolved bystanders" (Lewis, 2003: 39).

If there is nothing inherent in the Qur'an or other Islamic beliefs and values that constitutes social approval of terrorism, the rhetoric of Osama bin Laden and other terrorist leaders and the support their cause receives from various Muslim clerics, suggest otherwise. For example, one analyst argues that the Qur'an, unlike the Bible contains instructions even for the minutiae of everyday that were divinely vouchsafed therein (Horan, 2002: 53). Consequently in Sunni Islam, both the secular and the religious sides of the Prophet Mohammad's mission became equally sanctified and immutable and theoretically have remained so to the present day. One long-term consequence is that modern Arab societies "lack a tradition of self-criticism, of rational analysis" (ibid.: 54). Without the ability to analyze successfully the developments in the world around them or even in their own societies, the Arab public ego has experienced many setbacks. Hence Muslims in the Arab world tend to be "defensive and insecure," and inclined to blame any bad news on various "exterior, malevolent powers" (ibid.).

That diagnosis is certainly plausible and may in large measure be correct. But it does not by itself explain the widespread social approval of terror in the Middle East. Islamic values and beliefs cannot explain why the Muslims did not produce suicide bombers in previous decades, say in the 1960s, or why millions of Muslims around the world joined others in expressing their shock and disapproval of the events of September 11. Further, social support for terror is not confined to Muslim societies but exists in non-Islamic societies such as the Catholics and Protestants in Northern Ireland, and the largely Hindu Tamils in Sri Lanka.

If there is a link between Islamic cultural values and the social approval of global terrorism it may be a sense of pride that exists on two levels. Superficially modernity for the Arab world has been one failure after another. "Each path followed – socialism, secularism, nationalism – has turned into a dead end" (Zakaria, 2003: 139). People now associate the failure of their governments and their political and intellectual institutions to address the needs of their populations with the failure of secularism and of following the western path. Hence Muslims today see only a disastrous decline from former glory.

This long-term decline from former glory may provide a more enduring (albeit not complete) cultural explanation for the rise – if not the timing – of global terror in the Middle East that is directed toward the West and more specifically, towards the U.S. Historically the external environment validated Islamic precepts because a series of Muslim empires were supreme in world affairs. They were supreme because they were right and they were right because they were supreme. Only in the eighteenth century did this comfortable nexus between revelation and state power begin to unravel. It has continued to unravel at an accelerating rate ever since and confronts Muslims, especially those in the Arab world with some agonizing questions:

> "How do we reconcile the Qur'anic assurance of divine favor and worldly power with daily proofs that we Muslims are falling behind? That we are falling behind not just the United States and Europe, but even their despised 'step-child' Israel? Where today are the happy, successful and above all, *powerful* states of Islam? How can God allow his people to be so confounded? Are our tribulations a punishment for our flawed practice of his teachings?" An increasingly common answer to these doubts is this: "I should resolve to become ever-more-and-more intensely and rigorously observant."
>
> (Horan, 2002: 54)

One consequence is the growing attraction of Islamic fundamentalism. Fouad Ajami explains, "The fundamentalist call has resonance because it invites men to participate ... [in] contrast to an official political culture that reduces citizens to spectators and asks them to leave things to their rulers. At a time when the future is uncertain, it connects them to a tradition that reduces their bewilderment" (Ajami, 1981: 117).

Another consequence has been the intensification of the long-standing belief in Muslim societies that it is truly evil for infidels to rule over true believers. This state of affairs is unnatural and even blasphemous, since it leads to the corruption of religion and morality in society, and to the flouting or even the abrogation of God's law (Lewis, 1990: Part 2:2).

Religious versus secular terrorists

The explicit grievance on religious grounds is important since the salience of religion as the major driving force behind international terrorism in the 1990s is evidenced by the fact that the most serious terrorist acts of the decade – whether reckoned in terms of political consequences or in numbers of fatalities caused – have all had a significant religious dimension or motivation (Hoffman, 1998: 92). The list includes terrorist acts committed by all faiths. More significant is that terrorist acts that are motivated wholly or in part by religious imperatives have produced considerably higher levels of fatalities than the relatively more discriminating and less lethal episodes of violence perpetrated by secular terrorist organizations (ibid.: 93).

The reason why terrorist incidents undertaken for religious purposes result in so many more fatalities, Hoffman argues, "may be found in the radically different value systems, mechanisms of legitimization and justification, concepts of morality, and world-view embraced by the religious terrorist, compared with his secular counterpart" (ibid.: 94). For the religious terrorist, violence is a sacramental act executed in response to some theological demand or imperative. Terrorism assumes a transcendental dimension, and its perpetrators are unconstrained by the political, moral or practical constraints that may affect secular terrorists. Whereas even if the latter have the capacity to carry out large-scale indiscriminant mass killings they rarely do so because such tactics are inconsistent with their political aims and therefore considered counterproductive, if not immoral. By contrast religious terrorists may seek the elimination of broadly-defined categories of enemies and thus regard such large-scale violence not only as morally acceptable but also as a necessary expedient for the achievement of their goals. Religion – conveyed by scripture and imparted by clerical authorities claiming to speak for the divine – therefore serves as a legitimizing force for acts that might otherwise be deemed socially unacceptable.

Religious and secular terrorists also differ in the constituencies they claim to serve. Whereas secular terrorists attempt to appeal to a constituency variously composed of potential and actual sympathizers or members of the communities they profess to defend, religious terrorists "are at once activists and constituents engaged in what they regard as a total war. They seek to appeal to no other constituency than themselves" (ibid.: 95). Thus the constraints on violence that are imposed on secular terrorists by the need to appeal to a partially committed or only tacitly supportive constituency are not salient to the religious terrorist. The absence of a constituency other than themselves enables the religious terrorist to approve of almost limitless violence against a virtually open-ended category of targets. This includes anyone who is not a member of the terrorists' religion or religious sect.

Finally religious and secular terrorists have vastly different perceptions of themselves and their violent acts. Secular terrorists regard violence either as a way of bringing about the correction of a flaw in a system that is basically good or as a means of instigating the creation of a new system. By contrast the religious terrorists see themselves not as components of a system worth preserving but as "outsiders" seeking fundamental changes in the existing order. This sense of alienation leads the religious terrorist to contemplate a far more destructive and deadly array of terrorist operations than secular terrorists and to embrace a far more open-ended category of "enemies" for attack. These core characteristics are common to religious terrorists of all faiths, but they are most closely associated with Islamic terrorist groups in general.

Even if it is the Arab world, and not Islam, that is the wellspring of religious terrorism in the Middle East, neither rational nor cultural explanations enable us to accurately forecast when and where social support for terror is likely to materialize. Rational explanations have an advantage over cultural explanations with their focus on observable attributes – poverty, economic inequality, poor education and a lack of economic freedom and democracy – that facilitate the prediction of where social support for terror is likely to emerge. Explanations linking various social pathologies with terror, however, do not provide a close fit between theoretical expectations and observed behavior. The advantage that cultural explanations have over rational approaches is that they assume that those who engage in or support mass suicide attacks do not think like people in out-groups (in this case "out groups" refer to people in the United States, Israel and the rest of the western world). But these approaches do not help predict the kinds of values and beliefs that support terror. To isolate the origins of socially-approved terror, an approach is needed that combines the rationalist identification of observable conditions with the cultural emphasis on explaining why people think and act as they do.

Clientalism versus markets[3]

As stated earlier, the primary difference between the western world and the world in the Middle East is a difference of economic mental models, which are differentiated along approaches to socio-economic orientation. One approach suggested by Mousseau (2002/2003) is to refer to the two principal mechanisms of socioeconomic integration in history – clientalism and markets – and examine the relationships between the economic conditions in each with the sets of values and beliefs that emerged in each one.

In clientalist economies, the obligations of cooperating parties are implicit (and not made explicit) and based on reciprocity in the form of gift giving. This is a form of exchange that is supposed to reinforce a sense of mutual trust and enduring obligation among the parties. Obligations are enforced by the threat of punishment where violations of trust lead to severed relationships. Since mutual obligations are only implied and are socially enforced, patrons rather than states regulate economic cooperation. Examples of clientalist forms of social organization include feudal Europe, and more recently, mafias and the complex patronage systems that characterize the politics of redistribution in most developing countries (ibid.: 10).[4]

Because economic relations are long-term and open ended, clientalist economies are based on explicit social linkages such as kinship and ethnicity. These linkages make in-groups more important than out-groups and therefore clientalist communities tend to be more inward-looking than market communities in terms of identity, values and beliefs. One attribute that reinforces the in-group/out-group distinction is the lack of interpersonal trust outside the family as indicated by the rates of endogamous marriages. The rate of endogamous marriages varies in the Muslim world from 15 percent in Turkey to 25 percent in Egypt and Iran, to 50 and and 57 percent for Pakistan for Sudan respectively. The average rate for the Arab world is 25–35 percent (Root, 2006: 185). People turn to kinship and form intense attachments with family members in regions where the state cannot provide security or justice. It makes sense to rely on family members when the courts cannot enforce business agreements. Families can ostracize and otherwise punish disloyal members. One important implication is that the in-group/out-group distinction in clientalist economies limits the set of people with whom one can legitimately do business. The power of family networks provides advantages in illegal enterprises or mafia-like activities but weakens loyalties to the larger society (ibid.: 185). Clientalist societies are organized hierarchically. Patrons receive gifts from clients as expressions of loyalty in exchange for life-long protection.

By contrast, in market economies, mutual obligations among cooperating parties are made explicit in the form of contracts. The quid pro quo nature of the cooperation implies no obligation or commitment among the contracting parties beyond that expressed in the contract. Therefore, unlike clientalist economies, in market economies strangers or even enemies can cooperate in prescribed ways. A contract imposes an equitable relationship on all parties even those of highly diverse social standings. Since each party is consciously equally obligated to fulfill his side of the bargain and has choice and free will whether to enter the contract, the arrangement is explicitly equitable, even if it is between a prince and a peasant (Mousseau, 2000: 477–478).

The implications of this relationship are far-reaching. The norm of cooperating with strangers on the basis of legal equality is the logical precondition for respecting the rule of common law. Since contractual obligations are explicit, the state can enforce them and a market economy can emerge if the state is willing to enforce contracts impartially. By these mechanisms markets develop and the liberal[5] values of individualism, universalism, tolerance, and equity emerge concurrently with the rule of law and democracy. Economic norms appear to translate into social and political norms: "exchange-based cooperation, individual choice and free will, negotiation and compromise, universal equity among individuals, and universal trust in the sanctity of contract" (ibid.: 479).

The market economy and liberal values also account for the emergence of science over faith-based forms of knowledge. Science is based on the notion that "(1) some facts are universal (universalism), (2) any person can challenge another's assertions of fact, including those of his or her leader (freedom and equity), and (3) truth is sought through the competition of ideas (tolerance)" (Mousseau, 2002/2003: 11). The opposite of science is truth determined by an authority legitimized by loyalty and faith, the norm in clientalism.

Although neoliberal belief systems have cast an immense normative shadow across the post-cold war world, societies are still a combination of clientalist and market exchange. The lower the level of economic development (especially the lower the level of life expectancy), the more pervasive is the clientalist exchange likely to be. For markets to prevail, a majority of the population must engage regularly in contract-based exchanges. This requires a complex division of labor associated with higher levels of economic development. At lower levels of development and incomes, people engage in fewer exchanges and those that occur are less likely to be mediated by the market (where price is determined by supply and demand). Instead these may take the form of gifts by members of an in-group (with price determined by privileged discount). Consequently developing countries tend to have political cultures characterized by strong in-group/out-group feelings, less respect for individual freedom, stronger religious beliefs, more respect for loyalty and hierarchy than for the rule of law, and extensive informal patronage networks associated with high levels of corruption (ibid.: 12). More important, the idea of representative government, of elections, of popular suffrage, of political institutions being regulated by laws passed by a legislative assembly, of these laws being defended by an independent judiciary, not to mention the idea of a secular state, are all alien to the Muslim political tradition.

Although contracts may be officially enforced and regulated in many developing countries, the persistence of in-group/out-group cleavages can weaken impartiality and diminish the reliability of that enforcement. Further, since clientalist economies are informal they lie beyond the regulatory capacity of the state. In such mixed economies the clash of market and clientalist cultures can lead to illiberal and unstable democracy, authoritarian rule, state failure or sectarian violence – and intense anti-Americanism. Birthe Hansen, an associate professor at the University of Copenhagen, identifies one critical consequence of this social turmoil when she writes "the spread of free market capitalism and liberal democracy . . . is probably an important factor behind the rise of political Islam (as cited in Pipes, 2002: 19).

The promotion of market exchange and its liberal belief system disrupts clientalist linkages. In clientalist societies cooperation is maintained with the exchange of gifts, and trust is based on life-long friendships confined to in-groups. In market societies loyalty to the in-group is devalued, and cooperation with strangers is encouraged; trust is based less on friendship and more on the universal principal of the sanctity of contracts. Hence individuals from market cultures seek out cooperation across ethnic, religious or linguistic differences. Clientalist societies regard individuals with market values as being from out-groups and thus are untrustworthy. By expressing their self-interest, individuals with market values are viewed as selfish and decadent, lacking in culture, and interested only in the pursuit of material gain.[6] The latter perception may be partly true. A society undergoing economic change may experience a period where there is no common culture as clientalist linkages are ruptured prior to the emergence of market exchange. The social anarchy associated with this kind of transformation – and the concomitant anti-Americanism – has become magnified as a consequence of globalization.

Globalization and the clash of values

The clash between clientalist and market values and the bitter resentment Muslims experience over the decline of Islam in the face of continued western ascendancy has intensified as a consequence of globalization.[7] While many of the phenomena associated with globalization are not really new, the way in which the new technology carried liberal ideas and practices through a multitude of new global networks was revolutionary. Beginning in the late twentieth century liberal values had a presence and a plausibility that enabled them to penetrate non-western societies in ways that were totally unprecedented. Globalization includes such concepts as westernization, secularization, democratization, consumerism and the growth of market capitalism and represents an onslaught on less privileged people in clientalist cultures. Unfortunately, these less privileged people are often repelled by the fundamental changes that these forces are bringing – or angered by the distortions and uneven distributions of benefits that result (Cronin, 2002/03: 45). This is especially true of the Middle East.

Two categories of friction stand out. First liberalization threatened political and economic destabilization. Reducing controls on foreign trade, foreign exchange, pricing and the private sector almost always led to a spurt of consumption and inflation, followed by worsening trade balances and indebtedness, then by a real or de facto devaluation of the exchange rate, and finally a further stoking of inflationary pressures. Second, embracing market values relaxed cultural boundaries. While the cultural implications of global engagement were many and wide-ranging, "they included more contact with foreigners through business and tourism, more pressure to adopt secular ideas and market principles in society, and greater immersion in the products and images of global capital, many of which were explicitly of Western origin" (Murden, 2002: 103).

The breakdown of cultural boundaries does not necessarily have to take place in the Middle East, but could occur in other regions as well. In the case of the 9–11 hijackers, the breakdown of cultural boundaries occurred in Europe, not the Middle East. Thomas Friedman points out that the biographies of many of the key hijackers or al-Qaeda agents – Mohammed Atta, Ziad al-Jarrah, Marwan al-Shehhi – reveal a common theme: they grew up in middle-class families in the Arab world, were educated and went to Europe for more studies.

One of their Arab contemporaries who studied abroad with young Muslim men described them in this way:

> They are mostly men who grew up in an environment where the rules were very clear. They grew up never encountering anything that shakes their core. Suddenly they are thrown into Europe, and there are a whole different set of social rules that shakes their core. They don't know how to adapt because they've never had to, so they become more insular and hold onto their [Islamic] core even more.
>
> (Friedman, 2002a)

While in Europe, the would-be hijackers lived on the fringes of European society, eventually gravitating to a local prayer group or mosque where they became radicalized there by militant Islamists, went to Afghanistan for training, and voilà – a terrorist was born (ibid.).

The new and accelerated globalization that thrived in the 1990s has hit the Middle East in a perverse way. Middle Eastern societies are open enough to be disrupted by modernity, but not so open that they can embrace those values and use them to change their societies or even to improve their own situations. "Arabs see the television shows, eat the fast foods, and drink the sodas, but they don't see genuine liberalization in their societies, with increased opportunities and greater openness" (Zakaria, 2003: 140).

The liberalization as transmitted through new global networks almost always meant uprooting local socioeconomic arrangements: patron–client networks and bureaucratic states were under pressure to release their grip. True, states remained the preeminent influence on the lives of most people around the world, but markets and private actors were pressing on the state's control of its society and economy.

The United States stands at the center of the world of globalization and seems unstoppable. "If you close the borders, America comes in through the mail. If you censor the mail, it appears in the fast food and faded jeans. If you ban the products, it seeps in through satellite television" (Zakaria, 2001: 30). Americans are so comfortable with global capitalism and consumer culture that they cannot fathom just how revolutionary these forces are on societies transitioning from clientalism to a neoliberal system of market exchange. Globalization not only comes with the liberal politics and economics of the West, but also brings with it the prospect of cultural transformation.

Often this cultural transformation involves the breakdown of clientalism, based on friendship and in-group loyalties toward a zero-sum, winner-take-all culture before market values emerge. For the people living in this state of social anarchy the new winner-take-all culture has a thoroughly western or American character as seen on television, in the cinema and other forms of popular culture imported from Europe and the United States. Lacking an alternative set of market values and beliefs, millions of individuals in developing countries are convinced that the collapse of clientalist relationships and the emergence of zero-sum anarchy are the results of increasing westernization or Americanization of their societies and they bitterly resent it. Worse, a society with clientalist values and beliefs but with weakening protection from in-groups is highly vulnerable to any in-group system that promises an end to this deep-seated insecurity. This helps to explain the appeal of alternative value systems in developing countries that support ethnic sectarianism, extreme nationalism or various types of religious fundamentalism, *especially* Islamic fundamentalism.

For the last 300 years Muslims have watched in horror and humiliation as the Christian civilizations of Europe and North America have overshadowed them militarily, economically and culturally. Lewis (1990) describes this process of insecurity and rage as it applies to a burning desire to reassert Muslim values and Muslim greatness:

> The Muslim has suffered successive stages of defeat. The first was his loss of domination in the world, to the advancing power of Russia and the West. The second was the undermining of his authority in his own country, through the invasion of foreign ideas and laws and ways of life and sometimes even foreign rulers or settlers, and the enfranchisement of native non-Muslim elements. The third – the last straw – was the challenge to his mastery in his own house, from emancipated women and rebellious children. It was too much to endure, and the outbreak of rage against these alien, infidel, and incomprehensible forces that had subverted his dominance, disrupted his society, and finally violated the sanctuary of his home was inevitable.

It was also natural that this rage be directed primarily against the millennial enemy – the Christian civilizations of Europe and North America – and should draw its strength from ancient beliefs and loyalties associated with Islam. Another example of Muslim rage is reported by *New York Times* columnist Thomas Friedman. Whenever Arab Muslims would tell him of their pain at seeing Palestinians brutalized by Israelis on their TV screens, Friedman would ask back: "Why are you so pained about Israelis brutalizing Palestinians, but don't say a word about the brutality with which Saddam Hussein has snuffed out two generations of Iraqis using murder, fear and poison gas?" Friedman received no satisfactory answers. An American diplomat provided an important insight. "Israel – not Iraq, not India – is 'a constant reminder to Muslims of their own powerlessness.' How could a tiny Jewish state amass so much military and economic power if the Islamic way of life – not Christianity or Judaism – is God's most ideal religious path?" (Friedman, 2002b: A21). One might add that another reason is Israel's identification with the United States and with market forms of exchange. Clearly while identification with Islam is one expressed cause of this rage, the underlying cause is not Islam, so much as a deeply-rooted antimarket and therefore anti-American anger – a fury that extends beyond the Islamic world and whose origins are not understood even by those expressing hatred of the West (Mousseau, 2002/2003: 22).

Conclusions, implications and policy prescriptions

To win the war against international terrorism, the United States and other market democracies have to remove the underlying cause of terror – the deeply imbedded anti-market rage brought on by a clash of values between market exchange economies and clientalist societies and accelerated by the forces of globalization. The problem is that it is only through the development of a market economy that promotes liberal values – impartial enforcement of contracts and common law, destruction of clientalist networks that breed corruption, respect for individual freedom and legal equality – that there appears to be any chance of reducing the social approval of terror. However, it is this same advancement of market exchange that has created so much social anarchy that has led to the anti-market rage in the first place.

The options available to the U.S. are few given the mental model that drives the anti-market and anti-American rage underlying Islamic and other sources of terror. For example, extending more economic aid (Daalder and Lindsay, 2001; Abboud and Minow, 2002) and explaining U.S. policies more clearly as a signal of America's friendly intentions (Daalder and Lindsay, 2001; Peterson, 2002) are unlikely to be very effective. First, as was pointed out earlier, most of the terrorist leaders and their lieutenants are fairly wealthy or at least hail from middle class backgrounds. Poverty does not appear to be a motivating factor that attracts recruits to various terrorist organizations. Second, presumably the objective of increased economic aid would be to assist in laying the institutional foundations for a market economy. Among others, these include the subsidizing of small loans that enable people to buy homes or start small businesses to expand employment. The problem is that the countries that are the most permissive breeding grounds for terror (i.e. Egypt, Saudi Arabia, and Pakistan) are likely to be governed by leaders who hold clientalist rather than market values and beliefs. Maintaining themselves in power typically involves allowing the coalition of clientalist in-groups that keep them in power privileged access to state resources. In this way current forms of foreign aid may actually reinforce the clientalist values and beliefs that condone terror, since recipient governments may use the foreign aid to reward supporters and reinforce clientalist connections.[8] Indeed recent empirical evidence indicates that current forms of economic aid have no effect on promoting democracy (Knack, 2004: 257–260).

Third, and probably the most important, no matter how skillfully implemented a campaign of "public diplomacy" may be, it will not be listened to. Horan points out that there is no ecumenical tradition in Islam. "There are mosques all over America – there is even one in Rome – but Christians may not bring so much as a bible into Saudi Arabia.... In Islamic cultures, the foreigner's extended hand receives no response; indeed, the gesture is likely to be rebuffed or misconstrued" (Horan, 2002: 54). Even many educated people in the developing world believe the nonsensical claim[9] that 4,000 Jews in the New York area were warned not to go to work at the World Trade Center on September 11 (Friedman, 2002c: section 4:15).

Nor is the idea very persuasive that if only people who hate the United States and the liberal belief system had greater exposure to American values, their hatred would dissipate (Peterson, 2002: 84). Anti-American, anti-market rage is the result of knowing Americans too well and having their lives disrupted by the intrusion of market exchange and liberal values. If anything it appears that it is the cultural homogeneity associated with globalization that is stoking anti-American and anti-market rage. Many people view the whole process of cultural assimilation as a mortal threat, as something to be resisted and fought against (Barnett, 2004: 3). Many of these people not only do not embrace a market-based neoliberal orientation, but actually want to see such regimes overthrown or at least kept out of their territory (e.g. Muslim extremists who dream of a Middle East largely isolated from the "infidel" West).

The publication of cartoons satirizing the Prophet Muhammad by the Danish newspaper *Jyllands-Posten* in September 2005 can be interpreted as one skirmish in the running battle between neoliberalism versus a premodern patrimonial paradigm.[10] First, there is no Quranic injunction against depicting human images, whether of Muhammad or anyone else. Indeed there are many depictions of the Prophet, some of which can be seen in museums in the Muslim world including the Topkapi in Istanbul (Taheri, 2006: A16). Second, the widespread violent protests against the publication of these cartoons did not erupt until four months after their original publication to the fairly muted protests of Danish Muslims. Finally, in December 2005 an Egyptian newspaper reprinted the cartoons without drawing any noticeable wrath from Muslim clerics.

It was only after a December meeting of the 56 member states of the Organization of Islamic Conferences – the membership of which consists overwhelmingly of dictatorships or absolute monarchies – that widespread "outrage" against the cartoons began to surface according to Muhammad-el-Sayed, deputy director of the Ahram Center for Political and Strategic Studies in Cairo. No surprise there: as Sari Hanafi, an associate professor at the American University in Beirut noted, "for Arab governments resentful of the Western push for democracy, the protests presented an opportunity to undercut the appeal of the West to Arab citizens. The freedom pushed by the West, they seemed to say, brought with it disrespect for Islam" (Fattah, 2006). He added that the demonstrations "started as a visceral reaction ... and then you had regimes taking advantage saying, 'Look, this is the democracy they're talking about.' "

In short the demonstrations against the Danish cartoons are not an expression of the proverbial rage of the Arab street. They are an orchestrated effort by illiberal regimes in collusion with fundamentalist clerics to create the illusion of Muslim rage for their own political purposes. The protests also allowed Middle Eastern governments to outflank a growing challenge from Islamic opposition movements by appearing to defend Islam.

Most Middle Eastern citizens are undoubtedly aware of the fundamental differences between liberal and Islamic belief systems. Islam is a vision of religious community and social control, whereas the liberal vision is one of secularism, equality, individual autonomy and economic liberalization. God's writ governs social life in the Islamic ideal, whereas individual choice, self-interest and contingent social contracts do so under liberal governance (Murden, 2002: 159). In western Christian societies, God's will is largely unobtrusive in everyday life, engendering a contract, if you will, between individuals and God. As in Islam, Christianity also has its fundamentalist sects, yet these groups generally do not perceive market economies as inimical to their existence. These are bedrock differences over what constitutes the rights of the individual and the parameters of the community and how it should be governed. Clearly this liberal vision of how society should be governed is completely inconsistent with the beliefs held in the Islamic ideal.

In an Islamic theory of state, God rules man, instead of man ruling man. Sovereignty – the ultimate locus of power and authority – resides with God. Human governance exists to ensure submission of the community to God, so there can be no separation between religion and state. Humanity is not entitled to claim the right to legislate in a way that supersedes God's will as codified by the Qur'an and the *Sharia* (Islamic law). Thus the notion of majoritarian democracy is essentially heretical (Murden, 2002: 159).

Even if it is true that one political factor that motivates terrorism "is lack of opportunity for political participation" (Crenshaw, 2003: 95), it does not follow that the problems of terror will diminish if democratic reforms are introduced. Stable democracies emerge when they share the liberal beliefs and values that prevail in market economies – the very belief system that is the object of so much hatred in the Middle East. The simplest explanation for a new democracy's stability is its level of wealth expressed as high national income per capita. As Seymour Martin Lipset stated it in 1959: "the more well-to-do a nation, the greater its chances that it will sustain democracy" (Lipset, 1959: 75). Lipset argued that as countries develop economically their societies develop the capacity and skills to sustain liberal democratic governance. Among other things, wealth level affects the extent to which countries can develop "universalistic" norms among their civil servants and politicians (selection based on competence; performance without favoritism); by contrast, the poorer the country, the greater the incidence of nepotism (ibid.: 84). In other words, it is the level of per capita income and the development of market economies that "grow" neoliberal values. Lipset's thesis has spawned countless research efforts to support or disconfirm these causal linkages. After some 42 years of research, with some qualifications and caveats, Lipset's main point still holds.[11] Mousseau, for example, provides empirical evidence to show how market-based development can bring about the legitimacy of governing institutions that enforce contracts impartially and a political culture that upholds democratically-made common law, individual freedom, legal equality, and universal extensions of trust (Mousseau, 2003: 501–503). It is the interaction effect of democracy with wealth (GDP per capita) that creates the climate for liberal values. Democracy alone does not produce liberal values as evidenced by the existence of democracies (which may be termed as "illiberal") that afford the leader almost unlimited discretionary power and deprive citizens of their basic rights. Wealth alone is not a source of liberal values, either. Saudi Arabia is one of the world's wealthiest states, but remains a predominantly clientalist economy. The findings by Knack, reported earlier, suggest that the exogenous introduction of higher levels of wealth in the form of economic aid (as a percentage of GNP or as a percentage of government expenditures) cannot duplicate the causal linkages between levels of national wealth and democracy identified by Lipset and others. Historically, however, economic aid has not been provided with the primary intention of transforming recipient countries' institutions and belief systems.

Part of the problem is that most of the proposed solutions are grounded on the very liberal institutions – market economies, rule of law, liberal democratic governance and secularism – that local populations perceive as being responsible for their decline from former glory. Disillusionment with the West is at the heart of the Arabs' problem. It makes economic advance impossible and political progress fraught with difficulty (Zakaria, 2001). Worse, few if any feasible alternatives are offered by their own governments. Cronin summarizes the problem when she observes that the West must exploit the mechanisms of globalization to thwart the globalization of terrorism (Cronin, 2002/2003: 55).

The Chinese experience

At first glance, the prescription appears to be a contradiction as long as the purportedly benign intentions of the secular West do not appear at all benign to all those ill served by globalization and the extension of neoliberal values. One way to reverse this contradiction is to draw on China's experience. China has succeeded at capitalism without a firmly-based system of private property rights. China's discretionary officialdom and opaque procedures for political succession, recruitment and promotion are additional causes for uncertainty that in normal circumstances would have a significant negative impact on economic growth. China, however, has a strength that is rarely acknowledged. Root points out that before opening its markets, China's leaders took steps to alleviate the kinds of social imbalances that undermine support for markets and distort public policy in places such as Latin America, South Asia and the Middle East (Root, 2006: 187). The Chinese undertook programs to provide access to health, education and sanitation before liberalization, enabling a large fraction of the population to benefit from new opportunities. Consequently, China's development trajectory more closely resembles East Asia, where the social productivity gap was closed by deliberate government efforts to mitigate social risk (ibid.). Thus the economic opportunities that followed did not lead to a class or ethnicity-based struggle.

> China's population supports competition as an incentive to promote hard work as much as peers do in North America according to cross-national Surveys of contemporary attitudes.[12] The contradictions in the management of China's market economy such as the absence of private property rights, have not thwarted growth because prior reforms created initial social conditions that were hospitable to liberalization of the economy.
>
> (ibid.)

China's approach seems to work because it balances the need to increase the size of the economic pie with the need to address social equity and satisfy the interests of those already in power. This reduces social and political uncertainty which allows China to successfully foster liberalization without privatization even though it violates international norms for promoting growth.[13]

The prior theoretical and empirical work reviewed in this paper suggest that if there is a chance of reducing the social support of terror, market democracies need to use diplomacy and economic aid in more creative ways both as a means and an incentive for governments in developing countries to first create and enforce the bodies of common law that are essential to the functioning of market economies; and second, to equitably subsidize small loans to private enterprises (with fair bidding practices) with the aim of promoting widespread employment. The expansion of employment opportunities is crucial to gaining the acceptance of market values from leaderships in the developing countries whose tenure in office may still depend on heavily clientalist networks and for whom bad economics can be good politics. The availability of well-paying jobs in the market not only alleviates insecurity and reduces anti-market rage, it also legitimizes the values associated with market economies. The prerequisites of a market economy do not include privatization or deregulation.[14] Such measures could have the effect of strengthening, not weakening clientalist linkages and discouraging trust in contractual exchanges as they did in Russia.

Along with funding entrepreneurial activity, western leaders and international organizations could work at convincing Middle Eastern leaders to change the educational curriculum for its younger generation to be more inclusive of world history, sociology and economics and politics. To change the mental model, an internalized cultural change is necessary, not simply implementation of liberal market principles. The greatest difficulty for governments comes in overcoming fears of losing clientalistic networks, and also they must deal with Islamic clerics who will fear the loss of control over the population.

An interesting case in point is the current socio-political and economic cultural change taking place in twenty-first century Iran. The younger generation, beneficiaries of President Muhammad Khatami's more liberal approach to political participation and liberal economic policies, have now internalized the benefits of their condition and desire a more open and inclusive society. They have come to resent the intrusive presence of the Supreme Council in politics and society. The Supreme Council has taken steps to impede these liberal policies. Although it appears that the Council has won a small skirmish over who may serve in the legislature, the population's desires will most likely lead to further evolution of their society to one that is not inimical to outside ideas, but includes a form of Islam, one that is not radical, but recognizes and accepts a new mental model.

All of this is much more easily said than done for a number of reasons. One is that the continued imposition of the prerequisites of a market economy must, by definition, continue to threaten clientalist networks. A market economy expanding at the expense of influential clientalist communities can still trigger a political crisis even if an economic crisis is avoided by expanding employment opportunities and economic growth – for it does not take into account how the fundamentals of a market economy challenge the Muslim vision of religious community and social control.

Among the most critical challenges is how the prerequisites of a market economy are achieved and by whom. One reason why so many Iraqis and other Arabs resented the U.S. invasion of Iraq was not that they supported the Saddam Hussein regime. What they resented was that the Arabs and the Iraqis were too weak to put an end to such a brutal regime, and had to have the Americans do it for them. This is simply another reminder to Muslims of their own powerlessness even when it comes to reforming their own societies. In short, if the liberal values that emerge from higher levels of development and market exchange are to be legitimized, the introduction of a market economy will have to be accomplished by indigenous leaderships as much as possible.

Recall, however, that liberal values emerge as the result of the interaction between the fundamentals of a market economy and higher levels of development expressed as GDP per capita. This implies that a fairly long gestation period may be necessary before the interactive effects of wealth and market exchange register any significant embrace of liberal values.

The evidence reviewed in this paper strongly suggests that it is through the establishment of market economies that the United States and its allies can most effectively defeat global terror. But that is a long term objective. In the meantime, a deeply-embedded clash of cultures lies just beneath the surface: market civilization versus the rest of them.

Notes

* Special thanks to Kanishka Balasuriya for research assistance in connection with this paper and to Cheryl Van Den Handel and Maureen Belson for critiques and editorial assistance of an earlier draft.

1 For a discussion of rational choice in social modeling see Morrow, 1994: 7–9 and Basu, 2000: 36–39.

2 Muhammad Atta, the pilot of the first plane to strike the World Trade Center, came from a modern and reasonably well-to-do – and moderate – Egyptian family. His father was a lawyer. He had two sisters, one a professor, the other a doctor. Atta himself studied in Hamburg, as had several of the other terrorists (Zakaria, 2003: 136–137).

3 This section draws heavily on the work of Mousseau (2000), Mousseau (2002/03) and Zakaria (2003).

4 Another example of a clientalist community that has existed for centuries in the Middle East is the *suq* or bazaar. This form of exchange was apparently intended to operate with little or no government controls over marketplace activity. See North, 1990: 123–124.

5 I use the term "liberal" in the nineteenth-century sense, meaning a concern with individual economic political and religious liberty and the idea of limited government. This variant is sometimes called "classical" liberalism, "constitutional liberalism (Zakaria, 2003) and "Anglo-American" liberalism (Murden, 2002).

6 A similar dichotomy forms the basis of Benjamin Barber's characterization of *Jihad vs. McWorld. Jihad* (Islam is not the issue) is a metaphor for the forces of disintegral tribalism and reactionary fundamentalism. *McWorld* represents the forces of integrative modernization and aggressive economic and cultural globalization (Barber, 1995: xii).

7 For the purposes of this discussion, globalization is a gradually expanding

process whereby power is located in worldwide social formations and expressed through international networks rather than through territorially-based states.

8 This idea is developed at length in Bueno de Mesquita and Root (2002: 29) and Bueno de Mesquita *et al.* (2003).

9 The rumor originated from *Al-Minar*, the television station owned by Hizbollah in Beirut, Lebanon.

10 The distinction between "pre-modern" versus "modern" grew out of the realization by medieval scholars that reason could be a powerful tool, but they feared that using it would undermine faith, which was the basis for authority in all three monotheistic religions – Judaism, Christianity and Islam. This was an age in which the literate West, not unlike today's Islamists, still regarded theology as "the queen of the sciences" (Rutten, 2006). The great rabbi and physician Moses Maimonides and the philosopher Thomas Aquinas argued that there exists a single truth. Faith properly understood, cannot conflict with reason (the "modern" position). The alternative interpretation was championed by the philosopher and jurist Abu-al-Walid Ibn Rushd, known to the West as Averroes, who held that there are two truths – that of revelation and that of the natural world ("pre-modern"). There was no need to reconcile them because they were separate and distinct. This was a form of intellectual isolationism that cut off much of the Islamic world from centuries of scientific and political progress that followed.

11 One research effort that provides considerable empirical support for Lipset's core thesis is Przeworski and Limongi (1997) who looked at every country in the world between 1950 and 1990. Zakaria adjusted their original data expressed in 1985 dollars to a 2000 purchasing power parity (PPP) in U.S. dollars. A democratic country with a per capita income of under $1,500 (constant 2000 dollars) has an average longevity of eight years. With a per capita income of between $1,500 and $3,000 it had a life span of about 18 years. With an income of above $6,000 per capita, it became extremely durable. The probability of a democratic regime dying in a country with an income above $6,000 is 1 in 500 (Zakaria, 2003: 69–70). However, economic development does not "*cause*" democracy. Democracy is established by political actors pursuing their goals and it can be initiated at any level of development. Only after it is established do economic constraints play a decisive role and the chances for the survival of democracy are greater when a country is richer. Further it is not a country's current wealth that is decisive. Democracy is more likely to survive in a growing economy with a per capita income of less than $1,000 than in a country with an income between $1,000 and $2,000 that is in economic decline. If democracies succeed in generating development, they can survive even in the poorest nations (Przeworski and Limongi, 1997: 177).

12 www.worldvaluessurvey.org.

13 Similarly China's gradual and partial path of industrial reform was not decided by a few high-level officials. Root points out that industrial reform evolved from sequences of decisions made by tens of thousands of enterprises and millions of administrators, managers, and workers. The large number of participants and the lengthy duration of the reforms gave people ample time to evaluate alternatives and reconsider their initial views. Eventually this extended process "built a constituency for market-based change that was far stronger than any official announcement could have achieved (Root, 2006: fn. 3, 291–292).

14 A market economy is not to be confused with a free market. "A market economy is one in which the majority of people routinely engage in contractual exchange" (Mousseau, 2002/2003: 25). A market economy can be highly regulated and can involve public as well as private ownership. A free market refers to an unregulated or partially-regulated economy.

References

Abboud, A. Robert and Minow, Newton N. (2002) "Advancing peace in the Middle East," *Foreign Affairs* 81(5) (Sept./Oct.): 14–16.

Ajami, Fouad (1981) *The Arab Predicament: Arab Political Thought and Practice since 1967.* Cambridge, London and New York: Cambridge University Press.

Barber, Benjamin R. (1995) *Jihad vs. McWorld: Terrorism's Challenge to Democracy.* New York: Ballantine Books.

Barnett, Thomas P.M. (2004) *The Pentagon's New Map: War and Peace in the Twenty-First Century.* New York: The Berkley Publishing Group.

Basu, Kaushik (2000) *Prelude to Political Economy: A Study of the Social and Political Foundations of Economics.* Oxford and New York: Oxford University Press.

Bueno de Mesquita, Bruce and Root, Hilton L. (2002) "The political roots of poverty," *The National Interest* 68 (Summer): 27–38.

Bueno de Mesquita, Bruce, Smith, Alastair, Siverson, Randolph M. and Morrow, James D. (2003) *The Logic of Political Survival.* Cambridge, MA and London: the MIT Press.

Crenshaw, Martha (2003) "The causes of terrorism," in Kegley, Jr., Charles W. (ed.) *The New Global Terrorism: Characteristics, Causes, Controls.* Upper Saddle River, NJ: Prentice Hall.

Cronin, Audrey Kurth (2002/2003) "Behind the curve: globalization and international terrorism," *International Security* 27(3) (Winter): 30–58.

Daalder, Ivo H. and Lindsay, James M. (2001) "Nasty, brutish and long: America's war on terrorism," *Current History* 100(650) (Dec.): 403–409.

Fatah, Hassan M. (2006) "At Mecca meeting, cartoon outrage crystallized," *New York Times* (Feb. 9).

Friedman, Thomas L. (2002a) "The twin domes of Belgium," *New York Times* (Jan. 27).

Friedman, Thomas L. (2002b) "The core of Muslim rage," *New York Times* (Mar. 6): A21.

Friedman, Thomas L. (2002c) "Global village idiocy," *New York Times,* Section 4 (May 12): 15.

Fromkin, David (1975) "The strategy of terrorism," *Foreign Affairs* 53(4) (July).

Hoffman, Bruce (1998) *Inside Terrorism.* New York: Columbia University Press.

Horan, Hume (2002) "Those young Arab Muslims around us," *Middle East Quarterly* 9(4) (Fall): 51–58.

Huntington, Samuel P. (2001) "The age of Muslim wars," *Newsweek* (Dec. 17): 42–48.

Knack, Stephen (2004) "Does foreign aid promote democracy?" *International Studies Quarterly* 48(1) (Mar.): 251–266.

Krueger, Alan B. (2001) "Economic scene; to avoid terrorism, end poverty and ignorance. Right? Guess again," *New York Times* (Dec. 13): C2.

Krueger, Alan B. and Maleckova, Jitka (2002) "The economics and the education of suicide bombers," *The New Republic* (June 24).

Lewis, Bernard (1990) "The roots of Muslim rage," *The Atlantic Monthly* (Sept.); see also *The Atlantic Online* (Sept.) www.theatlantic.com/issues/90sep/rage2.htm.

Lewis, Bernard (2003) *The Crisis of Islam: Holy War and Unholy Terror,* New York: The Modern Library.

Lipset, Seymour Martin (1959) "Some social requisites of democracy: economic development and political legitimacy," *American Political Science Review* 53(1) (Mar.): 69–105.

Mousseau, Michael (2000) "Market prosperity, democratic consolidation and democratic peace," *Journal of Conflict Resolution* 44(4) (Aug.): 472–507.

Murrow, James D. (1994) *Game Theory for Political Scientists.* Princeton, NJ: Princeton University Press.

Mousseau, Michael (2002/2003) "Market civilization and its clash with terror," *International Security* 27(3) (Winter): 5–29.

Mousseau, Michael (2003) "The nexus of market society, liberal preferences, and democratic peace: interdisciplinary theory and evidence," *International Studies Quarterly* 47(4) (Dec.): 483–510.

Murden, Simon W. (2002) *Islam, The Middle East and the New Global Hegemony.* Boulder and London: Lynne Rienner.

North, Douglass C. (1990) *Institutions, Institutional Change and Economic Performance.* Cambridge: Cambridge University Press.

Peterson, Peter G. (2002) "Public diplomacy and the war on terrorism," *Foreign Affairs* 81(5) (Sept./Oct.): 74–94.

Pipes, Daniel (2002) "God and Mammon: does poverty cause militant Islam?" *The National Interest* 66 (Winter): 14–22.

Przeworski, Adam and Limongi, Fernando (1997) "Modernization: theories and facts," *World Politics* 49(2) (Jan.): 155–183.

Rutten, Tim (2006) "Drawn into a religious conflict," *Los Angeles Times* (Feb. 4).

Root, Hilton L. (2006) *Capital and Collusion: The Political Logic of Global Economic Development.* Princeton and Oxford: Princeton University Press.

Stern, Jessica (2001) "Being feared is not enough to keep us safe," *Washington Post* (Sept. 15): A27.

Taheri, Amir (2006) "Bonfire of the pieties," *The Wall Street Journal* (Feb. 8).

Wolfensohn, James D. (2002) "Making the world a better and safer place: the time for action is now," *Politics* 22(2) (May): 118–123.

Zakaria, Fareed (2001) "Why do they hate us?" *Newsweek* (Oct. 15): 22–40.

Zakaria, Fareed (2003) *The Future of Freedom: Illiberal Democracy at Home and Abroad.* New York and London: W.W. Norton.

12 Experiments with neoliberalism in India

Shattering of a mental model

Sunil Rongala

> India has 2,000,000 gods, and worships them all. In religion other countries are paupers, India is the only millionaire.
>
> Mark Twain[1]

> India is a muddle.
>
> E.M. Forster[2]

> India, said to have been "emerging" for years, has at last come out.
>
> *The Economist*[3]

Until the early 1990s, India was viewed as country where gods and religion took center stage, where cows blocked roads at every point and a name recognition that rarely extended beyond restaurants featuring Indian cuisines. India was always seen by outsiders as a tourist destination but never a place to invest their money. As far as economic planning was concerned, E.M. Forster's view that India is a muddle has been true from the time of independence to the present. However, in spite of this muddle, in a short time since the early 1990s, this view is changing rapidly. India is now viewed not as exotic but where the future lies.

Denzau and North (1994) write "The mental models are the internal representations that individual cognitive systems create to interpret the environment and the institutions are the external (to the mind) mechanisms individuals create to structure and order the environment.... The mental models that the mind creates and the institutions that individuals create are both an essential part of the way human beings structure their environment in their interactions with it."

The old mental model in India was a more socialist one, one that encouraged dirigisme policies and discouraged foreign investment. This model came about because policy-makers believed that economic growth and reduction of poverty would come about through directed investment by the government. They also believed that these policies would reduce India's dependence on foreign goods. These old mental models and institutions that led India to be considered a "backwater" are being shattered as neoliberalism, in its broad sense of economic liberalism, spreads across the Indian sub-continent.

This shattering of the mental model with regard to India has to be two-fold, however. First, investors have to change their mind about India. This is now taking place. Investors now believe that India is the future, and they are investing billions of dollars in India. However, arguably the more important shattering has to be that of the mental model in the minds of Indians, both policy makers and citizens. Politicians, business groups, and professionals are fueling rapid expansion by embracing deregulation and liberalism. How well the average urban citizen has embraced change is yet to be seen and the rural poor are yet to be convinced that liberalism will benefit them at all.

The paper will show how the old mental model of India came about and how some minor attempts were made to change this mental model. It also explains how this mental model is being shattered and the tasks ahead in order for India to complete its transition from its old mold. The paper concludes by highlighting recent efforts made in this direction.

The socialist years (1947–1984)

Between 1947 and 1984, India had five Prime Ministers but only two of them, Jawaharlal Nehru and his daughter Indira Gandhi, had any serious impact on the economic policies of India. There is no doubt that Nehru was responsible for planting the seeds of democracy in India and is perhaps also responsible for its current healthy situation. However, his contribution to the long-term economic progress and prosperity of the nation is a sadder story. At the time of independence in August of 1947, there were two competing economic ideologies. One was Gandhian Economics and the other was Fabian Economics. Mohandas Karamchand Gandhi propagated the former and the latter was by Nehru.[4] Gandhi was for a more decentralized economy with an emphasis on smaller and village industries rather than heavy industry while Nehru was for the opposite.[5] Eventually, Nehru's ideas won out but whether it did so because of his forceful nature or because Gandhi was assassinated within six months after Indian independence is debatable.

Nehru, from his days in Cambridge, was influenced by Fabian socialism, which called for the state to direct all planning while still having a democracy. [6] Nehru established a haphazard sort of economy, called a "mixed-economy", meaning that the economy would have elements of both capitalism and socialism. However, the objective of Nehru as well as the Indian National Congress (INC) was to create a "socialistic pattern of society" and the resolution of the INC in its 1955 session specified that "planning should take place with a view to the establishment of a socialistic pattern of society, where the principal means of production are under social ownership or control, production is progressively speeded up and there is equitable distribution of the national wealth."[7] Nehru, in 1959, said, "For us there is no other way except that we plan in a socialist way."[8]

This socialistic pattern of society was implemented through Five-Year Plans (FYPs) whereby the state would and could direct the path of the economy. On this issue, the 1955 INC resolution reads, "The First FYP was based on a public sector and a private sector. The public sector must play a progressively greater part, more particularly, in the establishment of basic industries." The duration of the First FYP was from 1951–1956, but it is the Second FYP (1956–1961) that pushed India into a command economy. Nehru called the First FYP as a "modest approach to planning" and described the second FYP as "the first organized attempt at real planning in India" (Bauer, 1961: 30). The objective of the plan was the development of heavy industry in an effort to raise living standards and reduce poverty. According to the Industrial Policy Resolution (IPR) of 1956,

> The state will progressively assume predominant and direct responsibility for setting up new industrial undertakings and for developing transport facilities. It will also undertake State trading on an increasing scale.... The adoption of the socialist pattern of society as the national objective, as well as the need for planned and rapid development, requires that all industries of basic and strategic importance, or in the nature of public utility services, should be in the public sector.[9]

The Second FYP states that the resolution had "to be governed by the principles laid down in the constitution and the objectives of socialism."[10] The Second FYP paved the way for the development of an autarkic system in India. If the resolution and the Second FYP resemble Soviet style planning, it is because it was consciously modeled after Soviet economic planning. Andrew Shonfield of the *Observer* newspaper remarked that

> It is a Soviet type plan. I do not use that label in any pejorative sense, but simply to indicate that it is a heavy-industry plan. And it is a Soviet type plan which errs towards Khrushchev rather than Malenkov; the consumer gets a small look in. Within the total set aside for industrial investment during the five-year period, rather more than half goes to steel alone, and a lot of what is left over goes into capital goods industries.... As far as the consumer is concerned no effort at all is made in the industrial sector to fulfill his needs.
>
> (Bauer, 1961: 106)

The statistics for the outlay of money for the public sector show that the original allocation for large and medium industries and mineral development was around 14.3 percent of the plan total. Agriculture received 7.1 percent, while education and roads received 6.3 and 5.1 percent respectively. However, the outlay for the plan changed and the total amount of the plan was reduced. The new allocation for different sectors pointed to what the planners had alluded to in the IPR. The outlay for large and medium industries was increased to 17.5 percent of the plan total, while agriculture, education, and roads were cut to 6.9, 6.1 and 4.8 percent, respectively (Bauer, 1961: 143–144).

What has not been mentioned so far was the role of the private sector or more accurately, the role that was assigned to the private sector. It is clear that the planners envisaged a subservient role for the private sector in the economic development of India. According to the IPR of 1956, the first category was industries for which the state would be exclusively responsible for their future development. The second category consisted of industries, which would progressively be state-owned, and in which the state would therefore generally take the initiative in establishing new undertakings, but in which private enterprise would also be expected to supplement the effort of the state. The third category included all the remaining industries, and their future development would, in general, be left to the initiative and enterprise of the private sector.

Thus began the start of government monopolies in India. These monopolies were involved in activities such as heavy machinery, shipbuilding, telephone companies, petroleum, and banking. There were also cases of state monopolies created by the nationalization of private companies. One such example is the case of Air India in 1953. Most of these monopolies continue to this day and are only now slowly being divested.

The public sector in India has become the byword for inefficiency. Of the hundreds of industries controlled by the government, only nine of them have shown a reasonable profit.[11] They are referred to as the "nava-ratnas" or nine jewels.[12] However, profits from these few companies were eaten up because of the lack of profitability of the other industries. The nava-ratnas are arguably profitable only because they are government mandated monopolies. Bhagwati (1993) reported that the average rate of return on capital from public sector enterprises was an astonishingly low 2.5 percent in the 1980s and the 14 petroleum companies, which accounted for 77 percent of all profits, heavily weighted this. Das (2000) explains "In India, we primarily focused on the numerator, that is, how to raise savings, thinking it to be the essential problem. We (Indians) ignored the denominator – capital productivity – and it turned out to be our Achilles heel.[13] Indian policy makers naively assumed that once the government made the investments, the return from the capital would come automatically" (p. 73). Citing his grandfather, he writes "the public sector has become the politician's cow – to be milked forever" (p. 86).

As for the private sector, it was also completely controlled by the government but differently when compared to the public sector. Every action by private entrepreneurs required a government license. The government intended to determine the pattern of economic activity and promote only certain industries, and those were mainly import-substituting industries. This led to an inefficient allocation of resources to the private sector companies resulting in low productivity, low quality of products, and limited consumer choice. An example is the automobile industry. Until the late 1970s, Indians could choose from only two widely available models. By the late 1980s, this number increased to five but they too were of low quality. Ordinary Indians had to suffer this ordeal because inordinately high tariffs made the option of importing goods prohibitively expensive. This was not the only reason; the structure and incentives that had set in were also responsible. The nature of the "license-*raj*" was such that it was first-come, first-served. The government would issue only a set number of licenses in a particular industry, so it was common for established businesses to buy them and then just hold on to them in order to prevent any new competition.

There were some early cracks in the Second FYP when receipts from taxation proved to be less than estimates and the government had to resort to deficit financing. The growing deficit led to the foreign exchange crisis in 1958. This was precipitated by a rise in prices, which led to an over-valuation of the real exchange rate leading to reduced exports. Critics also suggested that money was being spent ineffectively on the industrial sector. Milton Friedman, in an unpublished memorandum in 1955, commented about the problems of FYPs:

> India needs heavy industry for economic development; and two, that development of heavy industry uses up large amounts of capital while providing only small employment. Based on these facts, Mahalanobis proposed to concentrate on heavy industry development on the one hand and to subsidize the hand production cottage industries on the other.[14] The latter course would discriminate against the smaller manufacturers. In my opinion, the plan wastes both capital and labor and the Indians get only the worst of both efforts.

A problem in the Indian model was that it did not consider demand conditions while planning the supply of consumer goods. Another criticism of the plan, similar to Friedman's, is the disproportionate amount of money spent on heavy industry vis-à-vis agriculture. In the 1950s, over 80 percent of the population lived in rural areas and an arguable case can be made that most of these people were involved in agriculture. This leads to the criticism made by Friedman about the inefficiencies in the use of capital and labor. However, the biggest criticism of economic planning in India was that it blindly copied the Soviet model since the Soviet Union had plenty of natural resources to support their industries while India did not.

Nehru died on May 27, 1964 and his command economy policies went largely untouched by his successor, Lal Bahadur Shastri (June 1964–January 1966), chiefly because of the outbreak of war between India and Pakistan.[15] The furtherance of Nehru's policies was left to Indira Gandhi, his daughter, Prime Minister of India from January 1966 till March 1977. India then had two Prime Ministers from March 1977 to January 1980, Morarji Desai and Charan Singh. Mrs. Gandhi was re-elected as Prime Minister in January 1980 and remained so till her assassination in October of 1984. Looking at the timeline shows the influence that Nehru and Mrs. Gandhi had on the politics of India and by default, the economics of India.

Mrs. Gandhi, like her father, was a proponent of Fabian socialism. But that was where the similarity ended. She was an autocrat at heart who changed the body-politic of India and according to David Goodal, inflicted the most damage on it.[16] When she was first chosen by the "elders" of the INC in 1966 to be Prime Minister, they thought they could mold her but they failed rather spectacularly. She split the party and increasingly sidelined the old guard of the party. She was ruthless in achieving her objectives and dissidence was rarely tolerated.

She expanded the Nehruvian policies by nationalizing more industries. She once remarked in an interview that "I don't really have a political philosophy ... I wouldn't say I'm interested in socialism as socialism. To me it's just a tool."[17] In 1969, she ordered the nationalization of the 14 largest banks and the insurance companies. Subsequently in 1973, she nationalized the coal and oil industries. The nationalization of these sectors has not exactly contributed to the economic health of India. They became inefficient since the issue of profitability was a moot point and like almost all other state-run enterprises, these sectors became quasi-welfare states providing employment.

A good example of this mismanagement is the banking sector. Nationalization was supposed to ensure that banking services were available to all and this resulted in a massive increase in building of branches in all parts of India. An unfortunate consequence of the nationalization of banks was that it became a tool of the politicians. The banks were forced to do "priority-sector lending"; they had to lend a certain quota to the agriculture sector as well as sectors that were defined as a priority. Since almost no personal risk considerations were taken into account while lending, banks had a high level of non-performing loans leaving a lot of them in the red.

Kripalani (2002) comments, "Years of lax controls and politically dictated lending have left the banks holding $23 billion in bad debt; more that a fifth of their loan portfolios." She then states that

> The bad-loan problem largely afflicts the state-owned banks, which control more than 80% of the country's banking assets. The government has long misused these banks to rescue failing institutions or to funnel money to favored projects – the bailout of a bankrupt steel mill

> in one state, the construction of an unneeded chemical plant in another – that had little hope of paying off. And in a scathing indictment, a study to be released soon by McKinsey & Co finds that the productivity of Indian banks is a mere one-tenth that of U.S. banks.

She further comments that

> ... the government routinely bails out the banks that are in the deepest trouble. In February, IDBI (Industrial Development Bank of India) asked for, and got, $458 million. Last August, the government organized a $215 million bailout of the Industrial Finance Corporation of India. State-owned banks, in fact, have higher credit ratings than the Indian government because the market is confident that the government will always rescue them.

On the issue of poverty, Mrs. Gandhi campaigned on the slogan "garibi hatao" (remove poverty) during the 1971 elections, which she won convincingly. However, according to DeLong (2004),[18] "Politicians (chief of them Nehru's daughter Indira Gandhi) saw India's poverty not as a problem to be solved through economic growth but as an interest group to be appeased in an attempt to seize and maintain political power" (p. 16).

Before her assassination, Mrs. Gandhi began some reforms on licensing and taxes in an attempt to improve economic performance. Bhagwati (1993) called them "reforms by stealth". He, however, expressed doubt at Mrs. Gandhi's intention on long-term economic reforms and commented that

> Tentative moves towards delicensing had been planned as early as towards the end of Mrs. Gandhi's term before her assassination.... But, with her formative years spent in an intellectual atmosphere permeated with the Fabian thinking ... I suspect that Mrs. Gandhi would have been a reluctant reformer at best. It is hard to imagine that she would have proceeded steadily further down the road to liberalization if she had not been assassinated.... We will never know; but any speculation suggesting continued reforms by her cannot really be supported by cogent arguments.
>
> (p. 78)

However, in the end, what really matters is whether economic planning in India succeeded or not. The two stated objectives of the FYPs were rapid economic growth and the reduction of poverty in India and if the success of the FYPs is to be judged on those two objectives, they have failed on both counts. Figure 12.1 shows the annual rate of growth of GDP and the annual rate of growth of per capita GDP from 1961 to 1984. Though some years show spectacular growth, they seem to be aberrances rather than the norm and the growth patterns fluctuate wildly over years. The

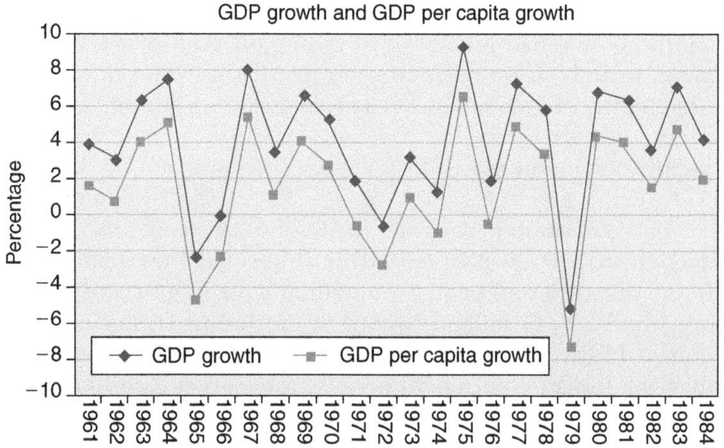

Figure 12.1 GDP growth and GDP per capita growth (source: World Bank, *World Development Indicators*).

average rate of GDP growth for the 25 years was a mediocre 3.8 percent (so called Hindu rate of growth), while the average per capita GDP growth rate was an abysmal 1.54 percent. Panagariya (2004) reports that the average growth rate during the First FYP (1951–1956) was 3.6 percent, while the Second FYP (1956–1961) was 4.3 percent.

Figure 12.2 shows the percentage of people below the poverty line from 1956–1983 and this portrays a very dismal situation too. In 1956, 57.55 percent of the population was below the poverty line while it was 62 percent in 1966. The poverty level did reduce to 43 percent in 1983 but that is still high if one of the stated objectives of the FYPs was the reduction of poverty.

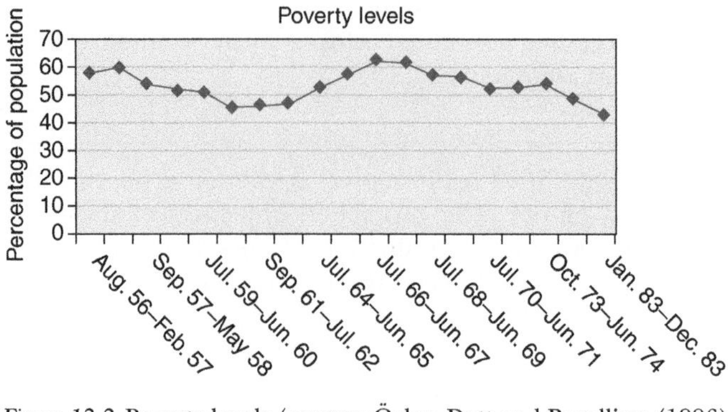

Figure 12.2 Poverty levels (source: Özler, Datt and Ravallion (1996)).

Bhagwati (2000) summarizing Lal (1999)[19] writes that:

> The professional "povertywallahs": the politicians who have mouthed slogans such as "garibi hatao" and the economists who write continually about "abysmal poverty". Both have generally espoused policies, such as defending public sector enterprises at any cost, discounting and even opposing liberal reforms, promoting white-elephant style projects that use capital-intensive techniques on unrealistic grounds as that they would create profits and savings when in fact they have drained the economy through losses that have stalled the effort to accumulate and grow and create more jobs to "pull up" the underemployed into gainful employment and hence out of poverty.

Returning to the issue of mental models, the question is how the old model formed in the minds of Indians and international investors. As far as investors are concerned, it is obvious since India was implementing socialist policies. There were a lot of restrictions placed on foreign investment and thus they never saw the country as having a good investment climate. The total foreign direct investment from 1970 to 1984 was a paltry $640 million (See Figure 12.3).

As far as Indian policy makers were concerned: the socialist policies as well as extensive regulation of the private sector gave the policy makers and bureaucrats enormous power over the daily lives of people. That, in turn, gave them the incentive to stick to more socialist policies and less liberalization. As for the elites, the protectionist policies were very suitable for them since the net result was that they had very little competition for their products.

What is trickier, however, is how the old mental model took its place in

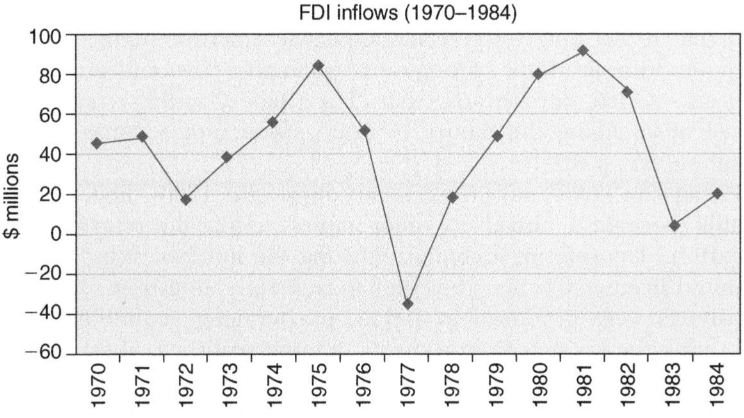

Figure 12.3 FDI inflows (1970–1984) (source: UNCTAD, Foreign Direct Investment database, *World Investment Report*).

the minds of ordinary people since the figures suggest that they did not really benefit from the socialist policies. There are two possibilities for this. One is Nehru himself. It should be understood that Nehru had near messianic status next only to Mahatma Gandhi. People trusted Nehru to do what was right since he had made a lot of personal sacrifices to join the freedom struggle.[20] To people in the rural areas, he was a demigod and to people in the urban areas, he was one of them; well-read and very sophisticated. This courtesy was surely passed down to his daughter. She was very popular in the rural areas because of her populist policies, and given the size of the population in the rural areas, it really didn't matter what people in the urban areas thought. The second possible explanation may simply be that the poor and uneducated lack the sophistication to be politically astute; they are always too busy finding food for their families.

The "liberalization by stealth" years (1984–1991)

India had three Prime Ministers between 1984–1991, Rajiv Gandhi (1984–1989), V.P. Singh (1989–1990), and Chandrashekar (1990–1991). After the assassination of Indira Gandhi in October of 1984, her son Rajiv Gandhi became the Prime Minister. In the elections that were held immediately after the assassination, the Congress party won a large majority of seats in the *Lok Sabha* (lower house of parliament).[21] Rajiv Gandhi started new economic reforms and continued some of the reforms that his mother had started just before her assassination. Bhagwati (1993) commented, "The liberalizing reforms tentatively begun at the end of Mrs. Gandhi's life, and pursued somewhat more energetically by Rajiv Gandhi but coming to naught within a year, were both undertaken for reasons other than because these Prime Ministers were looking down the barrel of a gun" (pp. 73–74). What Bhagwati meant is that, apart from the fact that both realized that India was heading towards financial disaster, they realized that it was time for reforms, especially microeconomic reforms, if there was to be any hope of long-term sustainable economic growth. Bhagwati also added the footnote that "His (Rajiv Gandhi's) reforms were aimed at changing the nature of intervention, not at emasculating it" (footnote on pp. 15–16).

Panagariya (2004) calls the reforms during the 1980s "liberalization by stealth" because of their very quiet nature, unlike the reforms initiated post-1991. The reforms included reducing the number of industries that required licenses to open (but they were mainly industries for which no substitutes were produced in India), encouraging commodity exports, reforming the tax system, introducing a more realistic real exchange rate and reducing duties on imports of capital goods.

However, continued reforms by the Rajiv Gandhi government came to a quick end for several reasons. One was that several factions within the Congress Party were not too keen about economic reforms; the other was the bribery scandal that eventually brought down the government. The scandal was related to a $1 billion-plus deal with the Bofors Company of Sweden for howitzer guns. It was alleged that a number of kickbacks were paid to close confidantes and friends of the Gandhi family. The result was that Gandhi increasingly secluded himself. The scandal also resulted in a bitter dispute with his Finance Minister, V.P. Singh. Singh, who was responsible for many of the reforms, eventually left the party. When Rajiv Gandhi lost the elections in 1989, India had two Prime Ministers between then and 1991 and no further reforms were done.

Whether the reforms done in the 1980s were a success or not and whether they changed mental models in and of India is debatable. DeLong (2004) commented on India's accelerating economic progress:

> What are the sources of India's recent acceleration in economic growth? Conventional wisdom traces them to policy reforms at the start of the 1990s. Yet the aggregate growth data tells us that the acceleration of economic growth began earlier, in the early or mid 1980s, long before the exchange crisis of 1991 and the shift of the government of Narasimha Rao and Manmohan Singh towards neo-liberal economic reforms.
>
> (p. 5)

Furthermore, he added, "The consequence of this first wave of economic reform was an economic boom. Real GDP growth grew at 5.6 percent per year" (p. 24). DeLong however acknowledges that this boom would not have lasted had the economic reforms of the 1990s not been implemented, but he added the caveat "hard evidence to support such a strong counterfactual judgment is lacking" (p. 6). This statement could suggest that reforms in the 1980s had gathered enough steam as well as support to move the Indian economy along in the right direction. Rodrik (2002), with reference to DeLong, writes,

> Furthermore, DeLong's back-of-the-envelope calculations suggest that the significantly more ambitious reforms of the 1990s actually had a smaller impact on India's long-run growth path. DeLong speculates that the change in official attitudes in the 1980s, towards encouraging rather than discouraging entrepreneurial activities and integration into the world economy, and a belief that the rules of the economic game had changed for good may have had a bigger impact on growth than any specific policy reforms.
>
> (p. 19)

Panagariya (2004), however, argues that the reforms started in the 1980s were unsustainable because official attitudes had not changed in India. He argues that the factors responsible for rapid economic growth in

India during the 1980s were borrowing abroad and rising government expenditures. The gross domestic savings and investment were 20.4 percent and 22.7 percent of GDP respectively during 1985–1990. The difference was made up largely through foreign debt. Figure 12.4 shows the rapid rise in foreign debt from around $33 billion in 1984 to over $80 billion in 1991. The debt service ratio rose from 18 to 27 percent from 1984 to 1990. Panagariya writes

> The growth in debt was also accompanied by a rapid deterioration in the 'quality' of debt between 1984–1985 and 1989–1990. The share of private borrowers in the total long-run debt increased from 28 to 41 percent. The share of non-concessional debt rose from 42 to 54 percent. The average maturity of debt declined from 27 to 20 years. Thus, while external debt was helping the country grow, it was also moving it steadily towards a crash.
>
> (p. 28)

As far as government expenditures were concerned, Panagariya gives a Keynesian argument that rising domestic public expenditures such as defense spending, interest payments on the debt, and subsidies provided the stimulus. Also, according to the Department of Disinvestment, the investment in public sector companies rose from Rupees 181 billion in 1980 to Rupees 426 billion in 1985 and then to Rupees 993 billion in 1990. The average fiscal deficit during the period, 1984–1991, was over 7 percent (see Figure 12.5). Panagariya concludes, "The eventual outcome of these developments was the June 1991 crisis."[22] Another problem with the GDP growth from 1984 to 1991, though it was a relatively high growth rate (see Figure 12.6), it had a relatively high variance.[23]

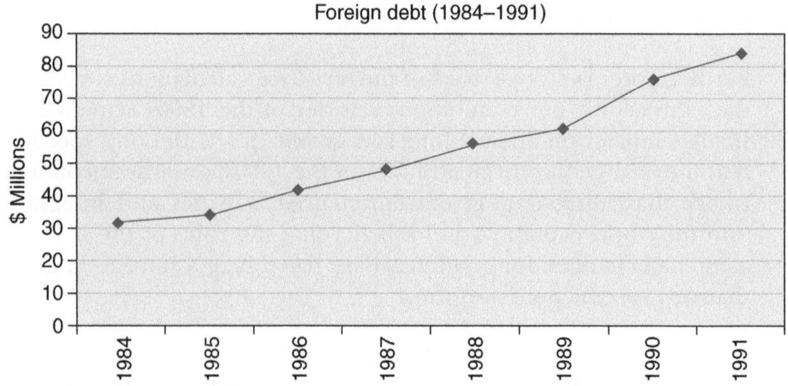

Figure 12.4 Foreign debt (1984–1991) (source: World Bank, *World Development Indicators*).

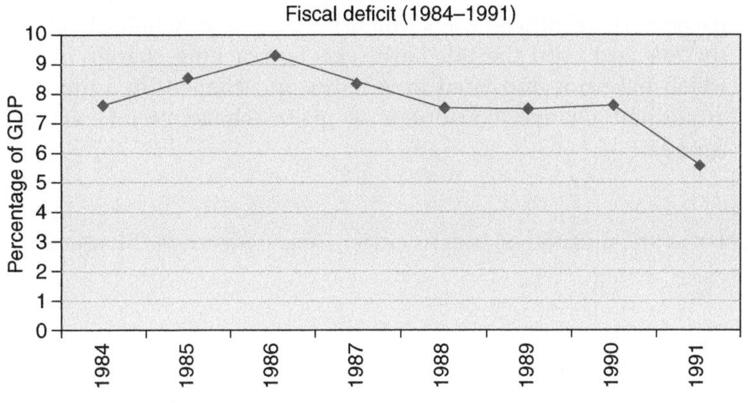

Figure 12.5 Fiscal deficit (1984–1991) (source: IMF, *International Financial Statistics*).

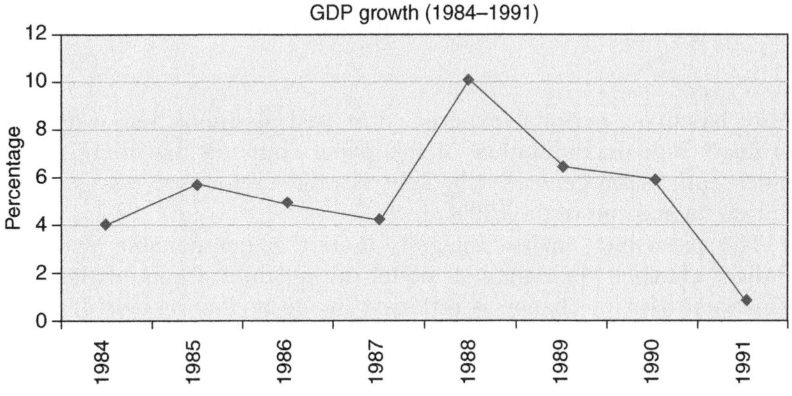

Figure 12.6 GDP growth (1984–1991) (source: World Bank, *World Development Indicators*).

Writing about official attitudes, Panagariya (2004) cites personal correspondence he had with N.K. Singh, a member of the Planning Commission of India. Singh wrote,

> I am somewhat intrigued by the statement of DeLong and Rodrik stressing change in official attitude over change in policies implying that if attitude changed for good, growth would have been sustained even without reforms in the 1990s. Even today, more than change in policies we are struggling with change in attitude. The first reflex of any observer of (the) Indian economy or potential foreign investor

> would be that while policies may not be so bad, it is the attitude particularly of official ones which becomes the Achilles heel. In fact the 80s and even the 90s have seen far-reaching change in policies which have not translated themselves into changes in attitudes. This attitudinal change constitutes a major challenge in our reform agenda.
>
> (p. 4)

Insofar as the attitude of Indian citizens was concerned, Bhagwati (1993) writes,

> By contrast, Indian expectations, while aroused, were somewhat modest. It is fair to say that the euphoria exhibited in the United States was not shared in the same degree by Indians, much as they supported their young Prime Minister's declarations and initiatives supportive of "liberal," market-oriented economic reform.... Yet many in India did feel that finally India had turned the corner and an "economic miracle" might well be at hand if only the Prime Minister could stay the course. In the event, he did not.
>
> (pp. 15–16)

Also, based on personal experience as well as interactions with many ordinary Indians, the author of this paper contends that there was not much enthusiasm generated by Rajiv Gandhi's reforms as was generated during the reforms of the 1990s.

The preceding analysis suggests that it is questionable that many Indians changed their mental model during the reforms of the 1980s. This same lack of change is reflected in the mental models of foreign investors also. A reasonable proxy for this attitude is foreign direct investment inflows. The aggregate FDI inflow into India from 1984 to 1991 was $1.1 billion (see Figure 12.7) which pales in comparison to China which had aggregate FDI inflows of $21.5 billion during the same period.

Bhagwati (1993) sums it up well writing, "Rajiv Gandhi's reforms were hardly revolutionary in conception or in execution. In retrospect, they amounted to acquiescence in the regime but a mild attempt at moderating its worst excesses. They were a small step in the right direction; they generated enthusiasm simply because India seemed finally to be going down the right road" (p. 80).

The neoliberal "reforms by storm" years (1991–present)

A suicide bomber assassinated Rajiv Gandhi during the election campaign in 1991. In the elections that followed, the Congress Party won 44 percent of the seats in the *Lok Sabha* and formed a minority government with Narasimha Rao as the Prime Minister. The "elders" of the Congress Party

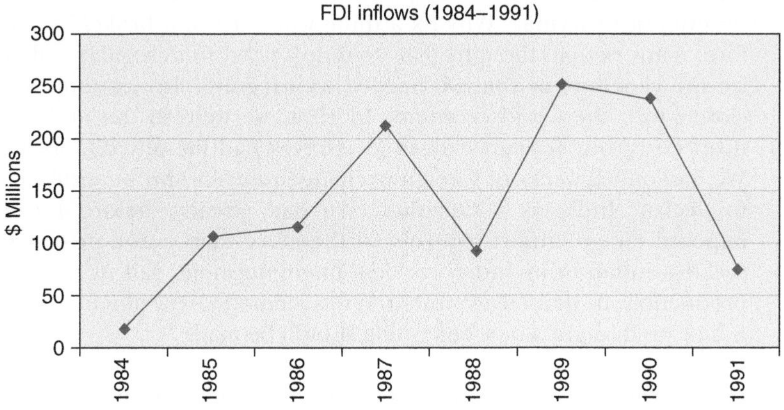

Figure 12.7 FDI inflows (1984–1991) (Source: UNCTAD, Foreign Direct Investment database, *World Investment Report*).

anointed Rao in much the same fashion as they had anointed Indira Gandhi. Although Rao did not have a support base in the party he would prove to be very agile and eventually outmaneuver much of the old guard. Rao appointed Manmohan Singh as the Finance Minister. Singh, a Ph.D. economist from Oxford, was largely unknown, having previously been an academic and civil servant; his appointment was a surprise to say the least. He surrounded himself with a group of technocrats and they set about implementing the most extensive set of economic reforms that had been attempted in the history on independent India. Bhagwati called these "reforms by storm."

Reforms were badly needed because India was suffering severe economic stresses and was heading to a fiscal crisis owing to the large public debt accumulated over the 1980s and this debt had reached 50 percent of GDP in 1991. The problem was that the debt had a large foreign component and, as mentioned previously, the quality of debt was poor. At the same time, foreign exchange reserves were falling and India was coming under increased pressure because of large debt service payments. By 1990 it was becoming apparent that India was, for the first time in her history, heading towards a default. The government was forced to approach the IMF to ask for an emergency loan of $1.8 billion. The lowest ebb was reached in mid 1991 when India's foreign reserves reached $200 million, sufficient for only two weeks'-worth of imports.[24] Manmohan Singh, in a personal interview with the author, said,

> We were in a crisis. We had tried all the old technologies and they didn't seem to work. I felt that the crisis was an opportunity to do things that many people thought should be done. When the economy

> was doing reasonably well in the 1980s with 5.5% growth many used the American saying, "Why fix a thing when it is not broken". Therefore, many people thought that we didn't need to deregulate, liberalize the economy or that we needed to integrate our economy more closely with the world economy. In 1991, we were in the midst of a deep crisis; our foreign exchange reserves had literally disappeared. We had only 2 weeks of foreign exchange reserves and we would have to declare India as a defaulter. We had already, before I came, imposed savage import controls, so therefore there was a prospect of reckless inflation in India, reckless unemployment, fall in industrial production. In that environment, it was a time to experiment and that is how we thought a new beginning should be made.

The reforms were implemented almost overnight. India had quite never seen anything like it before. According to Bhagwati (1993), "The reforms are being unfolded in a blitzkrieg of successive moves that both give them a momentum and keep opposition off-balance" (pp. 84–85). The reforms enacted since 1991 have included:

- Scrapping the requirement of licenses for almost all industries. The exceptions involved a few that were regarded as environmentally sensitive.
- Reducing tariffs on imports from an average of 85 percent to 25 percent.
- Making the Rupee convertible on the current account with steps being promised to make it convertible on the capital account.
- Encouraging foreign direct investment through a process of reduced approval time and increasing the ceiling on foreign stake-holds in Indian companies.
- Removing the obligation of the Reserve Bank of India to monetize the budget deficit.
- Removing punitive regulations against large corporations.[25]
- Privatizing a number of state owned industries.
- Granting permission to private enterprises to enter sectors previously open only to the government.[26]
- Reducing the Cash Reserve Ratio (CRR) that banks had to keep.[27]

However, the question that needs to be asked again is whether or not these reforms have successfully changed the attitudes or the mental models of investors, officials, and the common people. This change is needed for long-term continuity as well as the success of the reforms. As far as investors are concerned, the proxy of their perceptions of the prospects of India is FDI inflows. The total inflows from 1991 to 2004 totaled $34.6 billion (see Figure 12.8) as compared to $1.31 billion for the 13 previous years. The *Economist Intelligence Unit* (2004) estimates that

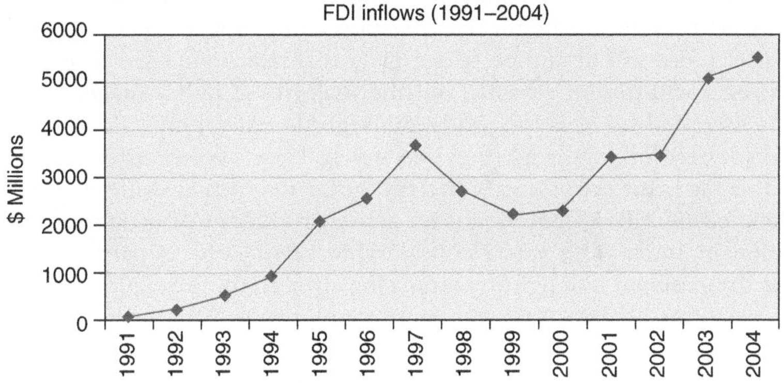

Figure 12.8 FDI inflows (1991–2004) (source: UNCTAD, Foreign Direct Investment database, *World Investment Report*).

India will receive yearly FDI inflows of $13 billion by 2008. The *EIU* also points to India being one of the key destinations for global foreign direct investment. This is a sign that investors no longer look at India as a backwater but it is currently debatable whether they have completely changed their minds or mental models since there are surely aware of the fact that there still need to be considerable changes made in the business environment.

Goswami (2005) sums this change of mental model of international investors saying:

> Of course, some commentators were aware of India's strides in software, information technology and business outsourcing from the late 1990s. Even so, the prognosis was, at best, cautiously optimistic; more typically, people believed that India specialized in flattering to deceive – a vibrant but unruly democracy that was congenitally adept at snatching defeat from the jaws of victory.
>
> Perceptions changed in late 2003, when it became apparent that for the first time since the advent of economic reforms in 1991, the country would achieve over 8 per cent in annual growth. The developed world was seeking an alternate growth pole to China, and the prospects of a strong, democratic, multicultural, youth-dominated nation with a population of more than 1 billion, was an attractive proposition indeed. Goldman Sachs's famous BRICs Report (Brazil, Russia, India and China) released in October 2003, upped the ante by forecasting that a modestly but steadily growing Indian economy would overtake Italy by 2016, France by 2019, the United Kingdom by 2022 . . . the *New York Times*'s columnist Thomas Friedman's book, *The World is Flat,* released in April 2005, did the rest.
>
> (p. 12)

As far as political attitudes are concerned, a sign that they may have changed is reflected in the last election campaign in April of 2004. Of course, there will always be fringe groups that are opposed to economic reforms for different reasons, but the majority of policy makers seem to have accepted reforms for good. Although the governments that followed Rao's lasted for two years, they did not roll back economic reforms that had so far been introduced. The BJP government that came to power in 1999, led by A.B. Vajpayee, was an active proponent of economic liberalization in India. This was a considerable *volte-face* for a party that came into the national limelight by espousing strong Hindu religious values. In the elections held in 2004, the main plank of the BJP was the success of the reforms and the strong performance of the economy while the plank of the Congress Party included the fact that it was responsible for the start of economic reforms in India.

What is debatable, however, is whether the mental model of the masses has been changed. Manmohan Singh said, "India has (had) for fifty years a mindset (that) more public intervention was considered good, right or wrong. We had changed the direction but we had to prepare our people for this change."[28] Based on personal experience, having lived in both rural and urban areas in India, the author contends that there has been considerable enthusiasm for the economic reforms in the country. However, this enthusiasm is certainly stronger in the urban areas, which have seen the tangible changes of economic liberalization. Many have interpreted the election defeat of the BJP, in 2004, as indicating that people, especially in the rural areas, were dissatisfied with economic reforms and didn't want them. The author argues that this dissatisfaction is not because rural people, who comprise 70 percent of the population, don't want economic reforms, but because they want the reforms to reach down to them too. An editorial in the *Financial Times* reads "Last month's electoral upset in India ... should not be construed as a vote against reform. It was a vote against the complacency of urban elites who have neglected the countryside where two-thirds of Indians live."[29] However, the reforms that need to be made in the rural areas are of a different nature and will be discussed later. A rapid expansion of media such as television and radio is responsible, to a large extent, for increasing political awareness among the rural population. Politicians will be forced to address their needs if they want to stay in power.

The blame game

While it may be instinctive to blame politicians for the poor and lackluster economic performance in India, there are many places where the finger must be pointed. There is no doubt that politicians bear some responsibility because they were enamored by the tenets of Fabian Socialism and implemented them in India with dismal results. They did not change their ways when early results from the FYPs showed that the goals of economic growth and reduction in poverty were not being reached. The politicians should also be blamed for using poverty as a political tool rather than something that must be reduced.

Another finger must be pointed at the economists. Bhagwati (1993) writes,

> The central role of economists, and their responsibility for India's failings, cannot be lightly dismissed. It is not entirely wrong to agree with the cynical view that India's misfortune was to have brilliant economists; an affliction that the Far Eastern super-performers were spared. There is a related but brilliant proposition that India suffered because her splendid economists were both able and willing to rationalize every one of the outrageous policies that the government was adopting: by ingeniously constructing models designed to yield the desired answers.
>
> (pp. 84–85)

Indian economists weren't the only ones to blame; many prominent western economists thought that India's model of economic development was the right model to pursue. India pursued the Rosenstein–Rodan, Harrod–Domar and Prebisch models. The first argued that industrialization could be regarded as the initiator of economic development. It advocated a massive plan of investment by the government to achieve balanced growth. The Harrod–Domar model argued that growth was a function of the savings ratio divided by the marginal returns to capital. Though these models were perfectly reasonable models to follow, they were incorrectly followed in India. One model that Indian policy makers followed was the "dependency theory" by Raúl Prebisch. This theory said that poor countries were better off developing import-substituting industries than trading with developed countries. The argument was that the poor countries would become dependent on the rich countries for those goods and be held hostage if they traded. Das (2000) likens this theory to "re-inventing the wheel" because indigenous companies would have to develop methods to produce these previously imported products making them even more costly to consumers.

Some big industrial houses in India can also be blamed. When India was under a "license-*raj*" system, there were only a limited number of licenses that were issued by the government for any industrial sector. Industrial houses regularly purchased many licenses in order to restrict competition. Because of prohibitive import duties, Indians were forced to buy durable goods from a very limited selection. It can be argued that this sort of behavior severely retarded economic growth as well as giving Indian consumers a very raw deal.

Another group which deserves some blame includes some politicians, "social activists", labor unions, etc. who are against any sort of economic reforms. They cannot be blamed for the poor economic performance before India's reforms but can certainly be blamed for constantly distracting the reformers from doing their job. This group has no real policymaking power but they do have influence because of their high profile. The problem with this group is that they have not offered any real solutions and alternatives to the economic liberalization process but have instead taken to expressing *schadenfreude* when there are glitches in the reforms.

Rajan and Zingales (2003) commenting on the impediments to a free market system write,

> Throughout its history, the free market system has been held back, not so much by its economic deficiencies, as Marxists would have it, but because of its reliance on political goodwill for its infrastructure. The threat primarily comes from two groups of opponents. The first are incumbents, those who already have an established position in the marketplace and would prefer to see it remain exclusive. The identity of the most dangerous incumbents depends on the country and the time period, but the part has been played at various times by the landed aristocracy, the owners and managers of large corporations, their financiers, and organized labor. The second group of opponents, the distressed, tends to surface in times of economic downturn. Those who have lost out in the process of creative destruction unleashed by markets ... see no legitimacy in a system in which they have been proved losers. They want relief, and since the markets offer them none, they will try the route of politics.
>
> (pp. 1–2)

The task ahead

The economic reforms, started in 1991, marked an important watershed for India. These reforms came about because of the will of a certain group of people who realized it was time for India to depart from her old habits if there was any chance of becoming an economic power and not sink into an economic quagmire. These reforms have resulted in an upward trend in GDP growth with less volatility in the years since 1991 (see Figure 12.9). Panagariya (2004) estimated the variance in GDP growth from 1998 to 2003 to be 0.96. However, there have been years, since 1991, where GDP growth rate has not been to par.

The foreign reserve levels in India are a very comfortable $130 billion plus. The exchange rate has been stable for several years and the inflation rate has been stable for some time. India did achieve a current account surplus but this has, of late, turned into a deficit because of sustained high oil prices. However, all these achievements could disappear if the fiscal deficit is not given enough attention; it is at a dangerous high of 10

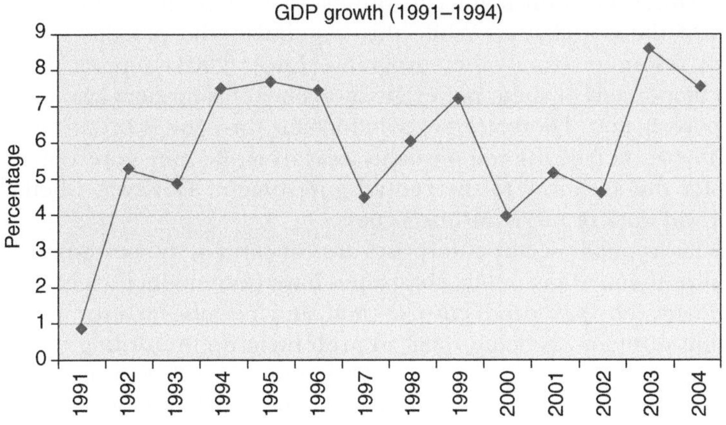

Figure 12.9 GDP growth (1991–2004) (source: World Bank, *World Development Indicators*).

percent of GDP. The poverty rate has declined to around 35 percent but that is still too high.

The perception that investors and Indians (policy makers and citizens) have of India is changing. However, for a successful transition from its old mold, there are a number of further reforms that need to be made. If this transition can be completed, and how it can be done is shown below, India will be able to perform at her full potential and set the stage to become a real economic power, as opposed to just potential, in the very near future.

The current stability of governments is tenuous because the large number of political parties necessitates coalition governments but there is no threat to democracy in India. The silver lining in the cloud, however, is that Manmohan Singh is the Prime Minister. Dr. Singh's challenges will be many, not the least of which is extending reforms to the rural areas. This is easier said than done because such programs are expensive and the federal government is cash-strapped. There are many reasons that can be pointed to for draining much of the cash. Some of them are the fiscally-irresponsible state governments, the inefficient power (electricity) sector, bankrupt public sector companies and a badly managed subsidy program. Another reason is the military expense but that is a necessary expense because of current tensions with Pakistan. However, recently improved relations with Pakistan could de-escalate this tension and possibly reduce military expenditure.

The solutions for India's problems are straightforward but require a lot of political will. The state governments need to be held responsible for their own finances instead of passing on the deficits to the federal government as they do now. Governments have so far used the power sector as an electoral tool with politicians promising free electricity to certain sections of the population. While this is popular, the practice is draining scarce resources from other programs. Luce (2004) reports that more than 90 percent of these power giveaways benefits farmers who are above the poverty line. There are two solutions for this: one is privatization and the other is to take the responsibility away from the state governments and transfer the authority to the central government. However, whether the latter will work or not is anyone's guess.

As far as public sector enterprises are concerned, the best solution is to privatize them. Many public companies have become inefficient by hiring too many, be they productive or not, and because a disproportionate amount of money is being spent to prop them up. According to the Economic Survey of India for 2002–2003, there are 3.26 million persons employed by the central government in the public sector, less than 0.5 percent of India's population.[30] The Department of Disinvestment of the Government of India reports that the total investment in central government owned public sector companies as of 2000 was Rupees 2.5 trillion or $56.01 billion.[31] It then becomes questionable why so much is being spent on so few.

Dr. Singh has come under political pressure to halt privatization, and he has expressed some reluctance to privatize the profitable enterprises. Since the profitable companies are so few in number, it should not really be a problem. If the government does keep the profitable companies, it needs to stop meddling and to outsource management in order to garner even higher returns on capital. Another avenue to stop unnecessary expenditures is to reform the current program of subsidies given to farmers. Like the power giveaways, a considerable percentage of these subsidies reach farmers who do not need them. This will require immense political will and skill and as Dr. Singh said, "Farmers make up 65% of the population and all political parties shy away from making hard decisions when it hurts 65% of the population which is in agriculture."[32]

If the government is able to initiate these meaningful reforms, it will have money to begin to address the other needs in society. The first priorities are education and health. Many studies point to the correlation between illiteracy and poverty; given that 40 percent of India's population is still illiterate, there is a great task ahead. Money effectively spent on public health, primary and secondary education will help people emerge from crippling poverty. A reduction in ignorance and poverty is a requirement for India to reach her full potential in terms of economic growth. A skilled workforce will also make India more attractive to investors. Manmohan Singh, commenting on government involvement in health and education, said

> Our reform process is in the first phase and we haven't moved beyond what was essentially concerted liberalization of industry, trade, and

> reform of the tax system. But, we have not had time to create an environment where reforms would change the lives of the ordinary people. Now that could only happen if we could improve the processes of governance at the grassroots where the central government has a very limited role to play and it is the state governments that are involved. Where the central government is concerned, our expectation was we would be able to restructure the fiscal system and get government out of business and industry and get government more actively involved in health and education so that people will feel that reforms have made a difference.[33]

Extending education and health programs to the rural areas is a critical necessity in the face of the looming AIDS crisis. Unfortunately, only lip service is being given to the AIDS crisis and is not being given the urgent attention it needs to be given by the policy makers. Experts in India believe that there are now around ten million HIV infected people in India, by far the highest in any nation, while the government's figure is less than half; about 4.5 million.[34] These experts believe that it reflects widespread ambivalence about AIDS. Another example of this ambivalence was reflected when Bill Gates, Chairman of Microsoft, gave $100 million to fight AIDS in India but it was met with indignation at the assumption it was needed; the sore point being Gates's prediction that HIV infections could double to 20 million by 2010.[35] Root (2005) reports that while India has 48 physicians per 100,000 persons. A simple cost versus benefit analysis will suggest that investing in education and health will be cheaper than having to deal with a full-blown epidemic later on.

The government needs to also invest money in infrastructure for long term sustained economic growth. This includes roads and electricity, which are currently in a bad state. India has so far attracted FDI in the service sector but not much in the manufacturing sector; most of which has found its way to China. Though expensive, developing this infrastructure will make India attractive to investment in the manufacturing sector, thus paying for itself. This is necessary since there is a large percentage of the population with a low educational skill set who will be better suited to the manufacturing sector than the service sector. As people gravitate away from agriculture and as the public sector is reorganized through privatization, increased manufacturing will be able to absorb workers, thus reducing unemployment.

On the banking sector, Kripalani (2002) writes:

> Now, the banking system has become so dysfunctional that it's slowing the economy. Banks are increasingly wary of lending to businesses, starving even promising sectors of capital. Real bank reform could boost economic growth by 1% to 2% a year, according to McKinsey. "These banks have all the symptoms – nonperforming assets, poor

> productivity, inability to raise capital from the market – that precede a crisis," says Joydeep Sengupta, a partner with McKinsey in India.

This may be overstating the case and Kripalani reports that some state-owned banks are trying to fix themselves by tightening their lending criteria and strengthening their accounting and corporate governance and also creating subsidiaries that aim to operate like private sector banks. However, of late, the Reserve Bank of India has stepped up its vigilance on banks and has been doing a remarkable job.

A serious image problem is the entrenched bribery and corruption, which has led many business magazines to mention India as a bad place to do business in. This corruption is the direct result of the extensive bureaucratic regulations and government monopolies. How to eliminate it is always a dilemma; however, there are some steps that can be taken to reduce it. The first obvious step is to reduce bureaucratic regulations thereby reducing patronage. A "mindset" change is also required among Indian citizens since they accept bribery as the norm. Obviously, change will take a long time. Another way to improve India's image will be to strengthen property rights, which the World Bank currently lists as inadequate. New and improved laws and institutions will bring about these improvements. Watchdog agencies and the courts will be required to enforce rights and contracts. An excellent example of a watchdog agency working well is the Reserve Bank of India, which is also the central bank. The RBI regularly audits banks and has in the process prevented many banks from defrauding investors.

Such reforms must be implemented in conjunction with the free market reforms currently in place. Regulations on labor, trade, and foreign investment must be reduced and reformed. Ethnic Indians around the world have shown that they are very resourceful when not hampered by bureaucrats. For long-term economic success, citizens in India need to develop a shared mental model that views economic liberalization as beneficial to all. From a policy standpoint, a shared mental model to emphasize that reforms will benefit all levels of society is imperative if the poor are to believe that they too will benefit.

Conclusions

There is ground, however, for considerable optimism over India's future for both Indians and foreign investors because the current government is committed to reforms. The Prime Minister, Manmohan Singh, as well as the Finance Minister, Chidambaram Palaniappan, have proven track records in bringing about free market reform. The recent budgets have moved in the direction where reforms are being spread to the rural areas as well as further free market reforms being introduced. A free market remains India's best bet for higher and sustained economic growth; this combined with increased educational opportunities will lower the incidence of poverty. The battle should not be over wealth division but over wealth creation. In conclusion, quoting *The Economist* (2004), "This is India's decade, crow the optimists; India's century, echo true patriots."

Notes

1 M. Twain (1897) *Following the Equator*, Ch. 43.
2 E.M. Forster (1924) *A Passage to India*, Ch. 7.
3 "A Survey of India," *The Economist* 21 February 2004.
4 M.K. Gandhi was also known as *Mahatma* Gandhi, *Mahatma* meaning "great soul".
5 The popular notion that Gandhi was opposed to industrialization and heavy machinery is wrong. What he was against was a rush towards mass industrialization. He permitted many exceptions to heavy machinery when they were necessary. The other popular notion that he was a socialist is wrong too. He was in fact opposed to publicly funded education.
6 A brief write-up on Fabian Socialism is available at cepa.newschool.edu/het/schools/fabian.htm
7 Source: "Congress Sandesh" which is a publication of the Congress Party in India. Congress Sandesh. "History of Congress Sessions", All India Congress Committee. Online. Available www.congresssandesh.com/november-2002/history.html (accessed on 5 June 2004).
8 Annual meeting of the INC in January 1959 held in Nagpur, India.
9 Government of India. Industrial Policy Resolution of 1956. Online. Available www.smallindustryindia.com/policies/iip.htm#Indus2 (accessed on 26 July 2004).
10 Source: Planning Commission of India. Second Five Year Plan. Online. Available planningcommission.nic.in/plans/planrel/fiveyr/welcome.html (accessed on 26 July 2004).
11 The Ministry of Disinvestment in India reports that there were 242 enterprises under government control as of March of 2001.
12 The list of Navaratna companies includes Indian Oil Corporation Ltd (IOCL), ranked 257 in Fortune's Global 500, and two other Indian oil companies, Bharat Petroleum Corporation Ltd (BPCL) and Hindustan Petroleum Corporation Ltd (HPCL); Oil and Natural Gas Corporation Ltd (ONGC), the premier oil exploration and crude oil producing company; Steel Authority of India Ltd (SAIL), India's largest integrated steel producer; Indian Petrochemicals Corporation Ltd (IPCL), the country's biggest integrated petrochemicals company; Bharat Heavy Electricals Ltd (BHEL), the biggest power equipment manufacturer in India; National Thermal Power Corporation (NTPC) which produces about one-fourth of the power generated in India; and Videsh Sanchar Nigam Ltd (VSNL), the sole provider of international telephone services in India. A partial stake in VSNL has been sold as of now.
13 The numerator and denominator are from the Harrod–Domar model which postulates that growth is a function of the savings ratio divided by the marginal capital:output ratio.
14 Professor Mahalanobis, an Indian statistician, who was a key advisor to the government on issues concerning economic planning and development, largely created the Indian economic model.
15 Gulzarilal Nanda was the interim Prime Minister from May 27 to June 9, 1964.
16 The imposition of "Emergency" in June of 1975 for almost two years is an

example of this autocratic behavior. She ruled by decree during these two years and it is generally recognized as the "darkest hour" in Indian democracy.

17 As cited in D. Goodal (2002) Lead Book Review of Indira: the life of Indira Nehru Gandhi by Katherine Frank (2002), HarperCollins. Online. Available www.thetablet.co.uk/cgi-bin/book_review.cgi/past-00020 (accessed on 22 June 2004).

18 Though DeLong's website states that this paper was written in 2004, it was actually written in July 2001 because Rodrik (2002), written in February 2002, makes a reference to it, www.j-bradford delong.net/Econ_Articles/India/India_Rodrik_DeLong.html

19 Lal, D. (1999) *Unfinished Business: India in the World Economy*, New York: Oxford University Press.

20 Nehru was born to a wealthy family and was schooled at Harrow and Cambridge.

21 This large majority by the Congress Party was largely the result of a sympathy vote in the wake of Indira Gandhi's assassination and should not be interpreted as an affirmation of the policies pursued by the Congress.

22 "These developments" refers to the deficits and interest payments feeding into the current account.

23 According to Panagariya (2004), the variance of GDP growth rates was 7.01 from 1986–1991 as compared to 0.96 for 1998–2003.

24 The IMF considers foreign reserves covering six months worth of imports as "safe" or "adequate."

25 The Monopolies and Restrictive Practices Act (MRTP) prevented "large" firms from entering certain sectors.

26 The airline sector is an example.

27 The CRR was as high as 50 percent in the 1980s and has now been reduced to around 5 percent. The reason for this high number was that the government could use the funds to finance its fiscal deficit on the cheap.

28 In an interview with the author.

29 Source: *Financial Times* (2004). "Reforming India," *Financial Times*, Editorial 23 June 2004.

30 The figure of 3.26 million employed by the central government may be lower since it also includes people employed in "Community, Social and Personal Services" who are technically not part of the workforce employed in industries owned by the central government. According to the ESI, there are 19.138 million persons employed by the public sector. However, this includes employees of the central and state Governments, quasi-governments, and local bodies.

31 The estimate of $56.01 billion was derived based on the 2000 exchange rate of $1 = Rupees 45.09. However, the dollar figure is considerably understated because the Indian Rupee was much stronger in earlier years.

32 In the interview with the author.

33 Ibid.

34 Source: Public Broadcasting Service (2003) "India's AIDS Epidemic." Shown on Newshour with Jim Lehrer, August 6, 2003. Online. Available www.pbs.org/newshour/bb/asia/july-dec03/indiaaids_8-6.html (accessed on 3 July 2004).

35 Ibid.

References

Bauer, P.T. (1961) *Indian Economic Policy and Development.* London: George Allen & Unwin Ltd.

Bhagwati, J. (1993) *India in Transition: Freeing the Economy.* Oxford: Clarendon Press.

Bhagwati, J. (2000) "Review of Sachs-Varshney-Bajpai and Lal books on India," *Times Literary Supplement.* Online. Available www.columbia.edu/~jb38/TLS_SV.pdf (accessed on 26 July 2005).

Congress Sandesh. "History of Congress sessions," *All India Congress Committee.* Online. Available www.congresssandesh.com/november-2002/history.html (accessed on 5 June 2005).

DeLong, J.B. (2004) "India since independence: an analytic growth narrative," in Rodrik, Dani (ed.) *Modern Economic Growth: Analytical Country Studies.* (Forthcoming).

Das, G. (2000) *India Unbound.* New York: Alfred A. Knopf.

Denzau, A. and North, D. (1994) "Shared mental models: ideologies and institutions," *Kyklos* 47: 3–31.

Department of Disinvestment (Government of India). *Evolution of Public Sector of India.* Online. Available divest.nic.in/manual03/chap3.htm (accessed on 8 May 2005).

Economist, The (2004) "A survey of India," *The Economist,* 21 February 2004.

Economist Intelligence Unit (2004) *World Investment Prospects: The Revival of Globalisation?* London: The Economist Intelligence Unit.

Friedman, M. (1955) "On the Nehru-Mahalonobis Plan." *Unpublished Memorandum to the Government of India.* Online. Available www.geocities.com/ecocorner/intelarea/mf6.html (accessed on 20 June 2005).

Financial Times (2004) "Reforming India," *Financial Times,* Editorial 23 June 2004.

Goodal, D. (2002) Lead Book Review of *Indira: the life of Indira Nehru Gandhi* by Katherine Frank (2002), HarperCollins. Online. Available www.thetablet.co.uk/cgi-bin/book_review.cgi/past-00020 (accessed on 22 June 2005).

Goswami, O. (2005) "Humility, not hubris, will make india great," *Far Eastern Economic Review* 168(11): 12–17.

Government of India. *Industrial Policy Resolution of 1956.* Online. Available www.smallindustryindia.com/policies/iip.htm#Indus2 (accessed on 26 July 2005).

International Monetary Fund. *International Financial Statistics.* Washington: IMF.

Kripalani, M. (2002) "Will India's banks be crushed by bad debt?" *Business Week,* June 10, 2002.

Luce, E. (2004) "India's polls teach World Bank a lesson," *Financial Times,* May 27, 2004.

Ministry of Finance (Government of India). *Economic Survey of India 2002–03.* Online. Available indiabudget.nic.in/ (accessed on 22 July 2005).

Özler, B., Datt, G. and Ravallion, M. (1996) *A Database on Poverty and Growth in India.* Washington: World Bank.

Panagariya, A. (2004) "India in the 1980s and 1990s: a triumph of reforms," *IMF Working Paper,* WP/04/43.

Planning Commission of India. *Second Five Year Plan.* Online. Available planningcommission.nic.in/plans/planrel/fiveyr/welcome.html (accessed on 26 July 2005).

Public Broadcasting Service (2003) "India's AIDS epidemic." Shown on *Newshour with Jim Lehrer*, August 6, 2003. Online. Available www.pbs.org/newshour/bb/asia/july-dec03/indiaaids_8-6.html (accessed on 3 July 2005).

Rajan, R. and Zingales, L. (2003) *Saving Capitalism From the Capitalists.* New York City: Crown Business.

Rodrik, D. (2002) "Institutions, integration, and geography: in search of the deep determinants of economic growth," in Rodrik, Dani (ed.) *Modern Economic Growth: Analytical Country Studies.* (Forthcoming). Online. Available ksghome.harvard.edu/~drodrik/growthintro.pdf (accessed on 30 May 2005).

Root, H. (2005) *Capital & Collusion: The Political Logic of Global Economic Development.* Princeton: Princeton University Press.

Singh, M. (2001) Personal Interview with the Author. 2 November 2001, New Delhi.

UNCTAD. *Foreign Direct Investment database, World Investment Report.* United Nations Conference on Trade and Development, Geneva.

World Bank. *World Development Indicators.* Washington: World Bank.

13 East Asia and neoliberal mental models

Arthur T. Denzau and Ravi K. Roy

Introduction

The past 20 years in East Asia have been turbulent, beginning with the rise of the East Asian economies documented in World Bank (1993) as a Miracle, through the crises of 1997–1998, and various recoveries. During the Miracle days, a combination of some neoliberal policies and strong government–business cooperation led to what was termed the Asian Development Model (Asian Development shared mental model – related to the Developmental State mental model of Chalmers Johnson of UC-San Diego). This shared mental model, espoused most publicly by PM Mahathir bin Mohamad of Malaysia, presented close government–business cooperation and communal values as the path to rapid economic growth. The economic collapses in the 1997–1998 Asian crises led this approach to be renamed "crony capitalism." These have been contending shared mental models for understanding economic development.

In general, most of the successful growth of the East Asian economies coincided with market-friendly policies at the macro-level and micro policies that usually allowed considerable scope for private businesses to choose how and where to invest – in a word, neoliberal. However, in all cases other than Hong Kong, a nationalist element often accompanied the purely economic approach, with governments attempting to build up specific industries, often attempting to pick economic winners. These approaches were all distinguished from the Latin American inward-oriented ideas by their explicit export orientation. Noteworthy, however, is that when such interventionist attempts ran into major troubles, governments usually returned to policies prescribed by neoliberal shared mental models.

We find this pattern in the early leader – Japan – and in later successes – Thailand and China. A similar pattern is developing now in Singapore, which started out with a government-led growth path of seeking FDI (Foreign Direct Investment) to gain capital and technology. The success of this policy combined with the realization of the large shift among developed nations into services, especially financial, has turned

Singaporean policy toward more neoliberal and market-friendly paths in order to foster the growth of a regional financial center that could overtake Hong Kong.

The paper proceeds first with a short history of Japanese political economy and the ideas, both the neoliberal shared mental model and others, behind their policies. The focus then shifts to later Southeast Asian NICs (Newly Industrializing Countries) to see how neoliberal ideas fared there. The new and huge Asian dragon, China, is then considered, along with the related case of Singapore.

Recent history and mental models – Japan

Japan's novel and partially successful reaction to being forced open by the West in the 1850s and 1860s was to search for a way to maintain their cultural and political identity against the onslaught of western ideas and weapons. The shared mental model of the leaders of the Meiji Restoration of 1867–1868 was that of finding the fastest way to bring Japanese technology and organizational skills up to the best the world possessed, without sacrificing Japanese identity and sovereignty. Agents were sent around the world to discover whose system was best in any particular area such as education, bureaucracy or the military, and then to learn how to adapt that system into Japan. Failures in the process were usually quickly discerned and changes made. For example, when the attempt to build new state-owned enterprises during the 1880s led to large fiscal deficits, the Japanese Minister of Finance, Matsukata Masaoyoshi, sold off the businesses, helping to found the original zaibatsu industrial groups.

This approach led to quick successes. A key achievement right in the mainstream of western science was the discovery of the bubonic plague bacillus after an outbreak in Hong Kong in 1894 (published as Kitasato 1894, in the British journal, *The Lancet*). In 1895, Japan's army defeated China in the First Sino-Japanese War to become a serious regional power. And in 1905, Japan's new navy beat a major western navy, Russia's, at the battle of Tsushima, which ended the Russo-Japanese war of 1904–1905. With this success, Japan became a major Pacific naval power, enabling its strategic policies that lead to the Pacific War of 1931–1945.

Japan's basic strategic problem is its lack of essential natural resources for a modern industrialized economy. With the successful creation of modern military systems, the climate of the times (the rapacious wave of colonialism of the late nineteenth century) led them to adopt a strategy of conquering those resources instead of trading for them. The First Sino-Japanese War of 1894–1895 resulted in Japan acquiring Taiwan as a colony and the 1905 Treaty of Portsmouth ending the Russo-Japanese War recognized Japanese control over Korea. These two colonies (with Korean formal colonial rule starting in 1910) provided some of the needed resources, but still lacked the essential minerals required for a steel industry, the basic industrial commodity of the Second Industrial Revolution. The Japanese Army's incursion into Manchuria in 1931 provided access to and ownership of these resources.

This strategy, however, lead to conflict with the dominant powers of the time, and with Japan's push to acquire the necessary energy resources of petroleum, led to war with the United States, Canada, the United Kingdom, Australia and the Netherlands. With the failure to win the Pacific War that ended in 1945, and the American occupation of Japan, the time was ripe for strategic rethinking, and a new set of shared mental models.

The peaceful export-based strategy of trading for the essential resources was now seen as the best, if not the only path, with the new Japanese Constitution banning all but self-defense forces. The new mental models devolved around catching up with the West in economic areas, once the necessary recovery from the war's devastation and absorption of former Japanese overseas colonists was completed. Industrial purchases to supply the Korean War effort sped up this recovery. The shared mental models developed in this era were descendants of the prewar government–business cooperation in building a military force, but now focused on consumer and industrial products. This cooperation was led by the large *keiretsu* industrial groups and the dominant LDP (Liberal Democratic Party) that won every election from 1955 on (except for 1993 to 1994).

By the late 1970s, Japan had caught up in several key industrial areas, hitting the technological and organizational frontier in productivity. At this point the old shared mental models no longer supported further rapid economic growth. Government–business cooperation now more resulted almost exclusively in rent-seeking and the use of government funds to prop up the LDP's power (see Calder on these money flows).

Growth slowed during the early 1980s (to less than 3 percent p.a.) and has been stop-and-slow-go since 1990 (under 1.5 percent p.a.). The problems that the old mental models helped deal with and solve were no longer as important as new problems. Slow growth in the 1980s and 1990s created challenges for the industrial labor system in the large firms. The older system had substantial payoffs for workers to learn and cooperate both with each other and with management as they produced large productivity gains and increasing market shares globally. Firm growth slowed and then went negative at the same time that the workforces aged for the large firms, putting great pressure on the *keiretsus* to maintain "permanent employment." More and more employees became non-core or contract employees, now about half the total, who were given no reason to expect to be permanent.

Responding to desperate exporting firms after the Plaza Accord of December 1985 caused the yen to rise substantially, accommodative monetary policy in the late 1980s exacerbated Japanese problems further by flooding the economy with liquidity, causing an asset bubble in land and stock prices. Japanese firms could obtain capital at almost a zero cost of capital, inducing them to overinvest in physical assets. Some firms shifted into *zaitech*, going into the investment business themselves as they tried to make profits from their financial activities. When the bubble burst, and cash flows slowed, the excessive leverage that the *keiretsus* had been able to afford during the high growth and bubble years now had become excessive risk. Entire *keiretsus* found financing their core permanent employees more and more difficult. Only the 1998 collapse of the huge Korean *chaebols* rivals this corporate collapse in East Asia.

During the decade of the 1990s, the Japanese government found its old remedies useless. The use of Keynesian fiscal deficits to pump up the economy resulted in the largest developed country national debt (as a share of GDP) without generating sustained recovery. An alternative remedy was finally sought with the zero-interest policy starting in 1999 and then in 2001 Quantitative Monetary Easing Policy, a policy of trying to force quantitative increases in the money supply. Japanese bank eligibility for clearing international transaction as their BIS risk-based capital ratio levels became questionable due to the large quantity of NPLs (Non-Performing Loans). At times, it appeared that the government was using off-budget funds (largely postal savings deposits) to prop up the stocks that the shaky banks held to help them meet the semiannual capital adequacy checks. Very little help was provided by the older shared mental models as to how to proceed to end the mess.

Japan's demography made recovery more difficult. The Japanese workforce was rapidly aging and started focusing on their retirement savings. Year after year, heavily weighted to bank deposits and postal savings accounts, these savings were earning returns below the inflation rate, putting aging workers further behind and induced to save more and more. This caused government attempts to raise consumption by various means usually only increasing savings instead. Business investment continued to fall in this environment and a large wave of business bankruptcies began. This further focused the aging worker's attention on getting an adequate return on their retirement savings and increased their search for higher return investments. With the Big Bang of 1998 opening up access to investing in other countries, the pressure on Japanese financial intermediaries increased and they also began further search and pressure for greater returns from their Japanese investments.

The demands by investors in Japanese firms were no longer to be ignored as was possible in the high-growth years. Firms wanting access to external capital now found it in their interest to respond by increasing dividends and maximizing profit in the present instead of promising future growth only. In response, the large exporting firms gradually restructured and began to act more like western firms. Some that did not went bankrupt or were taken over, at times by outsiders, even foreigners. The failure of the Long Term Credit Bank in 1998 led to its takeover in 2000 by Ripplewood Holdings and its being renamed as Shinsei Bank. Under the leadership of an American-trained Japanese manager, Hideki Kurashiga, this has been the only Japanese bank to consistently earn profits. It did this by following regular western banking practices – cutting off borrowers that could not repay (regardless of how long they had been a customer) and dealing more quickly with borrowers in default. This approach, consistent with neoliberal notions and not openly disfavored by the MoF (Ministry of Finance) or the FSA (Financial Supervisory Agency), has been regularly attacked by the other Japanese banks. Their solution, helped along by the government and its zero-interest policy, has been merger, possibly to get "too big to fail."

In other ways, the government has gradually been adopting neoliberal policies. Tightened accounting rules were adopted over the past ten years that increased the reporting and visibility of NPLs. Financial reporting for non-financial firms has similarly improved, making it easier for market discipline to operate effectively and efficiently.

A major event reflecting this neoliberal outlook has been Prime Minister Koizumi's 2005 actions to begin the privatization of the largest insurance company and largest deposit bank in the world, the Japanese Postal Savings system. This financial enterprise and postal insurance employs the majority of postal employees, who can take deposits or issue life insurance at any post office in the country. The pre-Big Bang system of financial repression and low interest rates enabled it to get deposits at very low deposit rates. Deposit rates since 1996 have been less than 1 percent, and since 2001 less than 0.1 percent!

The system also used to provide tax preferences, but these were reduced in the Big Bang for elderly savers, and removed for others at the same time. The funds in Postal Savings are invested by the government, and are a key means by which the government can intervene directly in the economy, off-budget. The funds have been used over the past 15 years to try to prop up the stock market, and apparently other non-neoliberal purposes. To privatize this system would be to take this powerful tool away from future Japanese governments and would reflect a major commitment to neoliberal policies. When Koizumi failed to get the privatization bill through the House of Councilors, the upper chamber of the Diet (the legislature), he dissolved the lower house and called a new election. After he substituted hand-picked candidates for those who had fought his policies, including those consistent with neoliberalism, his new reform-friendly LDP party won a larger majority than before in the lower chamber, and the privatization easily passed through both chambers.

But this apparent victory for neoliberalism deserves less than three cheers – the privatization enacted will take 11 years, to be completed only in 2017. Any failure by a future government to support the privatization could lead to a repeal of the policy, and a return to the old ways. The interests involved are the private banks who strongly favor privatization and the *zoku* or political tribe of Diet members who are closely associated with Postal Savings, their employees and very likely the older ways of seeing how government and business should interact. Notice that the support by the commercial banks for privatization may not be a preference for neoliberal policies, but rather an attempt to remove a low cost competitor. Again, motives for both sides may be difficult to disentangle as private interest and expressed mental models can both lead to the same result.

Major parts of the Japanese economy are internationally noncompetitive. Outside the large exporting firms, much of the rest of the economy contains businesses that would find it hard to compete with foreign firms. Most of the distribution system of wholesaling and retailing seems inefficient by international standards, with an average 3.9 transactions between the original producer and final consumer, versus 1.7 in the United States (Powell, 1987). Many American and European low-cost retailers have attempted to enter the market but have been thwarted by legislation (the Large Scale Retail Store Law in 1973), among other problems. Similarly impervious to attempts to improve efficiency are firms in the business services sectors, including logistics, finance and communications. The financial sector was opened up in a neoliberal manner by the Big Bang reforms of April 1998 and the pressure from customers has also induced changes in the financial intermediaries helping Japanese to save for retirement, but the basic pattern is one of a High Cost Economy in business services that the large exporters would like to change.

Overall, Japanese economic thinking is quite mixed, but some strong patterns are present. It is widely recognized that catch-up has been achieved, and that the often non-neoliberal policies of that era no longer serve the nation. But there are entrenched interests in many parts of the economy and government that would not be helped by neoliberal policy change, and are resisting changes. The political system, still largely dominated by the several factions of the LDP, was not able to surmount these interests until recently with the "triumph" of PM Koizumi's privatization bill for the financial parts of the Postal System.

The "High Cost Economy" of uncompetitive business services has also resisted most attempts at change beyond the Big Bang international financial reforms of 1998 and related domestic financial system reforms of 1998 and 1999. It is unclear whether the current populist PM, Koizumi, will attempt to make further changes, but this is a major area of government policy and private activity that is quite market-unfriendly.

On the other hand, changes to practices of many large exporting corporations have made them more responsive to investors. But corporate governance is in a state of flux and where this will lead is not clear with the end of the Main Bank System for many *keiretsus* due to the selling off of a large part of the old cross-shareholdings.

The Asian shared mental model in Southeast Asia

The Asian Development Model shared mental model involving the use of government–business cooperation to achieve catch-up development was also prevalent in policymaking circles in some Southeast Asian countries. In Indonesia, this set of beliefs may have been responsible for General Soeharto's re-engineering the Sukarno system of communitarian socialism. His Berkeley boys were quite similar in their views to those of the Chicago boys in Chile.

In Thailand, similar beliefs seem to be behind the push in the late 1970s to construct a new industrial region in the Eastern Seaboard. The intention was for the government to build major infrastructure projects with its state-owned enterprises. The large fiscal deficits induced by the policy (similar to the experience in Korea and Malaysia) lead to a shift in policy in the early 1980s. Japanese companies that had been investing in the Seaboard area brought in other Japanese companies to help construct the infrastructure on a new basis. Instead of public ownership, the firms contracted with the SOEs enabling them to recover their investments from revenues paid by their customers. The government of the period was headed by Prem Tinsulanonda, who provided some stability during his eight years as PM in spite of a changing set of coalitions supporting him. One unique stabilizing feature of Thailand that more easily enabled it to be credible was the stable, incorruptible monarchical institution.

Once again today, Thailand may be veering away from neoliberal policies under PM Thaksin Shinawatra. Khun Thaksin became the first elected non-coalition Thai PM with majority party support in January 2001. He campaigned on a platform of privatizing many of the SOEs (state-owned enterprises) resulting from previous governments' attempts to establish new industries in Thailand. But by 2002, Thaksin's government had given up its rapid privatization, and delay in the process was clearly the new policy. Since then, privatization has been quite slow, and much of government efforts seem to be the presentation of new government spending programs as pump-priming Keynesian policies. This move away from neoliberalism is termed *Thaksinomics*, quite the opposite of the earlier presentation of DJnomics (Government of Korea, 1999), a quite neoliberal set of policies for Korea by the Korean PM, Kim Dae Jung.

Aeusrivongse (2002) characterizes Thaksinomics as an attempt to build a political base of crony capitalists and grass-roots villagers, providing roads and other public works for the capitalists to build that may help the villagers. This policy, combined with the substantial slowing of privatization represents a clear shift from a neoliberal shared mental model. Domestic political incentives appear to be the driving force in this shift and future elections and economic outcomes will show if this is a sustainable policy approach.

Moving toward nationalism, but in very different economic directions is the largest nation of East Asia (and the world), China.

Recent history and mental models – China

China's interaction with the West was jump-started with the burning of all the opium owned by all foreign merchants in Canton (Guangdong) by order of Commissioner Lin Tse-Hsu in 1839, triggering the first of the Opium Wars. By the end of the first Opium War in 1842, Britain took control of Hong Kong Island and various other territorial concessions were extracted by external powers. China was less successful than Japan in gaining control of its opening up by the West.

With the end of the Qing Dynasty and the Time of Troubles in 1909–1912, a new attempt was made to create a government that could ensure Chinese sovereignty, led by Sun Yat Sen. His Three Principles of the People – Nationalism, Democracy and Livelihood – were intended to restore Chinese sovereignty and autonomy. With his death in 1925, the warlord era opened up, and Japan's increasing pressure lead to outright warfare in 1937. The 1945 end of the Pacific War did not lead to peace in China as the Kuomintang under Chiang Kai-Shek fought Mao Zedong and the CPC (Communist Party China) until Chiang and many of his people fled the mainland in 1949, shifting their capital to Taiwan, a former Japanese colony freed in 1945.

The people controlling the mainland were not using the Asian Development Model shared mental model of government–business cooperation, but rather the Stalinist shared mental model of SOEs and cooperative farming in the countryside. This model, with control coming from the top at Beijing from Mao led to a sequence of sharp policy shifts due to whims of Mao – the Great Leap Forward of 1958 to 1960, Let A Thousand Flowers Bloom of 1957 to 1958, the Cultural Revolution of 1966 to 1969 (officially, but actually continuing until the arrest of the Gang of Four in 1976). Finally came the fight for succession as Mao became ill and unable to maintain personal control (the battle of the Gang of Four and Deng Xiao Ping). Mao's death in 1976 ended in Deng taking control, and then beginning the introduction of a new set of Mental Models in 1979.

The gradual introduction of market-friendly policies reflected a very partial commitment to neoliberal notions, but they were unrelated to any real attempt to limit the still arbitrary power of the CPC. Opening up to foreign investment required such a commitment, and China became the largest recipient of FDI after the United States. This commitment is so well understood that many Chinese citizens utilize it to gain protection for their own investment. It is widely understood that much of the "foreign" direct investment funds going into joint ventures in China is "fake foreign investment" mainland Chinese money that has been sent out surreptitiously and comes back in with a "foreign" label on it that allows one to fund a joint venture with one's self. The size of such flows is substantial but no one seems to have attempted to estimate their size.

The Chinese savings is probably the highest in the world. But as with

Japan, much of that savings goes into government-linked financial intermediaries that use the funds in politically-desired ways. The rates of return in these investments are notably low, and imply a larger growth rate could be achieved with more efficient financial intermediation than now occurs. The aging of the Chinese and Japanese populations has helped to keep savings rates high, but when enough of the population retires, savings rates should rapidly fall, and this will be (or may already be in the case of Japan) a major source of reduced economic growth.

Some gradual opening up of the political side was greatly hindered by the Tiananmen Square troubles of June 1989. But even after this, further changes were introduced that ended, to some extent, the monopoly on power locally of the CPC – multiple candidates were allowed to run, and eventually non-party candidates began to win elections. The coming of the Internet and blogs opened up a degree of Civil Society, and some citizens began to peacefully challenge the government in court cases (see Kahn, 2005). To the extent these continue, they represent limits on the arbitrary power of the government and the CPC, and along with the market-friendly economic policies, resemble somewhat what a neoliberal shared mental model would recommend.

Neoclassical economics is now widely taught in Chinese universities, and even the New Institutional Economics of Douglass North. With many graduates of American Ph.D. programs coming back to teach, and the government's desire to upgrade its universities in terms of their research abilities, these neoliberal shared mental model ideas are gaining wider acquaintance within the nation. How far this influence may spread is unclear at this point.

As Chinese academics continue to engage the world more fully in China and when traveling in the West, party control may weaken. At a seminar held at Washington University (St. Louis) with Douglass North in attendance, the Chinese economists there were fully cognizant of the neoliberal approach, but were constrained by the presence of a CPC chaperone. A most remarkable interaction occurred when the chaperone translated one of the Chinese economists' remarks incorrectly, and a member of the audience pointed out the discrepancy. The unchallenged ability of the CPC to control its academics has its limits.

But the CPC is not without tools to slow this process. Internet access is heavily controlled and censorship ubiquitous. In February 2006, Google China was exposed as now censoring its search responses to words such as "freedom" and "democracy", much as Yahoo and others had previously done. The criticism in the West has been strong, and may make it more difficult for such firms to continue their acquiescence with such attempts to maintain the old closed information system. But so long as access to information is important to continuing China's amazing economic growth, the government and CPC will itself be under continual pressure to cut back their control of such flows.

Singapore, information and neoliberal policies

A clear example of such a process can be seen in Singapore. As of 1959, Singapore was very poor but had become independent. The government set up a system of tripartite cooperation among labor, business and government. The National Wages Council was created in 1972 to facilitate wage bargaining by consensus agreement on guidelines for each year's bargaining. The system has since enabled compensation to still be flexible in response to external shocks while giving both labor and management a means of gaining a hearing about their chief concerns (Root, 1996).

During the 1990s, the government of Singapore determined that it wished the nation move more firmly into being the Southeast Asia's financial center, displacing Hong Kong as its handover to the mainland loomed for 1997. In order to succeed in this endeavor, the government understood that it needed to free up access and communication of information, as financial markets are fundamentally ways to price such information. This involved a major reduction in governmental controls that had been imposed under PM Lee Kuan Yew partially in response to ethnic rioting in Malaysia in 1969 that tightened a clampdown on information dissemination that might lead to further ethnic tensions in Singapore. These reductions in control are not complete, but there will continue to be pressure for market-friendly reforms by some politicians and interest groups in this direction.

Other governmental policies in Singapore are far less neoliberal. The Central Provident Fund (CPF) started as a system of forced savings in 1955 and has been used by the government to finance off-budget projects. It was widened in 1973 in its coverage to most workers, and private voluntary savings then fell to less than 25 percent of national savings by 1983. Thus the government's role in allocating investment funds became very large in Singapore, not neoliberal at all. The size of forced savings has been used as a macroeconomic policy tool since then, following tripartite discussions. During economic downturns, as with the 1997–1998 crises, the government reduces the mandatory contributions to maintain consumption demand.

The CPF is now being used by the government of Singapore to deal with health, education and pension demands, enabling the government to finance them without budgetary resources. This heavy involvement of government in financial markets has not gone without challenge. Private financial interests have demanded a cutting back of the governmental role and greater transparency. Governmental response has been largely rhetorical, but Temasek, a GLC (Government-Linked Company) with $107 billion in assets, finally issued its first annual report in 30 years in October 2004. No response, however, has come from GIC, a government-owned investment fund manager with over $100 billion under its control. Looking at GIC's website, one discovers the site is copyrighted 2002, and announces its 2001 Yearbook as a *recent* option! No accounting data is provided in the 181 pages of the annual report. Transparency in reporting and governance has not yet reached the large GLCs of Singapore, although private market pressures are present.

Overall, the state is a much larger entity in the economy of Singapore than most other developed countries. The belief that they needed to receive foreign investment has constrained the government in what it does, and enables commitment to market-friendly policies in many areas. Thus, just as the desire to become a regional financial center has tempered many non-neoliberal policies, the desire to attract external capital and technology seems to have enticed Singapore to have put on Freidman's (2000; Chapter 5) Golden Straitjacket of neoliberal policies.

Summary and conclusions

The heyday of government-led growth proponents has now passed in East Asia, and more neoliberal beliefs are being expressed and acted upon by some governments in the region. But one of the wealthiest states in the region, Singapore, has largely pursued neoliberal shared mental model policies for development, but not exclusively. It continues to pursue non-transparent governance and policies with its financial sector GLCs. Several of the large nations, such as Japan and China, as well as Singapore, utilize public savings deposits to further governmental aims, allocating savings often into unproductive uses (this is more problematic in Japan and China than Singapore).

In all cases, problems and crises have lead to governments utilizing neoliberal shared mental models to create policies to turn things around, and the success of such remedies is likely to keep the neoliberal shared mental model and its ideas active even during the most interventionist of times. Academic training in all the countries is incorporating more and more of western economics. Douglass North's New Institutional Economic approach is being taught even in China, and the presence of these ideas in universities means that college-trained people with an understanding of neoliberal prescriptions are more widely present than in the past.

The old Asian Development shared mental model espoused by Mahathir of Malaysia and others has far fewer adherents, and has been reinterpreted in many places to mean crony capitalism, believed a major cause of the 1997–1998 crises. The glaring failures of the state-led economic systems in the DPRK (Democratic People's Republic of Korea, or North Korea) and Myanmar (a military kleptocracy) are obvious for all to see, compared to the stunning successes in most of the rest of East Asia. While the neoliberal shared mental model has not come to dominate the stage, they have pushed out several other shared mental models used to understand economic development, and are likely to continue their ascendance as long as further progress continues in the countries most adhering to this approach.

References

Aeusrivongse, Nidhi, (2002) "Thaksinomics," *Kyoto Review of Southeast Asia* 1 (March), kyotoreview.cseas.kyoto-u.ac.jp.

Calder, Kent E. (1991) *Crisis and Compensation: Public Policy and Political Stability in Japan.* Princeton: Princeton University Press.

Friedman, Thomas L. (2000) *The Lexus and the Olive Tree.* New York: Anchor Press.

Government of the Republic of Korea (1999) *DJnomics: A New Foundation for the Korean Economy.* Seoul: Korean Development Institute.

Kahn, Joseph (2005) "In China, rule of law may mean no verdict: people can sue the state but the system works against them," *New York Times,* December 27.

Kitasato, Shibasaburo (1894) "The bacillus of bubonic plague," *Lancet* 11: 35–36.

Powell, Jim (1987) "The new protectionism?" in Hudgins, Edward L. (ed.) *Freedom to Trade: Refuting the New Protectionism.* Washington, DC: Cato Institute.

Root, Hilton L. (1996) *Small Countries, Big Lessons: Governance and the Rise of Asia.* Oxford: Oxford University Press.

World Bank (1993) *The East Asian Miracle: Economic Growth and Public Policy.* Oxford: Oxford University Press.

14 Mental models of the economy and economic policy in Indonesia

Stephen V. Marks[1]

The vast and diverse archipelago nation of Indonesia is the fourth most populous nation in the world, and an arena in which neoliberal imperatives have run into resistance from traditional cultural orientations. Indonesian mental models of the economy tend to include suspicion toward free markets and private ownership of natural resources, and toward foreign and ethnic Chinese ownership. There is a concomitant belief in the importance of the state in economic affairs, not just as the guarantor of a secure basis for a market economy and as a regulator of economic activities in neoliberal terms, but also as an initiator of economic activities, manipulator of market prices, and owner of productive assets, particularly natural resources. Neoliberal tenets are often viewed in pejorative terms.

The differences between neoliberalism and the prevalent Indonesian mental models are not only about the details of the operation of the economy or the impact of economic policy, but also about how the world is interpreted at a deep level. The next section of this chapter will outline a framework for comparison of worldviews on this basis.

Denzau and North (1994) observe that cultural heritages provide a means for mental models to coalesce and pass from one generation to the next. Thus, to understand how the economy and policy are envisioned in Indonesia, it is useful to consider the history of the archipelago. I will focus on three major influences on shared mental models: indigenous patron-client traditions, the colonial period under the Dutch, and Islam as a world view and a normative guide. I will also touch on the influence of foreign education of various elites.

One of my goals is to understand how the prevalent mental models have translated into policy approaches. A variant of neoliberalism is followed in Indonesia by the "economic technocrats," but at least three other ideological frameworks for economic policy can be identified: "industrial nationalism," "economic populism," and "welfare interventionism."

I will also offer some observations on mental models in Indonesia with respect to two important issue areas, competition and corruption. First, I will examine the ideological basis for resistance to the free play of competition, and how this has shaped preferential policies for indigenous and small business. I will then discuss corruption from the Indonesian viewpoint, and how the slow pace of fundamental reforms can be understood in part in terms of shared mental models.

Deep biases in western thought

Examination of the deep tendencies of modern western worldviews provides a benchmark against which other belief systems can be compared and contrasted. Jones (1971) outlines a simple typology of five major dimensions across which worldviews may vary:

- Static–Dynamic: Does one tend to view the natural state of the world as at rest or in motion?
- Continuity–Discreteness: Does one see phenomena as interrelated and contextual or does one perceive sharp distinctions between ideal types? Does one see the world as an organic whole or in terms of constituent parts?
- Simplicity–Complexity: Does one have a preference for "the obvious, the easily readable, the easily legible" or "the devious, the rich, the esoteric" (Jones, 1971: 15)?
- Abstract–Concrete: Does one emphasize general characteristics or that which is particularistic and unique?
- Immediacy–Mediation: Does one prefer to be inherently engaged in the world or more detached? Does one prefer the informal and natural, or protocol and distance?

Jones notes that these biases will only represent statistical tendencies in any society. Nevertheless, he generalizes about the worldview behind western scientific thought, and his observations apply remarkably well to economics as a social science. The analysis is abstract. Economists see themselves as observers rather than participants. Their tendency to cut the world into distinct variables reflects a bias toward discreteness. The world typically is viewed as static, particularly as embodied in the concept of equilibrium; even dynamic analyses may look for steady-state growth paths.

In anticipation of later postmodernist perspectives, Jones notes that, if westerners seek to examine eastern worldviews, western biases will necessarily shape the analysis. Also, there is certainly no single worldview in Indonesia, or in any society. There are variations among and within social strata based on educational background, income, gender, religion, race, age, location, occupation, and experience.

Despite these reservations, I will offer a few generalizations. First, Indonesians tend to have an affinity for the particularistic rather than the abstract. Thus, a concept such as the rule of law is not well established, and tends to be trumped by social relationships or political imperatives, as in much of East Asia. Second, the world tends to be perceived more as an interconnected continuum than as a composite of discrete parts. I will revisit these points later in this chapter, and offer some additional conjectures within this framework.

A sketch of the history of Indonesia

Although Indonesians tend to be suspicious of free markets, it was not always thus. Historians recognize extensive trade and diplomatic relations between coastal city-states of the Indonesian archipelago and China as early as 1400 (Reid, 1993).[2] The introduction of Islam to the archipelago was driven by the spread of the trade from the Red Sea area and India.

In the sixteenth century the foreign trade of the archipelago languished, however. Anthony Reid (1984) argues that part of the problem was that intense rivalry among coastal city states on the islands of Sumatra, Java, and Sulawesi allowed the Dutch to exert military control. As the Dutch gained domination over coastal ports of Java, indigenous power tended to shift more to the interior of the island, in particular to the Mataram sultanate of central Java, which became the preeminent political force on the island from the late 1500s to the mid 1700s. It too was eventually contained by the Dutch.

Dutch domination clearly had an effect on the prevalent mental models within the archipelago, as Java in particular became more mystical and turned inward, away from the dynamic force of international trade (Reid, 1984).

A hierarchical society

Although all of the early states of the archipelago were absolutist,[3] their power bases were often tenuous (Reid, 1993). More than any other historical culture of Indonesia, Java featured an institutionalized hierarchy.[4] Java has been the predominant source of political and economic elites for the modern archipelago, and the Javanese aristocratic tradition has provided much of the institutional framework upon which the nation is governed. Java today boasts more than half the population and gross domestic product of Indonesia.

The Javanese aristocratic tradition, embodied in the *priyayi* class, was a tradition of bureaucratic formalities and obligations, cemented through an economic system in which patronage flowed from superior to inferior officials, and tribute (*upeti*) was returned to higher elites.[5] At the top of the system was the ideal of the *ratu adil* or just ruler, who through profound and even mystical insight was able to provide for the best interest of the people, but who might as a side effect of wise rule gain worldly riches of his own (Anderson, 1990).

Along the immediacy–mediation spectrum, the Javanese elite were not of the world, particularly not the rough and tumble of commerce, but above it. Entrepreneurship was not valued. Natural resources were abundant – initially spices but later forest products, metals, and cash crops (Reid, 1984). For these products, control was critical.

The Dutch colonial history

The Indonesian archipelago was colonized by the Dutch only in a very limited sense. Not long after its inception as an official monopoly in 1602, the Dutch United East India Company (*Vereenigde Oostindische Compagnie* or VOC) dominated much of the area militarily, through conquest of a few key port cities. Its economic goals were to dominate the most lucrative aspects of trade in the archipelago, not to establish a colonial administration. The dissolution of the VOC in 1798 was in part a product of its corrupt administration.[6]

The Netherlands resumed control of the archipelago in 1816, but indirectly through Dutch supervision of local rulers. In the colonial hierarchy, with the Dutch at the top and the indigenous Indonesians (*pribumi*) at the bottom, the ethnic Chinese emerged in an intermediate position, as petty traders, money lenders, and tax collectors. The shared mental model that the world was hierarchical was retained, but reshaped by circumstances.

Like the VOC, the Dutch colonial administration had extractive goals for the archipelago, especially in the early years of its occupation. Forced cultivation of crops such as sugar cane and coffee was initiated on Java in 1830.[7] By 1870 this *cultuurstelsel* was on its way out, but forced cultivation of sugar cane on Java was replaced by forced leases of the irrigated land on which the cane could be grown (Houben, 2002).

Furnival (1939) argues that market forces would have worked within the agrarian economy of the archipelago early on:

> But the VOC found it more profitable to resort to forced labour, compulsory cultivation and arbitrary destruction than to depend for produce on the law of supply and demand; the bitter experience of two hundred years dulled the economic sense of the people and, after living for two centuries in a land where the laws of economics did not run, it is not strange that they ceased to recognize them.
>
> (Furnival, 1939: 45)

It is easy to see how Indonesian shared mental models of the economy might envision markets inherently in terms of power relations and as potentially dangerous or oppressive. Nevertheless, the extent to which the mental models of Indonesian peasants might have become warped as Furnival asserts is debatable. Although a Dutch dualism school posits inherent cultural differences between Indonesians and westerners, as will be discussed further later in this chapter, Lindblad (2002) notes that recent case studies point to successful entrepreneurship among smallholder farmers in Indonesia. Benjamin (1992) presents econometric evidence from Java in 1980 that labor supply and demand decisions within farm households are separable: labor demand decisions depend on characteristics of the farm, while labor supply decisions depend on characteristics of the household. This is an implication of a rational actor model in which markets are complete and efficient. Thus, even if the mental models shared by Indonesian farmers includes distrust of foreigners or markets in general, there is some evidence that markets work, farmers utilize them, and the neoclassical model has explanatory power.

Islam and economic norms

Islam spread eastward within the archipelago along major trade routes, as Islamic traders settled and intermarried in coastal areas. By the year 1500, Islam had substantial numbers of adherents among the city-states of Sumatra, Java, Sulawesi, and Maluku (Reid, 1993). The reform movements that periodically swept through the Islamic world had their greatest influence in these coastal areas. In some states, such as Aceh at the northern tip of Sumatra, strict *syariah* law was practiced. In such situations, Islam required strong local rulers who could enforce Islamic laws that ran counter to local traditions (Reid, 1988). The Islam practiced in the interiors of the islands was less strict and more adapted to local animistic traditions. Today 88 percent of Indonesians view themselves as Islamic, but a great diversity of practices and beliefs remains.

World War I gave birth to the realization that eventually the European powers would not be able to maintain their empires.[8] The development of an Islamic economic tradition around the world was partly a response to this recognition,[9] though it also had roots in earlier efforts to grapple with the challenges posed by the modern industrial economy. Nationalists in the Indonesian independence movement against the Dutch and in other similar movements around the world responded to these developments in their own ways, but Islamic scholarship clearly influenced many of the new nation states that emerged.

How are the economic world view and norms of Islam manifested in Indonesia? First, in neither the Islamic economic tradition nor the indigenous cultures of the archipelago is there an appreciation of the "invisible hand" of Adam Smith (1776), which allows individuals to advance a version of the good of society through the pursuit of their own selfish goals, if the proper foundations for a market economy are in place. In particular, the modern view of the invisible hand is that the operation of a competitive market economy implies economic efficiency: in a competitive equilibrium, no one can be made better off without others being made worse off.

In the typology of world views introduced earlier, the modern formulation of the invisible hand requires a bias toward abstraction and discreteness. Specifically, it requires a conceptual separation of efficiency from concerns related to the distribution of income and wealth. This is problematic in non-western world views in general.[10] It also requires a view of society as consisting of individual entities in pursuit of their own interests rather than as a more organic whole, a theme that will be pursued in the next section. Finally, it requires a separation of the sacred from the profane, so that humans in their day-to-day affairs are not under a continual obligation to act in ways consistent with religious precepts. In contrast, Islam is about the totality of religion, state, and law. Its ideals are egalitarian,[11] and one of the basic tenets of Islam is that one must curb selfish behavior.[12]

Throughout its history, Islam has been one of the religions most predicated on the prayer relationship between the individual and God, and on the importance of individual ethics and discipline. Timur Kuran (2004) notes how Islamic economic norms determine the moral responsibilities of the individual:

> The intended effect of the norms is to transform selfish and acquisitive homo economicus into a paragon of virtue, homo Islamicus. Homo Islamicus acquires property freely, but never through speculation, gambling, hoarding, or destructive competition. And although he may bargain for a better price, he always respects his trading partner's right to a fair deal.
>
> (Kuran, 2004: 42)

The prophet Muhammad himself was a trader: to be Islamic and a trader is not only acceptable but virtuous. In Indonesian society, however, acquisitive behavior, speculation, hoarding, gambling, and fierce competition are all attributes associated with the stereotypical ethnic Chinese entrepreneur. In the liberal mental model, there are rationales for these practices, variations on the theme of the invisible hand. Profitable speculation and hoarding can stabilize prices: to profit one must buy low and sell high, adding to demand when prices are low and adding to supply when prices are high. Efficient allocation of risks requires that some parties have insurance, and thus that others take on gambles to provide this insurance, if risks are not all diversifiable. Competition benefits consumers and promotes efficiency.

The historical identification of the ethnic Chinese with the reviled attributes of homo economicus, and their insularity from the indigenous population, has led to hostility toward them in much of the country, but particularly among Muslims.[13] In the early twentieth century, an association of Muslim traders, *Sarekat Dagang Islam*, was formed to provide economic solidarity against "aggressively competitive Chinese entrepreneurs"

(Booth, 1998: 292) and grew into a nationalist movement. This mental model of the ethnic Chinese has also led to recurrent legal actions since independence against Chinese traders accused of hoarding. During the economic crisis of 1997–1998, it was announced that hoarding of essential commodities would be subject to the death penalty. Though this sanction was never enforced, the police raided the warehouses of some ethnic Chinese merchants and seized stockpiles of their goods as evidence.

The Indonesian nation state

Indonesia arguably does not constitute a natural nation state. It encompasses five major islands and a total of about 6,000 inhabited islands, some 300 distinct languages, and a wide array of racial, ethnic, and cultural groups. To forge a national identity, the founders of the independent Indonesian state in the middle of the twentieth century made the calculation that "unity in diversity" would be the basis for the new state, in particular through opposition to the colonial rule of the Dutch. It was recognized that this could only work if a modern and secular nation state were created. The 1945 Constitution of Indonesia sets forth "belief in the one and only God" as the first of five basic philosophical principles of the Indonesian state. This is significant, and controversial among some Islamic intellectuals, in that it does *not* say that Indonesia shall be governed by *syariah* law.

Even if Indonesia is not an Islamic republic, values broadly consistent with Islamic ideals are deeply ingrained in the state. Article 33 of the 1945 Constitution sets forth communalism as the primary basis for the organization of the economy. It begins: "The economy shall be organized as a common endeavor based upon the principle of the family system."[14] An historical parallel is that the emergence of Islam in the seventh century was partly driven by the perceived threat of disintegration of the tribal culture of Arab lands. This made imperative the renewal of a communal ethos, and the rejection of the individualism and materialism that had begun to encroach into the area (Armstrong, 1994).

Article 34 of the Constitution further stipulates: "The poor and destitute children shall be cared for by the State." Obligations to the poor are embodied in the Islamic (and Indonesian) concept of *zakat* (alms). These obligations are not only consistent with Islamic ideals, but are also a product of the communalist cultures of the archipelago. One astute Indonesian intellectual calls the national culture a *kita* culture versus the *kami* cultures of the West.[15] The first of these terms is the inclusive form of "we" in the Indonesian language, the second is the exclusive form. These notions parallel the sociological concepts of *Gemeinschaft* (community, based on shared values and concerns) and *Gesellschaft* (society, based more on individual interests) (Tönnies, 1887). The implication is that Indonesian culture is more communalistic and inclusive, not so individualist and exclusive. These observations are more than norms or values: the prevalent mental model tends to see the world through a lens of continuity rather than discreteness.

Article 33 of the 1945 Constitution was contributed by Mohammad Hatta, a son of a prominent Sumatran family and Dutch-trained economist who later became the first vice president of Indonesia. Indonesian intellectuals differ about the degree to which Hatta was influenced by Islamism. Certainly his presentation of national ideals was packaged in the rhetoric of secular nationalism and social justice rather than religion. Like many early economists in independent Indonesia, Hatta received a university education in economics in the Netherlands, and was steeped in the relatively interventionist and even socialist mental models of continental Europe. Hatta biographer George Kahin (1980), who talked with Hatta many times from 1948 to 1976, noted that Hatta came from a strongly Islamic family and concluded that Hatta believed that Islam could play a progressive socioeconomic role in the attainment of social justice in Indonesian society.

State control of resources

The ideals of communalism and relief of the poor included in the 1945 Constitution both imply a significant role for the state in practice, as do the shared mental models based on the historic absolutist states of the archipelago and the extractive Dutch colonial presence. The remainder of Article 33 formalizes the role of the state in the economy:

- "Branches of production which are important for the State and which affect the life of most people shall be controlled by the State."
- "Land and water and the natural riches contained therein shall be controlled by the State and shall be made use of for the people."

There has been considerable debate among Indonesians and foreign observers of the country as to how state control of important branches of production should be understood – in particular whether it implied state ownership of the means of production or simply oversight and regulation.

Robert Rice (1983) compares the terms of this debate during the presidencies of Soekarno (1949–1966) and Soeharto (1966–1998). Soekarno was strongly inclined to believe that private, and particularly foreign, ownership of important branches of production would lead to oppression of the people. His vice president, Hatta, and his successor, Soeharto, believed that private investment across the economy was critical to economic growth and development, but that natural resource sectors such as forestry, mining, and oil and gas had to be subject to extensive state involvement, typically through state enterprises but also through regulation. State enterprises have had dominant positions in oil and gas as well as steel, and others are in cement, plantation agriculture, finance, telecommunications, and wholesale and retail trade. Many of these enterprises were the product of the nationalization of Dutch enterprises.

A number of Indonesian intellectuals have framed the management of the economy as a search for a middle road between the perceived excesses of capitalism and socialism. Hatta in particular was a forceful advocate of an idealistic alternative to both private and public ownership in the form of rural cooperatives (Hill, 2000). The cooperatives were also seen as an indigenous Indonesian alternative to the dominance of rural trade by the Chinese.[16]

In practice the cooperatives have tended to be top-down organizations that have been marked by their inability to compete and by their parasitical nature. Like the state enterprises, the cooperatives are hindered by weak institutional frameworks and the absence of an entrepreneurial tradition among the indigenous elite. At times coercive policies have been used to support the cooperatives, much in the way that the Dutch exploited the economy of the archipelago. One example is a 1990 decree of the Governor of Nusa Tenggara Timur (NTT) province, one of the poorest provinces in the country, which required smallholder farmers to sell up to 60 rural commodities to or through the village unit cooperatives. There was evidence that this monopsonistic system was burdensome to rural producers, as neoliberal mental models would presume. In many cases the managers of the cooperatives simply collected fees from local traders, which led to lower producer prices of the items (Marks, 1998).

The Indonesian approach to resource management has also led to the misuse of forest resources: the Indonesian principle of "property owned by all" usually becomes "property owned by none" in practice (Gillis, 1988: 49). In particular, the ownership claims of the original inhabitants of forest areas in much of Indonesia have been rejected in favor of state ownership. These persons are typically among the poorest in the country. In the neoliberal view, were such persons allowed secure property rights, their incomes and incentives to care for the forests would be enhanced.

In the context of shared mental models of the economic role of the state, one interpretation is that these failed approaches represent a perversion of the communal ideals that formed the basis for the Indonesian state. Economist Umar Juoro argues that the prevalent mental model of the economy and policy in Indonesia is not abstract, but that it is idealized and that not enough attention is paid to implementation issues.[17] An implication is that Indonesian comprehension of economic forces tends to be simplistic.[18] A cynical assessment is that these failed approaches are the routine exploitative activities of an absolutist state. Under this interpretation, the question is whether the movement toward democracy since 1998 can hold at the national and local levels and can correct such problems.

State economic policies

Soekarno, a revolutionary and visionary nationalist, took office as president upon independence from the Dutch in 1949. In his effort to repudiate the colonial capitalist occupation, he was drawn to a socialist or planned model of economic development, much like the approach in India (Booth, 1998). Soekarno saw Indonesia as an active participant in a global movement of less developed countries, but his mismanagement of the economy and confrontational foreign policy toward the West led to economic chaos.

With the ascension to power of Soeharto in 1966, the Javanese tribute–patronage tradition was restored. Soeharto has been described as general, president, and king (Schwarz, 2000). To maintain political power, Soeharto used patronage to secure the loyalty of armed forces officers and payments from various foundations under his control to co-opt political elites. He also used populist policies and other economic interventions to maintain support among the masses, as will be discussed below. His control over the economy extended all the way to approval of individual investment projects, and tribute flowed back to his cronies and family in various forms, notably through their equity participation in numerous domestic and foreign investment projects, but also through special state preferences. Consistent with the absolute power that Soeharto wielded in economic matters, there was not much discussion in official documents of options and tradeoffs (Hill, 2000).

In line with the shared mental model of the absolutist indigenous ruler and the extractive colonial state, but in sharp conflict with neoliberal precepts, Soeharto reinstated mandatory periodic cultivation of sugar cane by small farmers on Java in 1975. The practice continued even after a 1992 referendum of the national legislature banned it. The 1998 agreements with the International Monetary Fund (IMF) explicitly outlawed the forced cultivation of sugar cane, but even now some farmers may be pressured by village officials or rural cooperatives to supply cane to the state-owned, and in some cases antiquated, sugar mills on the island.

Nevertheless, in the mental models of Java, a ruler provided for the people, and ultimately Soeharto derived legitimacy from the performance of the economy (Liddle, 1985). In contrast to Soekarno, he understood the importance of allowing markets to function to some degree and engaging with the West on its own terms. To combat the hyperinflation of the later years under Soekarno, the budget deficit was brought under strict control. Foreign donors were cultivated, and aid was used to finance the budget deficit. Monetary growth was restrained, and the extensive price controls were mostly removed. The exchange rate was unified and financial capital flows were virtually unimpeded by 1970.[19] Between 1986 and 1991 the coverage of non-tariff trade barriers was significantly reduced, and thinking within government and industry became more outward and less inward oriented (Hill, 2000).

Soeharto ruled for 32 years until being forced aside in the midst of the East Asia economic crisis in 1998. Since that time Indonesia has had four presidents. Despite the brevity of their tenures, certain themes have marked the economic policy approaches of each administration. Rather than recount the history in detail,[20] I will seek to characterize the principal ideological frameworks that have influenced the formulation of economic policies.

The technocrats and their rivals

One of the principal economic ministers under both Soekarno and Soeharto, Sumitro Djojohadikusumo, sent a generation of top Indonesian economists at the University of Indonesia to be educated at the University of California at Berkeley, a number of which subsequently became the "Berkeley Mafia" of economic technocrats within the bureaucracy.[21] Many of the technocrats are viewed in Indonesia as strongly market oriented. Nevertheless, their orientation has been more pragmatic than ideological, though certainly their shared mental models of the economy have pushed them toward liberal policies. Moreover, their views typically do not conform fully with liberal precepts. They have tended, for example, to view the existence of poverty as a market failure, while in the neoliberal formulation market failures are confined to those problems that hinder the attainment of economic efficiency.

Under Soeharto, macroeconomic management was more consistent with technocratic prescriptions than was microeconomic management. In the shared mental model of Javanese tradition, the latter reflected more the prerogatives of the ruler. It also reflected the noneconomic goals described below. However, for many years the performance of the economy was impressive, with average growth of gross domestic product close to seven percent until the last year of the Soeharto era.

An old adage in Indonesia is that bad times make for good policies. Under Soeharto the particular mental model that carried the greatest weight at any moment was partly a function of economic conditions, as technocratic and other imperatives and elites contested for primacy. This was demonstrated in 1985 and afterward, when Soeharto enacted a series of economic policy reform packages that were consistent with neoliberal precepts, mostly in response to a persistent downturn in oil export revenues.[22] Similarly, although policy toward foreign direct investment served to ration foreign access to the economy throughout the Soeharto era, the terms of foreign direct investment were relaxed during periods in which foreign businesses showed less interest in Indonesia. However, during much of the 1990s, with the economy doing well, liberal ideology was less in favor, as Soeharto extended favors to state enterprises and businesses of his family and other cronies. Although much of this activity can be understood in terms of the perquisites and obligations of the traditional

Javanese ruler, one can identify three distinct ideological frameworks that were also involved: "industrial nationalism," "economic populism," and "welfare interventionism."

The term "industrial nationalism" was posited for Indonesia by Thee (1994), along with "technological nationalism." It reflects the ideology of a number of senior economic bureaucrats in Indonesia who have been engineers or technologists, many whom have been strong economic nationalists. Foremost in this group was B.J. Habibie, long a close Soeharto protégé who earned a doctorate in engineering in Germany, worked for an aircraft company there, then returned to Indonesia to become State Minister for Research and Technology in 1978. He became Vice President in 1998, and succeeded Soeharto as president in May of that year.

Habibie was a visionary who believed that Indonesia could leap ahead in technological development to become a manufacturer of commercial aircraft in particular.[23] This vision was realized with the establishment in 1976 of a state venture in the aircraft sector, *Industri Pesawat Terbang Nusantara* (IPTN), which Habibie managed. Adam Schwarz in 1994 discussed the ideological appeal to Soeharto:

> Habibie's vision of Indonesia as a technologically advanced industrial powerhouse is carefully crafted to appeal to Soeharto. Habibie portrays the technocrats' economic policies as turning Indonesia into a mere pawn of international capital, a nation to be exploited for its natural resources just like the Dutch did for centuries before independence. His approach, on the other hand, promises to make Indonesia a more independent and powerful actor on the world stage.
> (Schwarz, 2000: 88)

This approach resonated in a country in which shared mental models of the economy were influenced strongly by the colonial experience under the Dutch. Indeed, for decades a number of Dutch scholars led by Julius Herman Boeke (1953) had subscribed to their own model of the dualistic tropical economy, in which a dynamic western sector contrasted with a stagnant indigenous one (Lindblad, 2002). This division was attributed to innate cultural differences: "The inhabitant of the tropics is further removed from the classical *homo oeconomicus* than the Westerner" (van Gelderen, 1961: 144). Prominent Indonesian economists such as Sumitro Djojohadikusumo were well aware of this formulation, and resented it.[24] One can imagine how satisfying it would be to prove these Dutch observers wrong.

Certainly Habibie's vision of the role of the state in development was a dynamic one, in comparison with the more static traditional role of the state in natural resource management. The engineer tends to see the world more in terms of possibilities, the economist more in terms of constraints. IPTN was a costly endeavor, however, and persistent management problems kept it from financial viability (McKendrick, 1992). In 1998 one of the agreements with the IMF ended state budgetary and other financial support for IPTN and for a more recent National Car Project run by the youngest son of President Soeharto. Today the former barely survives in a much downsized form; the latter was shut down in 1998.

Industrial nationalism has also manifested itself in policy interventions in less glamorous sectors of the economy. In trade policy, there have been protectionist policies on the import side – to favor local automobile assembly and petrochemical development during the Soeharto years, for example. Less constrained by international agreements have been export restraints, which have been applied extensively to primary products in the agricultural and natural resource sectors. Export bans on logs and raw and semi-processed rattan, and export restraints on crude palm oil, have been among the most notable of these restraints. The goal behind these measures has been to promote the development of value-added in downstream industries, such as plywood, wood and rattan furniture, and cooking oil and oleochemicals by lowering their input costs. Along the way many favored parties have reaped great benefits.[25]

The broader vision behind these interventions has been to transform Indonesia from a natural resource based economy into an industrial one. Although Habibie sometimes referred to technological spillover benefits from advanced industries, the advocates of such policies have not in general considered whether there is evidence to support the sophisticated market-failure rationales for infant-industry protection that can be accommodated within a neoliberal framework, or even whether such protection met the basic test of being only temporary.[26] Instead, the industrial nationalists have tended simply to privilege the development of value-added in industry over agriculture and natural resources.

Economic populism has emerged in a variety of forms in Indonesia. In the next section, in the broader context of competition policy, I will focus on a populist theme that has persisted for decades, and that seems to be directly related to shared mental models on the economy: protection for indigenous Indonesian and small businesses against the ethnic Chinese, particularly the large conglomerates, and other large businesses.

A final economic policy framework that can be identified is welfare interventionism, a term offered by Anne Booth (1998) to describe Dutch colonial policy in the early twentieth century. The underlying mental model posits that a primary role of the state is to control markets for the sake of social welfare, which can be seen through the lens of Islamic economics, traditional Javanese culture, or even the welfare states of modern capitalism, particularly the *dirigiste* continental European variety. Specifically, the Indonesian state has intervened in certain commodity markets in order to stabilize or manipulate prices.

In late 1997 and early 1998, during the worst of the economic crisis, the government restricted and for a time even banned exports of cooking oil in an effort to hold down consumer prices. These measures led to rampant smuggling. From a neoliberal perspective, the advocates of these and other burdensome trade restrictions have failed to acknowledge that, as a porous archipelago nation with weak governance, Indonesia is a natural haven for the smuggler. Within the shared mental models that posit a strong role for the state, however, the customary response to poor outcomes is to cite a failure in implementation and impose even tighter controls. The cynical interpretation is that such interventions have been intended to generate income for state officials and favored traders, by clamping down on market forces.

Not all welfare interventionism in Indonesia has worked to the advantage of consumers. Rice policy has been intended to stabilize and, particularly in recent years, raise real rice prices, primarily through the imposition of import barriers. The official rationales have been that the policy promotes food security and benefits poor rice farmers. However, there is evidence that high rice prices hurt the poor – not only poor residents of urban areas but also smaller landholders in rural areas, who may be net buyers of rice (Timmer, 2004).

These policies have exhibited a remarkable degree of continuity with late Dutch colonial policies. For example, in the midst of the Great Depression of the 1930s, the colonial government joined various international commodity price stabilization programs and tried to regulate the output of rubber, tea, and other products (Booth, 1998). The putative goals were stabilization of farm incomes as well as food security.

The role of competition in society

The idea that competition is a force for social good is not part of the prevalent mental models in Indonesia, and in particular runs counter to the communalistic, egalitarian ethos of Islam. The primacy of the consumer in general is not well established, nor is the concept of efficiency enshrined as it is in neoliberal economic analysis, as discussed earlier.

Robert Rice (1983) notes that the aversion to competition was partly learned from the colonial period. The Dutch colonial government used recession cartels and entry barriers to limit competition perceived to be destructive and to protect indigenous manufacturers, mostly small and medium sized, in certain sectors from being displaced by mechanized production.

One of the arguments commonly made against market liberalization in Indonesia is that it could result in the emergence of “free fight competition” in which some businesses could be wiped out, particularly small businesses owned by indigenous Indonesians, in competition with the ethnic Chinese or foreign companies. This rhetorical device goes back at least to the early days after independence. It does not require that stronger parties engage in unfair conduct, but rather simply that the outcome perceived to be unfair.[27] It can be viewed especially as part of the shared mental model of those who were at the bottom of the social and economic order during the Dutch colonial period.

In parallel with the efforts to promote the cooperatives, there have been repeated efforts to shelter small businesses and indigenous businesses from competition, particularly from the ethnic Chinese or larger enterprises. For example, the infamous *Benteng* (Fortress) Program was launched in 1950 to create a set of Indonesian entrepreneurs to offset the economic clout of Dutch and Chinese interests.[28] The program reserved subsidized credit and import licenses for certain easily-marketable goods exclusively for indigenous Indonesian importers. In practice, however, many of the supposed entrepreneurs sold their licenses to Chinese importers, who continued to operate almost as openly as in the past. Others defaulted on their loans from state banks, and few of the indigenous businesses survived the end of the program in 1957.

Popular discontent under Soeharto focused mostly on the economic power and special favors received by large foreign and ethnic–Chinese conglomerates, and in later years of his regime on the favored economic position of his family. There had been calls within Indonesia since the late 1980s for development of an anti-monopoly law, but such an initiative was a no-go as long as Soeharto was in office. Partly as a political offset to this discontent, Soeharto offered various preferential programs for indigenous entrepreneurs.

Even now there remain restrictions on entry by large firms into some traditional sectors occupied mostly by small businesses, such as the manufacture of soybean curd or prawn crackers, as well as restrictions on entry into some areas in which state enterprises have operated, such as the steel industry. The regulations that have reserved sectors for small enterprises have allowed medium and large enterprises to enter certain sectors, but only in partnership with small firms.[29] In practice, such partnerships have tended to be in name only, but it is not clear that the regulations are strictly enforced.

As noted earlier, Indonesian thought tends toward the particularistic rather than the abstract. One manifestation of this tendency is that economic policies appear not to be based on a clearly-delineated philosophy (Hill, 2000). Although the policy preferences for small businesses over larger ones can be seen as the product of an egalitarian world view in Islam or as a residual defensiveness from the colonial period, from a neoliberal perspective the policy preference for indigenous Indonesian entrepreneurs over ethnic Chinese businesses is difficult to distinguish from political favoritism. More generally, competition policy seems intended to protect competitors more than the process of competition (Thee, 2005b).

It is ironic that some of the worst excesses of the Dutch colonial administration – such as forced production of sugar cane to supply the local sugar mill – were fundamentally harmful to Indonesians not because there was too much competition but because there was not enough. But also Indonesian officials learned too well from the Dutch the allure of manipulation and monopolization of sectors of the economy. Indeed, there are many examples of measures to restrain competition that have benefited political and economic elites, but not most of the population and particularly not lower-income persons.[30]

The clove distribution monopoly of 1991–1998, awarded by President Soeharto to his youngest son and the rural cooperatives, is one of the most egregious examples. The vast majority of cloves produced in Indonesia are purchased by the *kretek* cigarette companies, the largest of which are Chinese owned. The distribution monopoly was supposed to boost the prices received by clove farmers. In practice it had the opposite effect (Bennett, Marks, and Muslimin, 1998). The most charitable interpretation is that, based on a concern that even wise policies could be undermined by poor implementation, Soeharto put someone he trusted in charge of the policy, though clearly such an interpretation could be used to rationalize crony capitalism in general.[31] A neoliberal perspective is that some competition (multiple buyers of cloves) ought to be better for farmers than no competition (a single buyer of cloves).

One of the structural reforms negotiated by the IMF in Indonesia in 1998, in addition to many other changes broadly consistent with neoliberal tenets, was the establishment of a competition law.[32] Consistent with the mental model that business size differences per se could be unfair, whether or not anti-competitive conduct was present, the new law stipulated that a firm could be deemed a monopoly if it had a market share of greater than 50 percent. Similarly, two or three firms with a combined market share of greater than 75 percent could be deemed an oligopoly. Any of these firms could be subject to millions of dollars in fines. In contrast, small businesses and cooperatives were explicitly exempted from the new law, and state enterprises were to be regulated separately.

From a neoliberal perspective, strict enforcement of the market-share provisions could create disincentives for firms to realize economies of scale, or could lead to less rather than more competition, if low-cost firms hesitated to expand beyond some point. The extensive powers granted to the new Business Competition Supervisory Commission (KPPU) were also a concern, given the weakness of governance in Indonesia. The worst concerns have not been realized so far.[33] The KPPU at times has acted on its mandate to point out anti-competitive government regulations. However, its effectiveness has been limited, partly due to the external judicial review process, which has put it at the mercy of the unreliable legal system.

Corruption, collusion, and nepotism

Indonesia by all accounts is one of the most corrupt societies in the world. In the government and politics, this corruption occurs at all levels, and permeates state enterprises, political parties, the judiciary, and law enforcement – from the petty corruption of the traffic police to large-scale corruption in government procurement, taxation and regulation. Much of this corruption is of a parasitical character and undermines productive activities. The arbitrariness of the legal system deters both domestic and foreign investment.[34] Official corruption makes it difficult for the government to muster resources for any purpose.

Corruption is one of the concerns most on the minds of the Indonesian people. A credible poll conducted for the 2004 presidential election found that 30 percent of the public believed the single most important policy issue to be reducing corruption, while 30 percent were most concerned with keeping prices low and 26 percent with creating jobs.[35] The poll indicated that older persons (above age 55) tended to be more concerned with keeping prices low and were less concerned with reducing corruption, consistent with traditional mental models of the role of the state, while younger persons (below age 25) were more concerned with creating jobs and reducing corruption. Those with at most an elementary education were less concerned about reducing corruption than were those with a secondary education or higher.

I have noted the Javanese tribute–patronage tradition. Through a neoliberal lens, this system would be viewed as the embodiment of corruption. To many Indonesians, it is a natural state of affairs. It is significant that in modern Indonesia the term commonly used to described corrupt behavior is KKN, or *korupsi, kolusi, dan nepotisme.* All three of these terms derive from western cognates: corruption, collusion, and nepotism.

It turns out that there are terms in the Indonesian language that are more or less equivalent to corruption and collusion. For corruption, there is *penyelewengan,* which also means deviation from task or duty, or irregularity. For collusion, there is *persekongkolan.* The root of this term, *kongkol,* means to talk or chat. This root word is similar to *kongko,* a term of ethnic Chinese origin with a similar meaning. Thus, *persekongkolan* is associated socially and even linguistically with the ethnic Chinese, perceived to be a group that connives to take unfair advantage of outsiders.[36] For nepotism, however, there is no counterpart in Indonesian: there could be nothing more natural than to take care of one's family![37]

The new anti-corruption initiative of President Susilo Bambang Yudhoyono, who was elected in 2004, is primarily a law-enforcement effort. New investigative bodies have been created, and a number of high-profile convictions of senior figures in the central and regional governments have been handed down. The overall progress against corruption has been modest, however, and there are concerns that the corruption may simply spread to the new investigative institutions or further permeate the judiciary as it handles these cases.

This approach is consistent with the legalistic tradition in Islam that focuses on the moral responsibilities of the individual. Indeed, the President has called upon Islamic organizations to join the campaign to strengthen moral resistance to corruption.

Given human imperfections, social and economic institutions emerge to constrain and direct our behavior in certain ways. Timur Kuran notes in the context of Islamism that there are information and coordination problems in an approach to socioeconomic mobilization that focuses on the process of perfection of the individual, and depends on some degree of altruism and jointness of purpose. In small, simple societies (with a *kita* flavor) anti-social behavior may be surmountable through kinship and other social relations, but in large, complex societies (with a *kami* flavor) communalistic values are limited in their capacity to influence behavior.[38] Indonesia seems to be a *kami* society that imagines itself as a *kita* society.

Consistent with these observations, the new anti-corruption initiative, and the legalistic and moralistic mental model on which it is based, seem not very cognizant that improved institutions are required as part of a comprehensive effort against corruption.[39]

- There have been some public discussions of the importance of providing remunerative incomes to civil servants or political office holders, but these have focused mostly on higher-level elites, while lower-level civil servants, police, and military personnel must get by on relatively low official incomes.[40]
- There have been no concerted public discussions of the large numbers of low-productivity employees in government service, or how most of these persons earn substantial portions of their incomes in the form of discretionary payments that confer a high degree of control to their superiors, a modern version of the traditional tribute–patronage system.

On both of these accounts, the pursuit of supplemental income tends to distract government employees from service of the broader public interest. McLeod (2005) points out how difficult it is to remove incompetent or even corrupt officials from the civil service, and notes the impracticality of a law enforcement approach, given that so many persons are implicated in various corrupt activities.

There also seems to be only limited official recognition of the way that distortive economic policies contribute to corruption. An example is the fuel subsidies, which have been in effect since 1975. In September 2005 the differential between the retail price of regular gasoline in Indonesia and the wholesale price in Singapore rose to as high as 146 percent,[41] and the subsidies threatened to absorb 30 percent of the central government budget. The subsidies have led to extensive smuggling, evidently in part by officials of Pertamina, the state oil and gas company. On the first day of October, President Yudhoyono dramatically reduced the subsidy, and subsequent changes in energy prices and the value of the rupiah eliminated it altogether. The measured consumption of gasoline in Indonesia, which included any amounts being smuggled out of the country, dropped substantially.[42]

Even with the recent reforms, distortive policies remain. The price of kerosene for household use in Indonesia is only 31 percent of the price for industrial users, and so illegal arbitrage activities and chaotic market conditions have continued. Fertilizer subsidies similarly have been targeted for small-scale rice farmers, but there have been extensive diversions to other users.[43] Perhaps these targeted price subsidies can be understood via a mental model in which welfare interventionism must be conducted subject to a tight budget constraint. A neoliberal take is that these policies run starkly counter to market forces, and that the lawlessness that has followed was preordained. However, durable mental models typically include mechanisms for their own defense. If a policy that flows logically from some mental model fails, it can be argued that the policy experiment was flawed in some way. In Indonesia a familiar refrain has been that the policy was good, but that the people who implemented it were bad, or that the problem was a lack of enforcement (Bennett, Marks, and Muslimin, 1988). The cynical view is that these interventions have been intended precisely to generate illicit income for state officials and their cronies.

State enterprises, long treated as cash cows by various elites, remain for the most part immune from the privatization pushed by the IMF and other donors. Some Indonesians are concerned that the public missions of some of the state enterprises would be forsaken under privatization. Ministers in charge of privatization have also argued that, due to the sluggish recovery since the economic crisis of 1997–1998, the prices that state assets can fetch are too low.[44] In the meantime, assets like state-owned Bank Mandiri and Bank Negara Indonesia continue to be eroded through corrupt activities.[45] In the search for a balanced approach, minority stakes in some enterprises have been offered.[46] Like the middle road that led to the rural cooperatives, this approach is problematic from a neoliberal perspective, which predicts that vulnerability of minority shareholders under partial privatization would cause share prices to be discounted.

In summary, the slow pace of fundamental reforms is in part a function of Indonesian mental models on the economy. The absence so far of major bureaucratic reforms reflects the durability of a tradition that allows senior officials control over various forms of patronage. The resistance to reform of distortive economic policies reflects the historic role of the state and aversion to the free play of market forces. The slowness of privatization of state enterprises reflects the historic aversion to foreign and Chinese domination.

The slowness of these reform processes is also a function of their political difficulty. The bloated civil service provides employment for many, while proposals for increased salaries for corrupt public officials have been widely condemned. Fuel price increases have met with public protests, as the Indonesian people have played their own role in support of a continued interventionist state. Privatization has been resisted because a great many persons have a stake in enterprises that, for better or worse, are managed by indigenous Indonesians rather than ethnic Chinese or foreigners.[47]

Concluding remarks

The old adage that bad times make for good policies was evident in the economic crisis of 1997–1998: under an IMF program, Indonesia adopted not only changes to macroeconomic policies and financial regulations but also many structural reforms that from a neoliberal standpoint should have contributed to efficiency, equity, and freedom. However, subject to criticism both inside and outside Indonesia for the intrusiveness, excessive breadth, and initial ineffectiveness of its mandated reform program, the IMF limited its attention after 1998 mostly to macroeconomic policies and financial regulation. Since then, subsequent governments have backtracked in some reform areas, notably in domestic and foreign trade policies and through the expansion of subsidies under President Megawati Soekarnoputri during 2001–2004.

The old adage also seems to have been in force during the last quarter of 2005, as serious weakness in the rupiah and associated inflationary pressures, as well as the prospect of huge budget deficits due to the costly fuel subsidies, induced President Susilo Bambang Yudhoyono to pare down the subsidies and replace the two most powerful economic ministers in the cabinet with market-oriented technocrats.[48] In addition, the central bank tightened monetary policy. Markets responded favorably, as a flood of new money into equity and bond markets drove up the value of the rupiah against the dollar by 11 percent from the end of September 2005 to early February 2006.

The advantages of full participation in the global economy, and the disciplines imposed by the global market, could provide further impetus for liberalization of economic policies in Indonesia. Certainly the education of more and more Indonesian economists in graduate programs in Australia and the United States has planted the seeds for neoclassical economic analysis, and neoliberal mental models, to continue to work their way into the economic discourse.

Nevertheless, the ties between contemporary Indonesia and its past remain strong, and the deep suspicions of market forces and private ownership of resources will not easily be assuaged. Indeed, given the economic, social, and political upheavals of 1997–1998, and the subsequent diminishment of foreign direct investment, Indonesia has to some extent turned inward. Islamic fundamentalism has attracted new adherents, there is evidence that Islam in Indonesia has become less tolerant, and terrorism is a constant threat. The fragile legislative coalition of President Susilo Bambang Yudhoyono includes no fewer than seven political parties, five of which are based in Islam, and one of which is the successor to the formidable political machine that President Soeharto directed for many years. In the midst of all these uncertainties, continued constructive engagement by the United States and the broader international community will be critical to the future of this important and turbulent nation.

Notes

1 Pomona College, Claremont, CA. I thank Ross McLeod, Lynn Rapaport, Ravi Roy, Thee Kian Wie, and Frank Wykoff for helpful comments on earlier drafts, and Tahir Andrabi and James Likens for helpful discussions. I am also grateful for the financial support of the Freeman Program in Asian Political Economy at the Claremont Colleges.

2 Indonesian economist Faisal Basri (2005) cites an even earlier history of trade with other parts of Asia. He advocates greater reliance on markets and expansion of trade with Asia in particular, but argues that without appropriate "market regulating," "market stabilizing," and "market legitimizing" mechanisms there could be a backlash. His analysis reveals the suspicion with which markets are viewed. Basri is a U.S.-trained economist who is a member of the Business Competition Supervisory Commission as well as a committed reformer and progressive Islam-oriented politician.

3 For example, the Balinese aristocracy exported slaves through the early nineteenth century (Ricklefs, 2002).

4 Less stratified tribal or other forms of social and political organization persisted in some areas. Examples include the clan, village, and village federation structures of the Minangkabau ethnic group of West Sumatra, and the village irrigation associations of Bali (van Leur, 1967).

5 Even the Javanese language embodied hierarchy: social superiors used a familiar, informal, style with their social inferiors, who were obliged to use a polite, formal style in return.

6 Furnival (1939) and Houben (2002) provide useful accounts of the demise of the company.

7 There is evidence of a significant decrease in per capita rice production on Java between 1815 and 1836, which implies that forced cultivation of cash crops was burdensome to the population (Booth, 1998).

8 Several of Indonesia's early nationalist leaders were also impressed by the Japanese victory over the Russians in the Russo-Japanese war of 1904–1905, which showed that an Asian nation could defeat a European power (Thee Kian Wie, personal communication).

9 In his analysis of Islamism and economics, Timur Kuran (2004) calls this an invented tradition rather than an ancient tradition of either Islamic texts or practice.

10 It is not a coincidence that one of the most trenchant critiques of this separation comes from a non-western economist, Amartya Sen (2000).

11 Adi Sasono, a former State Minister of Cooperatives and Small Business, and an Islamist and populist, put it this way in an interview with me in July 2005:

"rules in the mosque are like rules in the market – there are no privileges for anybody."

12 Kuran (2004) considers the extensive literature on whether Islam hinders economic development, focusing on the tendency toward communalism rather than individualism, inhibitions on public discourse conducive to change, and whether it entails an inherently static world view.

13 Thee (2005a) chronicles discriminatory Indonesian government policies toward ethnic Chinese businesses since independence. Also see Schwarz (2000).

14 Some sardonic observers have characterized the principal "family system" of Indonesia as the rent-seeking practices of the wife, children, and grandchildren of former President Soeharto, particularly during the latter years of his 32-year rule. Some estimates put the accumulated family wealth on the order of $40 billion prior to the economics crisis of 1997–1998.

15 This was the characterization used by Emil Salim, an elder statesman, Ph.D. economist from the University of California at Berkeley, Muslim intellectual, and former cabinet minister under Soeharto, in an interview with the author in July 2005.

16 Government Regulation Number 10 of 1959 banned foreigners from participation in rural trade, but in practice it was targeted at the ethnic Chinese, many of whom had been in Indonesia for generations. Its enforcement cost many Chinese their businesses and even their lives.

17 Interview with the author in July 2005. Juoro is an Islamist and was economic adviser to President B.J. Habibie during his 1998–1999 term in office. He has a masters degree in political economy from Boston University.

18 In contrast, the Javanese elite saw the social and political worlds as complex. The overworked metaphor of Javanese shadow puppetry remain apt: complex subterfuges were perceived to be at work behind a screen.

19 This reversed the conventional neoliberal wisdom that the current account should be opened before the capital account (Thee, 2002).

20 Hill (2000), Schwarz (2000), Thee (2002), and Borsuk (1999) examine economic policy-making in Indonesia in recent decades. Boediono (2005) (also see note 48 below) offers perspectives almost up to the present, and a vision for the future.

21 See, for example, Bresnan (1993) on the rise of the technocrats. Thee (2003) presents a series of interviews with top economic policy makers of the Soekarno and Soeharto eras.

22 Richard Borsuk (1999) argues that Soeharto became adept at the development of periodic economic reform packages to assure continued external finance. Basri and Hill (2004) econometrically examine the political economy of trade policy reform in the Soeharto era.

23 He was also an Islamist and was appointed by Soeharto to head the Alliance of Indonesian Muslim Intellectuals (ICMI) at its creation in 1990. Islamic modernism enjoyed an ascendancy in Indonesia in the 1990s. One interpretation of ICMI is that it represented primarily an effort by President Soeharto to coopt Islamic intellectuals, though certainly a number of the Islamic intellectuals who have participated in the organization have harbored considerable ambitions for it. Schwarz (2000) examines ICMI in detail.

24 Based on a 1986 interview by Anne Booth and Thee Kian Wie, reprinted in Thee (2003). A cogent critique of the dualism theory was offered by Mohammad Sadli (1957), who did graduate study in economics at MIT and the University of California at Berkeley, but completed his doctoral degree at the University of Indonesia, and later became a respected economist and minister under Soeharto.

25 One of these was Bob Hasan, an ethnic Chinese crony of Soeharto who converted to Islam and dominated the timber and plywood businesses for decades. He was recently released from prison after serving time for misuse of state funds.

26 For a modern presentation of the infant-industry analysis, see, for example, Krugman and Obstfeld (2005).

27 Based on my interviews in July 2005 with Mohammad Sadli (note 24 above) and Pande Radja Silalahi, a Japan-educated Ph.D. economist and member of the Business Competition Supervisory Commission.

28 For an excellent discussion, see the introductory chapter of Thee (2003). See also Schwarz (2000).

29 The latest is Presidential Decree Number 127 of 2001, on Sectors/Types of Business Reserved for Small Business and Sectors/Types of Business Open for Medium or Large Business on the Condition of Partnership, enacted by President Megawati Soekarnoputri on 14 December 2001.

30 Faisal Basri (2002) (note 2 above) catalogues some of the worst cases of state-sponsored monopolies in recent decades.

31 The son, Hutomo Mandala Putra, is currently imprisoned in Indonesia for paying for the murder of a supreme court justice, a case related to his earlier conviction on corruption charges.

32 As a consultant to the Ministry of Industry and Trade during 1997–1999, sponsored by the US Agency for International Development (USAID), I assisted in the development of the new law, which eventually became Law Number 5 of 1999 on the Prohibition of Monopolistic Practices and Unfair Business Competition, 5 March 1999.

33 Thee (2005b) offers an overview and critique of the law and its initial implementation under the KPPU.

34 This problem is worse than in the past. Under Soeharto, the judiciary was corrupt, but in a more directed manner, so that most companies could find a way to do business. Similarly, although the overall level of corruption may or may not be higher, it tends to take a greater toll on business nowadays, because of its unpredictability, in part a function of the decentralization of fiscal and regulatory authority since 1999.

35 International Foundation for Election Systems, Results from Waves XI–XII of Tracking Surveys, 31 May 2004. These polls were sponsored by USAID.

36 Confirmed through personal communication with John U. Wolff, Professor Emeritus of Linguistics, Cornell University.

37 The Indonesian terms *perkoncoan* or *koncoisme* from the Javanese root *konco* refer to cronyism, however.

38 Emil Salim (note 15 above), who served for a time as State Minister for the Improvement of the State Apparatus under Soeharto, told me that *kita* societies have not yet found institutional arrangements that work effectively to achieve societal goals, while *kami* societies have extensive internal checks and balances. He also noted how Islamic practices and obligations could be reconciled with corrupt behavior: people pray five times a day, but the corruption is in between!

39 Teten Masduki, a respected long-time activist against corruption in Indonesia and director of Indonesia Corruption Watch, agreed with this characterization in my July 2005 interview with him. See also, for example, "Tax Chief Says Graft the Work of Individuals, Not the Institution," *Jakarta Post*, 19 January 2006.

40 Teten Masduki (note 39 above) states that higher salaries are a necessary, but not sufficient condition for control of official corruption, which has continued in governmental institutions in which salaries have been relatively high. Moreover, applicants are required to pay bribes to obtain employment in many

governmental or police positions, so that increased salaries may be offset by increased up-front payments.

41 Calculations by the author based on daily Singapore gasoline price data from the U.S. Department of Energy and daily exchange rate data from the Pacific Exchange Rate Service of the University of British Columbia.

42 See Leony Aurora, "Subsidized Fuel Consumption Down," *Jakarta Post*, 19 October 2005. The fuel subsidies have benefited primarily middle and upper income groups, but direct payments to the poor have been instituted, despite technical issues and concerns about financial leakages, to soften the economic and political impact of the reductions in the subsidies.

43 These subsidies were ended under an agreement with the IMF in early 1998, but were reintroduced in 2003.

44 Economist Faisal Basri (2002) (also see note 2 above) argues, along lines reasonably consistent with neoliberal analysis, that whether privatization will improve resource allocation depends on factors such as the market structure of the industry and whether the regulatory framework is adequate.

45 See Assif Shameen, "Indonesia: A Scandal That's Almost Welcome," *Business Week Online*, May 16, 2005; or Bill Guerin, "Just Another Indonesian Bank Scandal," *Asia Times Online*, November 27, 2003.

46 A 31 percent share of Bank Mandiri was sold to the public in 2003. A similar step may be taken this year for Bank Negara Indonesia, after delays of several years.

47 Former minister Mohammad Sadli (note 24 above) argues that managers and employees of state enterprises also resist privatization because they fear that their involvement in corrupt activities will be disclosed (Prasetiantono, 2004).

48 Sri Mulyani Indrawati, a senior lecturer at the University of Indonesia and recently an executive director at the IMF, was appointed Minister of Finance. The President had reportedly wanted her at Finance from the outset, but she was too tainted by her IMF post in the view of some nationalists, and so she initially settled for a lesser cabinet position. Boediono, the former Minister of Finance, returned from his duties as senior lecturer at Gadjah Mada University to become Coordinating Minister for the Economy. A third respected economist, Mari Pangestu, from the Centre for Strategic and International Studies in Jakarta, has been Minister of Trade throughout the Yudhoyono administration. All three earned doctorates in economics in the United States.

References

Anderson, Benedict R. O'G. (1990) *Language and Power: Exploring Political Cultures in Indonesia.* Ithaca, NY: Cornell University Press.

Armstrong, Karen (1994) *A History of God: The 4000-Year Quest of Judaism, Christianity and Islam.* New York: Alfred A. Knopf.

Basri, M. Chatib, and Hill, Hal (2004) "Ideas, interests and oil prices: the political economy of trade reform during Soeharto's Indonesia," *The World Economy* 27(May): 633–655.

Basri, Faisal (2002) *Perekonomian Indonesia: Tantangan dan Harapan bagi Kebangkitan Indonesia.* Jakarta: Penerbit Erlangga.

Basri, F. (2005) "*Liberalisasi perdagangan yang mencelakakankah?*" in *Kita Harus Berubah: Analisis Ekonomi Faisal Basri.* Jakarta: Kompas.

Benjamin, Dwayne (1992) "Household composition, labor markets, and labor demand: testing for separation in agricultural household models," *Econometrica* 60 (March): 287–322.

Bennett, Christopher P.A., Marks, Stephen V., and Muslimin, Lukman (1998) "The clove monopoly: lessons for the future," unpublished manuscript, TIP Project, USAID and Ministry of Industry and Trade, Republic of Indonesia, Jakarta (November).

Boediono (2005) "Managing the Indonesian economy: some lessons from the past," *Bulletin of Indonesian Economic Studies* 41 (December): 309–324.

Boeke, Julius Herman (1953) *Economics and Economic Policy of Dual Societies, as Exemplified by Indonesia.* New York: International Secretariat, Institute of Pacific Relations.

Booth, Anne (1998) *The Indonesian Economy in the Nineteenth and Twentieth Centuries: A History of Missed Opportunities.* New York: St Martin's Press.

Borsuk, Richard (1999) "Markets: the limits of reform," in Emmerson, Donald K. (ed.) *Indonesia Beyond Suharto: Polity, Economy, Society, Transition.* Armonk, NY: M.E. Sharpe.

Bresnan, John (1993) *Managing Indonesia: The Modern Political Economy.* New York: Columbia University Press.

Denzau, Arthur T. and North, Douglass C. (1994) "Shared mental models: ideologies and institutions," *Kyklos* 47(1): 3–31.

Dick, Howard, Houben, Vincent J.H., Lindblad, J. Thomas, and Kian Wie, Thee (2002) *The Emergence of a National Economy: An Economic History of Indonesia, 1800–2000.* Crows Nest, New South Wales: Allen and Unwin.

Furnival, John Sydenham (1939) *Netherlands India: A Study of Plural Economy.* Cambridge, UK: Cambridge University Press (1967 reprint).

van Gelderen, Jacob (1961) "The economics of the tropical colony," in *Indonesian Economics: The Concept of Dualism in Theory and Policy.* Amsterdam: The Royal Tropical Institute, Selected Studies on Indonesia by Dutch Scholars, vol. 6.

Gillis, Malcolm (1988) "Indonesia: public policies, resource management, and the tropical forest," in Repetto, Robert C. and Gillis, Malcolm (eds) *Public Policies and the Misuse of Forest Resources.* Cambridge, UK: Cambridge University Press.

Hill, Hal (2000) *The Indonesian Economy,* second edition. Cambridge, UK: Cambridge University Press.

Houben, Vincent J.H. (2002) "Java in the 19th century: consolidation of a territorial state," in Dick, H., Houben, V.J.H., Lindblad, J.T., and Thee, K.W. (eds) *The Emergence of a National Economy: An Economic History of Indonesia, 1800–2000.* Crows Nest, New South Wales: Allen and Unwin.

Jones, Will T. (1971) "Worldviews – West and East," *Journal of the Blaisdell Institute* 7: 9–24.

Kahin, George McT. (1980) "In memoriam: Mohammad Hatta (1902–1980)," *Indonesia* 30 (October): 113–120.

Krugman, Paul R. and Obstfeld, Maurice (2005) *International Economics: Theory And Policy,* 7th edn. Boston: Addison Wesley.

Kuran, Timur (2004) *Islam and Mammon: The Economic Predicaments of Islamism.* Princeton, NJ: Princeton University Press.

van Leur, J.C. (1967) *Indonesian Trade and Society: Essays in Asian Social and Economic History.* The Hague: W. van Hoeve Publishers.

Liddle, William (1985) "Soeharto's Indonesia: personal rule and political institutions," *Pacific Affairs* 58 (Spring): 68–90.

Lindblad, J. Thomas (2002) "The late colonial state and economic expansion, 1900–1930s," in Dick, H., Houben, V.J.H., Lindblad, J.T., and Thee, K.W. (eds)

The Emergence of a National Economy: An Economic History of Indonesia, 1800–2000. Crows Nest, New South Wales: Allen and Unwin.

Marks, Stephen V. (1998) "Restrictions on commodity trade in Nusa Tenggara Timur Province," unpublished manuscript, TIP Project, USAID and Ministry of Industry and Trade, Republic of Indonesia, Jakarta (February).

McLeod, Ross H. (2005) "The struggle to regain effective government under democracy in Indonesia," *Bulletin of Indonesian Economic Studies* 41 (December): 367–386.

McKendrick, David (1992) "Obstacles to 'catch-up': the case of the Indonesian aircraft industry," *Bulletin of Indonesian Economic Studies* 28 (April): 39–66.

Prasetiantono, Tony (2004) "Political economy of privatisation of state-owned enterprises in Indonesia," in Basri, M. Chatib and van der Eng, Pierre (eds) *Business in Indonesia: New Challenges, Old Problems.* Singapore: Institute of Southeast Asian Studies (ISEAS).

Reid, Anthony (1984) "The pre-colonial economy of Indonesia," *Bulletin of Indonesian Economic Studies* 20 (August): 151–167.

Reid, A. (1988) *Southeast Asia in the Age of Commerce 1450–1680,* vol. 1, *The Lands Below the Winds.* New Haven: Yale University Press.

Reid, A. (1993) *Southeast Asia in the Age of Commerce 1450–1680,* vol. 2, *Expansion and Crisis.* New Haven: Yale University Press.

Rice, Robert C. (1983) "The origins of basic economic ideas and their impact on 'New Order' policies," *Bulletin of Indonesian Economic Studies* 19 (August): 60–82.

Ricklefs, M.C. (2002) *A History of Modern Indonesia Since* c.*1200,* 3rd edn. Palo Alto: Stanford University Press.

Sadli, Mohammad (1957) "Reflections on Boeke's theory of dualistic economies," *Ekonomi dan Keuangan Indonesia* (June), reprinted in Bruce Glassburner (ed.) *The Economy of Indonesia: Selected Readings.* Ithaca: Cornell University Press, 1971.

Schwarz, Adam (2000) *A Nation in Waiting: Indonesia's Search for Stability,* 2nd edn. Boulder, CO: Westview Press.

Sen, Amartya (2000) "The discipline of cost-benefit analysis," *Journal of Legal Studies* 29 (June): 931–952.

Smith, Adam (1776) *An Inquiry into the Nature and Causes of the Wealth of Nations,* Campbell, R.H. and Skinner, A.S. (eds). New York: Oxford University Press, 1979.

Thee Kian Wee (1994) "Reflections on Indonesia's emerging industrial nationalism," Working Paper no. 41, Asia Research Institute, Murdoch University, Western Australia.

Thee Kian Wee (2002) "The Soeharto era and after: stability, development and crisis, 1966–2000," in Dick, H., Houben, V.J.H., Lindblad, J.T., and Thee, K.W. (eds) *The Emergence of a National Economy: An Economic History of Indonesia, 1800–2000.* Crows Nest, New South Wales: Allen and Unwin.

Thee Kian Wee (ed.) (2003) *Recollections: The Indonesian Economy, 1950s-1990s.* Singapore: Institute of Southeast Asian Studies (ISEAS).

Thee Kian Wee (2005a) "The Indonesian government's economic policies towards the ethnic Chinese," paper presented at the ISEAS Workshop on the Ethnic Chinese Economy and Business in Southeast Asia in the Era of Globalisation, April 21–22.

Thee Kian Wee (2005b) "Indonesia's first competition law: issues and experiences," in Lee, Cassey (ed.) *Competition Policies and Deregulation in Asian Countries.* Kuala Lumpur: University of Malaya Press.

Timmer, C. Peter (2004) "Food security in Indonesia: current challenges and the long-run outlook," Center for Global Development, Working Paper no. 48 (November).

Tönnies, Ferdinand (1887) *Community and Society* [Gemeinschaft und Gesellschaft], translated and edited by Charles P. Loomis. New York: Harper & Row, 1963.

15 The usefulness of the shared mental model framework for understanding Latin American economic history

From dependencia to neoliberalism

Anil Hira

Introduction

This chapter seeks to address whether Denzau and North's shared mental models framework can successfully explain different periods in Latin American economic history (Denzau and North, 1994). We take as our guideposts for evaluation four key points from their article. First, that individual rationality alone can not explain Latin American economic policy choices (p. 3). Second, that in situations of uncertainty, ideas, dogmas, tacit knowledge, and ideologies inform both policy reactions and normative evaluations (3, 15–16, 20–21). Third, however, that learning is possible (13–15), and that it tends to follow a pattern of "punctuated equilibiria," due to the "stickiness" of shared mental models (22–26). Punctuated equilibria suggests slow evolutionary change or stagnation, followed by moments of revolutionary change. Overall, we would expect a trajectory of steady but periodic change. Change could result from incoherence, "surprise," "contradictions," and/or as the result of the efforts of "ideological entrepreneurs. Fourth, applying this model can explain the reasons for suboptimal performance of Latin American nations over long periods of time (3, 27). Through a perusal of Latin American economic history, we shall demonstrate the usefulness of the shared mental models framework to explain simultaneous learning, stickiness, and punctuated equilibria in the fit between ideas and interests, as well as its limitations, principally the neglect of political variables, including discount rates. Our conclusion is that the shared mental models framework can be modified to accommodate these limitations.

Before evaluating the shared mental models framework on Latin American (LA) economic history, we must describe two of the most important limitations of the model. The first is how to evaluate suboptimality and the second related question of how to evaluate if "learning" is actually taking place. The answer to these questions may be more subjective than meets the eye. Clearly, a perusal of LA historical economic statistics (see Thorp, 1998) demonstrates that advances in education (literacy), health, and overall standards of living have increased significantly over time. However, macroeconomic volatility, vulnerability to international economic shocks, and income and wealth inequality remain as major vulnerabilities in the region. The way to evaluate the performance of Latin American economies depends, therefore, in part on the criteria for the perspective which one employs.

In development studies, there have been two contending shared mental models on development, modernization and dependency. Without fully explicating these well-known (So, 1990) perspectives, we can delineate their general criteria for evaluating economic performance. It is interesting to note that both modernization and dependency agree on the general end goal for development – that of an advanced industrial society in which every person has a standard of living on a par with those of citizens in the First World. While this view is increasingly challenged (Escobar, 1995), no clear alternative paradigms as yet have emerged or taken hold in regard to the region. The neoliberal shared mental model and the modernization shared mental model are highly contiguous and are treated as such in this chapter. Neoliberal policies, including the liberalization of trade, exchange, and financial accounts, and the general reliance upon market forces wherever possible, would fit into the modernization shared mental model.

The neoliberal shared mental model expects that the adoption of modern policies will lead naturally to development. More recently, this view has been modified to include the need to develop modern institutions as well (North, 1990; Krueger, 2000). Therefore, the evaluation of optimality from a modernization point of view would be the adoption of market-based economic policies that will lead to sustained economic growth. On the other side, the well-known dependency shared mental model looks primarily to measures of equity and a reduction of dependence upon external forces, including both trade and investment, and the exploitation that accompany them (Frank, 1978). That is, for a dependentisa, Latin American development can only occur if redistribution of some form leading to greater equity and an improvement in the ability of Latin American countries to produce their own financial, technical, and industrial capabilities. Neoliberals would tend to focus, therefore, upon the macroeconomic accounts for their measures of performance, while dependentistas would focus on measures of distribution and autonomy from the world economy.

Latin American historical economic performance

Beginning with the first guidepost, we can clearly see that rationality alone can not explain Latin American economic policy choices or performance.

We begin with a brief review of LA economic history using the suggested evaluative criteria from both perspectives. Rosemary Thorp's seminal work, *Progress, Poverty and Exclusion* (1998), contains the only comprehensive source of historical statistics for LA. Her statistical annexes provide a great deal of proof that modernization and some learning has taken place in Latin America. Across the region, improvements in literacy, health care, and other measures of absolute living standards as well as industrialization and a limited degree of export diversification (though this varies greatly by country) have undoubtedly improved over the course of the century. In addition, a fragile yet functioning democracy seems to have taken hold, and the degree of tolerance and moderation for political differences has apparently increased with the recent elections of Lagos, Lula, Kirchner, all moderate leftists in Chile, Brazil, and Argentina. Moreover, from the 1990s, inflation ceased to be a constant fear through most of the region. By economic logic, we would expect that a developing country would seek increasing investment; a positive or at least neutral trade balance; a balanced government budget, especially in light of the need to repay crushing external debts and the phantom of hyperinflation; corresponding improvements in the ability to tax; and investments in human capital both for reasons of increasing human capital and dealing with social and political polarization. However, the following tables (analyzed by author from Oxford University's Latin American economic database built upon Thorp's work), point to a number of puzzles from this logical perspective.

Table 15.1 shows that there is no evidence that total investment has increased in LA countries over time. Even in the case of the neoliberal "miracle" economy of Chile, there is no real evidence of differential economic performance over the course of the century.

Table 15.2 shows a very pessimistic story for most of the region, as net trade deficits have increased in four of the seven major countries. This is an odd finding given the resource wealth and dependency on exports of LA countries. It underscores the importance of the external debt to finance current expenditures (or more recently interest on past expenditures), rather than achieving a surplus for long-term investment.

Table 15.1 Gross domestic fixed investment

Year	*Argentina*	*Brazil*	*Chile*	*Colombia*	*Mexico*	*Peru*	*Venezuela*
1900–1920 ave	21	17	22	14	n/a	n/a	n/a
1920–1940 ave	17	13	18	17	9	n/a	23
1940–1960 ave	16	14	19	17	15	n/a	29
1960–1980 ave	22	20	18	17	20	16	24
Ave 1980–2000	18	20	21	18	20	21	19

Source: Author calculations from Oxford University Latin American Database.

Table 15.2 Trade balance: exports minus imports

Year	*Argentina*	*Brazil*	*Chile*	*Colombia*	*Mexico*	*Peru*	*Venezuela*
Ave 1900–1920	107.2	91.4	117.8	4.3	51.5	19.4	3.9
Ave 1920–1940	160.2	76.7	57.9	8.7	83.6	30.2	63.9
Ave 1940–1960	86.5	24.6	15.3	−5.3	−169.1	−9.6	416.6
Ave 1960–1980	265.5	−1,493.1	−133.3	−41.3	−1,432.1	143.0	1,631.4
Ave 1980–2000	797.4	3,923.5	−411.8	−1,011.1	−3,183.5	−1,183.1	5,506.4

Source: Author from Oxford University.

Note
Balance is in current millions $.

Table 15.3 also shows a disconcerting trend towards increasing government budget deficits. While the figures are undoubtedly inflated due to the dollar-denomination of much of the external debts acquired amidst high inflation and currency volatility, the point is that only in Chile is there any sign that LA governments have made the basic step of balancing government budgets. This step is at the heart of basic learning about economic management and is obviously a key for providing macroeconomic stability and growth.

Table 15.4 demonstrates a mixed picture. The ability to collect direct taxes through income and property taxes is perhaps the most revealing

Table 15.3 Central government budget deficit

Year	*Argentina*	*Brazil*	*Chile*	*Colombia*	*Mexico*	*Peru*	*Venezuela*
Ave 1900–1920	26	125	29	1	−14	2	−4
Ave 1920–1940	139	380	193	10	−8	43	1
Ave 1940–1960	7,738	17,173	14,549	30	1,151	106	−7
Ave 1960–1980	437,070	390,718	2,631	1,590	23,158	23,753	−3,232
Ave 1980–2000	5,495,843	293,163,888	−109,888	1,893,510	5,883,208	22,591,930	144,074

Source: Author from Oxford University.

Note
Deficits are reported in millions of LCU.

Table 15.4 Ratio of customs tax revenue to direct income tax revenue

Year	*Argentina*	*Brazil*	*Chile*	*Colombia*	*Mexico*	*Peru*	*Venezuela*
Ave 1900–1920	17.71	n/a	64.01	n/a	n/a	6.35	n/a
Ave 1920–1940	8.68	9.43	4.60	5.97	2.19	3.29	n/a
Ave 1940–1960	0.27	0.42	0.63	0.62	1.11	1.12	11.92
Ave 1960–1980	1.02	0.31	0.37	0.47	0.45	0.80	0.21
Ave 1980–2000	1.39	0.14	0.51	0.44	0.19	0.66	0.19

Source: Author from Oxford University.

sign of a government's capacity. With direct taxation, governments can stabilize their revenues and, in turn, social investments and expenditures. While it appears initially that over time the ratio of indirect revenue collection to direct taxation decreases over time, the early part of the century is deceiving for the obvious reason that in most places internationally an income tax was not passed until later in the century, including in LA. If we thus limit our consideration to the latter part of the century, Brazil, Venezuela, and Mexico appear to have made substantial progress, while the other major countries in the hemisphere have not. Nonetheless, if we further consider the continuing strong levels of commodity reliance for both exports and taxes (as noted in Thorp, 1998) is greater than direct sources of revenue, it is clear that LA government capacity is still weak and vulnerable.

Tables 15.5a and 15.5b, accumulated from very limited data, demonstrate that LA governments' dedication to human capital development remains rather limited in comparison with their military spending (though military spending in isolation is not exceptional internationally). While there are some exceptions, such as Brazil recently with education, there is no indication of a trajectory of investment for the future. This is especially tragic since most income distribution studies of the region (Thorp, 1998) show a stable or worsening picture over time. Furthermore, while not demonstrated here, Cuba has emerged in the popular imagery as a guiding light for the region's poor and middle classes, in terms of its supposed superiority in social development. However, a perusal of the UN Human Development Index reveals that while Cuba's historical improvement on social indicators is impressive, but not distant from other leading market-based countries with stable growth periods such as Costa Rica, Uruguay, and Chile. This is just one example of how false myths feed into regional shared mental models, as Denzau and North discuss.

In sum, the above tables show us that, by both neoliberal and dependency criteria, LA economic performance has been suboptimal and even irrational. If we include the mere consideration of military expenditures, justified for potential international conflicts, in a region that has seen almost none in recent years, we can immediately point to the seeming irrationality of Latin American economic priorities. The diagnosis for poor LA economic performance for neoliberal economists tends to be reluctance or unwillingness to see "economic logic," or inability to sustain such policies (Edwards, 1995). In other words, they seem to be at a bit of a loss to explain the choice of policies that clearly have been inimical to creating stable economic growth. On the dependency side, there is no surprise that, as predicted, the existing power structures do not redistribute. Dependency is more holistic and less prescription-oriented than neoliberalism in that it considers power relationships. For dependentistas, the key power relationships tend to be the alliance among elite owners of capital in both the North and the South. However, a bit of reflection reveals that

Table 15.5a Comparing social expenditures: defense vs. health

	Defense	*Health expenditures*		
	ave 1985–1997	*1990*	*1994*	*1997*
Argentina	14.40	10.54	10.64	9.80
Brazil	3.44	6.99	6.83	7.32
Chile	14.80	4.57	4.68	4.08
Colombia	16.15	4.77	5.91	9.41
Mexico	3.29	3.59	4.66	4.73
Peru	18.13	6.59	5.01	5.59
Venezuela, RB	9.92	6.87	7.49	

Source: Author from World Bank WDI 2000.

Notes
Defense = % of central government expenditures; Health = private + public % of GNP.

Table 15.5b Public spending on education (% of GNP)

	1960	*1965*	*1970*	*1975*	*1980*	*1985*	*1990*	*1995*
Argentina	1.88	4.13	1.49	1.82	2.67	1.47	1.12	3.33
Brazil	1.81	2.61	2.89	3.05	3.60	3.78	4.55	5.07
Chile	2.57	3.47	5.07	4.11	4.63	4.38	2.67	3.10
Colombia	1.69	2.23	1.93	2.22	1.86	2.89	2.52	3.67
Mexico		2.25	2.28	3.53	4.73	3.94	3.73	4.87
Peru	2.25	4.31	3.28	3.31	3.09	2.86	2.29	
Venezuela, RB	2.29	3.34	4.11	4.46	4.40	5.08	3.14	

Source: Author from World Bank, WDI 2000.

Note
Brazil's 1990 figure is from 1989.

even this compelling view of power relationships can not explain LA economic performance historically. That is, even if we posit that an alliance of elites between the North and the South runs the system for their own benefit, LA economic performance has still been suboptimal. LA elites suffer from macroeconomic volatility, including the need to rely upon foreign currencies and banks, an inability to invest in their own national means of production, an inability to borrow domestically, and a host of other symptoms. Even LA militaries would like a stable economy so that they can steadily maintain or grow their budgets. Moreover, clearly the levels of corruption and crime considerably lower the quality of life for LA elites who spend billions annually for private security, live in constant fear for their safety, and dream of sending their children abroad for study and often to stay.

From our analysis, we can reach some interesting conclusions. The first is that, surprisingly, there is no real contradiction between the dependency and modernization shared mental models. Both can see the same picture of economic performance over time and satisfactorily explain it. Neoliberals can explain poor macroeconomic performance by the lack of will and/or adequate or well-developed institutions. In the case of institutions, the question of why institution-building is neither apparent nor has brought palpable results over time remains. Dependency theorists can explain egregious income and wealth distribution by a concentration of economic and political power, on all geographic levels. However, neither party can explain the inconsistencies between poor LA economic performance and the expectations of each paradigm. We shall attempt to explain these paradoxes using the shared mental models framework and a recognition of power distribution.

Do shared mental models explain Latin American economic history?

This brings us to guideposts 2 and 3, that situations of high uncertainty can lead to the adoption of dogmas, ideas, and ideologies which impede adjustment to reality, but that learning can still take place in punctuated fashion. Clearly the indicators from the tables above indicate that LA operates in a context of extreme uncertainty in terms of economics and politics. Following a general consensus of Latin American economic historians, we can identify several general periods of ideology and the alliance of economic elites. We can also identify examples of certain "ideological entrepreneurs," who are in positions of power, though their role is not clear in every country or case. Table 15.6 summarizes these findings (Hira, 1998).

We should particularly note the very limited number of ideological frameworks that have been offered by ideological entrepreneurs. In many ways, the basic ideas of either relying on the market, now called neoliberalism, or relying on the state, whether of the socialist or structuralist variety, reverberate throughout LA history. Indeed, there is not much difference in principle between the reliance on market forces during the primary product boom at the end of the nineteenth century and the current market-oriented ideology of neoliberalism. Second, there is not much difference between the goals of structuralism, which were to change the reliance on commodity production, and to promote the development of the domestic market through a variety of mechanisms, including land reform and integration of LA countries, and the moderate export promotion and industrial promotion policies of contemporary LA states. In terms of alternatives to market-reliance, the refrain has, throughout much of this century, been that of proposing socialism. Even today, guerrillas groups like the FARC, the MST, the Sendero Luminoso, and the Zapatistas all refer to the ideas of Marx for legitimacy and as a signal for their

Table 15.6 Historical–ideological periods of Latin American economic history

Historical–ideological period	*Dominant political–economic groups*	*Innovative economic policies and epistemic communities*	*Dominant economic ideology*	*Crisis which ended period*
Colonial (1500–1800)	King and his delegates, large agricultural and mining owners.		Colonial mercantilism	Political independence wars.
Independence* (1800–1870)	Creoles: caudillos and centralizers; Conservatives and Liberals; primary product owners; foreign investors.		Classical liberalism	Consolidation of governments, end of civil wars.
First export boom (1870–1930)	Primary product exporters, foreign direct investors, and exporters.	Mexico – Diaz's *cientificos***	Neo-liberalism	Closure of international export markets with the Great Depression and World War I and II.
National populism (1930–1955)	Populist dictators, organized labor, consumer goods, industrialists.	Mexico – ruling PRN; Peru – APRA; Uruguay – Batlle; Argentina – Peron; Vargas – Brazil.	ISI1	Exhaustion of easy ISI, political and inflationary crises.
State-led industrialization (1955–1980)	Military, high-tech/capital industrialists, foreign finance and capital goods exporters, U.S. aid; economists.	Brazil & Peru – military-led development; Cuba – Marxist development; ECLA**.	ISI2***	Inflationary and debt crises.
Neo-liberalism (1980–present)	Military transition to civilian state, economists; international finance; foreign investors; industrial and primary product exporters.	Pinochet – Chicago Boys**	Neo-liberalism	

Notes

* The Independence period was one of upheaval, with continual political discontinuities, but a stable economic ideology, namely laissez-faire.

** These are the economic epistemic communities which we discuss in this dissertation, though we suggest that they exist more and more often in more places in Latin America.

*** ISI2 refers to a strategic period of import substituting industrialization in which capital- and technology-intensive goods are produced domestically through government assistance.

utopia. While there is much theorizing about social movements, civil society, and social capital (Alvarez), that would provide an autochthonous development path, free from both globalization and the state, such an alternative has yet be clearly articulated or put into practice. Indeed, one can argue that not only from the point of view of the strong dependence on external agencies to provide both financial and political resources, such as media coverage, but also from the point of view of internal politics, social movements will likely measure their success by the degree to which the state responds with new policies and resources and their ability to improve their living standards in modernist fashion. Furthermore, these ideas are really not removed from the populist ideas of self-sufficiency that go back centuries into agrarian and religious societies and reverberate with the regional metanarratives around anti-colonial and anti-imperialism.

Thus, these historical periods do reflect the punctuated equilibrium predicted by the shared mental models framework, but in a limited fashion. In almost every case, region-wide paradigms and the policies that stem from them, tend to be sticky, even as economic conditions suggest adaptation. The paradigms tend to fall apart when there is a major economic crisis. However, the palette of human economic ideas seems severely limited for reasons on which we can only speculate. Thus, in practice, we find ideological entrepreneurs have historically relied upon the same time-proven paradigms, albeit modernized in creative and hybrid applications, rather than engaging in noticeable innovation. Moreover, both simple policy adjustments, such as balancing budgets, increasing taxes and public education expenditures, or engaging in serious land reform, or more complex long-term reforms, such as developing stable institutions, that would lead to a much more sustainable economic model, and indeed a better quality of life for all involved, have yet to be implemented.

Conclusion: extending the shared mental models framework to explain the dynamic of Latin American economic history

Having shown the usefulness of the shared mental models framework to explain the dynamic of Latin American economic history, we also acknowledge the shortcomings. We have already pointed out the most important one, namely the distribution of power in a society can lead to a different sense of optimality than that measured purely by economic indicators. Indeed, as there is both a concentration of power and high degrees of instability (unlike East Asia in the 1960s–1990s) and uncertainty, we can understand why the discount rates for LA elites are extremely high. Another factor that must be taken into account to explain high discount rates, resulting in long-term suboptimality, is the extreme fragmentation of LA societies. LA societies are rife with class, ethnic, and patron–client fault lines. The protection of those lines, in the context of high volatility, thus outweighs the possibility of short-term sacrifice to expand the long-term economic pie. In this sense, cultural attitudes and levels of "social trust" as suggested by social capital theorists (Putnam, 1993; Fukuyama, 1992) deserve further incorporations. This would mean that the shared mental models framework should consider group rationality and social networks as well as individual or singular group rationality. In other words, there is a degree of ambiguity as to what networks (e.g. nationalism, class, religion) kick in as priority loyalties, responsibilities, and interests, in which situations. The social nodes of these strands, where they excessively overlap, as is the case in LA, will stifle creativity and the possibilities for social fluidity and adaptation. As a result, we tend to see the main unifying and perhaps most potent political force in LA tends to be anti-imperialism. Whenever a politician is in trouble, the anti-imperialism card tends to be the strongest weapon. This is true not only for the left (Castro, Chavez), but also for the right (Toledo, the Argentine military). Whenever there is a need to gain power, one can count on anti-U.S. and anti-imperialist rhetoric to flourish. In many respects, Castro's longevity, given the fact that most serious reforms were accomplished by the early 1970s, rests almost exclusively upon his personal charisma and on the incredible potency and imminent threat of the external enemy. Thus, anti-imperialism is buttressed not only by negative U.S. policies towards the region, which are short-term in their own right, but by the usefulness of this card for LA elites, to deflect criticism and potential change from their own poor performance. In this sense, we can suggest that the shared mental models framework can be both highly unproductive and adaptable. That is, if the shared mental models framework is not held to account, in this case, a continuing credible story that the U.S. is the ultimate source of all local problems, and is sufficiently adaptable over time, the punctuated equilibrium may not lead to a clear trajectory of economic learning. Thus, both fractal political and economic optimization as well as a self-reinforcingly high discount rate must be considered simultaneously to explain the lack of historical progress in Latin America.

References

Denzau, Arthur T. and North, Douglass C. (1994) "Shared mental models: ideologies and institutions," *Kyklos* 47(1): 3–31.

Edwards, Sebastian (1995) *Crisis and Reform in Latin America: From Despair to Hope.* New York: Oxford University Press.

Escobar, Arturo (1995) *Encountering Development: The Making and Unmaking of the Third World.* Princeton: Princeton University Press.

Frank, Andre Gunder (1978) *Dependent Accumulation and Underdevelopment.* London: Macmillan.

Fukuyama, Francis (1992) *The End of History and the Last Man.* New York: Avon Books.

Hira, Anil (1998) *Ideas and Economic Policy in Latin America.* Westport, CT: Greenwood.

Krueger, Anne O. (2000) *Economic Policy Reform: the second stage.* Chicago: University of Chicago Press.

North, Douglass C. (1990) *Institutions, Institutional Change, and Economic Performance.* New York: Cambridge University Press.

Putnam, Robert (1993) *Making Democracy Work: Civic Traditions in Modern Italy.* Princeton: Princeton University Press.

So, Alvin Y. (1990) *Social Change and Development: modernization, dependency, and world-systems theories.* Newbury Park, California: Sage.

Thorp, Rosemary (1998) *Progress, Poverty and Exclusion: An Economic History of Latin America in the 20th Century.* New York: Inter-American Development Bank.

16 The absence of social capital and the failure of the Ghanian neoliberal mental model

Nicholas Amponsah, Arthur T. Denzau, and Ravi K. Roy*

> The rules of the game should be transparently played. We still have a system that operates on the basis of persons rather than principles. It is like a village.[1]

In the 1980s, Ghana sought to institute market liberalization reforms based on policy prescriptions outlined by the IMF (International Monetary Fund) and the World Bank known as Structural Adjustment Programs (SAPs). SAPs were designed in accordance with a neoliberal framework known as the Washington Consensus (WC). The WC, a strand of the neoliberal shared mental model that was first coined by John Williamson, articulated a set of market-oriented policy prescriptions and goals that if pursued faithfully, would help encourage countries on the path to greater economic performance and prosperity. Such prescriptions included instructing governments to pursue policies and strategies aimed at promoting fiscal discipline, interest rate liberalization, privatization, deregulation of entrance and exit barriers, and establishing transparent and public-seeking institutions that are established to enforce and abide by a rule of law that would secure property rights and discourage predatory rent-seeking practices.

Thus far private business entrepreneurs generally have not responded favorably to Ghana's neoliberal reforms with increased investment as expected. In this chapter, we draw on core concepts from Denzau and North's (1994) shared mental models framework in conjunction with core tenets of the social capital thesis (Putnam, 1993a, b; Neace, 1999; Onyx, 2000) to examine the failure of neoliberal reforms in Ghana. We argue that while following sound economic mental models or ideas are critical for development and growth, they are not enough. We assert that even "sound mental models" or ideas will likely fail when applied in poor institutional environments. Such environments are those lacking in sufficient levels of social capital or public trust in political and economic institutions. Sound economic mental models may flourish more easily in certain institutional environments – those that enjoy a certain degree of social capital, where institutional credibility is high. The key ingredients in the recipe for economic policy success that leads to entrepreneurial growth and development are having both "the correct ideas" and applying them in the "correct institutional environments." Upon a first glance, this point may appear to be obvious and yet strategies for developing social trust have not been sufficiently emphasized in the policy prescriptions outlined in SAPs. Such policy frameworks appear to assume that government institutions will automatically faithfully carry out well meaning, public seeking policies and that their citizens and affected groups will automatically and naturally accept the legitimacy of institutions charged with carrying out these reforms and behave accordingly. We argue that neither should be automatically assumed. The presence of public trust is an essential but by no means automatically assured phenomenon.

We argue that government strategies for developing social capital be a critical feature of neoliberal-based policy frameworks such as SAPs that are aimed at promoting entrepreneurial development and investment-led growth. Building social capital among affected economic and political actors is crucial to implementing neoliberal reform. This is because the presence of strong levels of public trust and credible institutions are required for faithful execution of public-seeking reforms that promote entrepreneurial growth. This is, of course, much easier said than done. African states seeking to reform their economies under the current neoliberal dispensation have a major battle to wage. Because of several years of ruinous statism they have huge deficits in *social capital*. For contemporary governments to succeed in their efforts to improve the economic productivity of their economies through neoliberal reforms, they would need the cooperation of their most critical actors – private business entrepreneurs. Ghana's experience with decades of neoliberal reforms that have focused on market liberalization supports the recent work of social scientists that cooperation is facilitated if there is abundant social capital. This paper utilizes survey data to analyze the variations in responses of domestic private business in six sectors of the Ghanaian economy to market liberalization reforms that were once proclaimed to be the most successful in sub-Saharan Africa. This study demonstrates first, that a lack of social capital, rather than the inadequacy of the neoliberal shared mental model or the Washington Consensus, is the major culprit in explaining why domestic private businesses have not responded favorably to neoliberal reforms being undertaken for their own benefit. The failure of the neoliberal mental model and SAPs is due to the poor political and economic institutional environments in which these ideas and prescriptions were attempted, rather than the ideas and prescriptions themselves. Secondly, it shows that where a modicum of social capital exists, as in the case of the transportation sector in Ghana, there tends to be some amount of mutual trust that in turn promotes cooperation between state and societal economic actors in facilitating neoliberal economic reforms and prescriptions.

Although they have tried hard to follow neoliberal prescriptions outlined in the numerous structural adjustment programs (SAPs) aimed at boosting their economies through market liberalization, they have not been able to secure the cooperation of various economic actors, especially, domestic private entrepreneurs. For these governments to succeed in their efforts to improve the economic productivity of their economies through liberalization reforms, they would need the cooperation of these most critical actors, private entrepreneurs. Thus far, the indications are that reform governments of Africa have not delivered the desired goal of invigorating the private business in their countries as the case of Ghana amply demonstrates (Amponsah, 2000; Gyimah-Boadi, 1995). Private business, in most sectors of the Ghanaian economy (1983–2003) did not respond to the country's two decades of implementing profound SAP reforms by increasing investment. For historical reasons including wanton expropriation, private entrepreneurs in Ghana feel that it is a risky endeavor to sink more resources into their businesses. Private business in Ghana has no trust for the prevailing economic model of neoliberal-based prescription for development, nor the institutional framework. Our research in this paper indicates that economic mental models, even the most sound ones, are not enough. Rather a shared mental model of social capital must be incorporated into neoliberal SAP strategies and prescriptions if they are to be successful. Cultivating social capital among the entrepreneurs is essential for shoring up institutional credibility that is required for faithful implementation of genuine market reform. Where this is absent even the most "correct" or competent ideas or models will likely fail. Therefore, SAPs must be designed in a manner that includes dynamic strategies that are focused on building social trust in formal institutional arrangements as well as making those institutions trustworthy. This is especially critical for those institutions directly involved in carrying out entrepreneurial reforms.

The success of entrepreneurial investment and growth in Ghana's transportation sector in response to the SAP reform initiatives might offer some essential clues about how to do this. We found that while domestic private businesses in Ghana were generally lukewarm in their response to the country's reform program, those in the transportation sector exhibited a relatively warmer attitude and were more inclined to commit their resources to investment. Why are some entrepreneurs, notably those in the transport sector, more inclined to participate in the program of shared-growth by investing than others in different sectors of the economy?

Governments of many sub-Saharan African countries are content with the abundant natural resources they have to run the business of government. They have not felt the urgent need for the cooperation of private business in contributing towards the national endeavor through taxes and other resources (Bates, 1999: 86). At best, African governments ignore private economic entrepreneurs, considering them simply as malevolent, and at worst, try to tyrannize them out of existence (Tangri, 1992; Amponsah, 2001). How can these critical actors – state functionaries and societal economic entrepreneurs – cooperate for the mutual benefit of their nation's economic growth and development? Recent work of social scientists demonstrates that cooperation is facilitated by the prevalence of social capital – features of social organization such as networks, norms, and trust that facilitate coordination and cooperation (Putnam, 1993a; Neace, 1999).

We analyze the variation in responses of domestic private business in six sectors of the Ghanaian economy to the country's neoliberal reforms based on market liberalization using primary survey data. These reforms were once lauded to be the most successful in sub-Saharan Africa (Leechor, 1994). The study demonstrates first, that the lack of social capital – norms of mutual engagement that assure institutionalized reciprocal expectations (Putnam, 1993a), is a major reason why domestic private business in general continue to adopt a lukewarm attitude towards reforms (Amponsah, 2000). Secondly, it shows that where a modicum of social capital exists, as in the case of the transportation sector in Ghana, there tends to be some amount of mutual trust that in turn promotes cooperation between state and societal economic actors in the process of shared growth.

The chapter is presented as follows. After this introduction, the next section discusses the data obtained from a field study that serves as the factual basis for this chapter. It is followed by a brief interpretation of the notion of social capital and its significance for social progress and development in section three. After that, we discuss some of the salient explanations that have been given about Ghana's mixed market reforms in the fourth section. Emphasis is placed on the particular problem of lack of private sector participation in Ghana's two-decade old neoliberal reforms that have been focused on market liberalization. In the next section, we provide empirical data to show the anomalous case of private business in the transportation sector in contradistinction to the other five sectors of the Ghanaian economy. The final section draws conclusions.

The data and methodology

In the fall of 1997 and spring of 1998, Amponsah conducted a survey of certain Ghanaian private businesses[2] with the view to inquiring into the factors accounting for the low private business response to Ghana's then decade and a half market liberalization reforms. Again, in the spring of 2003 and the fall of 2004, this project of investigating the institutional environment and its impact on domestic private investment was replicated as a way of affirming the previous findings.[3]

The Ghana case was empirically disturbing in the light of the general

Table 16.1 Sectors of Ghanaian private business selected for the study

Type of business	*Survey Data I 1997–1998*		*Survey Data II 2003–2004*	
	Frequency	*Percent*	*Frequency*	*Percent*
Transportation	66	14.7	61	14.5
Textiles/garments	69	15.4	64	15.2
Construction	62	13.8	61	14.5
Metal works	94	21.0	86	20.4
Wood works	74	16.5	70	16.6
Food processing	83	18.5	80	19.0
Total	448	100.0	422	100.0

Source: Survey Data I, see Amponsah, 1999; Survey Data II which is a repeat of Survey Data I was conducted in Fall, 2003 and Spring, 2004.

consensus that its reform regime had, to a greater extent, followed the dictates of market rationality as demanded by the International Financial Institutions (IFIs), including the IMF and the World Bank (World Bank, 1994; Herbst, 1993). After an initial enumeration exercise, six sectors of business including food, textiles, transportation, construction, metal works and wood processing, were randomly selected for the study. The breakdown of respondents is shown in Table 16.1.

Amponsah (2001: 375) records the problems of domestic investment in Ghana even under neoliberal reforms. The paucity of domestic private investment is such that there are no significant records of it. Thus, to assess the propensity of Ghanaian private entrepreneurs to invest under the prevailing economic environment, two variables were employed. The first gauges the propensity of private business entrepreneurs to plow back profits as re-investment (PBP), while the second gauges the actual proportion of profits (APP) an entrepreneur is ready to risk in investment, should one decide to invest at all. These variables, representing the dependent variables, were measured against certain institutional variables – norms, practices and behavior that prevail in the Ghanaian polity especially with regard to doing business. These variables, which are used as approximate measures of social capital, are deemed to be among the crucial factors determining the investment actions of private entrepreneurs. They include the propensity of the state to wantonly expropriate property and business, the prevalence of certain covert or overt state actions that stall the smooth operations of a business, and the explicitness of existing business laws, rules and procedural regulations. Respondents included the owners and top managerial executive of these enterprises. Most of the businesses were of the medium and small-scale type.

The significance of social capital and shared mental models

The success or failure of mental models depends in large part, on the institutional, political, economic, and social context in which they are adopted and applied. Mental models promoting market reform tend to flourish in political economic environments where sufficient levels of social capital exist – where public trust is high and institutions enjoy wide legitimacy. Where this is wanting, such ideas have little chance of being successful. The case of neoliberal reform in Ghana provides a further example of this proposition. Several years of experience with wanton expropriation and deprivation under authoritarian regimes has made private business distrustful of political regimes. Private entrepreneurs are skeptical that surreptitious expropriations from the state will not reoccur. Putnam (1993a: 167) notes that "cooperation is easier in a community that has inherited a substantial stock of social capital, in the form of norms of reciprocity and networks of civic engagement." The existence of a generalized atmosphere of mutual trust, – norms of cooperation and previous experiences of successful collective endeavors within society (Serra, 1999; Fukuyama 1995; Putnam 1993a, 1993b), in short, trust among a host of economic entities and between them and the state authority, explains the success of economic entrepreneurship, growth and development. Although we do not impute a precise definition of social capital, the concept, in the sense deployed by Putnam (1993a), Fukuyama (1995) and Coleman (1988) implies the prevalence of norms of reciprocity and the certainty of principles and rules of practice. It also connotes, in particular, the prevalence of overwhelming trust for the institutional and regulatory climate of a society. These concepts of society and economy translate into institutionalized norms of behavior that are known and internalized. As Putnam (1993b: 167) succinctly notes, "social capital" refers to "features of social organization such as trust, norms, and networks," that facilitate coordination and cooperation for mutual benefit. An important implication is that social capital is created over a long period of time, through social interactions and state action.

When a regime provides a stable administrative and institutional environment that facilitates coordination and cooperation for mutual benefit, it creates a healthy social capital for prospective economic and social actors as they acquire a sense of trust and cooperative spirit. In such an environment, market oriented ideas can be expected to flourish. Thus, the propensity for individuals living in a society to join together to engage in issues of mutual concern is indicative of the presence of social capital in that society.

Shared mental models are an essential component in bringing actors together in support of collective goals. An equally important component that is essential to the successful implementation of any model is the existence of sufficient levels of trust and reciprocity where it is applied. Social capital engenders networks of organized reciprocity and civic solidarity. In the view of Neace (1999) social capital connotes the ability of a people to work together for common purposes in groups, organizations, and communities. It is the clearest manifestation of a harmonious coexistence of trust, prevalence of viable channels of communications, and norms and sanctions. He notes that in addition to human capital in the form of knowledge and skills, sufficient levels of social capital are essential for social and economic development. Where a modicum of trust exists, collective action is predictable. This is because the daily behavior of various actors in society will be underpinned by cooperation based on shared mental models or norms of society and polity. As Putnam (1993b) found out, the prevalence of longstanding traditions of civic engagement significantly affects the level of performance and effectiveness of social organizations.

Social capital, thus, exists in a society where social interactions are certain in that they follow laid down procedures and norms, and are therefore predictable. They are predictable because of the amount of trust that has been built up due to the historical experience of cooperation towards social goals. As Putnam (1993b) intimated, for a variety of reasons, life is easier in a community blessed with a substantial stock of social capital. This is because networks of civic engagement foster sturdy norms of generalized reciprocity and encourage the emergence of social trust. Such networks facilitate coordination and communication, amplify reputations, and thus allow dilemmas of collective action to be resolved.

Neoliberal reforms in Ghana: an overview of the market liberalization experiment

When African countries made the bold attempts to reform their decadent economies through IMF–World Bank sponsored neoliberal reform programs in the 1980s, concerned international observers as well as the peoples of their countries became optimistic about the future opportunities for Africans (Callaghy and Ravenhill, 1993). It was hoped that because a liberalized economy could assure unlimited freedom of enterprise, the reformed African economies would witness increased productivity since private societal actors would be galvanized into activity. It was also hoped that foreign investors would be forthcoming to augment domestic economic activity with the much-needed foreign capital. These hopes were based on the assumption that the demolition of the status quo collectivist state system implies more opportunities for the market to work. Above all, it was hoped that the living conditions of the people would be improved because the resurgence of vibrant economic activity and individual success would lead to employment opportunities and growing incomes. After nearly two decades, these hopes of achieving development have not been achieved as the case of Ghana, once touted as the best reformer, reveals (Alderman, 1994; Hutchful, 1995; Konadu-Agyemang, 2001). The unfettered market is yet to unleash the individual actions that create wealth. There is need for a critical explanation of the failure of market reforms to bring the desired growth and development.

As a result, neoliberalism and SAPs were regarded as a failure. But is the lack of potency of neoliberal ideas the cause for the failure of entrepreneurial development? We argue that they were not. The neoliberal reforms in Ghana since 1983 is yet another episode of the effort to unleash markets without seriously considering the institutional foundations necessary for private initiative in a market system to take root. The Ghanaian experience makes clear what needs to be done to restore confidence in an economy. While it is critical to ensure the free and unfettered working of the market – "a la invisible hand," it is equally important to erect a credible institutional framework characterized by mutual trust within which economic actors would operate.

To the extent that domestic private economic actors continue to be unresponsive to Ghana's reform, the goal of liberalization has not been achieved (Tangri, 1992). This is because private initiative is central to market liberalization reform. While the reasons for the negative private sector response are varied and numerous, a major area which requires serious consideration is the level of trust facilitated by the social, economic, political and institutional climate.

An examination of the level of social capital and other institutional prerequisites that stimulate private initiative is very necessary as an important first step for further examining the role private actors could possibly play in a process of shared growth. Ironically, several studies that have examined the private sector have always concentrated on their incapacity, without examining the fundamental causes of their weakness. In consonance with mainstream neoclassical thinking, Roger Ridell, for instance, maintains that the poor performance of African industry is due to the smallness and fragility of manufacturing enterprises, and more important, their non-competitiveness (Ridell, 1993). We argue that certain conditions must exist that assure individual entrepreneurs the willingness to participate in shared-growth that neoliberal reforms seek to bring. These conditions are embedded in the institutional climate. Where the institutional climate is not credible, as in Ghana, the goal of economic growth and development becomes an uphill battle.

Although the International Financial Institutions sponsoring neoliberal reforms have yet to comprehend the nature of reforms in Africa, and Ghana in particular, there is widespread recognition that the "market-as-magic-bullet" mechanism is not invigorating private initiative as expected. Aryeetey *et al.* (1994) aptly notes that even during the reform period, private investment did actually witness precipitous declines, well below planned targets. The decline in private investment he notes was particularly noticeable in the manufacturing sector where private entrepreneurship is predominant. In this sector, capacity utilization declined to a low of 37 percent after an initial rise. According to Aryeetey (ibid.), this low capacity utilization by private firms is one of the most vivid indications of the difficulty they face in responding to the macro-economic reforms.

While it is always easy to point out that the private sector's response to reforms has been poor, not much in-depth analysis has been done on why the response has not been forthcoming. The reason is due to perceived notions of their weakness. The explanation for the weakness is presented tautologically. Thus, while Hart (1996) rightly notes the necessity for exploring the reasons for the weak private sector response, her explanation is that they are simply weak. To be sure, the weakness of private business in Ghana, as elsewhere in Africa, is informed by the absence of the fundamental institutional preconditions that make the market work in all capitalist systems.

Social capital and market-oriented (neoliberal) shared mental models: analysis from survey data

The role of government in helping create abundant social capital necessary for cooperative endeavor cannot be overemphasized. This is particularly so in societies with little history of stable institutional development and cooperative endeavor. The long established practices, traditions and norms of the relationships between state agencies and private entrepreneurs are considered critical aspects of social capital that could enhance or dissuade entrepreneurial endeavor. The way state structures and institutions including rules of practice, laws, norms and procedural regulations have operated and impacted on entrepreneurial ventures in the past always serves as the basis for making any long term business decisions. Vigorous entrepreneurial activity will emerge in an atmosphere where experience points to abundant opportunities for unfettered business development.

Ghanaian private business entrepreneurs were surveyed on two sets of questions related to aspects of their interactions, traditions and norms of social interaction that prevail in their operations and interactions with the authorities. These traditions and norms of social interactions reflect the institutional and regulatory environment and serve as the basis of trust for the entire state system. They included: 1) the security of business and property, and; 2) pervasiveness of discretionary power by the state. These issues have so much affinity to the level of trust and hence, the social capital that exists. In addition, a set of questions was also asked to gauge the extent to which private entrepreneurs were actually ready to invest under Ghana's reforms. Before examining these specific perceptions, it is important to examine the general attitude of these entrepreneurs towards investment.

The tendency of Ghanaian private businesses to invest

The absence of well developed financial institutions in less developed countries such as Ghana means that reinvestment of profits may be the main or only source of private enterprise development and growth in these countries. In fact, Aryeetey *et al.* (1994) found that many small- and medium-sized enterprises (SMEs) in Ghana achieved substantial growth by reinvesting their accrued profits. The variable "reinvestment of profits" is thus used to gauge the propensity of the domestic private businesses in Ghana to commit their resources to investment. This is particularly useful because of the absence of reliable data on this important statistic. For instance, The World Bank and the IMF present different estimates of this measure. While some estimates from the Bank put domestic private investment at about 8 percent of GDP, IMF studies estimate the same at as low as 4.1 percent (Pattillo, 1997: 4). Worse still both estimates are distorted because they include foreign private investment. To be sure, local private investment rates are much lower.

For entrepreneurs, whose typical source of continued development is reinvestment of profits (Aryeetey *et al.*, 1994: 110–111), the motivation to plow back most of their profits as reinvestment will depend on the level of trust they share for the existing socio-economic and political environment. If they still must invest in a risky environment, given few other options, then they will do so by committing only the proportion of accrued profits, which, in their estimates, would not devastate them if lost. In other words, they will invest only insignificant proportions of profits. Two questions were asked to find out the tendency of domestic private business to invest under prevailing political and economic environment. The same questions were asked in two surveys conducted in 1997–1998 and 2003–2004, with the former referred to as Survey Data I, and the latter, Survey Data II. The responses to these questions are provided in Table 16.2.

In Question 1.1 we asked respondents: "Under present political and economic conditions, would you consider reinvesting a significant part of accrued profits?" The majority of entrepreneurs who responded to this question during the first survey (54.4 percent, Survey Data I) said they did not find it prudent to reinvest any accrued profits as a way of expanding or improving their production capacities under the existing political and institutional environment. Only 36.2 percent said they would reinvest accrued profits if they had to do so. This is surprising because it is quite atypical of entrepreneurship tradition in Ghana. From what Aryeetey *et al.* (1994: 110) discovered about entrepreneurship development in Ghana, "a common trend is that most started small, reinvested profits and other resources, and grew gradually, adapting or shifting product lines as need be." Thus, if private entrepreneurs are not motivated to reinvest their accrued profits, then something extraneous must account for their behaviour.

Table 16.2 The tendency of private business towards investing in Ghana

Question	*Survey Data 1: 1997–1998*							*Survey Data II: 2003–2004*						
	Yes	*%*	*No*	*%*	*DK*	*%*	*Total*	*Yes*	*%*	*No*	*%*	*DK*	*(%)*	*Total*
1.1 Would you reinvest accrued profits from your business under prevailing political and economic environment?	162	36.2	243	54.4	43	9.6	445	141	43.6	188	48.0	33	8.4	392

	1–9%		*10–29%*		*30–50%*		*51–100%*		*1–9%*		*10–29%*		*30–50%*		*51–100%*	
1.2 What percent of accrued profits would you reinvest under the present political and economic conditions?	210	47.8	76	17.3	75	7.1	78	17.8	80	19	79	18.7	40	9.5	52	2.3

Source: Survey Data I, see Amponsah, 1999; Survey Data II which is a repeat of Survey Data I was conducted in Fall, 2003 and Spring, 2004.

Note
DK=Don't Know.

The intensity of the responses to Question 1.1 was further reinforced in the subsequent question (1.2). This question probed further into the likely proportion of profits entrepreneurs would be prepared to reinvestment, in the event they had to do so because they lacked alternative options. Based on rudimentary estimates, which took into consideration inflationary spiral and other factors, a four-category ranking of proportions of profits that could be reinvested was drawn. A high figure would be if an entrepreneur was prepared to reinvest between 51–100 percent of accrued profits. Reinvesting less than 10 percent is the lowest category, while reinvesting 30–50 percent of profits is considered average.

As the responses revealed (Table 16.2, Data I), many respondents reported the lowest category of 1–9 percent as the proportion of accrued profits they would most likely sink into the business as investment. Among the 445 entrepreneurs who responded to this poll, 47.8 percent said they would reinvest less than 10 percent of profits in their business if they had to. In fact, only 24.9 percent considered reinvesting any range of profits above the (30–50 percent) category considered as average. Indeed, anecdotal inferences showed that many would prefer to invest their profits in real estate. Interestingly, even entrepreneurs in the other sectors are more inclined to divert accrued profits into some form of transportation. Five years later, when the survey was repeated (see Survey Data II), the responses, though appreciated, were not markedly different. In the second survey, 48 percent of respondents indicated that they were not motivated by the prevailing institutional environment to commit their resources to investment, while a lower figure of 43.6 percent said they were ready to reinvest their profits. In the same vein, these findings seem astonishing and a negative indicator of the prospects of improved investment. Yet, these results appear to tie with declining trends in investment in Ghana, especially in value-added terms. If Ghanaian entrepreneurs do not feel inclined to invest, as they should, what factors make them behave the way they do?

Private business and the problems of property rights and expropriation in Ghana

Among the potential factors that militate against unfettered entrepreneurship in modern societies are the problems of property rights, including the right to own and do business, own land and other movable or immovable assets without any hindrance or interference, as well as bureaucratic procedures that present entrepreneurs with unreasonable requirements that increase their transaction costs substantially. Four questions were posed to entrepreneurs to find out the extent to which problems related to property, business, and contract rights and bureaucratic bottlenecks constitute a hindrance to doing business. Table 16.3 summarizes the views expressed by Ghanaian private business entrepreneurs on the problems of

Table 16.3 Responses of Ghanaian private business entrepreneurs on problems of property rights and expropriation

Question	*Survey Data 1: 1997–1998*							*Survey Data II: 2003–2004*						
	Yes	*%*	*No*	*%*	*DK*	*%*	*Total*	*Yes*	*%*	*No*	*%*	*DK*	*(%)*	*Total*
Q. 2a. Do you think the authorities (state) can seize your business/property at anytime without any justification?	222	49.9	223	50.1	–	–	445	58	14.5	305	76.1	38	9.5	401
Q. 2b. Do you think the authorities can surreptitiously harm or interfere in your business operations?	274	61.4	160	35.9	12	2.7	446	174	42.8	168	41.3	65	16.0	407
Q. 2c. Are the levels of authority to traverse in order to formalize or register to start-up abusiness reasonable?	173	40.4	243	56.7	12	2.8	428	151	45.2	155	46.4	28	8.4	334
Q. 2d. Are existing laws for business regulation clear, and simple enough to understand and comply with?	149	35.0	230	54.0	47	11.0	426	163	42.7	175	45.8	44	11.5	382

Source: Survey Data I, see Amponsah, 1999; Survey Data II, Amponsah, Field Survey of Institutional Environment for Business, a repeat of Survey Data I, conducted in Fall, 2003 and Spring, 2004.

property rights and expropriation and bureaucratic bottlenecks during the two survey periods.

Aryeetey *et al.* (1994: 10) note that in Ghana the ability of a private enterprise to grow is "constrained by inadequate access to finance, or other market factors, product markets, and licenses needed to operate legally." State institutions must be crafted so as to ward off such constraints. Ironically, in some societies, such mundane obstacles to business operations may not be considered property rights problems in official circles, or their effects may be taken for granted. In the recent past, when Ghana was under "revolutionary" military rule, a common occurrence had been the capricious seizure of the properties of certain entrepreneurs, most often by the fiat of a decree. Under the era of political and economic liberalization that ushered in the Fourth Republic in 1992, and especially because the unfettered market was supposed to unleash a "golden age of business," such rapacious practices, a narrower view of the property rights problem, were supposed to be a thing of the past.

There is another conception of the property rights problem that is much more common, but subtle. This relates to situations in which the authorities commit certain surreptitious acts, extralegal, that impede, halt or thwart business operations. Instances of such situations include deliberate delays in processing licensing documents needed to carry on business operations, debiting certain entrepreneurs with unreasonable fees or charges, and even blunt refusal to grant state permits and licenses. Political authorities in a reforming Third World country may not directly or openly confiscate property as they did in the past, prior to reforms, but they could act covertly in much the same way. Borner, Brunetti and Weder (1995) observed a similar situation in Nicaragua where the political and bureaucratic elite referred to only instances of outright confiscation of property as the property rights problem.

The most direct kind of property rights problem is wanton expropriation by the leviathan (state) itself. In Question 2a, private entrepreneurs were asked, "Do you think the authorities can seize your business or property at anytime without any justification?" As the responses indicate, a significant number of respondents in both surveys said that outright confiscation of an individual's property or business by state authorities was not very likely. In the first survey (1997–1998), the majority of 50.1 percent of respondents said they believed the authorities could not come and seize their property or business without any justification, while 49.9 percent thought there was a possibility. In fact, the responses during the second survey (2003–2004), when the country had sustained more than a decade of stable democratic rule were more emphatic, as a whopping 76.1 percent said that direct confiscation of business or property in Ghana was unlikely. Only 14.5 percent believed direct confiscation of business or property may be likely. Thus, the narrow definition of property rights problem seems to have gained currency in Ghana. The reason, according to some entrepreneurs interviewed, was the democratization façade, which has ushered in a proliferation of business associations and a relatively critical media.

There was a consensus, however, that certain subtle actions by the state authorities could impede one's freedom or ability to carry on productive economic activity. Such surreptitious actions from the state could come in the form of delays in securing licensing and working permits (Aryeetey *et al.*, 1994: op. cit.). In Question 2b we asked: Do you think the authorities can surreptitiously harm or interfere in your business operations? To this question, a significant majority of respondents (61.4 percent) answered in the affirmative, with only 35.9 holding a contrary view during the first survey (see Survey Data I). Private entrepreneurs generally held the belief that the Ghanaian regime was intrinsically antagonistic to private business people (Hutchful, 1995; Tangri, 1992). Five years later in 2004, when entrepreneurs were prodded with the same question, there was a marked improvement in the perceptions about the general business environment. Fewer entrepreneurs (42.8 percent), held the view that the state could interfere or halt ones business operations. Yet, a near equal number, (41.3 percent) still held the belief that surreptitious interference of one's business by the authorities was likely. Anecdotal discussions from some entrepreneurs, notably in the construction and wood industry indicated that the state's monopoly over contracts in the public realm and over the wood industry makes an entrepreneur who is "not in the good books" of the regime highly vulnerable. The Ghanaian society is yet to rid itself of perceptions of institutional uncertainty, which we argue, is a source of the low tendency towards investment. These problems are further compounded by an environment and culture of bureaucratic ineptitude.

Bureaucratic bottlenecks as impediments to neoliberal reform

Bureaucratic bottlenecks constitute a major source of problems that confront entrepreneurs in less institutionalized developing nations, in their bid to initiate a business venture or maintaining and consolidating the business. This problem is particularly horrendous in situations with multiplicity and complexity of levels of authority that an entrepreneur has to traverse in order to formalize or register to commence a business venture. Added to the administrative jungle created by the multiplicity of conflicting levels of authority is the problem of ambiguity in the rules and procedures regulating business ventures. The constraining impact of these bureaucratic bottlenecks, especially for nascent entrepreneurs, cannot be overemphasized. These bureaucratic constraints on business are a major reason for the variations in industrial development between the Poorly Performing African Economies (PPAEs) and the Highly Performing Asian Economies (HPAEs). Thus, while Evans (1995: 43–50) describes the archetype of the developmental state as characterized by exceptional competence and coherence in organization, he notes that the archetypal predatory state is typified by rapaciousness of officialdom and a moribund bureaucratic organization which in itself places bottlenecks on induced economic decisions of private actors.

Two questions were asked to find out the extent to which problems of bureaucratic bottlenecks constitute a hassle in Ghana. First, we asked respondents: "Are the levels of authority to traverse in order to formalize or register to start-up a business reasonable?" (Q2c). And following from that (Q2d): "Are existing laws for business regulation clear, and simple enough to understand and comply with?" The responses as indicated in Table 16.3 showed that many Ghanaian entrepreneurs were not satisfied with the bureaucratic practice within which they operate. In the first survey, only a small proportion of respondents (40.4 percent) felt the levels of authority to traverse in order to complete official requirement was adequate and did not constitute a horrendous problem. A clear majority, (56.7 percent) indicated that they were dissatisfied with the levels of bureaucratic authority (both hierarchical and parallel) they had to traverse in order to formalize or register to start-up a business. Five years later, when respondents were prodded with the same issue (Survey Data II, Table 16.3) there had been some improvements in the perceptions about the problems emanating from bureaucratic bottlenecks as many more respondents than previously (45.2 percent as against 40.4 percent) said the levels of bureaucratic authority was relatively reasonable. Again, fewer also thought that the levels of authority were unreasonable. To be sure, the perception about bureaucratic bottlenecks, linger on. On the general view about the certainty of rules and regulations pertaining to business (Q2d), there had also been some improvements over time; yet, overall, entrepreneurs are still less sanguine. During the first survey 1997–1998, the overwhelming majority (54 percent) held the negative view that the rules and regulations pertaining to business were not clear, nor simple enough for entrepreneurs to comply with, while a minority of 35 percent held a positive view. Five years later, these perceptions, though slightly on the positive, still pointed to pervasive problems of institutional certainty. To be sure, a reasonably larger view (45.8 percent) held that the existing rules and regulations for doing business were unclear, full of ambiguity and moribund. Only a lesser percentage of respondents (42.7) thought that the rules and regulations for doing business were adequate.

The results of our study corroborate Aryeetey *et al.*'s (1994) speculations that risk-averse behavior resulting from an environment shrouded in institutional uncertainty, probably accounts for the reason why potential private investors shy away from long-term investment commitments. For instance entrepreneurs we surveyed for this study indicated high risk-aversion and thus the majority of 54.4 percent did not think it expedient to plow back profits as re-investment, as shown in Table 16.4. The data also indicates that the majority of Ghanaian private business entrepreneurs perceive the predatory tendency of the authorities (state) to be omnipresent despite reforms. They believe that even if the state in Ghana cannot overtly expropriate or seize one's business and property outright, there are several subtle or covert ways in which the actions of the state could interfere or halt the smooth operation of business. This weakness of the institutional climate in preempting any perceived potential predatory governmental actions is, therefore, very serious, and a major inhibiting factor for market liberalization to achieve the desired goals.

Explaining the success of neoliberal reform in the transportation sector

While businesses were generally lukewarm towards investment, we discovered that in some sectors of industry, notably the transportation sector, business had been invigorated and entrepreneurs were more enthusiastic towards investment. This was also the sector of industry where entrepreneurs seemed to be comfortable with the norms of social transactions such as the adequacy of the procedures and the general institutional climate. A modicum of social capital appears to exist within this business community. What could explain the apparent variant attitude of entrepreneurs in the transportation sector towards participation in shared growth? And what general lessons can we learn from Ghana's experience with market reforms?

The Ghanaian reform regime, especially during the first decade (1983–1992), did not consider the imperative of ensuring unfettered private initiative as its major task under the market liberalization reform (Amponsah, 2000: Tangri, 1992). Accordingly, private entrepreneurs also saw it as disdainful of individual profit accumulation and success. Indeed, the regime could not forge any functional mutual relationship with private entrepreneurs, especially in the manufacturing sector. The World Bank (1994) rightly noted, "*Trust and confidence* must be restored to enhance the private sector's response" (emphasis mine).

While the Ghanaian regime had a fractured relationship with most private economic actors, it shared some rapport with certain groups of business. The private transport business organization, under the umbrella of the Ghana Private Road Transport Union (GPRTU), was one sector of business that enjoyed a cordial relationship with the government. The goal of the regime's support and relationship with this business association was undoubtedly part of its search for groups to bolster its legitimacy and ensure its survival. Indeed, Rothchild and Foley (1988: 233) note that African regimes adopt such politics of cooptation in their vain effort to improve their capacity for governance. Nevertheless, the regime's partnership and commitment to the Ghana Private Road Transport Union (GPRTU), was indicative of what could be achieved when a reform regime secures the trust and confidence of private organizations. As Rothchild and Foley (ibid.: 241) surmised, even though such politics of inclusiveness result in political payoffs and back scratching for the regime, by creating coalitions and workable political and economic networks, it produces a positive effect of promoting cooperation. To be sure, the then PNDC regime was inherently patrimonial and made use of patronage as its most potent tool for securing support. Its approach to securing a modicum of support was to co-opt or woo certain groups in the Ghanaian society, for which the Private transport sector and its union presented an opportunity. This relationship was to benefit the GPRTU, its union and the transportation industry, immensely.

The transportation industry had the advantage that its assets were mobile and hence relatively safe, but not necessarily beyond the reach of predatory authorities. The industry also appeared to share lesser risks than other industries. Further, though by Ghanaian standards it is relatively less capital intensive, few in the Ghanaian society could secure the initial venture capital to enter the industry. Indeed, most Ghanaians saw transport owners as wealthy. This notwithstanding, the most pressing limitation to business venture and investment in Ghana, as in all less developed nations, is the problem of institutional uncertainty (Borner *et al.*, 1995). To be sure, the problems of ambiguity in rules for regulating and adjudicating business transaction and procedures, and the uncertainties about the predictability of the rules of the game, negatively affect business motivation (North, 1991; Putnam, 1993a; Keefer and Knack, 1997).

As Table 16.4 indicates, Ghanaian businesses in general perceive the institutional environment as not credible, and did not find it conducive for investment. Yet, businesses in the transportation sector shared a variant response to the perceived problems of institutional uncertainty. A majority of business entrepreneurs in this sector are among the few private entrepreneurs we interviewed who felt the legal climate was more conducive for an entrepreneur to commit his/her resources to investment in Ghana (Table 16.4). We posed the question: "Are you willing to plow back your profits as reinvestment?" The responses to this question are examined across the six business sectors using Survey Data II, 2004. The majority of respondents, 48.0 percent, perceived the institutional environment not conducive to commit their resources to investment. But 43.6 percent thought they were comfortable to reinvest resources. Undoubtedly, there had been an improvement over the previous situation some five years ago. In the first survey (see Appendix 16.A.1) 54.4 percent of respondents answered in the negative, indicating that the institutional climate was not secure for them to reinvest their profits. Only 36.2 percent indicated they were willing to reinvest profits. The improvement notwithstanding, the problem clearly persists.

What is of interest however is that while the majority of businesses were less motivated to reinvest, the majority of those in the transport sector

Table 16.4 Cross-tabulation, business type and readiness to invest

			Willing to plow back profits as reinvestment?			
			Yes	*No*	*Don't know*	*Total*
Business type	Transport	Count	39	12	4	55
		% of total	9.9%	3.1%	1.0%	14.0%
	Textiles	Count	21	33	8	62
		% of total	5.4%	8.4%	2.0%	15.8%
	Construction	Count	27	27	5	59
		% of total	6.9%	6.9%	1.3%	15.1%
	Metal	Count	28	43	7	78
		% of total	7.1%	11.0%	1.8%	19.9%
	Wood	Count	31	36	3	70
		% of total	7.9%	9.2%	0.8%	17.9%
	Food	Count	25	37	6	68
		% of total	6.4%	9.4%	1.5%	17.3%
Total		Count	171	188	33	392
		% of total	43.6%	48.0%	8.4%	100.0%

Source: Amponsah, Field Survey of Institutional Environment for Business, 2004.

were more favourably inclined to reinvest their resources to investment. The largest majority of respondents favorably inclined to invest (9.9 percent) came from the transport sector. Indeed, out of 55 respondents interviewed in that sector, the overwhelming majority of 39 (70.9 percent) were favourably disposed to invest. The explanation for this variant behavior of businesses in the transport sector can be gauged from the perceptions about the institutional environment. We have noted that perceptions of a credible institutional environment are very crucial for induced business initiatives. Such a credible and predictable institutional environment, Sandbrook and Oelbaum (1997) note, implies the existence of regularized patterns of social and economic interactions formulated into rules and codes of procedure. They also connote the prevalence of principles of behavior and regulations that are known, practiced and accepted (even if not necessarily approved), by firms and parties in the process of shared growth. It "refers to rules that, in actual practice, regulate behavior and expectations because they are widely shared." Institutional constraints such as bureaucratic bottlenecks all contribute to perceptions of institutional uncertainty (Aryeetey *et al.*, 1994: op. cit). We examined through a cross tabulation analysis, the extent to which problems associated to bureaucratic bottlenecks constitute a hassle across all business sectors. We asked respondents: "Are the levels of bureaucratic authorities to traverse in order to register or operate your business reasonable or fair?" The responses, which are summarized in Table 16.5, are important for gauging the extent to which various business sectors perceive the problems of

Table 16.5 Cross-tabulation, business type and perceptions bureaucratic bottlenecks

			Are levels of authority necessary to register business reasonable?			
			Yes	*No*	*Don't know*	*Total*
Business type	Transport	Count	32	14	9	55
		% of total	9.6%	4.2%	2.7%	16.5%
	Textiles	Count	19	26	4	49
		% of total	5.7%	7.8%	1.2%	14.7%
	Construction	Count	24	20	5	49
		% of total	7.2%	6.0%	1.5%	14.7%
	Metal	Count	30	27	4	61
		% of total	9.0%	8.1%	1.2%	18.3%
	Wood	Count	20	37	2	59
		% of total	6.0%	11.1%	0.6%	17.7%
	Food	Count	26	31	4	61
		% of total	7.8%	9.3%	1.2%	18.3%
Total		Count	151	155	28	334
		% of total	45.2%	46.4%	8.4%	100.0%

Source: Amponsah, Field Survey of Institutional Environment for Business, 2004.

bureaucratic constraints, and how these perceptions may likely affect their investment decisions.

Indeed, undue duplications or multiplicity of bureaucratic authority has been identified as the major source of the necessity for "go-betweens" and consequent corruption in some nations. The Institute for Liberty and Democracy conducted a simulated study on costs incurred by informal economic entities in securing formalization of their industry and businesses in Peru. The study found that, "a person of modest means must spend 289 days on bureaucratic procedures to fulfill eleven requirements for setting up a small industry" (De Soto, 1989: 134). These delays resulted in part from the number of hierarchies of authority (in this Peruvian case, eleven different levels) each of which must provide some different kind of authorization or permit.

The responses in Table 16.5 show that respondents were overall less enthusiastic about the bureaucratic constraints. A reasonably large majority, 46.4 percent shared the view that the levels of bureaucratic authorities one has to traverse in order to constitute or operate a business, including procedures necessary for "start-up" are unreasonable. A smaller figure, 45.2 percent said bureaucratic procedures and regulations were fair. Yet, as opposed to the other sectors, entrepreneurs in the transport sector again shared a variant view. For them, a majority of 32 or (58.1 percent out of a sample of 55), thought that bureaucratic procedures and regulations regarding their business was comparatively just or reasonable. This is not surprising in light of the evidence of strong mutual relationship between this sector and the regime over the years, especially under the PNDC and NDC period (1983–2000). Thus, as Ninsin puts it "most unions did not enjoy such government confidence" (Ninsin 1991: 56).

Onyx and Bullen (2000) draw attention to the important theme of reciprocity implied in the notion of social capital. They argue that an individual engages in economic activity, provides a service to others or acts for the benefit of others in anticipation that the action will be reciprocated. In providing his or her services, the entrepreneur expects the society and the state system to provide the requisite benefits – an orderly regulated environment, which will enhance or facilitate the smooth operation of business. In an environment without norms regulating social relations and interactions, people will have no trust for the system of authority. This is particularly so if authority could be used to impede the economic activity of individuals. Where actors believe that there exists some mutual trust based on established relations with the authorities as the private business sector in Ghana shared, especially during the PNDC/NDC period, they would also have trust for the "rules of the game" for transacting their business (an important source of shared social capital) as established by the authorities. Thus, Table 16.6 probes further the extent to which businesses believe that the prevailing business laws, that is, "the rules of the game," are just, explicit and fair. We asked: "Are the existing business laws for your business operations, clear, simple and fair enough to comply with?"

Table 16.6 Cross-tabulation, type of business and extent to which you think existing business laws are explicit?

			Are existing business laws, clear and simple?			
			Yes	*No*	*Don't know*	*Total*
Business type	Transport	Count	34	11	11	56
		% of total	8.9%	2.9%	2.9%	14.7%
	Textiles	Count	24	37	3	64
		% of total	6.3%	9.7%	0.8%	16.8%
	Construction	Count	29	25	4	58
		% of total	7.6%	6.6%	1.1%	15.3%
	Metal	Count	25	31	12	68
		% of total	6.6%	8.2%	3.2%	17.9%
	Wood	Count	20	34	6	60
		% of total	5.3%	8.9%	1.6%	15.8%
	Food	Count	27	38	9	74
		% of total	7.1%	10.0%	2.4%	19.5%
Total		Count	159	176	45	380
		% of total	41.8%	46.3%	11.8%	100.0%

Source: Amponsah, Field Survey of Institutional Environment for Business, 2004.

As we have noted, the prevalence of overwhelming trust for the existing institutional setting is indicative of the presence of social capital. For, trust for these institutions will emerge only when people feel they are practicable and credible. This institutional setting also includes issues pertaining to the specificity and flexibility of procedures for social interactions. Where social interactions are shrouded in ambiguous rules, norms and practices, social capital is greatly in danger. For these reasons, a good way of assessing the level of trust for the existing institutions, and hence, social capital is to examine the extent to which businesses perceive the explicitness of laws, rules and procedural regulations pertaining to doing business in a country. Where business entrepreneurs perceive the prevailing norms and practices as credible, they would have a measure of trust in dealing with themselves and the authorities. In the absence of such trust, the chances of entrepreneurs engaging in dynamic reciprocal activity will be slim.

As the responses indicate a reasonably large majority of respondents, 46.3 percent felt the rules of the game pertaining to business transactions were neither clear nor simple and hence, quite ambiguous. This cut across all business sectors with the exception, once again, of the transport sector. Only 41.8 percent of respondents indicated that they thought the existing business laws were explicit and fair. In the transport sector however, a noticeable number, 34 out of 56 respondents (60.7 percent) saw business laws as fairly explicit. The only other group where respondents said business laws were quite explicit was the construction sector, which obviously is made up of highly sophisticated business tycoons and engineers. For several reasons, including the development of mutual reciprocal relations between the reform regime (1983–2000) and the transportation sector and its union, various institutional mechanisms had been established simplifying procedures for coordinating expectations, thereby creating a modicum of social capital within that sector.

Campos and Root (1996) note the importance of establishing institutional mechanisms that facilitate the coordination of expectations. They write: "Regime leaders in the high-performing Asian economies (HPAEs) understood that the challenge of economic growth required the coordination of expectations of different sectors of the population (ibid.: 1)." Ninsin (1991) notes the mutual trust between the Ghana reform regime and the GPRTU. This trust, he argued, was so strongly grounded that the regime made legal provisions that simplified the collection of tax liabilities of entrepreneurs operating in this sector, thus lowering substantially, their transaction costs (Ninsin, ibid.: 55). The upshot of the matter is that, where a modicum of social capital – pervasive trusts for the regulatory environment exists, there tends to be confidence among people in transacting business. These issues need further elaborate analysis for definitive theory building, but they definitely do point to the need for rethinking the "market-as-the-bullet" notion associated with reforms, if fledging economies such as Ghana are to make any meaningful gains from such reforms.

Conclusion

The International Financial Institutions (IFIs), especially the World Bank and the IMF, governed by the neoliberal thinking have not sufficiently emphasized what must be done to activate private initiative. Thus, while the World Bank duly recognized that "trust and confidence must be restored to enhance the private sector's response," its prescriptions were the call "for eliminating the commercial advantage to public enterprises" which are perceived as the basis of state involvement in the economy.

Hart accurately notes that the current market reforms are right on target in addressing the problem of destructive statism in Africa, yet the same reforms could be used to reconstruct state domination (Hart, 1996: 5–6). This seems to be the case of Ghana's reforms during the 15-year period, 1983–1998. The state in Africa has obviously been predatory and ruinous. Nevertheless, there must be a way of capturing its benevolent and developmental roles that have been attained elsewhere in the industrializing societies of East Asia. The challenge for reformers therefore is how to ensure that the African states under reforms perform the alternative developmental role without drifting into their ruinous predatory past. There is need to create institutional mechanisms that facilitate coordination of expectations of economic actors, and to serve as the basis of social capital for enticing prospective entrepreneurs. The erection of credible economic and political institutional mechanisms may be one of the appropriate ways to ensure sustained economic success.

Appendix

Table 16.A.1 Cross-tabulation, business type and readiness to plow back profits as reinvestment

			Willing to plow back profits as reinvestment?			
			Yes	*No*	*Don't know*	*Total*
Business type	Transport	Count	40	17	9	66
		% of total	8.9%	3.8%	2.0%	14.8%
	Textiles	Count	19	46	3	68
		% of total	4.3%	10.3%	7%	15.2%
	Construction	Count	16	39	7	62
		% of total	3.6%	8.7%	1.6%	13.9%
	Metal	Count	26	57	11	94
		% of total	5.8%	12.8%	2.5%	21.0%
	Wood	Count	20	47	7	74
		% of total	4.5%	10.5%	1.6%	16.6%
	Food	Count	41	37	5	83
		% of total	9.2%	8.3%	1.1%	18.6%
Total		Count	162	243	42	447
		% of total	36.2%	54.4%	9.4%	100.0%

Source: Amponsah, 1999.

Notes

* Dr. Nicholas Amponsah is a lecturer at the Department of Political Science, University of Ghana, Legon.

1 These expressions about the institutional situation were made by this senior lecturer of the Department of Political Science in the University of Ghana, Legon. See Ofori, 1993: 70–71.

2 Mr. Osei Kwadwo and Mr. Adansi-Pipim, both graduate students of the Department of Political Science, University of Ghana, assisted in the data collection, as did Mr. Akwasi Addai-Boateng and Mr. Yaw Adjei-Sarkodie of Sunyani, Ghana. The survey was part of a major study. See (Amponsah, 1999), unpublished Ph.D. dissertation, Claremont Graduate University, Claremont, California.

3 The survey was conducted in the fall of 2003 and spring 2004. I am highly indebted to Mr. Daniel Appiah, and Mr. Desmond Tweneboah-Koduah, both Teaching Assistants in the Department of Political Science, University of Ghana (2003–2004) who assisted in the conduct of the field surveys.

References

Alderman, Harold (1994) "Ghana: adjustment's star pupil?" in Sahn, David E. (ed.) *Adjusting to Policy Failure in African Countries.* Ithaca: Cornell University Press.

Amponsah, Nicholas (1999) "Institutional credibility and entrepreneurial development: explaining Ghana's mixed structural adjustment results, 1983–1998," Ph.D. diss., Claremont Graduate University.

Amponsah, N. (2000) "Ghana's mixed structural adjustment results: explaining the poor private sector response," *Africa Today* 47(2). Spring, 8–34.

Amponsah, N. (2001) "Adjustment reforms in a poor business environment: why poor institutions persist under Ghana's reforms," in Konadu-Agyemang, Kwadwo (ed.) *IMF and World Bank Sponsored Structural Adjustment Programs in Africa: Ghana's Experience, 1983–1999.* Aldershot: Ashgate, 371–390. ISBN 0-7546-1396-8.

Aryeetey, Ernest (1994) "Private investment under uncertainty in Ghana," *World Development* 22(8): 1211–1221.

Aryeetey, Ernest, Amoah-Baah-Nuako, Duggleby, Tamara, Hettige, Hemamala, and Steel, William F. (1994) *Supply and Demand for Finance of Small Enterprises in Ghana.* Washington, DC: The World Bank.

Bates, Robert H. (1999) "The economic bases of democratization," in Richard, Joseph (ed.) *State, Conflict and Democracy in Africa.* Boulder, CO: Lynne Rienner Publishers.

Borner, Silvio, Brunetti, Aymo, and Weder, Beatrice (1995) "Policy reform and institutional uncertainty: the case of Nicaragua," *Kyklos* 48(1): 43–64.

Brunetti, Aymo, Kisunko, Gregory, and Weder, Beatrice (1998) *How Businesses See Government: Responses from Private Sector Surveys in 69 Countries.* Washington, DC: The World Bank, International Finance Corporation Discussion Paper no. 33.

Callaghy, Thomas M. and Ravenhill, John (1993) "Introduction, vision, politics and structure: Afro-optimism, Afro-pessimism or realism?" in Callaghy, Thomas and Ravenhill, John (eds) *Hemmed In: Responses to Africa's Economic Decline.* New York: Columbia Univesrsity Press, 1–17.

Campos, Jose Edgardo and Root, Hilton L. (1996) *The Key to the Asian Miracle Making Shared Growth Credible.* Washington, DC: The Brookings Institution.

Coleman, J. (1988) "Social capital in the creation of human capital," *American Journal of Sociology* 94: 95–120.

Denzau, A.T. and North, D.C. (1994) "Shared mental models: ideologies and institutions," *Kyklos* 47(1): 3–31.

De Soto, Hernando (1989) *The Other Path: The Invisible Revolution in the Third World.* New York: Harper & Row Publishers.

Evans, Peter (1995) *Embedded Autonomy: States and Industrial Transformation.* Princeton, NJ: Princeton University Press.

Fukuyama, Francis (1995) *Trust: The Social Virtues and the Creation of Prosperity.* New York: Free Press.

Gyimah-Boadi, E. (1995) "Explaining the economic and political successes of Rawlings: the strengths and limitations of public choice theories," in Harris, John, Hunter, Janet, and Lewis, Colin M. *The New Institutional Economics and Third World Development.* London: Routledge, 307–308.

Hart, Elizabeth I. (1996) *Liberal Reforms in the Balance: The Private Sector and the State in Ghana, 1983–95.* Ph.D. Dissertation, UMI: Princeton University.

Herbst, Jeffrey (1993) *The Politics of Reform in Ghana, 1982–1991.* Berkeley: University of California Press.

de Soto, Hernando (1989) *The Other Path: The Invisible Revolution in the Third World.* New York: Harper and Row.

Hutchful, Ebo (1995) "Why regimes adjust: the World Bank ponders its 'star pupil.'" *Canadian Journal of African Studies* 29(2): 303–317.

Keefer, Philip and Knack, Stephen (1997) "Why don't poor countries catch up? A cross national test of an institutional explanation," *Economic Inquiry* 25: 590–602.

Konadu-Agyemang, K. (2001) "Overview of structural adjustment programmes in Africa," in Konadu-Agyemang, K. (ed.) *IMF and World Bank Sponsored Structural Adjustment Programs in Africa: Ghana's Experience.* Aldershot: Asgate, 1–15.

Leechor, Chad (1994)"Ghana: front-runner in adjustment," in Husain, Ishrat and Faruqee, Rashid (eds) *Adjustment in Africa: Lessons from Country Studies.* Washington, DC: World Bank, 153–192.

Neace, M.B. (1999) "Entrepreneurs in emerging economies: creating trust, social capital and civil society," *Annals American Academy of Political Science* 565: 148–162.

Ninsin, Kwame A. (1991) "The PNDC and the problem of legitimacy," in Rothchild, Donald (ed.) *Ghana: The Political Economy of Recovery*, pp. 49–67.

Ofori, Ruby (1993) "Ghana: mixed messages," *Africa Report* (Sept./Oct.), 70–71.

Okwabi, Ayah (1996) "Inflexibility, bane of Ghana's economy," *West Africa* (March 25–31).

Onyx, Jenny and Bullen, Paul (2000) "Measuring social capital in five communities," *Journal of Applied Behavioral Science* 36(1): 23–43.

Pattillo, Catherine (1997) *Investment, Uncertainty, and Irreversibility in Ghana.* Washington, DC: International Monetary Fund, IMF Working Paper 97/169 (December).

Putnam, Robert D. (1993a) "The prosperous community: social capital and economic growth," *Current* Issue no. 356, October 4–9.

Putnam, Robert D. (1993b) *Making Democracy Work: Civic Traditions in Modern Italy.* Princeton: Princeton University Press.

Ridell, Roger (1993) "The future of manufacturing sector in sub-Saharan Africa," in Callaghy, Thomas and Ravenhill, John (eds) *Hemmed In: Responses to Africa's Economic Decline.* New York: Columbia University Press, pp. 215–247.

Rimmer, Douglas (1992) *Staying Poor: Ghana's Political Economy, 1950–1990.* Oxford: Pergamon Press.

Rothchild, Donald and Foley, Michael W. (1988) "African states and the politics of inclusive coalitions," in Rothchild, D. and Chazan, N. (eds) *The Precarious Balance: State and Society in Africa.* Boulder: Westview Press.

Sandbrook, Richard and Oelbaum, Jay (1997) "Reforming dysfunctional institutions through democratization? Reflections on Ghana," *Journal of Modern African Studies* 35(4): 602–646.

Serra, Renata (1999) "Putnam in India: is social capital a meaningful and measurable concept at Indian state level?" *IDS Working Paper 92,* August.

Tangri, Roger (1992) "The politics of government–business relations in Ghana," *Journal of Modern African Studies* 30(1): 97–111.

The World Bank (1994) *Adjustment in Africa: Reforms, Results and the Road Ahead.* Washington, DC: The World Bank.

Index

For Product Safety Concerns and Information please contact our EU representative GPSR@taylorandfrancis.com Taylor & Francis Verlag GmbH, Kaufingerstraße 24, 80331 München, Germany

* 9 7 8 0 4 1 5 4 5 8 6 6 5 *

T - #0055 - 230425 - C0 - 234/156/20 - PB - 9780415458665 - Gloss Lamination